CONTENTS

III

P9-CQJ-945

Fodor's 98

The U.S. & British Virgin Islands

The complete guide, thoroughly up-to-date

Packed with details that will make your trip

The must-see sights, off and on the beaten path

What to see, what to skip

Mix-and-match vacation itineraries

City strolls, countryside adventures

Smart lodging and dining options

Essential local do's and taboos

Transportation tips, distances and directions

Key contacts, savvy travel tips

When to go, what to pack

Clear, accurate, easy-to-use maps

Books to read, background essays

Fodor's Travel Publications, Inc.
New York • Toronto • London • Sydney • Auckland
www.fodors.com/

Fodor's U.S. and British Virgin Islands

EDITORS: Paula Consolo, Caroline Haberfeld

Editorial Contributors: Pamela Acheson, Rob Andrews, Carol M. Bareuther, David Brown, Gary Goodlander, Lynda Lohr, Heidi Sarna, Helayne Schiff, M. T. Schwartzman (Gold Guide editor), Dinah Spritzer

Editorial Production: Stacey Kulig

Maps: David Lindroth, *cartographer*; Steven K. Amsterdam, *map editor*

Design: Fabrizio La Rocca, *creative director*; Guido Caroti, *associate art director*; Jolie Novak, *photo editor*

Production/Manufacturing: Robert B. Shields

Cover Photograph: Bob Krist

Copyright

Special Sales

ON THE ROAD WITH FODOR'S

WE'RE ALWAYS THRILLED to get letters from readers, especially one like this:

It took us an hour to decide what book to buy and we now know we picked the best one. Your book was wonderful, easy to follow, very accurate, and good on pointing out eating places, informal as well as formal. When we saw other people using your book, we would look at each other and smile.

Our editors and writers are deeply committed to making every Fodor's guide "the best one"—not only accurate but always charming, brimming with sound recommendations and solid ideas, right on the mark in describing restaurants and hotels, and full of fascinating facts that make you view what you've traveled to see in a rich new light.

About Our Writers

Our success in achieving our goals—and in helping to make your trip the best of all possible vacations—is a credit to the hard work of our extraordinary writers and editors.

Pamela Acheson spent 18 years developing and marketing textbooks in New York City before heading south, where she now divides her time between Florida and the Virgin Islands. She writes extensively about both areas and is a regular contributor to *Travel & Leisure* and Fodor's guides, as well as other publications. Acheson is the author of *The Best of the British Virgin Islands, The Best of St. Thomas,* and *The Best Romantic Escapes in Florida.* She updated the Gold Guide, Chapter 1, and the British Virgin Islands chapter of this book.

St. Thomas-based writer and dietitian **Carol M. Bareuther** publishes two weekly columns on food, cooking, and nutrition in the *Virgin Islands Daily News* and serves as U.S. Virgin Islands stringer for the Reuters News Service International. She also writes about sports and travel for *Islands' Nautical Scene, Caribbean Week, Tropic Times,* and the *Virgin Islands Business Journal,* as well as other publications. She is the author of two books, *Sports Fishing in the Virgin Islands* and *Virgin Islands Cooking.* Bareuther updated the St. Thomas section of this book.

Longtime Virgin Islands resident **Gary Goodlander** has lived aboard sailing craft for more than 35 of his 46 years and currently resides with his wife and daughter on his 38-ft S&S sloop *Wild Card* in Great Cruz Bay, St. John. He is a freelance marine journalist for such publications as *Caribbean Herald, SAIL,* and *Yachting World* and is the author of *Chasing the Horizon* and *Sea Dogs, Clowns & Gypsies.* He updated the Sailing and Diving and Snorkeling chapters of this volume, as he has for many years.

Lynda Lohr spent the past 13 years as a St. John resident, much of it swimming at her favorite Hawksnest Beach. She's a veteran mainland and U.S. Virgin Islands journalist who works regularly for local, regional, and national publications. She lives with her two cats and her boyfriend in a tiny cottage overlooking Cruz Bay. She updated the St. Croix, St. John, and U.S.V.I. A to Z sections of this book.

We would like to thank the British Virgin Islands Tourist Board and the U.S.V.I. Government Tourist Offices for helping keep us up to date; Mike Kuich of Virgin Islands Charteryacht League, Kathy Mullen of Charter Services, and Verna Ruan of Crewed Charters for their expertise on the chartering industry; Mel Luff of Underwater Safaris and Patty and Marcus of Cruz Bay Diving for insider information about the diving industry; and old salt Christopher Gasiorek for sharing nautical knowledge and rum drinks, and for constant support.

New This Year

The U.S. and British Virgin Islands '98 has brand-new walking and driving tours and a timing section that tells you exactly how much time to allot for each tour. Also, the area code for the U.S. Virgin Islands has been changed from 809 to 340. Until June 30, 1998, both numbers will be operational. After that date, only 340 can be used.

And this year, Fodor's joins Rand Mc-Nally, the world's largest commercial mapmaker, to bring you a detailed color map of the Virgin Islands. Just detach it along the perforation and drop it in your tote bag.

On the Web, check out Fodor's site (www.fodors.com/) for information on major destinations around the world and travel-savvy interactive features. The Web site also lists the 85-plus radio stations nationwide that carry the Fodor's Travel Show, a live call-in program that airs every weekend. Tune in to hear guests discuss their wonderful adventures—or call in to get answers for your most pressing travel questions.

How to Use This Book

Organization

Up front is the **Gold Guide,** an easy-to-use section divided alphabetically by topic. Under each listing you'll find tips and information that will help you accomplish what you need to in the Virgin Islands. You'll also find addresses and telephone numbers of organizations and companies that offer destination-related services and detailed information and publications.

The first chapter in the guide, Destination: The Virgin Islands helps get you in the mood for your trip. What's Where gets you oriented, New and Noteworthy cues you in on trends and happenings, Pleasures and Pastimes describes the activities and sights that really make the Virgin Islands unique, Fodor's Choice showcases our top picks, and Festivals and Seasonal Events alerts you to special events you'll want to seek out.

Chapters in **The U.S. and British Virgin Islands '98** are broken down by island. For each major island, there is information on lodging, dining, beaches, outdoor activities and sports, shopping, nightlife and the arts, exploring, and also a section called A to Z. This section covers topics such as emergencies, getting around, guided tours, mail, opening and closing times, telephones, and visitor information. Price charts that we use to categorize the hotels and restaurants appear at the end of each chapter.

At the end of the book you'll find **Portraits,** wonderful essays about vacationing in the Virgin Islands, followed by sugges-

tions for pretrip reading, both fiction and nonfiction.

Icons and Symbols

★	Our special recommendations
✕	Restaurant
☷	Lodging establishment
✕☷	Lodging establishment whose restaurant warrants a special trip
⚠	Campgrounds
☺	Good for kids (rubber duckie)
☞	Sends you to another section of the guide for more information
✉	Address
☎	Telephone number
☉	Opening and closing times
⌑	Admission prices (those we give apply to adults; substantially reduced fees are almost always available for children, students, and senior citizens)

Numbers in white and black circles that appear on the maps, in the margins, and within the tours correspond to one another.

Hotel Facilities

We always list the facilities that are available—but we don't specify whether they cost extra: When pricing accommodations, always ask what's included. In addition, assume that all rooms have private baths unless otherwise noted.

Credit Cards

The following abbreviations are used: **AE,** American Express; **D,** Discover; **DC,** Diners Club; **MC,** MasterCard; and **V,** Visa.

Please Write to Us

You can use this book in the confidence that all prices and opening times are based on information supplied to us at press time; Fodor's cannot accept responsibility for any errors. Time inevitably brings changes, so always confirm information when it matters—especially if you're making a detour to visit a specific place. In addition, when making reservations be sure to mention if you have a disability or are traveling with children, if you prefer a private bath or a certain type of bed, or if you have specific dietary needs or other concerns.

Were the restaurants we recommended as described? Did our hotel picks exceed your expectations? Did you find a museum we recommended a waste of time? If you have complaints, we'll look into them and revise our entries when the facts warrant it. If you've discovered a special place that we haven't included, we'll pass the information along to our correspondents and have them check it out. So send us your feedback, positive *and* negative: email us at editors@fodors.com (specifying the name of the book on the subject line) or write the U.S. and British Virgin Islands editor at Fodor's, 201 East 50th Street, New York, NY 10022. Have a wonderful trip!

Karen Cure
Editorial Director

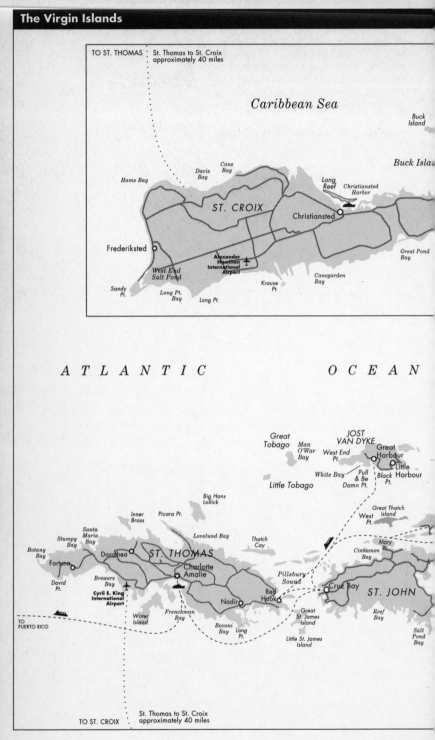

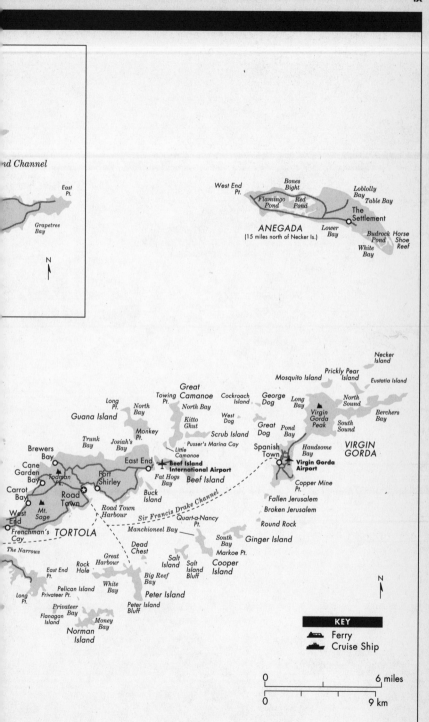

nd Channel

East
Pt.

*Grapetree
Bay*

N

West End
Pt.

*Bones
Bight*

*Flamingo
Pond* *Red
Pond*

Loblolly
Bay *Table Bay*

The
Settlement

ANEGADA
(15 miles north of Necker Is.)

*Lower
Bay*

*Budrock
Pond* Horse
Shoe
Reef

*White
Bay*

Necker
Island

Mosquito Island

Prickly Pear
Island

Eustatia Island

**Great
Camanoe**

Towing
Pt.

*Cockroach
Island*

*George
Dog*

*Long
Bay*

North
Sound

Virgin
Gorda
Peak

*Berchers
Bay*

Long
Pt.

North
Bay

North Bay

*West
Dog*

*Great
Dog*

*Pond
Bay*

South
Sound

Guana Island

*Kitto
Ghut*

Scrub Island

*Handsome
Bay*

**VIRGIN
GORDA**

*Trunk
Bay*

*Josiah's
Bay*

Monkey
Pt.

Pusser's Marina Cay

Spanish
Town

Brewers
Bay

*Little
Camanoe*

East End

**Beef Island
International Airport**

**Virgin Gorda
Airport**

Cane
Garden
Bay

Todman
Pk.

Fort
Shirley

*Fat Hogs
Bay*

Beef Island

*Copper Mine
Pt.*

Carrot
Bay

Road
Town

Buck
Island

Fallen Jerusalem

West
End

Mt.
Sage

*Road Town
Harbour*

Broken Jerusalem

Frenchman's
Cay

TORTOLA

Sir Francis Drake Channel

Quart-a-Nancy
Pt.

Round Rock

The Narrows

Manchioneel Bay

Dead
Chest

*South
Bay*

Markoe Pt.

Ginger Island

East End
Pt.

Rock
Hole

Great
Harbour

Salt
Island

Salt
Island
Bluff

**Cooper
Island**

N

Long
Pt.

Pelican Island Privateer Pt.

White
Bay

*Big Reef
Bay*

Peter Island

Privateer
Bay

Flanagan
Island

Money
Bay

Peter Island
Bluff

Norman
Island

KEY

Ferry

Cruise Ship

0 6 miles

0 9 km

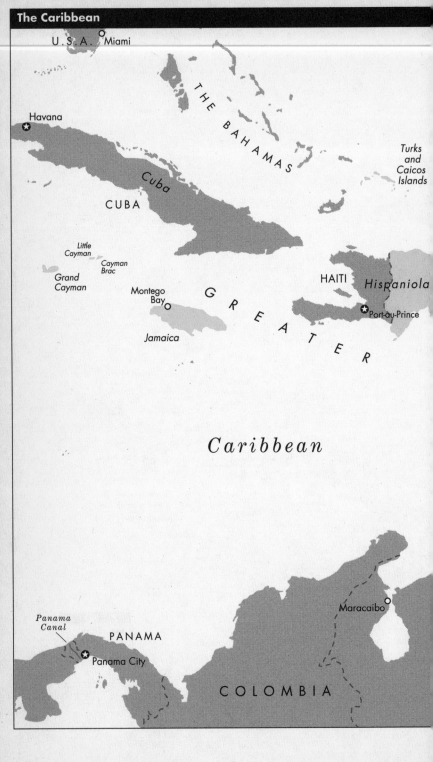

U.S.A. Miami

Havana

THE BAHAMAS

Turks
and
Caicos
Islands

Cuba

CUBA

Little
Cayman

Cayman
Brac

Grand
Cayman

Montego
Bay

G R E A T E R

HAITI *Hispaniola*

Port-au-Prince

Jamaica

Caribbean

Maracaibo

Panama
Canal

PANAMA

Panama City

C O L O M B I A

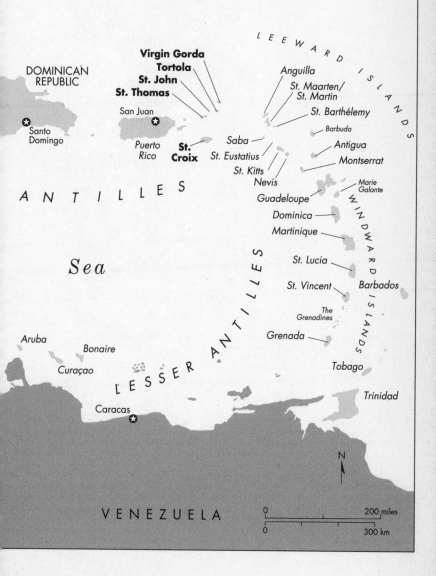

ATLANTIC OCEAN

LEEWARD ISLANDS

DOMINICAN
REPUBLIC

Virgin Gorda
Tortola
St. John
St. Thomas

San Juan

Anguilla

St. Maarten/
St. Martin

St. Barthélemy

Barbuda

Santo
Domingo

Puerto
Rico

**St.
Croix**

Saba

St. Eustatius

St. Kitts

Nevis

Antigua

Montserrat

A N T I L L E S

Guadeloupe

Marie
Galante

WINDWARD ISLANDS

Dominica

Martinique

Sea

St. Lucia

St. Vincent

Barbados

The
Grenadines

Grenada

LESSER ANTILLES

Aruba

Bonaire

Curaçao

Tobago

L E S S E R   A N T I L L E S

Trinidad

Caracas

N

VENEZUELA

0   200 miles

0   300 km

World Time Zones

Numbers below vertical bands relate each zone to Greenwich Mean Time (0 hrs.).
Local times frequently differ from these general indications,
as indicated by light-face numbers on map.

Mecca, **47**	Ottawa, **14**	San Francisco, **5**	Toronto, **13**
Mexico City, **12**	Paris, **30**	Santiago, **21**	Vancouver, **4**
Miami, **18**	Perth, **58**	Seoul, **59**	Vienna, **35**
Montréal, **15**	Reykjavík, **25**	Shanghai, **55**	Warsaw, **36**
Moscow, **45**	Rio de Janeiro, **23**	Singapore, **52**	Washington, D.C., **17**
Nairobi, **43**	Rome, **39**	Stockholm, **32**	Yangon, **49**
New Orleans, **11**	Saigon (Ho Chi Minh	Sydney, **61**	Zürich, **31**
New York City, **16**	City), **51**	Tokyo, **60**	

SMART TRAVEL TIPS A TO Z

Basic Information on Traveling in the Virgin Islands, Savvy Tips to Make Your Trip a Breeze, and Companies and Organizations to Contact

A

AIR TRAVEL

MAJOR AIRLINE OR LOW-COST CARRIER?

Most people choose a flight based on price. Yet there are other issues to consider. Major airlines offer the greatest number of departures; smaller airlines—including regional, usually have a more limited number of flights daily. Major airlines have frequent-flyer partners, which allow you to credit mileage earned on one airline to your account with another. Low-cost airlines offer a definite price advantage and fewer restrictions, such as advance-purchase requirements. Safety-wise, low-cost carriers as a group have a good history, but **check the safety record before booking** any low-cost carrier; call the Federal Aviation Administration's Consumer Hotline (☞ Airline Complaints, *below*).

On the small planes that fly from island to island, there is very limited carry-on space. Suitcases that fit under seats in big U.S. carriers just won't fit on these tiny planes. So **check your luggage and just bring the things you can't be without (medicine, bathing suit, etc.).**

➤ MAJOR AIRLINES: **American Airlines** (☎ 800/433–7300) to U.S.V.I., B.V.I. **Continental** (☎ 800/231–0856) to U.S.V.I. **Delta** (☎ 800/221–1212) to U.S.V.I., B.V.I. **United** (☎ 800/328–6877) to U.S.V.I. **US Airways** (☎ 800/428–4322) to U.S.V.I.

➤ SMALLER AIRLINES: From San Juan to U.S.V.I., B.V.I.: **American Eagle** (☎ 800/433–7300) to Beef Island/Tortola. **Four Star Aviation** (☎ 809/495–4389 or 809/777–9000) to Beef Island/Tortola and Virgin Gorda, via San Juan and St. Thomas. Service between St. Thomas and most Caribbean islands: **Leeward Island**

Air Transport (LIAT) (☎ 809/462–0701). Via St. Thomas: **Gorda Aero Service** (Tortola, ☎ 809/495–2271; a charter service).

➤ FROM THE U.K.: **British Airways** (☎ 0345/222–111) flies from London directly to Antigua, West Indies (an island south of the B.V.I.), four times per week. In Antigua you can connect with LIAT or VI Airways (☞ *above*) Alternatively, fly to Miami and board a connection with American Airlines; fly to Atlanta and board a Delta flight, or fly to San Juan in Puerto Rico, where you can board an Air Sunshine flight, in all cases landing at St. Thomas in the U.S. Virgins.

GET THE LOWEST FARE

The least-expensive airfares to the Virgin Islands are priced for round-trip travel. Major airlines usually require that you **book in advance and buy the ticket within 24 hours,** and you may have to **stay over a Saturday night.** It's smart to **call a number of airlines, and when you are quoted a good price, book it on the spot**—the same fare may not be available on the same flight the next day. Airlines generally allow you to change your return date for a $25–$50 fee. If you don't use your ticket you can apply the cost toward the purchase of a new ticket, again for a small charge. However, most low-fare tickets are nonrefundable. To get the lowest airfare, **check different routings.** If your destination or home city has more than one gateway, compare prices to and from different airports. Also price off-peak flights, which may be significantly less expensive.

To save money on flights from the United Kingdom and back, **look into an APEX or Super-PEX ticket.** Both should be booked in advance and have certain restrictions, though they can sometimes be purchased right at the airport.

DON'T STOP UNLESS YOU MUST

When you book, **look for nonstop flights** and **remember that "direct" flights stop at least once.** International flights on a country's flag carrier are almost always nonstop; U.S. airlines often fly direct. Try to **avoid connecting flights,** which require a change of plane. Two airlines may jointly operate a connecting flight, so ask if your airline operates every segment—you may find that your preferred carrier flies you only part of the way.

USE AN AGENT

Travel agents, especially those who specialize in finding the lowest fares (☞ Discounts & Deals, *below*), can be especially helpful when booking a plane ticket. When you're quoted a price, **ask your agent if the price is likely to get any lower.** Good agents know the seasonal fluctuations of airfares and can usually anticipate a sale or fare war. However, waiting can be risky: The fare could go *up* as seats become scarce, and you may wait so long that your preferred flight sells out. A wait-and-see strategy works best if your plans are flexible, but if you must arrive and depart on certain dates, don't delay.

CHECK WITH CONSOLIDATORS

Consolidators buy tickets for scheduled flights at reduced rates from the airlines then sell them at prices that beat the best fare available directly from the airlines, usually without advance restrictions. Sometimes you can even get your money back if you need to return the ticket. Carefully read the fine print detailing penalties for changes and cancellations, and **confirm your consolidator reservation with the airline.**

➤ CONSOLIDATORS: **United States Air Consolidators Association** (✉ 925 L St., Suite 220, Sacramento, CA 95814, ☎ 916/441–4166, ℻ 916/441–3520).

AVOID GETTING BUMPED

Airlines routinely overbook planes, knowing that not everyone with a ticket will show up, but sometimes everyone does. When that happens, airlines ask for volunteers to give up their seats. In return these volunteers usually get a certificate for a free flight and are rebooked on the next flight out. If there are not enough volunteers the airline must choose who will be denied boarding. The first to get bumped are passengers who checked in late and those flying on discounted tickets, **so get to the gate and check in as early as possible,** especially during peak periods.

Always **bring a photo ID to the airport.** You may be asked to show it before you are allowed to check in.

ENJOY THE FLIGHT

For more legroom, **request an emergency-aisle seat;** don't however, sit in the row in front of the emergency aisle or in front of a bulkhead, where seats may not recline.

If you don't like airline food, **ask for special meals when booking.** These can be vegetarian, low-cholesterol, or kosher, for example.

COMPLAIN IF NECESSARY

If your baggage goes astray or your flight goes awry, complain right away. Most carriers require that you file a claim immediately.

➤ AIRLINE COMPLAINTS: U.S. Department of Transportation **Aviation Consumer Protection Division** (✉ C-75, Washington, DC 20590, ☎ 202/366–2220). **Federal Aviation Administration (FAA) Consumer Hotline** (☎ 800/322–7873).

AIRPORTS & TRANSFERS

The major airport in the U.S. Virgin Islands is **Cyril E. King International Airport** (St. Thomas, ☎ 809/774–5100). The major gateway to the British Virgin Islands is **Beef Island International Airport** (Tortola, ☎ 809/495–2525).

C

CAMERAS, CAMCORDERS, & COMPUTERS

Always **keep your film, tape, or computer disks out of the sun.** Carry an extra supply of batteries, and **be prepared to turn on your camera, camcorder, or laptop** to prove to security personnel that the device is real. Always **ask for hand inspection of film,** which becomes clouded after successive exposure to airport X-ray machines, and **keep videotapes and computer disks away from metal detectors.**

➤ PHOTO HELP: **Kodak Information Center** (☎ 800/242–2424). *Kodak Guide to Shooting Great Travel Pictures,* available in bookstores or from Fodor's Travel Publications (☎ 800/533–6478; $16.50 plus $4 shipping).

CAR RENTAL

Rates in St. Thomas begin at $44 a day and $200 a week for an economy car with air-conditioning, automatic transmission, and unlimited mileage.

➤ MAJOR AGENCIES: **Alamo** (☎ 800/522–9696, 0800/272–2000 in the U.K.). **Avis** (☎ 800/331–1084, 800/879–2847 in Canada). **Budget** (☎ 800/527–0700, 0800/181181 in the U.K.). **Hertz** (☎ 800/654–3131, 800/263–0600 in Canada, 0345/555888 in the U.K.). **National InterRent** (☎ 800/227–7368; 0345/222525 in the U.K., where it is known as Europcar InterRent).

CUT COSTS

To get the best deal, **book through a travel agent who is willing to shop around.** When pricing cars, **ask about the location of the rental lot.** Some off-airport locations offer lower rates, and their lots are only minutes from the terminal via complimentary shuttle. You also may want to **price local car-rental companies,** whose rates may be lower still, although their service and maintenance may not be as good as those of a name-brand agency. Remember to ask about required deposits, cancellation penalties, and drop-off charges if you're planning to pick up the car in one city and leave it in another.

Also **ask your travel agent about a company's customer-service record.** How has it responded to late plane arrivals and vehicle mishaps? Are there often lines at the rental counter, and, if you're traveling during a holiday period, does a confirmed reservation guarantee you a car?

Be sure to **look into wholesalers,** companies that do not own fleets but rent in bulk from those that do and often offer better rates than traditional car-rental operations. Prices are best during off-peak periods. Rentals booked through wholesalers must be paid for before you leave the United States.

➤ RENTAL WHOLESALERS: **Auto Europe** (☎ 207/842–2000 or 800/223–5555, FAX 800/235–6321).

NEED INSURANCE?

When driving a rented car you are generally responsible for any damage to or loss of the vehicle. You also are liable for any property damage or personal injury that you may cause while driving. Before you rent, **see what coverage you already have** under the terms of your personal auto-insurance policy and credit cards.

For about $14 a day, rental companies sell protection known as a collision- or loss-damage waiver (CDW or LDW), which eliminates your liability for damage to the car; it's always optional and should never be automatically added to your bill.

However, **make sure you have enough coverage to pay for the car.** If you do not have auto insurance or an umbrella policy that covers damage to third parties, purchasing liability insurance and CDW or LDW is highly recommended.

BEWARE SURCHARGES

Before you pick up a car in one city and leave it in another, **ask about drop-off charges or one-way service fees,** which can be substantial. Note, too, that some rental agencies charge extra if you return the car before the time specified on your contract. To avoid a hefty refueling fee, **fill the tank just before you turn in the car,** but be aware that gas stations near the rental outlet may overcharge.

MEET THE REQUIREMENTS

In the U.S. Virgin Islands your own driver's license is acceptable for 90 days. The minimum age is 18, although many agencies will not rent to anyone under 25. In the British Virgin Islands a valid B.V.I. driver's license is required and can be obtained for $10 at car-rental agencies. You must be 25 and have a valid driver's license from another country.

You'll pay extra for child seats (about $3 per day), and for additional drivers (about $2 per day).

CHILDREN IN THE VIRGIN ISLANDS

Be sure to plan ahead and **involve your youngsters** as you outline your trip. When packing, include things to keep them busy en route. On sightseeing days try to schedule activities of special interest to your children. If you are renting a car don't forget to **arrange for a car seat** when you reserve. Most hotels in the Virgin Islands allow children under a certain age to stay in their parents' room at no extra charge, but others charge them as extra adults; be sure to **ask about the cutoff age for children's discounts.**

LODGING

➤ IN THE U.S.V.I.: Hotels that offer programs for children include the **Hyatt Regency** on St. John (☎ 800/233–1234), which offers supervised day and evening activity programs for children ages 3–15; the **Renaissance Grand Beach Resort** (☎ 809/775–1510 or 800/468–3571) on St. Thomas offers family room rates and a kids club (ages 4–12) that provides counselor-supervised activities; the **Sapphire Beach Resort and Marina** (☎ 809/ 775–6100 or 800/524–2090) on St. Thomas has a program in which children under 12 stay free and also offers daily supervised programs.

➤ IN THE B.V.I.: Resorts with notable family accommodations include the **Long Bay Beach Resort** (☎ 809/495–4252) on Tortola and the **Bitter End Yacht Club** (☎ 800/872–2392) and **Biras Creek Resort** (☎ 800/621–1270), both on Virgin Gorda.

➤ CAMPING: **Cinnamon Bay Campground** (☎ 809/776–6330) and **Maho Bay Campground** (☎ 809/776–6226), both on St. John, U.S.V.I. **Brewers Bay Campground** (☎ 809/494–3463) on Tortola, B.V.I. and **White Bay Campground** (☎ 809/495–9312) on Jost Van Dyke, B.V.I.

FLYING

As a general rule, infants under two not occupying a seat fly free. If your children are two or older **ask about children's airfares.**

In general the adult baggage allowance applies to children paying half or more of the adult fare.

According to the FAA it's a good idea to use safety seats aloft for children weighing less than 40 pounds. Airlines, however, can set their own policies: U.S. carriers allow FAA-approved models but usually require that you buy a ticket, even if your child would otherwise ride free, since the seats must be strapped into regular seats. Airline rules vary regarding their use, so it's important to **check your airline's policy about using safety seats during takeoff and landing.** Safety seats cannot obstruct any of the other passengers in the row, so get an appropriate seat assignment as early as possible.

When making your reservation, **request children's meals or a freestanding bassinet** if you need them; the latter are available only to those seated at the bulkhead, where there's enough legroom. Remember, however, that bulkhead seats may not have their own overhead bins, and there's no storage space in front of you—a major inconvenience.

GROUP TRAVEL

If you're planning to take your kids on a tour, look for companies that specialize in family travel.

➤ FAMILY-FRIENDLY TOUR OPERATORS: **Rascals in Paradise** (✉ 650 5th St., Suite 505, San Francisco, CA 94107, ☎ 415/978–9800 or 800/872–7225, FAX 415/442–0289).

Whenever possible, **pay with a major credit card** so you can cancel payment if there's a problem, provided that you can provide documentation. This is a good practice whether you're buying travel arrangements before your trip or shopping at your destination.

If you're doing business with a particular company for the first time, **contact your local Better Business Bureau and the attorney general's offices** in your state and the company's home state, as well. Have any complaints been filed?

Finally, if you're buying a package or tour, always **consider travel insurance** that includes default coverage (☞ Insurance, *below*).

➤ LOCAL BBBs: **Council of Better Business Bureaus** (✉ 4200 Wilson

SMART TRAVEL TIPS / THE GOLD GUIDE

Blvd., Suite 800, Arlington, VA 22203, ☎ 703/276–0100, FAX 703/525–8277).

CUSTOMS & DUTIES

When shopping, **keep receipts** for all of your purchases. Upon reentering the country, **be ready to show customs officials what you've bought.** If you feel a duty is incorrect, appeal the assessment. If you object to the way your clearance was handled, get the inspector's badge number. In either case, first ask to see a supervisor, then write to the port director at the address listed on your receipt. Send a copy of the receipt and other appropriate documentation. If you still don't get satisfaction you can take your case to customs headquarters in Washington.

ENTERING THE U.S. VIRGIN ISLANDS

Visitors arriving from the continental U.S. or Puerto Rico do not need to pass through customs. Visitors arriving from any other point of origin do. Items of a personal nature may be brought in to the U.S. Virgin Islands duty-free; any items of significant commercial value may be subject to a 6% duty.

ENTERING THE BRITISH VIRGIN ISLANDS

All visitors to the British Virgin Islands must pass through customs. Items of a personal nature may be brought in to the British Virgin Islands duty-free; any items of significant commercial value may be subject to a duty, which varies by the item.

ENTERING THE U.S.

U.S. citizens and residents may bring home $400 worth of foreign goods duty-free if you've been out of the country for at least 48 hours and haven't already used the $400 allowance or any part of it in the past 30 days.

Travelers 21 and older may bring back 1 liter of alcohol duty-free. In addition, regardless of your age, you are allowed 200 cigarettes and 100 non-Cuban cigars. Antiques, which the U.S. Customs Service defines as objects more than 100 years old, enter duty-free, as do original works of art done entirely by hand, including paintings, drawings, and sculptures.

You may also send packages home duty-free: up to $200 worth of goods for personal use, with a limit of one parcel per addressee per day (and no alcohol or tobacco products or perfume worth more than $5); label the package PERSONAL USE, and attach a list of its contents and their retail value. Do not label the package UNSOLICITED GIFT, or your duty-free exemption will drop to $100. Mailed items do not affect your duty-free allowance on your return.

➤ INFORMATION: **U.S. Customs Service** (Inquiries, ✉ Box 7407, Washington, DC 20044, ☎ 202/927–6724; complaints, ✉ Commissioner's Office, 1301 Constitution Ave. NW, Washington, DC 20229; registration of equipment, ✉ Resource Management, 1301 Constitution Ave. NW, Washington DC, 20229, ☎ 202/927–0540).

ENTERING CANADA

If you've been out of Canada for at least seven days you may bring in C$500 worth of goods duty-free. If you've been away for fewer than seven days but more than 48 hours, the duty-free allowance drops to C$200; if your trip lasts 24–48 hours, the allowance is C$50. You may not pool allowances with family members. Goods claimed under the C$500 exemption may follow you by mail; those claimed under the lesser exemptions must accompany you.

Alcohol and tobacco products may be included in the seven-day and 48-hour exemptions but not in the 24-hour exemption. If you meet the age requirements of the province or territory through which you reenter Canada you may bring in, duty-free, 1.14 liters (40 imperial ounces) of wine or liquor or 24 12-ounce cans or bottles of beer or ale. If you are 16 or older you may bring in, duty-free, 200 cigarettes and 50 cigars; these items must accompany you.

You may send an unlimited number of gifts worth up to C$60 each duty-free to Canada. Label the package UNSOLICITED GIFT—VALUE UNDER $60. Alcohol and tobacco are excluded.

➤ INFORMATION: **Revenue Canada** (⊠ 2265 St. Laurent Blvd. S, Ottawa, Ontario K1G 4K3, ☎ 613/993–0534, 800/461–9999 in Canada).

ENTERING THE U.K.

From countries outside the EU you may import, duty-free, 200 cigarettes or 50 cigars; 1 liter of spirits or 2 liters of fortified or sparkling wine or liqueurs; 2 liters of still table wine; 60 milliliters of perfume; 250 milliliters of toilet water; plus £136 worth of other goods, including gifts and souvenirs.

➤ INFORMATION: **HM Customs and Excise** (⊠ Dorset House, Stamford St., London SE1 9NG, ☎ 0171/202–4227).

D

DISABILITIES & ACCESSIBILITY

ACCESS IN THE VIRGIN ISLANDS

The Virgin Islands is a difficult destination for travelers with disabilities. Some hotels have ramps and moderately accessible facilities, but **make arrangements in advance** to ensure that ground-floor rooms are available. Taxis or specially adapted rental cars are the most practical option for island sightseeing. The Virgin Island Coalition of Citizens with Disabilities (☞ *below*) offers information on an islandwide Dial-A-Ride service and special parking permits.

Hotels and resorts will usually accommodate requests for ground-floor rooms, but it is wise to **inquire ahead** as to whether access to the beach, pool, lobby, and dining room requires the use of stairs and whether alternative ramps or elevators are available.

➤ LOCAL RESOURCES: **The Virgin Island Coalition of Citizens with Disabilities** (☎ 809/776–1277) offers information on accessible facilities, an islandwide Dial-A-Ride service, and special parking permits.

LODGING

➤ IN THE U.S.V.I.: **Hibiscus Beach Resort** (☎ 809/773–4042 or 800/442–0121), on St. Croix, has two wheelchair-accessible rooms, and the **Club St. Croix** (☎ 809/773–4800 or 800/524–2025) has limited facilities for people who use wheelchairs.

Caneel Bay Resort (☎ 809/776–6111 or 800/928–8889), on St. John, has two wheelchair-accessible rooms. Hotels on St. Thomas that accommodate travelers using wheelchairs include **Marriott's Frenchman's Reef and Morning Star Beach Resort** (☎ 809/776–8500 or 800/524–2000) and the **Renaissance Grand Beach Resort** (☎ 809/775–1311 or 800/468–3571).

➤ IN THE B.V.I.: a wheelchair-accessible property on Tortola is **Prospect Reef** (☎ 809/494–2512 or 800/356–8937).

TAXIS & FERRIES

Taxis—generally large safari vans with ample room for a wheelchair—are probably the best option for visitors who use wheelchairs. They are plentiful and relatively inexpensive. Although taxis are not fitted with ramps or lifts, drivers are generally happy to provide assistance. All ferries running between the islands can be fitted with roll-up ramps.

TIPS AND HINTS

When discussing accessibility with an operator or reservationist, **ask hard questions.** Are there any stairs, inside *or* out? Are there grab bars next to the toilet *and* in the shower/tub? How wide is the doorway to the room? To the bathroom? For the most extensive facilities meeting the latest legal specifications, **opt for newer accommodations,** which are more likely to have been designed with access in mind. Older buildings or ships may offer more limited facilities. Be sure to **discuss your needs before booking.**

➤ COMPLAINTS: **Disability Rights Section** (⊠ U.S. Department of Justice, Box 66738, Washington, DC 20035–6738, ☎ 202/514–0301 or 800/514–0301, FAX 202/307–1198, TTY 202/514–0383 or 800/514–0383) for general complaints. **Aviation Consumer Protection Division** (☞ Air Travel, *above*) for airline-related problems. **Civil Rights Office** (⊠ U.S. Department of Transportation, Departmental Office of Civil Rights, S-30, 400 7th St. SW, Room 10215, Washington, DC, 20590, ☎ 202/366–4648) for problems with surface transportation.

TRAVEL AGENCIES & TOUR OPERATORS

The Americans with Disabilities Act requires that travel firms serve the needs of all travelers. That said, you should note that some agencies and operators specialize in making travel arrangements for individuals and groups with disabilities.

➤ TRAVELERS WITH MOBILITY PROBLEMS: **Access Adventures** (✉ 206 Chestnut Ridge Rd., Rochester, NY 14624, ☎ 716/889–9096), run by a former physical-rehabilitation counselor. **Hinsdale Travel Service** (✉ 201 E. Ogden Ave., Suite 100, Hinsdale, IL 60521, ☎ 630/325–1335), a travel agency that benefits from the advice of wheelchair traveler Janice Perkins. **Wheelchair Journeys** (✉ 16979 Redmond Way, Redmond, WA 98052, ☎ 206/885–2210 or 800/313–4751), for general travel arrangements.

DISCOUNTS & DEALS

Be a smart shopper and **compare all your options before making a choice.** A plane ticket bought with a promotional coupon may not be cheaper than the least expensive fare from a discount ticket agency. For high-price travel purchases, such as packages or tours, keep in mind that what you get is just as important as what you save. Just because something is cheap doesn't mean it's a bargain.

LOOK IN YOUR WALLET

When you use your credit card to make travel purchases you may get free travel-accident insurance, collision-damage insurance, and medical or legal assistance, depending on the card and the bank that issued it. American Express, MasterCard, and Visa provide one or more of these services, so **get a copy of your credit card's travel-benefits policy.**

If you are a member of the American Automobile Association (AAA) or an oil-company-sponsored road-assistance plan, always **ask hotel or car-rental reservationists about auto-club discounts.** Some clubs offer additional discounts on tours, cruises, or admission to attractions. And don't forget that auto-club membership entitles you to free maps and trip-planning services.

DIAL FOR DOLLARS

To save money, **look into "1-800" discount reservations services,** which use their buying power to get a better price on hotels, airline tickets, even car rentals. When booking a room, always **call the hotel's local toll-free number** (if one is available) rather than the central reservations number—you'll often get a better price. Always ask about special packages or corporate rates.

When shopping for the best deal on hotels and car rentals in the B.V.I., **look for guaranteed exchange rates,** which protect you against a falling dollar. With your rate locked in you won't pay more even if the price goes up in the local currency.

➤ AIRLINE TICKETS: ☎ 800/FLY–4LESS. ☎ 800/FLY–ASAP.

SAVE ON COMBOS

Packages and guided tours can both save you money, but don't confuse the two. When you buy a package your travel remains independent, just as though you had planned and booked the trip yourself. Fly/drive packages, which combine airfare and car rental, are often a good deal.

JOIN A CLUB?

Many companies sell discounts in the form of travel clubs and coupon books, but these cost money. You must use participating advertisers to get a deal, and only after you recoup the initial membership cost or book price do you begin to save. If you plan to use the club or coupons frequently you may save considerably. Before signing up, find out what discounts you get for free.

➤ DISCOUNT CLUBS: **Entertainment Travel Editions** (✉ Box 1068, Trumbull, CT 06611, ☎ 800/445–4137; $28–$53, depending on destination). **Great American Traveler** (✉ Box 27965, Salt Lake City, UT 84127, ☎ 800/548–2812; $49.95 per year). **Moment's Notice Discount Travel Club** (✉ 7301 New Utrecht Ave., Brooklyn, NY 11204, ☎ 718/234–6295; $25 per year, single or family). **Privilege Card International** (✉ 201 E. Commerce St., Suite 198, Youngstown, OH 44503, ☎ 330/746–5211 or 800/236–9732; $74.95 per year). **Sears's Mature Outlook** (✉ Box

9390, Des Moines, IA 50306, ☎ 800/336–6330; $14.95 per year). **Travelers Advantage** (✉ CUC Travel Service, 3033 S. Parker Rd., Suite 1000, Aurora, CO 80014, ☎ 800/548–1116 or 800/648–4037; $49 per year, single or family). **Worldwide Discount Travel Club** (✉ 1674 Meridian Ave., Miami Beach, FL 33139, ☎ 305/534–2082; $50 per year family, $40 single).

G
GAY & LESBIAN TRAVEL

➤ TOUR OPERATORS: **R.S.V.P. Travel Productions** (✉ 2800 University Ave. SE, Minneapolis, MN 55414, ☎ 612/379–4697 or 800/328–7787), for cruises and resort vacations for gays.

➤ GAY- AND LESBIAN-FRIENDLY TRAVEL AGENCIES: **Advance Damron** (✉ 1 Greenway Plaza, Suite 800, Houston, TX 77046, ☎ 713/682–2002 or 800/695–0880, FAX 713/888–1010). **Club Travel** (✉ 8739 Santa Monica Blvd., West Hollywood, CA 90069, ☎ 310/358–2200 or 800/429–8747, FAX 310/358–2222). **Islanders/Kennedy Travel** (✉ 183 W. 10th St., New York, NY 10014, ☎ 212/242–3222 or 800/988–1181, FAX 212/929–8530). **Now Voyager** (✉ 4406 18th St., San Francisco, CA 94114, ☎ 415/626–1169 or 800/255–6951, FAX 415/626–8626). **Yellowbrick Road** (✉ 1500 W. Balmoral Ave., Chicago, IL 60640, ☎ 773/561–1800 or 800/642–2488, FAX 773/561–4497). **Skylink Women's Travel** (✉ 3577 Moorland Ave., Santa Rosa, CA 95407, ☎ 707/585–8355 or 800/225–5759, FAX 707/584–5637), serving lesbian travelers.

H
HEALTH

SUN PROTECTION

Even if you've never been sunburned in your life, believe the warnings and **use a sunscreen** in the Virgin Islands—especially if you've never been so close to the equator. If you're dark-skinned, start with at least an SPF 15 and keep it on. If you are fair-skinned, use a sunscreen with a higher SPF and stay out of the sun during the midday. Rays are most intense between 11 and 2, so move under a sea-grape tree (although you can still burn here) or, better yet, take a shady lunch break. You can also burn in this part of the world when it is cloudy, so putting sunscreen on every day no matter what the weather is the best strategy.

INSECTS

Mosquitoes can be a problem here. Off! insect repellent is readily available, but you may want to bring something stronger. Also a nuisance are the little varmints from the sand-flea family known as no-see-ums. You don't realize you're being had for dinner until it's too late, and these bites stay, and itch, and itch, and itch. No-see-ums start getting hungry around 3 PM and are out in force by sunset. They are always more numerous in shady and wooded areas (such as the campgrounds on St. John). **Take a towel along for sitting on the beach, and keep reapplying insect repellent.** If you can't find any repellent and are desperate, blot a cloth with vodka or gin and dab the itch.

MEDICAL PLANS

No one plans to get sick while traveling, but it happens, so **consider signing up with a medical-assistance company.** Members get doctor referrals, emergency evacuation or repatriation, 24-hour telephone hot lines for medical consultation, cash for emergencies, and other personal and legal assistance. Coverage varies by plan, so **review the benefits carefully.**

➤ MEDICAL-ASSISTANCE COMPANIES: **International SOS Assistance** (✉ Box 11568, Philadelphia, PA 19116, ☎ 215/244–1500 or 800/523–8930; ✉ Box 466, pl. Bonaventure, Montréal, Québec H5A 1C1, ☎ 514/874–7674 or 800/363–0263; ✉ 7 Old Lodge Pl., St. Margarets, Twickenham TW1 1RQ, England, ☎ 0181/744–0033). **MEDEX Assistance Corporation** (✉ Box 5375, Timonium, MD 21094, ☎ 410/453–6300 or 800/537–2029). **Traveler's Emergency Network** (✉ 3100 Tower Blvd., Suite 1000B, Durham, NC 27707, ☎ 919/490–6055 or 800/275–4836, FAX 919/493–8262). **TravMed** (✉ Box 5375, Timonium, MD 21094, ☎ 410/453–6380 or 800/732–5309). **Worldwide Assistance Services** (✉ 1133 15th St. NW, Suite 400, Washington, DC 20005, ☎ 202/331–1609 or 800/821–2828, FAX 202/828–5896).

THE GOLD GUIDE / SMART TRAVEL TIPS

SWIMMING & DIVING

In the water, **watch for black spiny sea urchins** on the bottom; stepping on their spines can really hurt. The good news is that they're usually found in reef areas where you'll be snorkeling, so you aren't likely to step on one by accident but they can be found next to an isolated rock, so be careful.

Familiarize yourself with the various types of coral before you go out. The fire coral, which can give you a bad burn if you scrape against it, is particularly nasty. **If you do get burned, apply ammonia** to the spot as soon as possible.

Scuba divers take note: **Do not fly within 24 hours of scuba diving.**

I

INSURANCE

Travel insurance is the best way to **protect yourself against financial loss.** The most useful policies are trip-cancellation-and-interruption, default, medical, and comprehensive insurance.

Without insurance you will lose all or most of your money if you cancel your trip, regardless of the reason. It's essential that you **buy trip-cancellation-and-interruption insurance,** particularly if your airline ticket, cruise, or package tour is nonrefundable and cannot be changed. When considering how much coverage you need, look for a policy that will cover the cost of your trip plus the nondiscounted price of a one-way airline ticket, should you need to return home early. Also **consider default or bankruptcy insurance,** which protects you against a supplier's failure to deliver.

Medicare generally does not cover health-care costs outside the United States, nor do many privately issued policies. If your own policy does not cover you outside the United States, **consider buying supplemental medical coverage.** Remember that travel health insurance is different from a medical-assistance plan (☞ Health, *above*).

Citizens of the United Kingdom can buy an annual travel-insurance policy valid for most vacations during the year in which it's purchased. If you

are pregnant or have a preexisting medical condition, make sure you're covered. According to the Association of British Insurers, a trade association representing 450 insurance companies, it's wise to buy extra medical coverage when you visit the United States.

If you have purchased an expensive vacation, particularly one that involves travel abroad, comprehensive insurance is a must. **Look for comprehensive policies that include trip-delay insurance,** which will protect you in the event that weather problems cause you to miss your flight, tour, or cruise. A few insurers sell waivers for preexisting medical conditions. Companies that offer both features include Access America, Carefree Travel, Travel Insured International, and Travel Guard (☞ *below*).

Always **buy travel insurance directly from the insurance company;** if you buy it from a travel agency or tour operator that goes out of business you probably will not be covered for the agency or operator's default, a major risk. Before you make any purchase, **review your existing health and home-owner's policies** to find out whether they cover expenses incurred while traveling.

➤ TRAVEL INSURERS: **Access America** (⊠ 6600 W. Broad St., Richmond, VA 23230, ☎ 804/285–3300 or 800/284–8300). **Carefree Travel Insurance** (⊠ Box 9366, 100 Garden City Plaza, Garden City, NY 11530, ☎ 516/294–0220 or 800/323–3149). **Near Travel Services** (⊠ Box 1339, Calumet City, IL 60409, ☎ 708/868–6700 or 800/654–6700). **Travel Guard International** (⊠ 1145 Clark St., Stevens Point, WI 54481, ☎ 715/345–0505 or 800/826–1300). **Travel Insured International** (⊠ Box 280568, East Hartford, CT 06128–0568, ☎ 860/528–7663 or 800/243–3174). **Travelex Insurance Services** (⊠ 11717 Burt St., Suite 202, Omaha, NE 68154-1500, ☎ 402/445–8637 or 800/228–9792, FAX 800/867–9531). **Wallach & Company** (⊠ 107 W. Federal St., Box 480, Middleburg, VA 20118, ☎ 540/687–3166 or 800/237–6615), in the U.S. **Mutual of Omaha** (⊠ Travel Division, 500 University Ave., Toronto, Ontario M5G 1V8, ☎ 416/598–

4083, 800/268–8825 in Canada).
Association of British Insurers (✉ 51
Gresham St., London EC2V 7HQ,
☎ 0171/600–3333, in the U.K.).

L
LODGING

APARTMENT AND VILLA RENTALS

If you want a home base that's roomy
enough for a family and comes with
cooking facilities, **consider a furnished
rental.** These can save you money,
however some rentals are luxury
properties, economical only when
your party is large. Home-exchange
directories list rentals (often second
homes owned by prospective house
swappers), and some services search
for a house or apartment for you
(even a castle if that's your fancy) and
handle the paperwork. Some send an
illustrated catalog; others send photographs only of specific properties,
sometimes at a charge. Up-front
registration fees may apply.

➤ RENTAL AGENTS: **At Home Abroad**
(✉ 405 E. 56th St., Suite 6H, New
York, NY 10022, ☎ 212/421–9165,
FAX 212/752–1591). **Europa-Let/
Tropical Inn-Let** (✉ 92 N. Main St.,
Ashland, OR 97520, ☎ 541/482–
5806 or 800/462–4486, FAX 541/482–
0660). **Property Rentals International**
(✉ 1008 Mansfield Crossing Rd.,
Richmond, VA 23236, ☎ 804/378–
6054 or 800/220–3332, FAX 804/379–
2073). **Rental Directories International** (✉ 2044 Rittenhouse Sq.,
Philadelphia, PA 19103, ☎ 215/985–
4001, FAX 215/985–0323). **Rent-a-
Home International** (✉ 7200 34th
Ave. NW, Seattle, WA 98117, ☎ 206/
789–9377 or 800/488–7368, FAX 206/
789–9379). **Vacation Home Rentals
Worldwide** (✉ 235 Kensington Ave.,
Norwood, NJ 07648, ☎ 201/767–
9393 or 800/633–3284, FAX 201/767–
5510). **Villas International** (✉ 605
Market St., Suite 510, San Francisco,
CA 94105, ☎ 415/281–0910 or 800/
221–2260, FAX 415/281–0919). **Hideaways International** (✉ 767 Islington
St., Portsmouth, NH 03801, ☎ 603/
430–4433 or 800/843–4433, FAX 603/
430–4444) is a travel club whose
members arrange rentals among
themselves; yearly membership is $99.

HOME EXCHANGES

If you would like to exchange your
home for someone else's, **join a home-
exchange organization,** which will
send you its updated listings of available exchanges for a year and will
include your own listing in at least
one of them. Making the arrangements is up to you.

➤ EXCHANGE CLUBS: **HomeLink
International** (✉ Box 650, Key West,
FL 33041, ☎ 305/294–7766 or 800/
638–3841, FAX 305/294–1148)
charges $83 per year.

M
MONEY

The U.S. dollar is the medium of
exchange in both the British Virgin
Islands and the U.S. Virgin Islands.

ATMS

Before leaving home, **make sure that
your credit cards have been pro-
grammed for ATM use in the Virgin
Islands.** Note that your ATM card
may not work in the British Virgin
Islands, and that Discover is accepted
mostly in the United States. Local
bank cards often do not work over-
seas or may access only your checking
account; **ask your bank about a
MasterCard/Cirrus or Visa debit card,**
which works like a bank card but can
be used at any ATM displaying a
MasterCard/Cirrus or Visa logo.
These cards, too, may tap only your
checking account; check with your
bank about their policy.

➤ ATM LOCATIONS: **Cirrus** (☎ 800/
424–7787). **Plus** (☎ 800/843–7587).

COSTS

In both the U.S.V.I. and the B.V.I., a
cup of coffee goes for 70¢–$1.50, a
beer costs $2–$5, and a cocktail runs
$3–$6.

N
NEWSPAPERS & MAGAZINES

There are several visitor-oriented
publications distributed free in hotel
lobbies, visitor centers, and shops.
The most current is *St. Thomas This
Week* (check the cruise-ship schedule
on the front cover and you'll know
when to avoid Charlotte Amalie) for
that island, and *St. Croix This Week*
for St. Croix. *Here's How* and *V.I.*

Playground are also good, comprehensive guides.

For the real inside scoop on St. John, get hold of Arne and Barbara Jakobsen's *St. John Guide Book* and Linda Smith-Palmer's detailed "St. John Map," both of which are published annually.

In the B.V.I., the *Island Sun* is the best local paper for everything from entertainment listings to local gossip. The *Welcome Tourist Guide* is comprehensive and available free at airports, hotels and resorts, and from some taxi drivers. The free *Limin' Times* covers all the entertainment in the B.V.I. and comes out weekly and you can find it in the lobby of almost any hotel or resort.

P

PACKING FOR THE VIRGIN ISLANDS

You won't need a suit and tie or a cocktail dress, but at the fancier resorts men will need a jacket (but not a tie) and women will need summery dresses or pant suits. Casual clothes are appropriate for almost everywhere. Natural materials that breathe work best in these warm climates, and there are few dry cleaners around so bring washable clothing. At many places you will spend the day in your bathing suit, wear a coverup to lunch, and then slip into something casual for dinner. If you plan to hike, be sure to bring along some sturdy shoes. You also may want to **bring a lightweight sweater or long-sleeve T-shirt** for breezy nights (or overly air-conditioned restaurants) or for the ferry ride home after a day in the sun.

One clothing tip that will go a long way in tourist-local relations: **Men, keep your shirts on, and women, get your tan on the beach, not in town.** You'll receive a much kinder reception from the prim Virgin Islanders if you are fully, albeit casually, dressed.

To avoid paying shockingly high drugstore prices in the Virgin Islands, **buy creams, lotions, insect repellents, sunscreens, and sunburn remedies before you leave home.** For the same reason, **buy your film at home.**

Bring an extra pair of eyeglasses or contact lenses in your carry-on luggage, and if you have a health problem, **pack enough medication** to last the entire trip or have your doctor write you a prescription using the drug's generic name, because brand names vary from country to country. It's important that you **don't put prescription drugs or valuables in luggage to be checked**: it might go astray. To avoid problems with customs officials, carry medications in the original packaging.

Also, don't forget the addresses of offices that handle refunds of lost traveler's checks.

LUGGAGE

In general you are entitled to check two bags on flights within the United States and on international flights leaving the U.S. A third piece may be brought on board, but it must fit easily under the seat in front of you or in the overhead compartment.

If you are flying between two foreign destinations, note that baggage allowances may be determined not by piece but by weight—generally 88 pounds (40 kilograms) in first class, 66 pounds (30 kilograms) in business class, and 44 pounds (20 kilograms) in economy. If your flight between two cities abroad *connects* with your transatlantic or transpacific flight, the piece method still applies.

Airline liability for baggage is limited to $1,250 per person on flights within the United States. On international flights it amounts to $9.07 per pound or $20 per kilogram for checked baggage (roughly $640 per 70-pound bag) and $400 per passenger for unchecked baggage. Insurance for losses exceeding these amounts can be bought from the airline at check-in for about $10 per $1,000 of coverage; note that this coverage excludes a rather extensive list of items, which is shown on your airline ticket.

Before departure, **itemize your bags' contents** and their worth, and label the bags with your name, address, and phone number. (If you use your home address, cover it so that potential thieves can't see it readily.) Inside each bag, **pack a copy of your itinerary.** At check-in, **make sure that**

each bag is correctly tagged with the destination airport's three-letter code. If your bags arrive damaged or fail to arrive at all, file a written report with the airline before leaving the airport.

Once your travel plans are confirmed, **check the expiration date of your passport if you're going to the B.V.I.** It's also a good idea to **make photocopies of the data page**; leave one copy with someone at home and keep another with you, separated from your passport. If you lose your passport, promptly call the nearest embassy or consulate and the local police; having a copy of the data page can speed replacement.

Upon entering the U.S. Virgin Islands, U.S. and Canadian citizens are required to present some proof of citizenship, if not a passport then a birth certificate, citizenship certificate, voter registration card, or driver's license. Upon entering the British Virgin Islands, it is best if U.S. and Canadian citizens have a valid passport but an expired passport *plus* a birth certificate, voter registration card, or driver's license with photo are acceptable. If you are arriving from the U.S. mainland or Puerto Rico, you need no inoculation or health certificate.

U.K. CITIZENS

Citizens of the United Kingdom need only a valid passport to enter the U.S. and British Virgin Islands for stays of up to 90 days.

➤ INFORMATION: **London Passport Office** (☎ 0990/21010) for fees and documentation requirements and to request an emergency passport. **U.S. Embassy Visa Information Line** (☎ 01891/200–290) for U.S. visa information; calls cost 49p per minute or 39p per minute cheap rate. **U.S. Embassy Visa Branch** (✉ 5 Upper Grosvenor St., London W1A 2JB) for U.S. visa information; send a self-addressed stamped envelope. Write the **U.S. Consulate General** (✉ Queen's House, Queen St., Belfast BTI 6EO) if you live in Northern Ireland.

S

During the off-season (April 15 to December 15), many hotels in the U.S. Virgin Islands offer substantial rate reductions for senior citizens. For a list of participating hotels, contact the U.S. Virgin Islands Department of Tourism (☞ Visitor Information, *below*).

To qualify for age-related discounts, **mention your senior-citizen status up front** when booking hotel reservations (not when checking out) and before you're seated in restaurants (not when paying the bill). Note that discounts may be limited to certain menus, days, or hours. When renting a car, **ask about promotional car-rental discounts,** which can be cheaper than senior-citizen rates.

➤ EDUCATIONAL TRAVEL PROGRAMS: **Elderhostel** (✉ 75 Federal St., 3rd floor, Boston, MA 02110, ☎ 617/426–7788).

To save money, **look into deals available through student-oriented travel agencies.** To qualify you'll need a bona fide student ID card. Members of international student groups are also eligible.

➤ STUDENT IDs AND SERVICES: **Council on International Educational Exchange** (✉ CIEE, 205 E. 42nd St., 14th floor, New York, NY 10017, ☎ 212/822–2600, or 888/268–6245, FAX 212/822–2699), for mail orders only, in the United States. **Travel Cuts** (✉ 187 College St., Toronto, Ontario M5T 1P7, ☎ 416/979–2406 or 800/667–2887) in Canada.

➤ HOSTELING: **Hostelling International—American Youth Hostels** (✉ 733 15th St. NW, Suite 840, Washington, DC 20005, ☎ 202/783–6161, FAX 202/783–6171). **Hostelling International—Canada** (✉ 400-205 Catherine St., Ottawa, Ontario K2P 1C3, ☎ 613/237–7884, FAX 613/237–7868). **Youth Hostel Association of England and Wales** (✉ Trevelyan House, 8 St. Stephen's Hill, St. Albans, Hertfordshire AL1 2DY, ☎ 01727/855215 or 01727/845047, FAX 01727/844126). Membership in the U.S., $25; in Canada, C$26.75; in the U.K., £9.30).

THE GOLD GUIDE / SMART TRAVEL TIPS

T

TAXES

➤ DEPARTURE: There is a $10 departure tax from the B.V.I. for travelers leaving by air; the tax is $5 for those leaving by sea. The tax for the U.S.V.I. is already incorporated into your airfare or cruise bill.

➤ HOTEL: An 8% tax is added to hotel rates in the U.S.V.I. In the B.V.I. there is a 7% tax, which will be added to your bill in addition to a 10% service charge.

➤ SALES: There is no sales tax in either the U.S. or British Virgin Islands.

TELEPHONES

The area code for the U.S. Virgin Islands has been changed from 809 to 340. Until June 30, 1998, both numbers will be operational.

LONG-DISTANCE

Before you go, **find out the local access codes** for your destinations. AT&T, MCI, and Sprint long-distance services make calling home relatively convenient, but you may find the local access number blocked in many hotel rooms. First ask the hotel operator to connect you. If the hotel operator balks, ask for an international operator, or dial the international operator yourself. One way to improve your odds of getting connected is to travel with more than one company's calling card (a hotel may block Sprint, for example, but not MCI). If all else fails, call your phone company collect in the United States or call from a pay phone in the hotel lobby.

➤ TO OBTAIN ACCESS CODES: **AT&T USADirect** (☎ 800/874–4000). **MCI Call USA** (☎ 800/444–4444). **Sprint Express** (☎ 800/793–1153).

TIPPING

In the U.S.V.I. some hotels and restaurants add a 10% or 15% service charge to your bill, but generally only if you are part of a large group. In the B.V.I. hotels on Tortola add a 10% service charge to your bill and on Virgin Gorda it can be 12%.

TOUR OPERATORS

Buying a prepackaged tour or independent vacation can make your trip to the Virgin Islands less expensive and more hassle-free. Because everything is prearranged you'll spend less time planning.

Operators that handle several hundred thousand travelers per year can use their purchasing power to give you a good price. Their high volume may also indicate financial stability. But some small companies provide more personalized service.

A GOOD DEAL?

The more your package or tour includes, the better you can predict the ultimate cost of your vacation. Make sure you know exactly what is covered, and **beware of hidden costs.** Are taxes, tips, and service charges included? Transfers and baggage handling? Entertainment and excursions? These can add up.

If the package or tour you are considering is priced lower than in your wildest dreams, **be skeptical.** Also, **make sure your travel agent knows the accommodations** and other services. Ask about the hotel's location, room size, beds, and whether it has a pool, room service, or programs for children, if you care about these. Has your agent been there in person or sent others you can contact?

BUYER BEWARE

Each year consumers are stranded or lose their money when tour operators—even very large ones with excellent reputations—go out of business. So **check out the operator.** Find out how long the company has been in business, and ask several agents about its reputation. **Don't book unless the firm has a consumer-protection program.**

Members of the National Tour Association and United States Tour Operators Association are required to set aside funds to cover your payments and travel arrangements in case the company defaults. Nonmembers may carry insurance instead. Look for the details, and for the name of an underwriter with a solid reputation, in the operator's brochure. Note: When it comes to tour operators, **don't trust escrow accounts.** Although there are laws governing charter-flight operators, no governmental body prevents tour operators from raiding the till. For more information, *see* Consumer Protection, *above.*

➤ TOUR-OPERATOR RECOMMENDA-
TIONS: **National Tour Association**
(✉ NTA, 546 E. Main St., Lexington, KY 40508, ☎ 606/226–4444
or 800/755–8687). **United States
Tour Operators Association** (✉
USTOA, 342 Madison Ave., Suite
1522, New York, NY 10173, ☎
212/599–6599, FAX 212/599–6744).

USING AN AGENT

Travel agents are excellent resources.
When shopping for an agent, however,
you should **collect brochures from
several sources**; some agents' suggestions may be skewed by promotional
relationships with tour and package
firms that reward them for volume
sales. If you have a special interest,
**find an agent with expertise in that
area** (☞ Travel Agencies, *below*).
Don't rely solely on your agent, who
may be unaware of small-niche operators. Note that some special-interest
travel companies only sell directly to
the public and that some large operators only accept bookings made
through travel agents.

SINGLE TRAVELERS

Prices for packages and tours are
usually quoted per person, based on
two sharing a room. If traveling solo,
you may be required to pay the full
double-occupancy rate. Some operators eliminate this surcharge if you
agree to be matched with a roommate
of the same sex, even if one is not
found by departure time.

PACKAGES

Like group tours, independent vacation packages are available from
major tour operators and airlines. The
companies listed below offer vacation
packages in a broad price range.

➤ AIR/HOTEL: **American Airlines Fly
AAway Vacations** (☎ 800/321–2121).
Delta Dream Vacations (☎ 800/872–
7786, FAX 954/357–4687). **US Airways
Vacations** (☎ 800/455–0123).

➤ FROM THE U.K.: **British Virgin
Islands Holidays** (✉ 11-13 Hockerill
St., Bishops Stortford, Herts. CM23
2DH, ☎ 01279/656111) acts as agents
for all major airlines and hotels in the
B.V.I. They can arrange multicenter
holiday stays, bare-boat charters and
crewed-yacht charters, and inclusive
package holidays. Also look into
Caribbean Connection (✉ Concorde

House, Forest St., Chester CH1 1QR,
☎ 01244/341131), **Caribtours** (✉ 161
Fulham Rd., London SW3 6SN, ☎
0171/581–3517), **Harlequin Worldwide** (✉ 2 North Rd., South Ock-
endon, Essex RM15 6QJ, ☎ 01708/
852780), and **Hayes and Jarvis Ltd.**
(✉ Hayes House, 152 King St., London W6 0QU, ☎ 0181/748–5050).

THEME TRIPS

➤ SAILING SCHOOLS: **Annapolis Sailing School** (✉ Box 3334, 601 6th St.,
Annapolis, MD 21403, ☎ 410/267–
7205 or 800/638–9192). **Offshore
Sailing School** (✉ 16731-110
McGregor Blvd., Fort Myers, FL
33908, ☎ 941/454–1700 or 800/
221–4326, FAX 941/454–1191).

➤ SCUBA DIVING: **Rothschild Dive
Safaris** (✉ 900 West End Ave., #1B,
New York, NY 10025-3525, ☎ 800/
359–0747, FAX 212/749–6172).

➤ VILLA RENTALS: **Unusual Villas &
Island Rentals** (✉ 101 Tempsford
La., Penthouse 9, Richmond, VA
23226, ☎ FAX 804/288–2823). **Villas
International** (✉ 605 Market St., San
Francisco, CA 94105, ☎ 415/281–
0910 or 800/221–2260, FAX 415/
281–0919).

➤ YACHT CHARTERS: **Alden Yacht
Charters** (✉ 1909 Alden Landing,
Portsmouth, RI 02871, ☎ 401/683–
1782 or 800/662–2628, FAX 401/
683–3668). **Huntley Yacht Vacations**
(✉ 210 Preston Rd., Wernersville, PA
19565, ☎ 610/678–2628 or 800/
322–9224, FAX 610/670–1767). **Lynn
Jachney Charters** (✉ Box 302, Marblehead, MA 01945, 617/639–0787
or 800/223–2050, FAX 617/639–
0216). **The Moorings** (✉ 19345 U.S.
Hwy. 19 N, 4th floor, Clearwater, FL
34624-3193, ☎ 813/530–5424 or
800/535–7289, FAX 813/530–9474).
Nicholson Yacht Charters (✉ 78
Bolton St., Cambridge, MA 02140-
3321, ☎ 617/661–0555 or 800/662–
6066, FAX 617/661–0554). **Ocean
Voyages** (✉ 1709 Bridgeway, Sausa-
lito, CA 94965, ☎ 415/332–4681 or
800/299–4444, FAX 415/332–7460).
Russell Yacht Charters (✉ 404 Hulls
Hwy., #175, Southport, CT 06490,
☎ 203/255–2783 or 800/635–
8895). **SailAway Yacht Charters**
(✉ 15605 S.W. 92nd Ave., Miami, FL
33157-1972, ☎ 305/253–7245 or
800/724–5292, FAX 305/251–4408).

TRAVEL AGENCIES

A good travel agent puts your needs first. **Look for an agency that specializes in your destination, has been in business at least five years, and emphasizes customer service.** If you're looking for an agency-organized package or tour, your best bet is to choose an agency that's a member of the National Tour Association or the United States Tour Operator's Association (☞ Tour Operators, *above*).

➤ LOCAL AGENT REFERRALS: **American Society of Travel Agents** (✉ ASTA, 1101 King St., Suite 200, Alexandria, VA 22314, ☎ 703/739–2782, FAX 703/684–8319). **Alliance of Canadian Travel Associations** (✉ Suite 201, 1729 Bank St., Ottawa, Ontario K1V 7Z5, ☎ 613/521–0474, FAX 613/521–0805). **Association of British Travel Agents** (✉ 55–57 Newman St., London W1P 4AH, ☎ 0171/637–2444, FAX 0171/637–0713).

TRAVEL GEAR

Travel catalogs specialize in useful items, such as compact alarm clocks and travel irons, that can **save space when packing.**

➤ MAIL-ORDER CATALOGS: **Magellan's** (☎ 800/962–4943, FAX 805/568–5406). **Orvis Travel** (☎ 800/541–3541, FAX 540/343–7053). **TravelSmith** (☎ 800/950–1600, FAX 800/950–1656).

U

U.S. GOVERNMENT

The U.S. government can be an excellent source of inexpensive travel information. When planning your trip, **find out what government materials are available.**

➤ ADVISORIES: **U.S. Department of State American Citizens Services Office** (✉ Room 4811, Washington, DC 20520); enclose a self-addresses, stamped envelope. Interactive hot line (☎ 202/647–5225, FAX 202/647–3000). Computer bulletin board (☎ 202/647–9225).

➤ PAMPHLETS: **Consumer Information Center** (✉ Consumer Information Catalogue, Pueblo, CO 81009, ☎ 719/948–3334) for a free catalog that includes travel titles.

VISITOR INFORMATION

For general information on the islands contact these tourist offices before you go.

➤ U.S. VIRGIN ISLANDS: **United States Virgin Islands Department of Tourism** (✉ 500 N. Michigan Ave., Chicago, IL 60611, ☎ 312/670–8784, FAX 312/670–8789). In Los Angeles: (✉ 3460 Wilshire Blvd., Suite 412, Los Angeles, CA 90010, ☎ 213/739–0138, FAX 213/739–2005). In Florida: (✉ 2655 Le Jeune Rd., Suite 907, Coral Gables, FL 33134, ☎ 305/442–7200, FAX 305/445–9044). In New York: (✉ 630 Fifth Ave., New York, NY 10111, ☎ 212/332–2222, FAX 212/332–2223). In Washington, DC: (✉ 444 Capitol St., Washington, DC 20006, ☎ 202/624–3590, FAX 202/624–3594). In Puerto Rico: (✉ 1300 Ashford Ave., Condado, Santurce, Puerto Rico 00907, ☎ 787/724–3816, FAX 787/724–7223). In Canada: (✉ 33 Bloor St. W., Toronto, Ontario M5V 1C2, ☎ 416/233–1414). In the U.K.: (✉ Molasses House, Clove Hitch Quay, Plantation Wharf, York Pl., London SW11 3TN, ☎ 0171/978–5262, FAX 0171/924–3171).

➤ BRITISH VIRGIN ISLANDS: **British Virgin Islands Tourist Board** (✉ 630 Fifth Ave., New York, NY 10111, ☎ 212/696–0400 or 800/835–8530, FAX 212/949–8254). **British Virgin Islands Tourism Bureau** (✉ 1804 Union St., San Francisco, CA 94123, ☎ 415/775–0344 or 800/232–7770, FAX 415/775–2554). In the U.K.: (✉ 110 St. Martins La., London WC2N 4DY, ☎ 0171/240–4259, FAX 0171/240–4270).

W

WHEN TO GO

Traditionally, high season in the Virgin Islands has been in the winter, from about December 15 to the week after the U.S.V.I. Carnival, usually the last week in April. This is the most fashionable, the most expensive, and the most popular time for cruising or lolling on the beaches, far from the icy north, so most hotels fill up. **Make your reservations at least two or three months in advance** for the very best places. There is usually a lull in the middle to end of January, when it can be easier to get last-minute reservations and sometimes even slightly lower rates.

Summer is one of the prettiest, greenest times of the year; the sea is even calmer, it's cheaper, and things generally move at a slower pace (except for the first two weeks of August on Tortola when the B.V.I. celebrates Carnival.

CLIMATE

Weather in the Virgin Islands is a year-round wonder. The average daily temperature is about 80°F, and there isn't much variation from the coolest to the warmest months. Unlike Stateside coastal areas, the nights, even on the beach, are warm, so **don't bother to pack bulky sweaters.**

Rainfall averages 40–44 inches per year. But in the tropics, rainstorms tend to be sudden and brief, often erupting early in the morning and at dusk.

In May and June what's known as the Sahara Dust sometimes moves through. That's dust that literally blows across the oceans from the African desert, making for hazy spring days and spectacular sunsets.

Toward the end of summer, of course, hurricane season begins in earnest, with the first tropical wave passing by in August. Since the advent of Hurricane Hugo, islanders have paid closer attention to the tropical waves as they form and travel up from Africa. In an odd paradox, tropical storms passing by leave behind the sunniest and clearest days you will see year-round. (And that's saying something in the land of zero air pollution.)

What follows are average daily maximum and minimum temperatures for the Virgin Islands.

Climate in the Virgin Islands

Jan.	86F	25C	May	88F	31C	Sept.	92F	33C
	74	23		75	24		76	24
Feb.	86F	25C	June	88F	31C	Oct.	92F	33C
	74	23		75	24		76	24
Mar.	87F	30C	July	95F	35C	Nov.	86F	25C
	71	22		77	25		72	22
Apr.	87F	30C	Aug.	95F	35C	Dec.	86F	25C
	71	22		77	25		72	22

➤ FORECASTS: **Weather Channel Connection** (☎ 900/932–8437), 95¢ per minute from a Touch-Tone phone.

1 Destination: The Virgin Islands

SOMETHING FOR EVERYONE

SEPARATED BY ONLY a narrow channel of shimmering water patrolled by flotillas of pelicans and pleasure craft, the United States and British Virgin Island groups are nevertheless a world apart. It isn't just the obvious: a tale of two traditions and governments. Indeed, clearing customs is usually a formality (although it is taken very seriously), and the U.S. dollar is the official currency on both sides of the "border." Rather, it's the individual look and feel that set them apart, the atmosphere they determinedly cultivate—and the differing breeds of visitors this attracts—an atmosphere perhaps too glibly defined as American verve versus British reserve.

Though the islands are closely grouped, the vegetation and terrain vary widely. The U.S.V.I. are largely lush and tropical. On St. John, where two-thirds of the land is under U.S. National Park Service protection, there are more than 250 species of trees, vines, shrubs, flowers, and other plant life. Each of the three major U.S. Virgin Islands—St. John, St. Thomas, and St. Croix—is really a collection of ecosystems, ranging from tropical seacoast to mountain, rain forest to desert. The flowering trees are particularly superb: Frangipani, flamboyant, hibiscus, and lignum vitae blanket the hills and rolling fields with a dainty blue, pink, yellow, and white quilt.

In contrast, the B.V.I.'s largest island, Tortola, lost lots of its vegetation to the farmer's field. This gives it a very different look than that of the heavily forested St. John, just a 2-mi boat ride away. Its high peaks culminate with see-forever views at Sage Mountain National Park. Virgin Gorda is fringed with monumental boulders whose exact origins are still shrouded in mystery. These are the "cactus tropics," dotted with agave and other spiny plants and enlivened by the vibrant colors of an occasional wild hibiscus or bougainvillea tree.

Both island groups are steeped in history. The U.S.V.I. are graced with the rich architectural legacy of the original Danish settlers, including the picturesque ruins of their sugar plantations. St. Croix is par-

ticularly notable. Christiansted and Frederiksted, the two main towns on St. Croix, feature delightful red-roofed gingerbreads in coral and canary yellow, fronted by shaded galleries and stately colonnades. The old sugar estates on St. Croix are the islands' best preserved and most elegant. Caribbean ghost towns unto themselves, they are crawling and cracked with undergrowth, the haunting grandeur of their double stairways eloquently attesting to St. Croix's former prosperity.

If their architectural remains are not as spectacular, the B.V.I. boast an incomparable *air* of history. In the 17th and 18th centuries the islands' numerous cays, rocks, secret coves, and treacherous reefs formed the perfect headquarters for raiding corsairs and privateers, among them the infamous Edward "Blackbeard" Teach, Captain Kidd, and Sir Francis Drake. Norman Island is the reputed locale of Robert Louis Stevenson's classic *Treasure Island*. The tiny island Dead Chest is said to have inspired the chantey of the same name: "Fifteen men on a dead man's chest, yo ho ho and a bottle of rum."

The nautical spirit lives on, and today these pirate hideaways attract legions of "yachties." The calm, iridescent waters of the B.V.I. are one of the world's most popular sailing destinations. In fact, the islands, forested by masts and flecked with sails, are perhaps best experienced by boat—what better way to explore every rainbow-colored coral reef or gleaming scimitar of white sand (replete with beach bar)? The favorite sport may well be motoring to a private cove, waving if it's occupied, and cruising to the next.

But ultimately the greatest differences between the U.S.V.I. and the B.V.I. are the ways they have been developed. Step off the plane in St. Thomas and you know you're in a consumer society where bigger is better. There are more hotels per square mile here than anywhere else in the Caribbean. Posters hawking products and fast-food franchises dominate the lush surroundings. Charlotte Amalie, the bustling capital, pulsates with legendary duty-free shopping and by far the most active nightlife in the area. You'll discover more pristine pockets on pastoral St. Croix, which by comparison resembles a friendly small town. The odd isle out in the U.S.V.I. equation is tranquil, sleepy St. John, the closest American island to the B.V.I. in distance and temperament. But even here the development and pace often exceed that of its British cousins.

With so many options for the tourist dollar, competition among U.S.V.I. properties is fierce. The constant upgrading of facilities, added amenities, and attractive package rates translate into tremendous value for vacationers. If you want all the comforts, conveniences (and convenience stores) of home—with tropical sun and exotic accent—head for the U.S.V.I.

Although tourism is as much the number-one industry on the B.V.I. as it is on the U.S.V.I., you'd never know it in these quiet, unhurried islands, where there are few major developments and where the largest hotel has only 131 rooms. There are no high-rises here, and no traffic lights. Cruise ships do visit regularly now, but far fewer stop here than at the U.S.V.I. Though there are repeated promises (viewed more as threats by locals) from the tourist office to deepen the harbor and lengthen the airport runways (now scheduled to happen by 2003), there is a tacit understanding that it is precisely their comparatively undeveloped state that makes the B.V.I. such a desirable vacation spot.

By many tourism standards, the B.V.I. are *not* a bargain. The hotels tend to be small and exclusive; many were built by industrial barons and shipping magnates as hideaways for themselves and friends. But true luxury is often understated. It isn't necessarily blow-dryers and satellite TVs in every room. Rather, it's the privacy, the relaxed, easygoing pace, the personalized service, and the ambience.

Expatriates on both the U.S.V.I. and the B.V.I. often delight in taking potshots at their neighbors. You'll find many passionate devotees and repeat visitors who wouldn't dream of crossing the border. U.S.V.I. detractors point to the swarming crowds and comparatively high crime rate on St. Thomas and St. Croix. B.V.I. critics cite the boring lifestyle and the difficulty of getting top-notch goods even on Tortola. The U.S.V.I. have been disparaged as "entry-level Caribbean" and "Detroit with palm trees." Their aficionados will counter, "There's a reason the British Home Office once called the B.V.I. 'the least important part of the Empire.'"

The rivalry only demonstrates how popular the islands are with their respective fans. Luckily, whichever you prefer, there's always the advantage of proximity. In the Virgin Islands you can truly have the best of both worlds.

— Jordan Simon

A freelance writer who has traveled throughout the Caribbean, Jordan Simon has written for Elle, Travel & Leisure, Modern Bride, *and* Fodor's Caribbean.

WHAT'S WHERE

The U.S. Virgin Islands

ST. THOMAS➤ Because it's the transportation hub of the Virgin Islands, many visitors at least land on hilly St. Thomas. Those who stay longer may be there for its legendary shopping or the wide variety of water sports, activities, and accommodations. The bustling port of Charlotte Amalie is the main town, and up-and-coming Red Hook sits on the island's eastern tip. The west end of the island is relatively wild, and hotels and resorts rim the southern and eastern shores.

ST. CROIX➤ The largest of the U.S.V.I., St. Croix is 40 mi south of St. Thomas. Plantation ruins, reminiscent of the days when St. Croix was a great producer of sugar, dot the island. Its northwest is covered by a lush rain forest, its drier East End spotted with cacti. The restored Danish port of Christiansted and the more Victorian-looking Frederiksted are its main towns; Buck Island, off the island's northeast shore, attracts many day visitors.

ST. JOHN➤ Only 3 mi from St. Thomas but still a world apart, St. John is the least developed of the U.S. Virgin Islands. While two-thirds of its tropical hills remain protected as national parkland, a bit of hustle and bustle has come to Cruz Bay, the island's main town. Accommodations range from world-class luxury resorts to top-notch vacation villas to back-to-basics campgrounds.

TORTOLA➤ A day might not be enough to tour this island—all 10 sq mi of it—not because there's so much to see and do but because you're meant to relax while you're there. Time stands still even in Road Town, the island's biggest community, where the hands of the central square's clock occasionally move, but never tell the right time. The harbor, however, is busy with sailboats—this is the charter-boat capital of the world. Tortola's roads dip and curve around the island and lead to lovely, secluded accommodations.

VIRGIN GORDA➤ Progressing from laid-back to more laid-back, mountainous and arid Virgin Gorda fits right in. Its main road sticks to the center of the island, connecting its odd-shaped north and south appendages; sailing is the preferred mode of transportation. Spanish Town, the most noteworthy settlement, is on the southern wing, as are the Baths. Here smooth, giant boulders are scattered about the beach and form delightful sea grottoes just offshore.

OTHER ISLANDS➤ **Jost Van Dyke,** a sparsely populated island northwest of Tortola, has a disproportionate number of surprisingly lively bars and is a favorite haunt of yachties. Hilly **Peter Island** also attracts sailors with its wonderful anchorages. Flat **Anegada** lurks 20 mi northeast of Virgin Gorda. It rises just 28 ft above sea level, but its reef stretches out underwater, practically inviting wrecks. The scores of shipwrecks that encircle the island attract divers and a bounty of fish.

PLEASURES AND PASTIMES

You may choose to spend your tropical vacation lounging day and night, or you may want to plan a few activities. Below are some favorite pleasures and pastimes in the Virgin Islands. Refer to the appropriate chapters for more detailed descriptions of these and other things to do.

With their warm, clear days, unspoiled sandy strands, and beautiful turquoise water, the Virgin Islands are a beach bum's paradise. Even if you're not a connoisseur,

a day or two at the beach is central to a complete vacation here.

Your accommodation may border a beach or provide transportation to one nearby, but you have other options. You could spend one day at a lively, touristy beach that has plenty of water-sports facilities and is backed by a bar and another at an isolated cove that offers nothing but seclusion. Of course, these beaches are just jumping-off points to the underwater world.

In the U.S.V.I., public access to beach waters is guaranteed but land access to them is not, effectively restricting some areas to resort guests. On St. Thomas, Magens Bay is among the prettiest (but also the liveliest) public beaches, and Hull Bay is the only place to surf. St. Croix's west-end beaches are popular, and the calm waters of Isaac Bay, on the more isolated East End, can give you a stretch all to yourself. Beautiful Trunk Bay, St. John, gets a lot of day-trip cruise-ship passengers; Salt Pond Bay is remote and mostly undeveloped.

Nowhere in the B.V.I. will you find crowds to match those at the most popular U.S.V.I. beaches, but Cane Garden Bay on Tortola probably comes the closest. Apple Bay and Josiah's Bay, also on Tortola, are good for surfing, and Long Bay (West) is quieter. Virgin Gorda's beaches are easiest to get to from the water but are also approachable from land. Swimming among the rock formations at the Baths is a priority for many visitors, but this area can be crowded. On the smaller British Virgin Islands, the lovely beaches are most likely sparsely populated by those who have dropped anchor and made their way in.

Columbus, pirates, European colonizers, and plantation farmers and their slaves are among the people who have left their marks on these islands, all of which are benefiting the tourism industry, a relatively recent development.

In Charlotte Amalie, St. Thomas, Fort Christian (1672), Blackbeard's Castle (1679), the Synagogue of Beracha Veshalom Vegmiluth Hasidim (1833), and the Danish Consulate (1830) are some noteworthy sites that give glimpses into the town's past. St. Croix's countryside is dotted with ruins of plantation great houses and sugar mills. St. John, too, has several plantations in varying degrees of decay.

Die-hard sightseers will find less to keep them busy in the British Virgin Islands. Numbering among historic sites, however, are Tortola's Mt. Healthy National Park, an old plantation site, and Copper Mine Point, the ruins of a 400-year-old mine on Virgin Gorda.

Nightlife

The nights are just as important as the days to many Virgin Island vacationers, and though you'll never be too far from a Jimmy Buffett tune, the nightlife options do their share in providing something for everyone. Yachties congregate—not surprisingly—at the waterfront bars, where live guitar music may accompany the rum drinks. British Virgin Island watering holes, especially those on Jost Van Dyke, are most likely to be true beach bars. Island steel-drum, calypso, and reggae music, and broken-bottle dancing are most common in shows at larger hotels. Discos exist wherever there's a market, musicians often play impromptu in the street, and if you look around you may come across a piano bar or a jazz band.

Sailing

Traveling by boat is a relaxing and efficient way to enjoy the islands. And if you charter a boat for your whole vacation, you'll also have your accommodations. Charter companies on all the main islands can outfit you with exactly what you'll need; brokers can help you figure out what that is, whether it's hiring a full crew or setting sail on your own. Once you're off, you're sure to enjoy the restaurants, bars, and other businesses that cater to sailing vacationers.

If you're a landlubber who only wants a taste of the sea, consider renting a powerboat for a day or going for a day sail, usually organized through a charter company. This is a good way to see some of the other, smaller islands.

Shopping

Charlotte Amalie, St. Thomas, is the place to shop. As the Virgin Islands' main commercial center, it has the best selection of just about everything. Bargain hunters drool over the $1,200 duty-free allowance and the lack of sales tax; liquor, china, crystal, and jewelry are especially popular buys. But you should also seek out goods that are only sold locally, from artwork to spices to crafts. Stores carrying such items are more liberally divided among the islands.

Snorkeling and Diving

Reefs, wrecks, and rife vegetation make the islands as interesting underwater as above. Convenient anchorages, conditions suitable to different levels of ability, and a plethora of outfitters add to the appeal of diving and snorkeling here. Chapter 2 has all the information you'll need to plan your time underwater, as well as maps detailing the best dive and snorkel sites.

NEW AND NOTEWORTHY

WATER ISLAND➤ In St. Thomas's Charlotte Amalie harbor, this quiet island is now part of Virgin Islands territory. Ownership of 50 of this island's acres was transferred from the U.S. Department of the Interior to the territorial government on December 12, 1996, making Water Island the fourth largest Virgin Island. A hotel is planned, as are concessions for Honeymoon Beach. Back in the 1940s, Water Island was the site of the U.S. Army's Fort Segarra. There was a hotel here from the 1960s until 1982.

ST. CROIX➤ **Casinos** are in the wind. The Legislature in 1995 approved six casino hotels in hopes of jumpstarting the island's economy. When they'll begin building is anyone's guess, but at press time insiders expected action sometime in 1997.

ST. JOHN➤ Look for improved rest room facilities at **Trunk Bay,** the premier attraction at Virgin Islands National Park. Recent construction replaced the old, barely functioning rest rooms with new toilets and showers.

A new **shopping center** opened in spring 1996 right next to the Westin Resort of St. John. Unlike most of St. John's shopping areas, Palm Plaza has ample parking. It has a host of shops including Island Made, a cooperative that sells made-in-St. John artwork. The plaza also has a video store, a convenience if you're renting one of the island's 350 vacation villas.

TORTOLA➤ Work continues on the **four-lane highway** that, when completed, will run from Port Purcell to Fort Burt right through the heart of the Road Town waterfront. All work should be completed by the summer of 1998.

FODOR'S CHOICE

Scenic Views

★ **Moonrise over Sapphire Bay, St. Thomas,** a relaxing and romantic way to close out a day.

★ **Sailing into Red Hook from St. John at sunset,** perfectly positioned for a mellow evening in town.

★ **The view from the Skyworld observation tower, Tortola,** on clear days, for especially colorful sunsets.

Beaches

★ **Magens Bay, St. Thomas,** a long, lovely loop of white sand.

★ **Palm-fringed Deadman's Bay, Peter Island,** conducive to romance.

★ **Smuggler's Cove, Tortola,** for its good snorkeling and view of Jost.

★ **Spring Bay or the Baths,** where you can swim among unique rock formations—essential to a Virgin Gorda vacation.

★ **Trunk Bay, St. John,** beautiful, if at times crowded. Its snorkeling trail is a big draw.

Hotels

★ **Bitter End Yacht Club, Virgin Gorda.** The extremely hospitable staff is what makes a stay here so memorable. *$$$$*

★ **Caneel Bay Resort, St. John.** Civilized and luxurious, Caneel Bay draws the same visitors year after year. *$$$$*

★ **Westin Carambola Beach Resort, St. Croix.** Room decor is tasteful but not overdone, and all rooms look out on a garden or an exquisite ecru beach. *$$$$*

★ **Colony Point Pleasant Resort, St. Thomas.** Different-size accommodations blend into the trees here, and all have great views. *$$$–$$$$*

★ **Villas at Fort Recovery Estates, Tortola.** These bungalows, built around the remnants of an old Dutch fort, have all the essentials: kitchens, patios facing the ocean, air-conditioning, and good management. *$$–$$$$*

Restaurants

★ **Le Château de Bordeaux, St. John,** in what is basically a glorified tree house. Drawing on different culinary traditions the chef produces such delicacies as macadamia-coated salmon with dill-crème fraîche glaze. *$$$$*

★ **Top Hat, St. Croix,** for its delicious Danish fare. The menu and the delightful Danish owners are a reminder of the time when Denmark ruled St. Croix. *$$$$*

★ **Virgilio's, St. Thomas,** an intimate, elegant hideaway that serves the best northern Italian food on the island, right down to its cappuccino. *$$$$*

★ **Brandywine Bay, Tortola,** for Tuscan food in a romantic setting. *$$$*

★ **Kendricks, St. Croix,** for jazz playing in the background, waiters wearing bow ties, and a stylish Continental menu. *$$$*

★ **Skyworld, Tortola,** where stunning views accompany outstanding cuisine and service. *$$$*

★ **Miss Lucy's, St. John,** is worth every part of the out-of-the-way drive for its authentic Caribbean fare. *$–$$*

Special Moments

★ **Watching pelicans dive for their supper** at twilight from Cruz Bay, St. John.

★ **The beautiful parade of cruise ships** out of Charlotte Amalie harbor.

★ **Listening to Quito Rhymer's love songs** drift across the water at Cane Garden Bay, Virgin Gorda. You won't find a more romantic evening.

★ **Phosphorus lighting up the water's edge** at night at Savannah Bay, Virgin Gorda—it's worth a trip.

Music, Nightlife, Bars

★ **Bath and Turtle, Virgin Gorda.** Good island bands play on Wednesday and Sunday evenings.

★ **Barnacle Bill's, St. Thomas.** Local entertainers, Caribbean bands, and well-known musicians have all performed here.

★ **Blue Moon, St. Croix.** Great live jazz every Friday night.

⭐ **Bomba's Surfside Shack, Tortola.** One of the island's liveliest spots.

⭐ **Quito's Gazebo, Tortola.** The surf is the perfect accompaniment to whatever's playing, whether it's ballads, love songs, or reggae.

⭐ **Sugar's Nightclub at the Old Mill, St. Thomas.** Rock till you drop.

⭐ **Any bar on Jost Van Dyke.** You can't go wrong on this island, which does its best to entertain the charter-yacht crowd.

FESTIVALS AND SEASONAL EVENTS

WINTER

DEC.➢ **St. Croix Christmas Fiesta.** Christmas and the day after (Christmas Second Day) are legal holidays and mark the start of 12 days of celebrations on St. Croix.

JAN.➢ **Martin Luther King, Jr. Day** is observed on all three U.S. Virgin Islands.

SPRING

MAR.➢ **Horticultural Society Show.** Tortola's Botanical Gardens (☎ 809/494–4557) displays breathtaking examples of the local foliage.

Virgin Gorda Festival. Calypso music, a parade, and a beauty pageant are the highlights of this local festival, which culminates on Easter Sunday.

APR.➢ **St. Croix's International Triathlon.** Athletes from around the world head for St. Croix to participate in this grueling annual swimming, biking, and running race.

Rolex Cup Regatta. This is part of the three-race Caribbean Ocean Racing Triangle (CORT) that pulls in yachters and their pals from all over.

St. Thomas Carnival. A weeklong, major-league blowout of parades, parties, and island-wide events. The date changes from year to year but always follows Easter.

B.V.I. Spring Regatta. For more than 20 years, this internationally known race has drawn sailing enthusiasts from all over the world.

MAY➢ **Sportfishing tournaments.** Throughout the month, several locally sponsored fishing events are held (St. Thomas is home to some 20 world sportfishing records), kicking off the summer-long fishing season.

SUMMER

JUNE➢ **Organic Act Day** commemorates U.S. Virgin Islanders' equivalent of a constitution (drawn up in 1945), which allows them to elect a legislature and enact laws.

JULY➢ **St. John Carnival.** This small but colorful carnival, complete with bands and parades, is characteristic of St. John's laid-back style; the final day coincides with the Fourth of July.

July 4th Tournament. St. Thomas Gamefishing Club sponsors this Independence Day fishing tournament.

Hurricane Supplication Day. U.S. Virgin Islanders gather in churches in mid-July to pray for deliverance from the ravages of storms.

Bastille Day. Descendants of the French settlers on St. Thomas celebrate the French Revolution with a minicarnival in Frenchtown.

AUG.➢ **Texas Society Chili Cook-Off.** That's right, a Texas-style chili contest in the U.S. Virgin Islands. It's a beach party with country music, dancing, chili tasting, and a variety of fun and games.

U.S.V.I. Open Atlantic Blue Marlin Tournament. Marlin anglers from around the world compete for big-money prizes for landing the biggest marlin.

B.V.I. Sportfishing Tournament. The B.V.I. Yacht Club hosts this event in which anglers compete to bring in catches such as marlin, wahoo, or grouper. ☎ 809/494–3286.

B.V.I. Summer Festival. This two-week free-for-all celebrates the season with local music, arts, and crafts, as well as a beauty pageant and a parade. ☎ 809/494–2875.

AUTUMN

SEPT.➢ **B.V.I. International Rugby Festival.** If rugby's not your thing, something in the whirlwind of social events surrounding this competition surely will be.

Foxy's Wooden Boat Regatta. This event attracts sailors the world over, who come to Jost Van Dyke for several days of racing and carousing.

OCT.➢ **Columbus Day/U.S.V.I.–Puerto Rico Friendship Day.** Parades and festivities commemorate both events at once.

Hurricane Thanksgiving Day. A legal holiday during which U.S.V.I. residents give thanks for being spared.

Bacardi Rum Beach Party. Cane Garden Bay Beach on Tortola hosts this day filled with seaside activities, from a tug-of-war to a bikini contest. ☎ 809/495–4639.

Nov.➤ **Liberty Day.** A legal holiday in the U.S. Virgin Islands honoring Judge David Hamilton Jackson, who secured freedom of assembly and freedom of the press for the Danish Virgin Islands in 1915.

St. Thomas–St. John Agricultural Fair. Tropical bounty at its best. There's fresh produce, home-grown herbs, and such cooked local delicacies as callaloo, salt fish and dumplings, and fresh fish simmered with green banana, pumpkin, and potatolike tannia.

The Thanksgiving Regatta in Coral Bay, St. John, is a chance for local sailors to compete against each other. The event culminates with a big blow-out at the Skinny Legs Bar.

B.V.I. Boat Show. Boat dealers from around the world assemble in the British Virgin Islands to display and sell boats. ☎ 809/494–3286.

Fast Tacks. Hosted by the Bitter End Yacht Club on Virgin Gorda, this is a six-week series of races, games, and special events, including the world-class Bitter End Invitational Regatta.

2 Diving and Snorkeling in the Virgin Islands

The only thing more beautiful than the Virgin Islands are the tropical reefs that surround them like brightly colored coral necklaces.

DIVING

By Marcia
Andrews

Updated by
Gary
Goodlander

Sliding down beside the anchor line, we could see the shape of the wreck. The *Rhone*'s bow was dark against white sand, even in 80 ft of water. We leveled off at the midsection, taking in the scene; the stern, its big propeller dug into rocks and coral, was uphill in a distant gloom. As we neared the bottom, a small striped fish nosed my buddy's elbow, like a puppy. There were several of them, hand-size sergeant major fish, objecting to us larger creatures invading their territory; then they darted off. Bigger fish were milling about below, parading through the ship's hatches and broken hull, showing silvers and blues—about the only colors visible at this depth. We were looking for the big barracuda that like to hang around and watch divers. "They're curious," say the dive guides. "Just don't wear anything shiny. If you don't look like a lure, you're okay."

Sure.

Our guide, an instructor from a Tortola dive shop, tapped a section of the ship's hull, drawing our attention to a hole. When the resident spotted moray eel poked out six inches of ugly head, all five divers danced back in a startled chorus line. The guide slipped the Central Casting eel something from her pocket, then continued the tour. She led the way to an opening in the ship's side, and, grinning—as well as a person can through a mouthpiece and mask—she urged us to follow her into the ship. My dive buddy and I, by mutual hand-signal agreement, hovered over the deck instead, watching the others enter the hulk, then reemerge, swimming across a patch of purple fan coral.

The wreck of the RMS *Rhone,* just off the western tip of Salt Island in the British Virgin Islands, is the region's star dive attraction. Not only is it old (sunk in 1867 in sheltered water), large (a more-than-300-ft, 2,434-ton steamer), and accessible (a short trip from Road Town Harbour, Tortola); it also was made famous in an '80s wet-T-shirt movie, *The Deep.* For nearby dive shops, it's a bonanza, the perfect place to launch student divers in open-water diving. Once they've seen the *Rhone* and a nearby reef covered with coral, sponges, and fish, most new divers are very enthusiastic about the sport.

There's a lot of dive excitement in both the British and United States Virgin Islands. The waters are ideal for discovering marine life—whether you snorkel (swim with mask, snorkel, and fins on the surface) or are trained to dive and explore reefs close-up with scuba gear and air tanks. Though seasoned divers may pursue wilder dive sites in the lower Caribbean, the Virgin Islands have variety—caves, walls, wrecks, lush reefs, pinnacles—and more than their share of practical advantages:

- Most anchorages are close to live reefs. Whether they're charted dive sites or not, nearby coral heads are mini-ecosystems, home to the region's rich mix of fish and coral. (Waterproof booklets on flora and fauna are widely available.)

- Dive shops are generally well equipped and operate with high standards, thanks, in part, to strong competition in the area and to a high volume of experienced divers who would know a second-rate dive shop when they saw one.

- Great beginner-level diving conditions include warm, calm seas (80°F at the surface and waves seldom more than 3 ft); excellent visibility, up to 120 ft (especially late spring through summer); and shallow coral reefs full of life. Experienced divers will find dramatic drop-offs, caves, and canyons.

- Full-service dive operations are on all major islands, with experienced guides to spot tidal currents and sea conditions, then lead you to any of 100 dive sites. Guided dives are the norm here—"because we get so many novices," say dive professionals.

- Attractions for nondivers make this a more versatile place than the "divers' camps" on islands with few beaches, resorts, or historic sites.

Certification

In all but a few remote backwaters, scuba divers are required to show certification of training—a C-card—from an internationally recognized program in order to obtain the essential air tanks. With the C-card, you can rent equipment and get air fills, and join others on guided dives virtually anywhere in the world. If you're an old hand, then diving on your own—off your boat or from a beach—is just a matter of renting filled air tanks (no one flies his or her own tanks from home to well-supplied resort areas). Even experienced divers, however, and especially those on their first Virgin Islands dive, do hire guides, if only for their knowledge of local attractions and for the convenience of well-equipped dive boats.

It is possible to accomplish the entire 32- to 40-hour scuba open-water certification course (to get a C-card) in as few as three days of vacation, but it's hard work. Professionals suggest new divers take a two-part approach: Do the classroom study and pool exercises (basic swimming and equipment skills) through a dive school or a YMCA program at home, or even with mail-order materials and an 800 number for a certified instructor. Then, with a transfer from your home instructor, Virgin Islands dive instructors trained and certified by one of the U.S. organizations will lead you through four open-water dives and check your qualifications for a C-card. The National Association of Underwater Instructors (NAUI) and the Professional Association of Diving Instructors (PADI) both provide reputable toll-free and mail-order services, which allow you to study independently before taking your tests. But keep in mind that it's better to do all this in advance. No one wants to spend romantic tropical evenings doing scuba homework.

Most dive operations are connected to retail/rental shops and are affiliated with NAUI or PADI. The latter is most evident in the Virgin Islands.

The YMCA also trains and certifies divers in the United States but isn't involved in resorts and shops. All three training groups give internationally recognized certification courses, and NAUI or PADI shops in resort areas will take you open-water diving to complete classroom and pool instruction begun by another group in the states. (You bring a letter or form from your hometown instructor. The local instructor notes your skills and signs your diving log.) Though each has its own style, you don't have to match organizations.

For lists of hometown dive shops, as well as introductory and safety information, each scuba training group has a national office: **PADI** (⊠ 1251 E. Dyer Rd., Suite 100, Santa Ana, CA 92705, ☎ 800/729–7234, 𝔽𝔸𝕏 714/540–2609), with the most instructors and training facilities; **NAUI** (⊠ Box 14650, Montclair, CA 91763-1150, ☎ 800/553–6284, 𝔽𝔸𝕏 909/621–6405); and the **National YMCA SCUBA Program** (⊠ 5825–2A Live Oak Pkwy., Norcross, GA 30093, ☎ 770/662–5172, 𝔽𝔸𝕏 770/292–9059), which will locate the nearest YMCA instructor in your area.

The Virgin Islands have many resort courses that are ideal for anyone who wants to try scuba. Typically such a course lasts from 2 to 4 hours and starts on a beach or poolside with a lecture about the equipment and the basics of diving. Students put on the equipment and use part of a tank of air, or the first of two tanks, to try breathing underwater. After a pause to regroup or to move to a dive site, divers explore a reef, usually at 30- to 40-ft depths. A single-tank resort course costs from $55 to $70. Also, this is just a sample dive and doesn't count toward certification—that requires classroom work. Many hotels promote a package deal or have a direct line to a nearby dive shop. But, be aware that the experience could be discouraging if you find a bored instructor handing out ill-fitting equipment and sloppy advice. There are a number of simple questions to ask both yourself and staff to judge the quality of a dive operation quickly. Are the facilities neat, clean, and businesslike? Are the boats custom-built for diving? Is the rental equipment in good shape? Are the instructors interested primarily in providing you with a quality dive experience and not constantly trying to sell you another dive gadget? Do they repair their own gear in their own workshop? Do they dive frequently, and are all dives guided? Are they safety conscious, rescue trained, and do they know (without the slightest hesitation) where the nearest hyperbaric chamber is located—and how to get there fast? Is the boat captain properly licensed; does the vessel have a tank of oxygen aboard? Is the information on the dive sites precise and specific? Is the staff friendly, knowledgeable, and helpful? The answers to all these questions should be yes.

The minimum age for PADI scuba instruction is 12, and that's for limited certification. The young diver must upgrade his or her training at age 15 in a brief course with an instructor. Dive-boat operators usually require that children younger than 12 remain in their parents' charge while on the boat or snorkeling. Some shops do have real (not toy) fins, masks, and snorkels to fit children age two and up. To encourage young people, "Discover Scuba" programs developed by PADI allow 12-year-old children to try on equipment and breathe underwater in a swimming pool. Ask your local dive shop about similar opportunities.

Part of any scuba-training program is a review of the sea life and the importance of respecting the new world you're exploring. Dive professionals recognize the value of protecting fragile reefs and ecosystems in tropical waters, and instructors emphasize look-don't-touch diving (the unofficial motto is: Take only pictures, leave only bubbles). Government control and protection of dive sites is increasing, especially in such heavily used areas as the Virgin Islands. Both the British and U.S. territories have active park departments with programs to place moorings in some of the most popular anchorages and dive locations (the objective is to keep too many anchors from tearing up the coral).

Park services in both territories are working with local charter companies, divers, and fishers to protect the area and inform visitors. The placement of moorings, regulations for their use, and fees are published in pamphlets found at customs offices, dive operations, and park-service offices: **B.V.I. National Parks Trust** (✉ Box 860, Road Town, Tortola, B.V.I., ☎ 809/494–3904) and **Virgin Islands National Parks** (✉ 6310 Estate Nazareth, St. Thomas, U.S.V.I. 00802, ☎ 809/775–6238).

Safety

Everyone gets excited about the perils of diving: "the bends" (decompression sickness) and large killer fish. This is why all diving certification courses stress accident prevention and diver safety. But the basic rules for safe diving are both simple and easily understood; fools ignore them at their own peril. Physical requirements for diving are general fitness and the ability to swim comfortably. Scuba training is widely available, and hundreds of thousands of new American divers are certified annually. About a third of them are women.

On the most-feared list are sharks, barracuda, and moray eels. But it's the sea urchins and fire coral that cause pain—when you accidentally bump them. It's easier to remember to be cautious about the big or defensive fish, knowing not to attract them with shiny jewelry or taunt them by poking into crevices.

Serious diving accidents are becoming increasingly rare these days, thanks largely to the high level of diver training. However, they *do* still occur occasionally. Surfacing too rapidly without exhaling—or going too deep for too long—can result in a diver's suffering from an air embolism or a case of the bends.

Placing the patient in a recompression chamber as soon as possible, and then bringing him or her "back down" to the pressure where the accident occurred, allows for a gradual reduction of that pressure.

A word of caution: There was recently a small but vocal group of "deep dive" advocates in the region. It maintained that deep diving was not nearly as dangerous as it had been perceived. A number of these divers are no longer with us, having expired somewhere below the 400-ft mark. *Never* exceed the PADI or NAUI recreational "sport diving" depth limits of 60 ft.

For information about scuba safety and direct assistance in diving emergencies through medical professionals, you can contact **Divers Alert Network (DAN)** (⊠ 3100 Tower Blvd., Suite 1300, Durham, NC 27707, ☎ 919/684–2948 or 800/446–2671). In a dive emergency contact the **U.S. Coast Guard** (VHF Channel 16, or ☎ 809/776–3497 on St. Thomas; 809/729–6800, ext. 140, in San Juan). The **St. Thomas Decompression Chamber** can be reached directly at ☎ 809/776–2686 or through the St. Thomas Hospital at ☎ 809/776–8311, ext. 2226. Ask your dive shop about its emergency plan and about nearby facilities.

Diving Vacations

Access to diving in the Virgin Islands is easy, and you can buy dive trips a day at a time or in packages. Vacationers with C-cards who prefer serendipity to schedules can walk into a dive shop at 8 AM and sign on for the next departure of a day-trip dive boat—or, if that's full, book the afternoon trip. The dive operator will discuss experience levels to make sure the planned dive suits you (for example, a dive with two tanks to a 60-ft-deep wreck and then a reef at 35 ft). He or she will outfit you with needed gear (no vacationers lug their own tanks or weight belts) and point you to the soda machine for après-dive refreshment. That typical two-tank, two-location day trip takes about three hours and costs $60–$80. Though a long wait is rare, in high season you may have to reserve several days in advance for space on a boat. Most people who want diving to be a focus of their trip avoid this by buying a dive package, whether it's directly from a dive operator, through a travel agent, or through a specialist.

A couple of travel agents specialize in diving vacations. **Rascals in Paradise** (⊠ 650 5th St., Suite 505, San Francisco, CA 94107, ☎ 415/978–9800 or 800/872–7225) tracks resorts worldwide that specialize in family vacations for divers with children. **East Coast Divers** (⊠ 280 Worcester Rd., Framingham, MA 01701, ☎ 508/620–1176 or 800/649–3483) is another that specializes in affordable dive packages.

To say prices vary is an understatement. Would you believe from $400 to $2,000? One of the least expensive packages we've noted is for hotel and diving, ". . . from $400, four nights/six dives." The other extreme is the ultimate scuba-training experience: private lessons, one-on-one, more than five days for $750 plus accommodations. Since hotels range from spartan to haute, Baskin-in-the-Sun quotes hotel-dive packages, such as seven nights/eight days, at prices ranging from $750 to $2,000 per week, per person.

Remove the hotel from the equation, and dive-package prices are influenced by whether or not you need instruction and whether you contract for a package or day-by-day diving. The most popular packages are for one week. A four-day certification course may cost from $350 to $425; sometimes it can be completed in as few as three days. If you've done your classroom and pool work you can schedule the required four open-water certification-completion dives in just two days, for as little as $225. Here's a representative day-trip dive package: six dives over several days, $200–$250, or an average $32–$38 per dive. That price buys you the dive leader's knowledge of the area, the boat ride, six full tanks, and use of any other equipment you need.

Rates for diving trips, equipment, and instruction don't vary from season to season—demand is evened by smart locals (summer means uncrowded dive boats and calmer, clearer waters) who dive until the northerners return in winter. Reduced rates for live-aboard dive boats and hotel/dive packages reflect low-season rates for living space, not diving guides and equipment.

Dive Operators

Dive-shop operators provide the visiting certified diver with knowledge of local conditions and guidance to dive sites, boats, rental equipment, and tanks and fills. Instruction and equipment are available from most shops, and many will arrange reduced-price hotel/dive packages. Many dive operations now offer custom underwater videos for as low as $40.

The U.S. Virgin Islands

ST. THOMAS

Aqua Action Watersports (✉ 6501 Red Hook Plaza, Red Hook, ☎ 809/775–6285, FAX 809/775–1501), a full-service PADI shop at the Secret Harbour Resort, offers all levels of instruction. It also rents sea kayaks and Windsurfers.

Chris Sawyer Diving Center (✉ 6300 Frydenhoj, Suite 29, Compass Point Marina, Red Hook, 00802-1411, ☎ 809/777–7804 or 800/882–2965, FAX 809/775–9495) has a custom 42-ft dive boat. It caters to small groups for daily two-tank dives and night dives as well as bi-weekly one-tank dives. It also runs a weekly trip to the *Rhone*. It has outlets at the American Yacht Harbor in Red Hook, the Renaissance Grand Beach Resort, and the Wyndham Sugar Bay Resort.

Dive In (✉ Sapphire Beach Resort & Marina, Red Hook, ☎ 809/775–6100 or 800/524–2090, ext. 2144, FAX 809/775–4024) has a PADI dive center running beach or boat dives and night tours. It emphasizes beachfront suites and villas with complimentary water sports and tennis, and children ages 12 and under get free food and lodging. In addition, there is a free daylong "kiddy club" for children of diving parents.

Seahorse Dive Boats (✉ 505 Crown Bay Marina, ☎ 809/774–2001, FAX 809/777–9600) is a PADI operation that runs both day and night dives at 58 different sites.

St. Thomas Diving Club (✉ 7147 Bolongo Bay, ☎ 809/776–2381 or 800/538–7348, FAX 809/777–3232) is a divers' resort at Bolongo Bay.

It's a PADI five-star facility with sales, rentals, and introductory and certification courses. It welcomes people who have completed their dive certification class work at home and wish to take their open-water dives. The club has three dive boats, one of which is USCG licensed to carry more than 40 passengers.

Underwater Safaris (☎ 809/774–1350, 𝖥𝖠𝖷 809/777–8733) is conveniently located at the Ramada Yacht Haven Marina in Long Bay and at the nearby Frenchman's Reef Resort. It is a PADI five-star dive operation that specializes in Buck Island dives to the wreck of the WWI cargo ship *Cartenser Sr.* The vessel rests in 30 to 50 ft of clear water and is St. Thomas's most popular wreck dive. It offers both morning and afternoon dives seven days a week, and a popular "resort dive" (which doesn't include certification) off Buck Island for only $69 per person.

ST. CROIX

Anchor Dive (✉ Sunny Isle, ☎ 809/778–1522 or 800/532–3483) offers both wall and boat dives. It's a five-star PADI Instructor Development Center in the Salt River Marina with a strong background in resort and certification instruction.

Cane Bay Dive Shop (✉ Kingshill, ☎ 809/773–9913, 𝖥𝖠𝖷 809/778–5442) is a five-star PADI operation on the north shore.

Cruzan Divers (✉ 330 Strand St., Frederiksted, ☎ 809/772–3701 or 800/352–0107, 𝖥𝖠𝖷 809/772–1852) serves divers on the West End. It's a PADI operation and has both 40- and 20-ft dive boats.

Dive Experience, Inc. (✉ 1 Strand St., Christiansted, ☎ 809/773–3307 or 800/235–9047, 𝖥𝖠𝖷 809/773–7030) is a PADI five-star training facility providing the range from certification to introductory dives. It specializes in groups of 2 to 12 and offers regularly scheduled morning, afternoon, and night dives. Its popular 2 PM fish-feeding frenzy features toothsome barracudas being hand-fed (with chain-mail gloves).

Dive St. Croix (✉ 59 King's Wharf, Christiansted, ☎ 809/773–3434 or 800/523–3483, 𝖥𝖠𝖷 809/693–9405) takes divers to walls and wrecks—more than 50 sites—and offers introductory, certification, and PADI, NAUI, and SSI C-card completion courses. Dive St. Croix is the only dive operation on the island allowed to run dives to Buck Island. It has custom packages with five hotels.

V.I. Divers, Ltd. (✉ Pan Am Pavilion, Christiansted, ☎ 809/773–6045 or 800/544–5911, 𝖥𝖠𝖷 809/773–2859) is a PADI five-star training facility with a 32-ft dive boat and hotel packages. It has operated on St. Croix since 1971.

ST. JOHN

Coral Bay Watersports (✉ 10–19 Estate Carolina, Coral Bay, ☎ 𝖥𝖠𝖷 809/776–6850) is on the eastern tip of the island, close to many of the lesser visited dive sights off the island. It offers both PADI and NAUI certifications and conducts daily dive trips in season.

Cruz Bay Watersports Co., Inc. (✉ Cruz Bay, ☎ 809/776–6234 or 800/835–7730, 𝖥𝖠𝖷 809/693–8720) is a PADI and NAUI five-star dive center with three locations. Owner-operators Patty and Marcus Johnston offer reef, wreck, and night dives aboard four custom dive vessels. Dive packages include cozy villas, luxury condos, and private homes. Certifications and group rates are available. Daily dive trips leave from both Cruz Bay and the Westin Resort in Great Cruz Bay.

Hurricane Alley (✉ Cruz Bay, ☎ 809/776–6256, 𝖥𝖠𝖷 809/693–9841) is a PADI center in the Mongoose Junction shopping mall. It does a number of different reef and wreck dives around St. John and is owned by Caribbean chartering pioneer Stu Brown of Proper Yacht Charters.

Low Key Water Sports (✉ Cruz Bay, ☎ FAX 809/693–8987, ☎ 800/835–7718), at the Wharfside Village, is a PADI Five Star IDC Training Facility that conducts daily reef, wreck, and night dives. It also offers special afternoon dives that specifically cater to scuba novices, as well as unique kayaking, fishing, and snorkel tours. Various dive packages feature waterfront condos, private coastal homes, and shoreside guest cottages.

The British Virgin Islands

TORTOLA

Baskin-in-the-Sun (✉ Prospect Reef, Road Town, ☎ 809/494–2858 or 800/233–7938, FAX 809/494–5853), run by Lisa Mitchell, is Tortola's only five-star PADI dive center. It has two locations (Soper's Hole and Prospect Reef), three dive vessels, and links with four Tortola hotels. Specializing in package tours, it is the largest such operation on the island. Its hotel/dive packages range from economical to sky's-the-limit.

Blue Water Divers (✉ Road Town, ☎ 809/494–2847, FAX 809/494–0198), at both Nanny Cay and Maya Cove, is operated by Mike and Keith Royle, both PADI instructors. Their services include dive tours, introductory courses, instructors' courses, air fills, and tank and equipment rentals. They'll meet an anchored sailboat and take divers to reefs or wrecks.

Underwater Safaris Ltd. (✉ Road Town, ☎ 809/494–3235 or 800/537–7032, FAX 809/494–5322) runs wreck-of-the-*Rhone* and reef dives daily and offers PADI and NAUI training, equipment sales, and rentals. It will fashion sail-and-dive or hotel/dive packages for you. In the Mooring Yacht Charter Marina (and on Cooper Island), it is associated with three hotels and has three dive boats of various sizes.

VIRGIN GORDA AND ANEGADA

Dive B.V.I. (✉ Virgin Gorda Yacht Harbour, ☎ 809/495–5513 or 800/848–7078, FAX 809/494–5347) provides tours, instruction, air fills, and equipment sales/rentals and will rendezvous with your boat. Of special interest are the snorkel trips to Anegada on Tuesdays and Fridays. Also located at Leverick Bay, Peter Island, and Marina Cay.

Kilbrides Underwater Tour (✉ North Sound, ☎ 809/495–9638 or 800/932–4286, FAX 809/495–7549), at Bitter End Yacht Club, is that resort's operator of daily dive and snorkel trips. This company was founded by the legendary treasure hunter Bert Kilbride, now retired.

Dive-Boat Trips

Live-aboard dive boats used to offer spartan bunks and gung-ho diving. Those listed below are full of other cruising amenities, so nondivers may happily come along. Since live-aboards are less popular in the Virgin Islands than in regions where dive sites are far-flung, some of the boats merely visit the B.V.I. on their way from other parts of the Caribbean. Other special operations include instruction in basic scuba and in photography.

Travel agents can direct you to the hotel that fits your vacation needs and has connections to a nearby dive operator. In the Virgin Islands no beachfront resort is more than a few minutes from a dive boat.

Trimarine (✉ Road Town, ☎ 809/494–2490 or 800/648–3393, FAX 809/494–5774) operates a large, 105-by-44-ft trimaran, *Cuan Law,* based at Road Town, Tortola. It focuses on scuba but offers windsurfing, catamaran sailing, kayaking, snorkeling, and shore trips. Basic scuba gear and tank fills are included; regulators and buoyancy jackets are rentable. Rates are approximately $1,500 per person per week (including meals), double occupancy, with private bath and twin or double beds.

Club Med (⊠ 7975 N. Hayden Rd., Scottsdale, AZ 85258, ☎ 800/453–7447, FAX 602/948–4562) is a cruise ship that caters to divers. Only certified divers have access to scuba gear and dive instructors, as well as lavish cruising quarters. The 191-cabin ship is unique for carrying five masts, electrically controlled sails, and a landing-craftlike stern deck that serves as a marina at any anchorage. Four large, inflatable boats transport as many as 40 people to dive sites. Weekly in-season cruises depart and return to Martinique and spend three days of the trip in waters off Virgin Gorda, Jost Van Dyke, and St. Thomas. Rates vary from $2,000 to $2,600, depending on the season; New Year's week costs about $3,000.

Rainbow Visions Photography (⊠ Prospect Reef, Road Town, Tortola, ☎ 809/494–2749, FAX 809/494–6390) teaches underwater photography and provides video or still equipment for rental or sale, plus film processing.

Dive Sites

The U.S. Virgin Islands

ST. THOMAS

The north shore holds the most attractions, prompting several dive shops with stores in St. Thomas Harbor to locate their boats in Red Hook Bay, close to **Thatch Cay** and **Hans Lollik Island.** Thatch Cay is famous for tunnels and arches that are full of light and sea life. Hans Lollik offers plenty of pinnacles and ledges.

When weather conditions favor the eastern and southern parts of the island, dive boats frequent **St. James Bay** and rocks called Cow and Calf. **French Cap,** south of St. Thomas, is another attractive pinnacle, standing in 80 to 100 ft of water. Sea and anchoring conditions here make it more suitable for experienced boat handlers.

Beach dives are rare on St. Thomas because runoff from land development has altered the sea life close to shore. One exception, **Coki Point,** across from Thatch Cay, is a 20- to 30-ft dive popular for resort courses.

The *Rhone,* in the B.V.I., exerts its pull in St. Thomas, and many dive operations plan weekly, all-day trips to the wreck, adding about $30 to the normal dive package and requiring a 7 AM departure for a 4:30 PM return.

ST. CROIX

From Christiansted the dive sites are abundant, starting with the most popular beach dive and resort-course site at **Cane Bay,** a 25-minute van ride away. From the beach divers can swim or take a dinghy about 300 ft to a dramatic wall that's covered in a coral garden.

Salt River Bay, nearer Christiansted, is remarkable for its submarine canyon ending in a waterfall. The trench provides exciting walls, and there's a pinnacle in 90 ft of water.

St. Croix's East End is lined with reefs, and **Buck Island Reef National Monument,** operated by the park service, is a lush protected area with shallow, marked coral gardens, particularly attractive for snorkelers.

ST. JOHN

Since about two-thirds of St. John is Virgin Islands National Park, its beaches and rocky points are less changed than those of the more developed islands. The points, outside anchorages all around the island, are attractive to snorkelers and divers. **Lind Point,** just north of Cruz Bay, was one of the first sites in the area for which buoys were provided for dive boats. For more information on anchorages and moorings, check the Virgin Islands National Park Visitor Center in Cruz Bay.

If you're diving on your own along the rocks south of **Coral Harbor,** then **Coral Bay Watersports** (☎ 809/776–6850) can help arrange tank refills and dive trips. The company also specializes in underwater videos. On the south-central shore, around **Lameshur Bay,** there's a Virgin Islands Ecological Research Station and a lot of pristine reefs to explore.

The British Virgin Islands

TORTOLA

The wreck of the RMS *Rhone,* in depths ranging from 30 to 80 ft, is a major destination for Tortola dive shops. The beaches of Tortola itself are left largely to snorkelers in favor of dive sites on nearby **Norman, Peter, Salt, Cooper,** and **Ginger islands.** There are caves that are easily accessible along **Treasure Point** on Norman, and most of the yacht-threatening rocks are great places to explore coral gardens and canyons.

VIRGIN GORDA AND ANEGADA

The Baths, those large boulders that litter the western tip of Virgin Gorda, are attractive for snorkeling but too shallow for divers. Most of the diving is around **the Dogs,** west of Virgin Gorda, and at the reef along **Eustatia,** at the north end of the island.

Great Dog features a grotto, mostly in 45 ft of water and covered with hard and soft corals, schooling reef fish, and lobster. The south side of Great Dog is known for sightings of turtles and for its stands of magnificent elk-horn coral. Nearby **Cockroach Island** has a feature called **the Visibles,** a pinnacle in 80 ft of water that starts about 15 ft from the surface. Dive shops usually time this dive to minimize the effect of a fairly swift current when the tides change.

An important thing to remember when diving the reefs around private islands is that you are not invited to come on shore. **Necker Island—** one of the most private islets in the Caribbean—is popular with celebrities and royalty who pay a lot of money for seclusion. Sites surrounding Necker Island can be challenging because of their exposure to the Atlantic surge, but dive guides also know how to time the trips to such sites as **the Invisibles,** another spectacular pinnacle. The reefs behind **Eustatia Island** are especially interesting because their northern sides are open to deeper water, drawing larger fish specimens, including eagle rays.

Anegada's wreck-strewn waters (about 300 recorded mishaps) contain six wonderful wrecks. However, much of this area (Horseshoe Reef) is currently closed to anchoring and fishing by the B.V.I. Fishery Department. Although diving here is technically not against the law, diving without anchoring your boat is unsafe. Thus, this area is effectively closed to both fishing and diving. However, this could change. Check with the local divers on Anegada or Virgin Gorda for up-to-date information. Caution: diving or snorkeling off the beach through "paths" in the coral can be dangerous to both diver and coral, especially if a large swell builds up while you are in the water.

JOST VAN DYKE

The reefs most mentioned in the area by divers are the same ones that confound sailors entering **White Bay** on the south shore.

U.S. Virgin Island Dive and Snorkel Sites

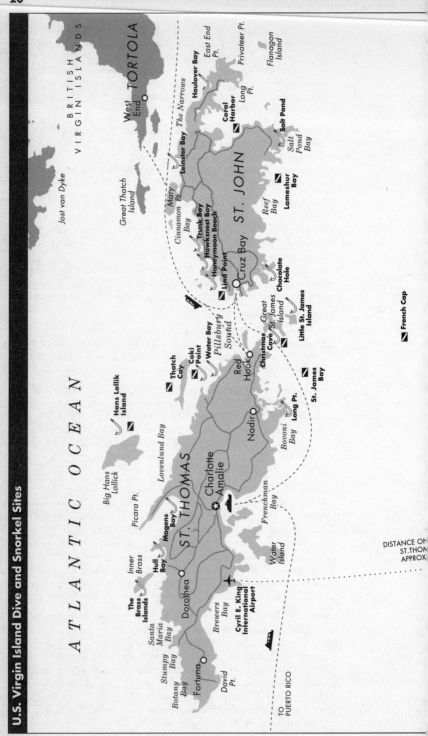

ATLANTIC OCEAN

BRITISH VIRGIN ISLANDS

TORTOLA

West End

Jost van Dyke

Great Thatch Island

Cinnamon Pt.

Mary Bay

Leinster Bay

The Narrows

Haulover Bay

East End Pt.

Privateer Pt.

Flanagan Island

Long Pt.

Coral Harbor

Salt Pond

Salt Pond Bay

ST. JOHN

Reef Bay

Lameshur Bay

Trunk Bay
Hawksnest Bay
Honeymoon Beach
Lind Point

Cruz Bay

Chocolate Hole

Great St. James Island

Little St. James Island

St. James Bay

Christmas Cove

Pillsbury Sound

Water Bay

Coki Point

Red Hook

Thatch Cay

Hans Lollik Island

Big Hans Lollik

Picara Pt.

Lovenlund Bay

Nadir

Bovoni Bay

Long Pt.

ST. THOMAS

Magens Bay

Hull Bay

Inner Brass

The Brass Islands

Santa Maria Bay

Stumpy Bay

Botany Bay

David Pt.

Fortuna

Dorothea

Charlotte Amalie

Frenchman Bay

Water Island

Brewers Bay

Cyril E. King International Airport

TO PUERTO RICO

French Cap

DISTANCE ON
ST. THOM
APPROX

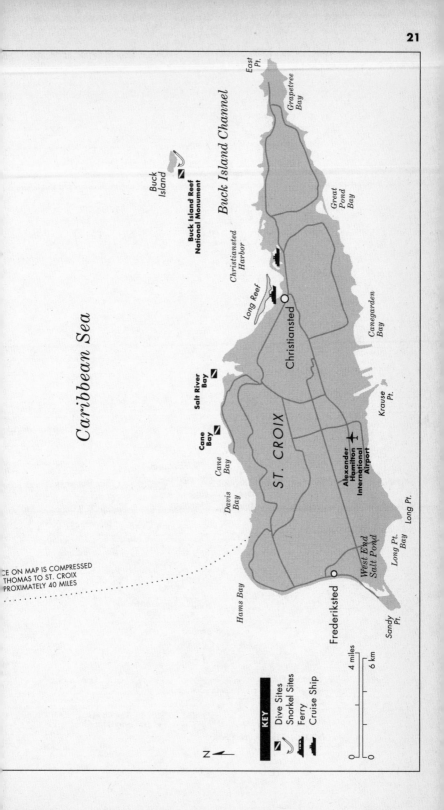

Caribbean Sea

Buck Island Channel

East Pt.

Grapetree Bay

Buck Island

Buck Island Reef National Monument

Great Pond Bay

Christiansted Harbor

Canegarden Bay

Long Reef

Christiansted

Salt River Bay

Krause Pt.

Cane Bay

ST. CROIX

Cane Bay

Alexander Hamilton International Airport

Davis Bay

Long Pt.

Long Pt. Bay

Long Pt.

West End Salt Pond

Hams Bay

Frederiksted

Sandy Pt.

CE ON MAP IS COMPRESSED
THOMAS TO ST. CROIX
PROXIMATELY 40 MILES

KEY

Dive Sites
Snorkel Sites
Ferry
Cruise Ship

4 miles
6 km

0

N

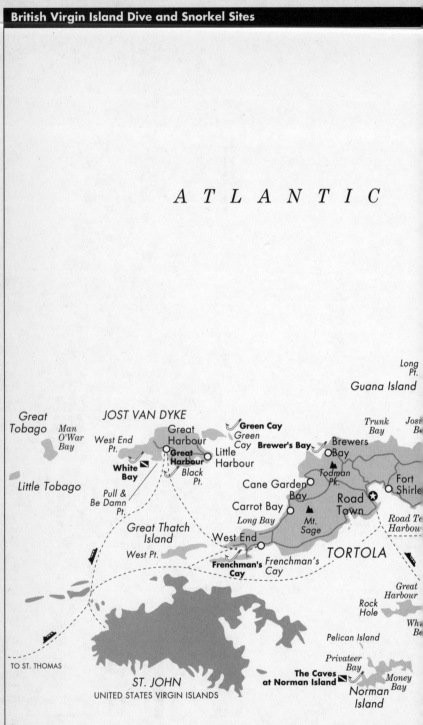

ATLANTIC

Long Pt.

Guana Island

Great Tobago

Man O'War Bay

JOST VAN DYKE

West End Pt.

Great Harbour

Great Harbour

White Bay

Little Harbour

Green Cay

Green Cay

Brewer's Bay

Trunk Bay

Josi Be

Brewers Bay

Black Pt.

Todman Pk.

Fort Shirle

Little Tobago

Pull & Be Damn Pt.

Cane Garden Bay

Carrot Bay

Road Town

Road Te Harbou

Great Thatch Island

West Pt.

West End

Long Bay

Mt. Sage

TORTOLA

Frenchman's Cay

Frenchman's Cay

Great Harbour

Rock Hole

Wh Be

TO ST. THOMAS

Pelican Island

Privateer Bay

The Caves at Norman Island

Money Bay

ST. JOHN
UNITED STATES VIRGIN ISLANDS

Norman Island

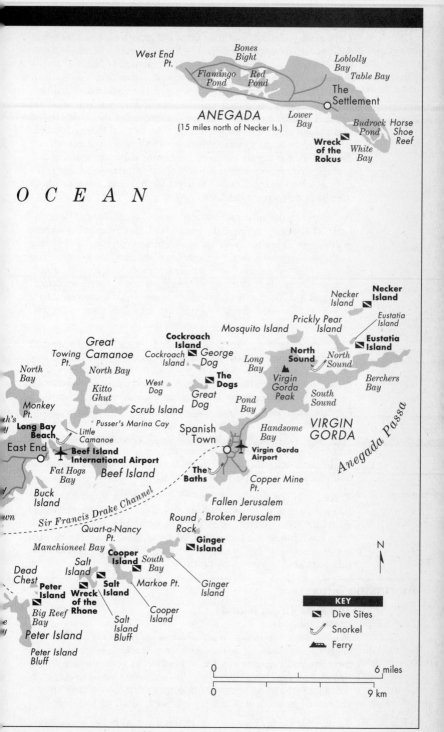

SNORKELING

The majority of today's sport divers spend more time with snorkels in their mouths than scuba regulators—for good reason. Snorkeling provides a maximum of enjoyment with a minimum of hassle. There is no heavy, expensive, complicated equipment involved; many divers enjoy the naturalness of being nearly naked underwater. Scuba diving always requires advance planning; snorkeling can be a far more casual affair. There is usually no need for a boat, since many of the finest snorkel sites are adjacent to a beach. Because most tropical marine life lives fairly near the water's surface, there is no link between the depth of a dive and the participant's enjoyment. Many avid water-sports enthusiasts progress from swimming to snorkeling to scuba—and then gradually drift back to snorkeling. The Silent World is even quieter without the hiss of a two-stage regulator.

Few places on this planet are as convenient to snorkel as the Virgin Islands. The dangers are few and easily avoided. Don't step on sea urchins or stingrays. Don't touch red or reddish brown coral; for that matter, don't touch *any* coral. Don't put your hand into dark holes—unless you want to play "patty cake" with a defensive moray eel. If spear fishing, remove all wounded fish from the water immediately. Ignore sharks and barracudas unless they act particularly aggressive; if so, retreat calmly without excessive splashing. Never snorkel alone. Don't wear shiny jewelry. Avoid areas with heavy surf or strong currents.

The biggest danger to snorkelers today is being struck by a small powerboat or high-speed dinghy while resurfacing for air. To avoid this, snorkel as far away from boats as practical. Avoid busy harbors, dock areas, or navigational channels. Never snorkel at dusk or night. If you hear a motor vessel approaching, surface immediately, and clasp both hands together over your head. This makes you clearly visible and means "Diver Okay." (Waving your hands rapidly back and forth over your head means "Diver in Trouble. Need Help!") In addition, make sure you don't get hit by one boat while watching another. Sound direction can be confusing underwater. Finally, towing a floating dive flag is your best protection against getting run down.

There are hundreds of great snorkeling sites in the Virgins. It would take a large book to describe each in detail, and a dozen "experts" would give you a dozen different expert opinions on which was the best. Below are a few of these top-notch sites. Many of the dive operators listed above offer boat trips that include snorkeling at a number of these sites. Call individual operators for details.

Snorkeling Sites

The U.S. Virgin Islands

ST. THOMAS

Magens Bay—the largest, most breathtaking bay along St. Thomas's rugged north coast—has all the conveniences (parking, lifeguards, equipment rental, changing rooms, freshwater showers, restaurants, and bars) of civilization and yet still offers excellent snorkeling within an easy walk. Ask a lifeguard where he or she recommends that day—certain areas in the bay are better than others if strong north winds are blowing.

Farther east on St. Thomas's north shore is **Coki Point,** where famed Caribbean diver Joe Vogel of Chris Sawyer Diving has been diving for more than 24 years. "It's still one of the nicest beach dives in the Caribbean," he reports. "Plenty of reef; plenty of fish!" Check out the coral ledges close to the Coral World Underwater Tower.

Southeast from Coki is **Water Bay.** Its windswept beach can be approached through the lovely Stouffer Renaissance Grand Beach Resort.

Elsewhere on St. Thomas, **Hull Bay, Long Point,** and numerous other locations provide excellent areas for snorkeling, depending on sea and wind conditions. By boat, **Cow and Calf, Christmas Cove,** the **Brass Islands, Little St. James, Buck,** and **Hans Lollik** all have wonderful areas.

ST. JOHN

St. John offers more pristine dive and snorkel sites closer together than any other of the Virgin Islands. The best are all within the boundaries of the national park.

Nearly everyone would agree that **Trunk Bay**'s Underwater Trail, within the national park on St. John, is the best location on the island for beginning divers. There are changing rooms, freshwater showers, equipment rentals, a snack bar, plenty of off-street parking, and even a professional lifeguard on duty. St. John resident Cynthia Smith gives a basic equipment demonstration on the beach daily and will help you adjust your mask and snorkel gear properly. The self-guided 675-ft trail itself has large underwater "road" signs that clearly identify nearby coral life and other areas of special interest. This is a perfect "first snorkel" for the whole family. The fact that it is at one of the world's most beautiful beaches is an additional bonus.

Leinster Bay is a particularly interesting snorkel. The water is usually calm, clear, and uncrowded. Access is easy by land or sea. The shallow ocean floor offers a little bit of everything within easy view, and sea life is abundant. Caution: This area is a popular overnight anchorage, so be especially careful of approaching power craft.

Farther to the east is **Haulover Bay.** This small bay—usually rougher than Leinster—is often deserted. The snorkeling here is highly dramatic, with ledges, walls, nooks, and sandy areas close together. It's a favorite spot for snorkelers who live on St. John.

West of Leinster and Trunk Bay is **Hawksnest Bay.** Usually calm except in large northerly swells, it has some interesting reefs along the rocky shore that surrounds the sandy beach. Elsewhere on St. John, **Salt Pond, Chocolate Hole,** and **Honeymoon Beach** offer excellent snorkeling.

The National Park Service (☎ 809/776–6201) on St. John regularly offers a wide variety of park ranger–guided marine-related tours. Walking and wading along the coast is always an enjoyable interlude; accompanied by an expert, it can also be a highly educational experience.

ST. CROIX

The premier snorkeling site here is the **Buck Island Reef National Monument.** This 850-acre island-and-reef system, 2 mi north of St. Croix, is particularly pristine, thanks to its protected status. The 1-mi-long eastern barrier reef is especially impressive, as is the entire north side of the island. An excellent snorkel for the beginner, Buck Island also provides nice drop-offs for the experienced diver. More than 250 species of fish have been recorded here, as well as a wide variety of sponges, corals, and crustaceans.

The British Virgin Islands

TORTOLA

Many tourists to the British Virgin Islands arrive by ferry at Soper's Hole, West End, Tortola, and there are a couple of snorkeling sites within walking distance of the ferry terminal. The southwest side of the harbor (actually the western tip of **Frenchman's Cay**) has some interesting coral and sea life close to the shore. Caution: Keep a wary eye on fast yacht tenders and power craft zipping too close to shore. Occasionally, a strong current in this area makes diving or snorkeling unadvisable.

Perhaps the best spot in good weather is **Brewer's Bay** on Tortola's north side. You can spend a few hours or a few days snorkeling here. The anchorage is seldom used, yet picture perfect. Just ashore is Mount Healthy, where the ruins of an old windmill make for an interesting, if dry, excursion. Farther to the east is **Long Bay Beach** on Beef Island. Heading east toward the airport, take the first road on your left after the tiny bridge. This area is usually calm and uncrowded—only the sound of the planes taking off from the nearby airport occasionally mars its perfection.

OTHER ISLANDS

Elsewhere in the Virgin Islands, countless dive sites are still almost untouched. The most popular snorkeling and swimming area in Virgin Gorda is the **Baths.** Swimming from the bright blue ocean through dark underwater openings and then quietly surfacing into the dimly lit caves is a thrill never to be forgotten. The **North Sound** area of the island has dozens of good spots.

On Jost Van Dyke, **White Bay, Great Harbour,** and, just offshore, **Green Cay** are all excellent snorkeling sites, as are the **Caves** on **Norman Island.** The islands of Salt, Peter, Ginger, Cooper, and Anegada all combine to present a lifetime of snorkeling possibilities.

FURTHER READING

Guide to Coral and Fishes of Florida, the Bahamas and the Caribbean, by Idaz and Jerry Greenberg (⊠ Seahawk Press, 6840 SW 92nd St., Miami, FL 33156), uses more than 200 color illustrations of coral and fish with brief, understandable text. Saltwater-reef fish are vibrantly painted as they appear in shallow water and sunlight. The book is softbound and waterproof.

St. John: Feet, Fins & Four-wheel Drive, by Pam Gaffin (⊠ American Paradise Publishing, Box 37, Cruz Bay 00831), is a delightfully quirky book about all the little-known beaches, hiking trails, and snorkel sites of that pristine island.

Fishwatcher's Guide to West Atlantic Coral Reefs, by Charles C. Chaplin and Peter Scott (⊠ Harrowood Books, 3943 North Providence Rd., Newtown Square, PA 19073), shows 184 species of fish, drawn in detail and color as they appear through a face mask—including head-on and top-down views. The text is concise and offers tips on how to spot elusive varieties. The softbound book is printed on plastic.

Skin Diver Magazine (⊠ 8490 Sunset Blvd., Los Angeles, CA 90069) is a thick (average 180 pages) monthly with regular features on dive locations, equipment, photography, and safety issues. Its advertisements for dive locations and packages are helpful. It is available at newsstands and is truly the dive traveler's guide.

Diving and Snorkeling in the B.V.I., by Jeff Williams (⊠ DIVEntures Publishing, Box 115, Hopkinton, MA 01748), is an excellent diving guide written by an experienced local diver.

3 Sailing in the Virgin Islands

The best way to see the Virgin Islands—to truly observe them with the proper laid-back reverence—is from the deck of a small sailing vessel snugly anchored in a quiet bay.

By Marcia
Andrews

Updated by
Gary
Goodlander

WITHIN A FEW HOURS after you alight in St. Thomas and unload the taxi at Red Hook Bay, you can sail across Pillsbury Sound, anchor in St. John's Caneel Bay, have dinner on deck, watch the sun set behind an age-softened, jungle-covered volcano, and simply forget whatever plagued you that morning. It sounds like a lot to accomplish in one day, but you wouldn't be rushed. On a chartered boat, you can set your own pace, but it doesn't take long to get to the most beautiful locations in the islands.

Caneel Bay, for instance, is a quiet, natural area, little more than an hour's sail from Red Hook's busy harbor. Viewed from a moonlit deck, the bay is a Gauguin scene in silhouette. A few sailboats float in the foreground, their masts tracing slow S-curves in the sky. Beyond the ghostly white hulls, a crescent of white sand is fringed with palm trees. The lights of the Caneel Bay Resort sprinkle the hillside, and faint arpeggios of a steel band ride the offshore breeze.

If a bright moon illuminates the packed white sand under your anchored boat, you'll be amazed by what you can see through the still, gin-clear water. Starfish and sea slugs and schools of minnows dart in and out of the boat's shadow. Scenes from *Jaws* may come to mind as you watch something huge slide from under the boat and glide out to sea. Chances are it's only a prowling, curious barracuda, and much smaller than the 6-ft maxi-specimens that can hover around nearby reefs. But, water magnifies things. So does the spell of your first night on a boat in the tropics.

With a sailing fleet of several hundred boats, based mostly in harbors on St. Thomas, Tortola, and Virgin Gorda, access to the island attractions is remarkably easy, year-round and from all directions. There's no prescribed itinerary, no best boat to charter. You can sail aboard a fully crewed boat with an experienced captain and cook, or sail independently on a bare-boat charter. The selection of high-quality, professionally run operations competing for your business in the Virgin Islands is unrivaled.

The Virgin Islands can match every cruising sailor's wish list:

- Sunny days, in the 70°F to 80°F range

- Dependable trade winds of 12 to 20 knots from the east-southeast

- Varied, exotic scenery, from the Danish-built harbor towns of Charlotte Amalie, Road Town, and Christiansted to small, remote beaches along jungle shores to the boulder-strewn moonscapes of Virgin Gorda

- Protected anchorages that are free; slips to rent for about $1 per foot of boat; moorings for about $15 per night

- Tides of less than 2 ft; generally predictable currents

- Short passages between islands. The archipelago—except for St. Croix and Anegada—is about 40 mi long, crow-flying style, and could be circumnavigated in two days of serious sailing.

- Easy access to on-shore attractions, most of which cluster around harbor towns

And St. Thomas is the current home of the Virgin Islands America's Cup Challenge. A fleet of mega-million-dollar 80-ft racing yachts (with towering 110-ft masts) is sailing within Charlotte Amalie harbor on a daily basis. The only thing more exciting than sailing alongside one of these majestic vessels is attempting to capture it on film.

If reliable winds (which keep general summer temperatures below those in the United States), lower prices (as much as 50% off), and uncrowded anchorages were the only drawing points, summer chartering would be more popular. But since everyone wants to escape northern snows, high season persists, December through April. If you chartered in August through October (hurricane season), you'd be nearly alone—and nervous.

Though all of the islands are your cruising playground, crewed charter operations are concentrated in the American territory and bare-boat charters dominate in the British islands. In fact, the B.V.I. reportedly are home to more boat bunks than hotel beds. The British half also has an amazing array of anchorages, with one impressive statistic to make the point: There are 16 good anchorages within one hour's sail of Tortola's Road Harbour, home base for the Moorings, the Caribbean's biggest bare-boat fleet.

The more developed U.S. ports, full of duty-free treasures, cruise-ship crowds, and tourist-worthy night spots, contrast with the quieter British islands. The B.V.I.'s lower population density means quieter anchorages, smaller towns, and easygoing people. Avid cruisers set out to sample both man-made and natural attractions on all the islands. They sail across borders, taking in stride immigration and customs rules as well as the British visitor's tax—an effort to make up for the B.V.I.'s lack of hotel-room income. Some U.S. sailors are reluctant to cross territories because of the customs formalities. This is a shame, considering that doing so costs so little in time and money and pays off many times over in experiencing the diversity of this intriguing area.

Whatever type of vessel you charter, make sure that it is allowed to go where you want it to go. The U.S.V.I. and the B.V.I. are parts of separate countries with distinctly different marine regulations. Not all charter vessels in the B.V.I. are legally allowed to visit the U.S.V.I. Some B.V.I. bare-boat companies actively discourage their customers from entering U.S.V.I. waters. Check in advance.

To visit the British Islands, a passport is highly recommended. Although a U.S. voter's registration card in conjunction with a photo ID often suffices, its acceptance seems to depend upon the mood of the immigration official. Also, American citizens often have numerous problems clearing back into the United States with only a voter's registration card as identification. U.S. boats entering British territory for a visit of less than five days usually are allowed to check in and out simultaneously. You'll find the office at one of the ports listed below and will meet for a few minutes with officials to complete forms. The skipper must show officials the crews' identification (passports) and the boat's papers and must pay a visitor's tax of $4 per person per day and $20–$50 per visit for the boat. British-registered boats pay $2 per person per day visitor's tax in high season and 75¢ per person per day, May 1 through November 30. If the vessel you've chartered has not paid its annual Commercial Recreational Cruising Permit fee, you'll have to pay an additional $25–$45 charge (depending on the length of the vessel) per charter.

British customs/immigration offices operate 8:30–3:30 weekdays, 8:30–12:30 Saturday. Holiday clearances cost more for overtime—and that's if you can reach anyone. It's best to plan your arrival and departure to avoid overtime charges. Always ask for a receipt. Avoid attempting to clear within an hour of opening or closing: Government offices in the Caribbean tend to open slowly and close quickly. Impatience can be misconstrued as rudeness here. Instead, begin all conversations with a warm smile, a friendly greeting, and a brief chat. Proper dress is required—no bare feet or bare chests. Offices are on Tortola (Road Town, West End ferry dock), Jost Van Dyke (Great Harbour), and Virgin Gorda (Virgin Gorda Yacht Harbour).

British-registered boats entering U.S. waters pay no fees, but the skipper must visit the customs/immigration office and present the crew and boat papers to clear in and out. U.S. customs-office hours are Monday–Saturday 8–5. The easiest clearance is through Cruz Bay on St. John, where officers are on the waterfront. The St. Thomas harbor offices are at the Blyden Ferry Terminal on the Charlotte Amalie waterfront, where the Tortola passenger ferries tie up. St. Croix clearance is at wharfside, Gallows Bay, but you call customs (☎ 809/773–1011) for directions and notify immigration (☎ 809/778–1419) to have an inspector come over from the airport. This is one reason that so few cruising yachts bother with St. Croix.

Just outside any of the charter harbors lies the world's most popular cruising playground, with six large islands and dozens of smaller cays. The Virgin Islands are a cluster of old volcanoes. They're distinct and visible on every horizon and perfect for line-of-sight navigation. As one charter outfit puts it, the United States and British Virgin Islands combined—excluding St. Croix and Anegada—could be transplanted into the waters of New York's Long Island Sound. Good visualization, bad idea.

Why exclude St. Croix? Although its shoreline might be great fun to explore, the island sits alone, about 35 mi south of the group. Plus, the prevailing winds from the east make it more work to visit than most vacationers will bother with. Hence, St. Croix has a fleet of smaller day-sail boats but few live-aboard charters. Anegada is counted out because it is some 15 mi north of the group and is surrounded by reefs, coral heads, and unpredictable currents. Most bare-boat charter contracts specify Anegada as off-limits, but its utterly pristine and usually deserted beaches make it a prime attraction for beachcombers and sun worshipers who cherish their privacy.

Winnowing your cruising options in the Virgin Islands starts with deciding between a crewed or a bare-boat charter. Crewed charters can be for everyone, even old salts who sometimes choose to sail with a captain or with a captain and a cook, to guarantee a relaxed vacation. Though cruising unassisted is reserved for people with at least basic sailing skills, it's not cut and dried. If you've mastered the basics of sailing a dinghy, you and your party can take a learn-to-cruise vacation, to train with internationally recognized instructors at the Offshore Sailing School (☎ 800/221–4326), in Tortola's Road Harbour, or Annapolis Sailing Schools (☎ 800/638–9192), in St. Croix. You'll live on a cruising boat and, after some courses, graduate by sending the instructor to shore for the last days of your vacation.

Crewed Charters

The captain and mate of our chartered 54-ft ketch knew how to cast the island spell immediately. They met us on the docks of American Yacht Harbor in Red Hook on St. Thomas, double-checked our special provisioning orders (nouvelle and local cuisine, French wines and diet soda), then began a gentle patter about the quirks of living aboard their classic mahogany boat: "Stow anything that might roll off the bunks and break, wear soft-sole shoes, if any." While we surveyed the boat's three private cabins, poked into lockers, checked the plumbing and the stereo system, they eased us away from the mooring and into the island tempo—no hurry.

Crewed sailboats are run by an intriguing international subculture of old salts and young adventurers. Our captain and his wife—both Canadians—sail around the Caribbean on a boat that represents their net worth and are available for the Virgin Islands charter season through a U.S. broker. Like most other cruising matchmakers, the broker had auditioned this crew and boat at a gathering of local skippers a couple of years before. Since we six were sharing about 600 sq ft of space for 10 days, matching us for group chemistry was important.

Starting months in advance, with a list of options and a questionnaire, the broker probed our wishes (white-knuckle sailing? raucous parties? marine biology? quiet therapy?). Based on our reaction to size and price, the broker furnished brochures showing boats, cabin layouts, and crew resumés. We asked for a fast boat with moderate amenities. As soon as we met at the marina, our crew sensed what we needed. They sailed us to their favorite spot for a swim and a quiet evening.

The transition to cruising was easy: out of city clothes; into bathing suits and deck shoes. With T-shirts and shorts for shore cover, that's about all you'll need except for casual dining-out clothes and a windbreaker in case the evening is cool. Men won't need blazers except in the most formal resort dining room. For women a skirt or easy dress is optional—you're going to be climbing ladders in and out of the boat's dinghy to get to restaurants that cater mostly to "yachties" whose uniform is knit shirts and khaki shorts. Even in some of the most luxurious surroundings, dress is casual—maybe *upscale* casual, but casual.

Since we four were a mix of sailors and potential sailors, the crewed charter was ideal: The captain's local knowledge meant we didn't have to worry about where the underwater rocks were hiding or whether the anchorage would be comfortable. But our captain never shooed anyone away from the wheel or discouraged us from turning a winch or hauling on a jib sheet. The mate's skill as sail handler, cook, and concierge guaranteed that we could play all day—sail a few hours to the next anchorage, survey sea life with snorkeling gear, embarrass ourselves on their sailboard, join a scuba trip on a boat from a shore-based dive shop, take the dinghy ashore to beachcomb—or simply decorate the deck of our own boat. Sure, there was time for activities in whatever town we were near, but the main attraction was the boat.

Crewed-charter costs vary greatly. A relatively modest boat with a small crew can be quite affordable; however, the Caribbean has a number of palatial vessels that charter for more than $20,000 a week. One megayacht that often headquarters out of the Crown Bay Marina in St. Thomas during the winter asks for $26,000 a *day*! (One would assume they throw in a complimentary glass of champagne at that price.)

The average cost for comparison purposes—based upon a charter party of six and a typical fully crewed charter boat of around 50 ft— is from $1,000 to $1,800 per person per week, with all food, beverages, water-sports equipment, and port fees included. A tip of between 10% and 15% is appreciated for captain and crew.

A couple can expect to pay between $1,600 and $2,300 each for a top-of-the-line 41-ft boat—not bad considering they are getting the most private, most exclusive "catered" vacation in the world.

Another option is to hire a bare boat and then allow the company to recommend an experienced skipper. In this case, you pay for all provisions, do all the cooking and cleaning, and the captain is your guest for all dinners ashore. This can save money, but bear in mind you are only hiring a "navigational" captain and thus will not be enjoying the same level of personalized service most fully crewed charter boats offer. While this option can be a good choice for the experienced charterer, it has all the disadvantages of both fully crewed chartering and bare boating while offering few of the advantages of either. Usually the money saved isn't worth it.

Remember: A bare boat is totally under the charterers' command—they (temporarily) have all the rights and responsibilities of a yacht owner. However, a boat with a licensed captain is under that *captain's* command. Of course, that captain will usually attempt to accommodate the charterers' wishes in every way—but the final decision on all matters rests with the captain.

When you sign a crewed-charter contract, there will be language about the company's insurance liability and yours. If you hire a captain and a boat, the owner's insurance covers his actions, not yours (if you fall overboard, for instance, only your personal insurance applies).

Bare-Boat Charters

A sailboat, with or without crew, is the individualist's choice. It assumes you'll set your own pace and enjoy sailing, even tacking half a day on a zigzag course to a beach you could see with binoculars from the start.

The popularity of bare-boat charters, designed for people who'd rather plan, sail, and explore on their own, has steadily increased in the Virgin Islands since the early '60s, when the first boat owner handed over the keys, untied dock lines, and waved bon voyage to a visiting sailor. The charter business has become very sophisticated, with formalized applications from sailors, including a sailing-experience resumé and references. There are competitive offerings such as rate reductions from charter companies, extra amenities to boost low-season summer business, and everything's signed and sealed, with a deposit of up to 50% of the charter cost, months in advance.

Not for beginning sailors, bare boating is an excellent way to graduate from sailing a boat of twentysomething feet at home to spending two weeks on a 32-ft cruiser. Many sailors quickly move up to the most popular cruising setup—a 42-ft boat, with six people sharing the cost, the work, and the fun.

The boats aren't exotic. Bare-boat fleets are fairly homogenous, with low-maintenance fiberglass boats predominating, though some companies specialize in ultraluxury bare boats—in case you want to try out your dream boat. Standard cruising equipment includes a furling headsail that rolls up on a cable at the front of the boat (so you never have to drag a sail to and from the bow). Everyone tows a dinghy or carries it on the boat—you may not ever take the big boat to a dock, unless you require water or fuel. Many boats also have a windlass to lift the anchor mechanically, and all have swim ladders, off-the-stern charcoal grills, and the standard two-burner, one-oven marine stoves below. On larger boats, you may find air-conditioning and a refrigeration unit, as well as the ice-cooled chest for food storage, but many people decide it's too annoying to run the boat's engine the required number of hours to power all that refrigeration.

Though the Virgin Islands are famous for making navigation easy, every bare-boat charter party needs willing, able sailors and at least one member whose boat handling and anchoring experience meets the charter company's minimum standards. (They're adept at spotting pretenders.) For your own enjoyment of the adventure, someone in your party must have the expertise to read charts and avoid obstructions, anchor the boat securely, and confidently operate such boat systems as the VHF radio and diesel engine. If such a person is not aboard, then you will not have an enjoyable vacation. Damaging the vessel—and possibly injuring yourself at the same time—can turn even the nicest vacation into a salt-stained nightmare.

Many companies or brokers will arrange airline bookings, suggest itineraries, and stock the boat with food, drink, supplies, and optional toys. After that, you're on your own. The charter base may ask that you check with them daily by radio for messages or call if you need advice or assistance. But remember that the primary job of a bare-boat company is to provide you with a well-functioning seaworthy boat— not to instruct you on basic seamanship by radio. Some charter companies have chase boats; any will arrange to send another boat to you in a pinch (no one wants to declare an emergency). If you're unsure of your skills, some companies will assign a captain to spend a day or two aboard your boat (for $90–$150 per day) to show you the ropes.

Bare-boat chartering is often a congenial gathering of four to six people who enjoy sailing and one another—and who can divide the costs of a 30- to 50-ft boat. Researching and planning together adds to the fun. Most sailors select a boat and make reservations at least six months in advance for high-season charters, or earlier to guarantee holiday dates. Our ritual is to book a boat, then call a planning meeting to discuss the optional activities (fishing, shopping, diving), a rough itinerary, and the food and drink. We prefer to buy partial provisioning (about half the dinners for the trip and most of the breakfasts and lunches) or less (a starter kit to get us through the first day) for highly personal reasons:

- Many charter companies still load the boat with canned foods, processed meats, frozen beef, and other less-than-gourmet items.

- There are restaurants at or behind every marina, and we enjoy sampling island food.

- Local markets, within walking distance of many marinas, can yield great fruit, seafood, and local specialties. We like to explore the communities and replenish our supply of fresh foods.

Provisioning costs about $18–$26 per person per day if you let the charter company supply every meal. Beverages are extra. Partial provisioning, for about $16, assumes you'll have three of seven dinners ashore.

Bare-boat cruising in style costs about the same as staying in a mid-range resort—and with less opportunity to run amok in bars or duty-free shops. The bare boat costs from $60 to $100 per person, per day, assuming you fill every bunk—and some people prefer the luxury of a foursome on a five-bunk boat. However, it is still possible to rent a cramped, hard-used 30-ft sloop for $1,200. The price range reflects such things as the optional equipment (refrigeration) and the age or reputation of the boat: It's prudent to ask for a boat in charter service under five years.

When you charter a bare boat, be aware that the boat owner's liability insurance doesn't cover your errors. In bare-boat contracts, there is usually a security deposit against property damage, from $500 to half the charter cost. To avoid problems, don't anchor too close to other vessels; topside damage is the primary reason most bare-boat charterers lose their deposits. Always put down two anchors, and "set" them carefully with a seven-to-one scope (seven times as much line as the depth of water you're in) so there is no possibility of dragging. Keep a sharp eye on your vessel's dinghy, or your security deposit will disappear along with it.

Sailing with Children

You've seen the ads showing only romantic young couples and no children. They're missing a major point. If you cruise at home with children, you'll love doing it in the tropics: Steady sailing breezes, relaxed beach time, colorful towns, and accessible snorkeling can make this a rich and memorable family vacation. The transition to Caribbean sailing will be easiest if you charter a boat like the one you sail at home. Bring your children's safety gear, too—the harness and tether to keep them inside the lifelines, the comfortable life jackets they'll wear constantly.

If family cruising is an experiment you'd like to try on vacation, start with a crewed charter and a boat the broker believes will foster safety for children and relaxed sailing for you. For example, a cockpit with an open stern (rare, anyway) would pose an absurd risk for a toddler. Though you may have to challenge a broker or two to arrange a toddler-friendly charter, there are crews that are especially good with youngsters. Note that the crews may insist, up front, that they haven't the time or skills to be baby-sitters. If a crew seems even mildly resistant to the idea of children on board, select another. You will still need to bring safety gear for your child. Captains can usually round up small-size snorkeling gear.

On land, casual open-air restaurants, shops, and entertainment can help parents relieve their restless children.

Selecting a Charter

Boats and captains operating in the U.S.V.I. (or picking up passengers from U.S. ports) must be U.S. Coast Guard–licensed or SOLAS (Safety of Life at Sea) approved. Crewed charters in the B.V.I. are usually (but not always) operated by people with British Yacht Masters' Tickets, a system comparable to Coast Guard licensing.

In either case, besides confirming the boat's and crew's status with a broker, you can verify their good standing by contacting voluntary associations in both U.S. and British territories. Yearning for repeat customers, these groups discourage contact with sloppy operators who could ruin your vacation. The U.S. fleet belongs to **Virgin Islands Charteryacht League** (⊠ Flagship, 5100 Long Bay Rd., St. Thomas, U.S.V.I. 00802, ☎ 800/524–2061, FAX 809/776–4468). The VICL will send you a "Sail the Virgins" brochure and the "How to Book a Boat" guide free of charge. The British fleet works with **Charter Yacht Society of the B.V.I.** (⊠ Box 3069, Road Town, B.V.I., ☎ FAX 809/494–6017).

Most sailboats in the Virgin Islands are 42 ft long and chartered to bareboat sailors, but the companies will find a captain for any boat. Figure out what size boat and crew situation you'll be most comfortable with and proceed from there. On Virgin Gorda, Bitter End Yacht Club has 30-ft boats (great for two people). Crewed boats are often 50 ft or longer.

With so many high-profile charter companies around, few private boats are offered for bare-boat charter in the Virgin Islands. If you decide to check the sailing-magazine classified ads hoping for a bargain in a freelance, transient boat, you should focus on getting a strict contract and references. We rented a private boat out of Palm Beach to sail to the Bahamas with good results. But that gamble didn't risk the disappointment of finding an unworthy boat in a foreign port after a long flight. Occasionally these can be great deals. But far too often the hassles endured are not worth the money saved.

All else being okay, ask private-boat owners for names of several recent customers, and check with them for their experiences. In more than 16 years of chartering, we've relied on personal recommendations but have never been asked to give a reference.

Brokers

Brokers are extremely important when it comes to selecting a fully crewed vessel. There are about 200 *independent* brokers worldwide, and all have access to the same fleet of 300 boats operating in the Caribbean. The differences among them are in personal experience and up-to-the-minute information. The single most important decision a charterer in search of an enjoyable crewed charter can make is selecting a reputable broker.

How? Make sure your broker regularly attends the annual Caribbean charter yacht "viewing" shows on Tortola and St. Thomas—and has actually been aboard the vessels he represents. The best brokers are on a first-name basis with their captains. Reputable brokers never offer "additional" discounts on fully crewed charter vessels; charter fees are a matter of public record and nonnegotiable. Good brokers are interested in making sure you have ". . . the sailing vacation of a lifetime!" so you'll re-book with them next year; bad brokers are interested primarily in "selling" you on any boat—so they can collect their commission.

Five or 10 years ago, it was fairly uncommon to be able to call a broker company and have information sent. Most companies these days do send fact sheets on request as a matter of course, but you should not be surprised if the person you talk to tries to make sure you're a "live one" before taking the time and money to send you an extensive packet.

A broker's general services:

- An interview at the time of your initial inquiry to determine your vacation expectations, budget, and other pertinent information

- A timely response with specific brochures on recommended boats

- A timely follow-up to narrow the selection and to make knowledgeable suggestions based on customer input

- Matching crew "personalities" with the potential charterers' needs

- Advice and help with island travel arrangements, including air and hotel

- Coordinating with the crew all details in regard to the actual charter contract: special food and beverage preferences, any special occasions to be celebrated during the voyage, etc.

Blue Water Cruises (⊠ Box 1345, Bayview St., Camden, ME 04843, ☎ 800/524–2020, ℻ 207/236–2132) has an excellent worldwide reputation; owner Nancy Stout lived on St. Thomas for more than 20 years. She knows the industry inside and out and provides an extensive information packet on request.

Charterboat Center (⊠ 6300 Smith Bay, 16-3, St. Thomas 00802–1304, ☎ 809/775– 7990 or 800/866–5714, ℻ 809/779–6116) is in Red Hook. It books both bare and fully crewed charter boats and is particularly knowledgeable about the growing sportfishing fleet tied up just outside the office window.

Crewed Charters (⊠ 5100 Long Bay Rd., St. Thomas 00802, ☎ 809/776–4811 or 800/522–3077, ℻ 809/776–4811) has been around since

1981 and is right in Yacht Haven Marina. Charter broker Verna Ruan knows all the captains and crews on a first-name basis.

Ed Hamilton & Co (✉ Box 430, N. Whitefield, ME 04353, ☎ 800/621–7855, FAX 207/549–7822) has booked both bare and crewed boats since 1972.

Lynhollen Yacht Charters (✉ Box 489, Fair Oaks, CA 95628, ☎ 800/821–1186, FAX 916/863–6637) is one of the top West Coast brokers.

Lynn Jachney (✉ Box 302, Marblehead, MA 01945, ☎ 800/223–2050, FAX 617/639–0216) is widely experienced and has been booking quality charters for 28 years. Her husband, Dick Jachney, owns Caribbean Yacht Charters (CYC), which is the largest bare-boat company on St. Thomas. She has extensive contacts throughout most of the Caribbean and is very up-to-the-minute on boats and crews; she is consistently one of the top three brokers in the world.

Regency Yacht Vacations (✉ 5200 Long Bay Rd., St. Thomas 00802, ☎ 809/776–5950 or 800/524–7676, FAX 809/776–7631) in St. Thomas is on the Yacht Haven marina. This brokerage team, headed up by Kathy Mullen, has an excellent reputation for keeping close tabs on its boats. It is also among the top three brokers in the world.

Russell Yacht Charters (✉ 404 Hulls Hwy., Suite 27, Southport, CT 06490–1020, ☎ 800/635–8895, FAX 203/255–3426), established nearly 26 years ago, has a solid reputation.

Ann-Wallis White (✉ Box 4100, Horn Point Harbor, Annapolis, MD 21403, ☎ 410/263–6366 or 800/732–3861, FAX 410/263–0399) is hardworking and ultraselective with her boats and crews—very knowledgeable about the global chartering industry.

Charter Companies

Bare-boat charter companies own and operate fleets of boats in the Virgin Islands, maintaining local facilities and services for customers. Many have offices in the United States or Canada, as well as at their island fleet locations. They're all quick to respond with brochures, boat layouts, questionnaires, and price sheets. Although you can still rent a small, basic bare boat for less than $1,200 a week, most bare boats in the Virgins cost $2,400–$4,900 a week. Generally speaking, bigger boats with more "toys" are more expensive. Many bare-boat companies offer extraordinary discounts (up to 50%) during the slowest summer months.

The U.S. Virgin Islands

ST. THOMAS

Caribbean Sailing Charters Inc. (✉ 3883 Andrews Crossing, Roswell, GA 30075, ☎ 770/641–9640 or 800/824–1331, FAX 707/992–0276), at Yacht Haven Marina in St. Thomas Harbor, has a 12-boat fleet, including Beneteau, Morgan, and Catalina yachts. Boats are all relatively new and range in size from 35 to 50 ft.

Caribbean Yacht Charters (✉ Box 583, Marblehead, MA 01945, ☎ 800/225–2520, FAX 617/639–0216) at Compass Point, East End, has a fleet of 35 yachts, including a Sabre 36 and a Frers 51. It is currently the largest bare-boat operation on St. Thomas, and the majority of its fleet is relatively new.

Caribbean Yacht Owners Association (✉ 62 Honduras, Frenchtown Marina, St. Thomas 00802, ☎ 809/777–9690 or 800/944–2962, FAX 809/777–9750), in the Charlotte Amalie harbor is connected with the International School of Sailing. It offers some of the lowest prices in the area for a generally well tended 22-boat fleet. In addition to sailboats in the 35- to 50-ft range, it charters Mainship 35 Trawlers. Ask the boat's age—under five years is preferred.

Island Yachts (✉ 6100 Red Hook Quarter 18B, Suite 4, Red Hook 00802, ☎ 809/775–6666 or 800/524–2019, FAX 809/779–8557), is a midsize operator with a diverse fleet of 15 boats, ranging from a 30-ft S2 to a Beneteau 50 and an Albin 43 Trawler. The bulk of its fleet is made up of 32-ft Island Packets, sturdy cruising vessels with plenty of room below deck.

Ocean Incentives (✉ American Yacht Harbor, Red Hook 00802–1303, ☎ 809/775–6406 or 800/344–5762, FAX 809/775–6712) is a newer operation with a 15-boat fleet ranging from 32 to 50 ft.

Trawlers in Paradise (✉ 6161 Estate Frydenhoj #67, 00802–1402, ☎ 809/775–9002 or 800/458–0675, FAX 809/775–9003) offers a new fleet of 12 Grand Banks Trawlers from 36 to 49 ft.

VIP Yacht Charter (✉ 6118 Frydenhoj, Suite 58, 00802, ☎ 809/776–1510 or 800/524–2015, FAX 809/776–3801), at Saga Haven Marina, has powerboats in the 34- to 53-ft range, with skippers and instruction available. Boats are loaded with amenities, such as microwave ovens, cellular phones, and TVs. Prices are generally 20% higher than for sailboats of comparable size.

ST. CROIX

Annapolis Sailing School (✉ Box 3334, 601 6th St., Annapolis, MD 21403, ☎ 800/638–9192, FAX 410/268–3114), Christiansted, offers one-week live-aboard cruising courses, including a sail from St. Croix to the B.V.I.

ST. JOHN

Proper Yacht Charters (✉ Box 1570, Cruz Bay, 00831, ☎ 809/776–6256, FAX 809/693–9841), Mongoose Junction, is a small operation on the quiet island, specializing in the finely made, luxuriously finished 40- to 51-ft Hinkleys many sailors covet. Few Hinkleys are available for bare-boat charters—so book early.

The British Virgin Islands

TORTOLA

Catamaran Charters (✉ 141 Alton Rd., Miami Beach, FL 33139, ☎ 800/262–0308, FAX 305/538–1556) rents catamaran sailboats. Its 39- to 50-ft Privilege cats have four double cabins, numerous heads, and double showers. Sunning mattresses and trampolines between hulls make the most of the deck.

Freedom Charters (✉ 305 Oliphant La., Middletown, RI 02842, ☎ 800/999–2909, FAX 401/848–2904), at the Village Cay Marina in Road Town, has a fleet of 10 especially-easy-to-sail vessels ranging from 35 to 45 ft.

The Moorings (✉ 19345 U.S. 19 N, 4th Floor, Clearwater, FL 34624–3193, ☎ 800/535–7289, FAX 813/530–9747), conveniently based at Wickham's Cay II in Road Town, is the largest operator in the islands, with a generally new, well-maintained fleet of 150 cruise-design boats. It has the most high-performance Beneteau yachts, and they're backed by an excellent staff. This company is generally considered to be the best-managed bare-boat operation in the world.

North South (✉ 655 Dixon Rd., Suite 18, Toronto, Ontario, Can. M9W 1J4, ☎ 800/387–4964, FAX 416/242–8122) has 30 boats in its fleet; it's based out of Nanny Cay.

Sun Yacht Charters (✉ Box 737, Camden, ME 04843, ☎ 800/772–3500, FAX 207/236–3972), at Maya Cove, has 41 sailing vessels ranging from 36 to 51 ft.

Sunsail Worldwide Charters (✉ 908 Awald Rd., Suite 302, Annapolis, MD 21403, ☎ 800/327–2276, FAX 410/280–2406), at West End, has more than 90 well-maintained boats ranging from 30 to 55 ft. This is one of the most rapidly expanding companies in the Caribbean.

Tortola Marine Management Ltd. (✉ Road Town, ☎ 809/494–2751 or 800/633–0155, FAX 809/494–5166; ☎ 203/854–5131, FAX 203/838–9756 in the U.S.), at Road Reef Marina, has an unusual selection of boats. Besides 35- to 51-ft monohulls, TMM's 33-boat fleet includes several shallow-draft catamarans that allow exploration of bays deeper hulls can't reach.

Tropic Island Yacht Management Ltd. (✉ Box 532, Maya Cove, ☎ 809/494–2450 or 800/356–8938, FAX 809/495–2155) has an interesting range of boats, from a 37-ft catamaran to a Beneteau 51. The cats are lower priced, but ask for the newest boats in the fleet of 25. It also offers a few midsize power vessels.

VIRGIN GORDA

Bitter End Yacht Club (✉ 875 N. Michigan Ave., Suite 3707, Chicago, IL 60611, ☎ 800/872–2392, FAX 312/944–2860), North Sound, is a 90-room resort with 8 charter boats and more than 100 daysailers and sailing dinghies available at no extra charge to resort guests. Charter boats include Freedom 30s, which are very easy to handle. Charter rates are average, but these include provisioning. Check land-and-water-combination vacation deals.

Misty Isle Yacht Charters (✉ Virgin Gorda Yacht Harbour, ☎ 809/495–5643, FAX 809/495–5300) has a fleet of four boats, both power and sail.

Small Powerboat Rentals

Another interesting way to see the islands is by small rental powerboat, a surprisingly affordable option. A 40-hp, outboard-driven, open 18-footer rents for less than $150 a day, while a twin-engine, mega-muscle powerboat is correspondingly higher. Most companies (but not all) require you to top off the fuel tanks at the end of the day—remember marina fuel is very expensive here. Slower boats are safer and more economical, but generally considered not as much fun.

The Virgin Islands have numerous regattas, yacht races, fishing contests, board-sailing events, and organized "booze cruises," which can only be enjoyed on watercraft. The New Year's Eve bash on Jost Van Dyke is world renowned for its wildness. Small rental boats can provide an ideal way to join the party or to get away from it all—depending on whim. A small deposit is usually required, as is a major credit card. Some companies are restricting rentals to persons 25 and older.

A couple of safety rules to remember: Don't ever "beach" the boat even momentarily, since sand (like sandpaper) is an ideal medium to scratch Fiberglas. All boats come with good anchoring gear, as well as all USCG-required safety equipment. In shallow water, be especially careful not to nick the prop. Watch your engine gauges, as well as the color of the water ahead. Never operate any vessel while intoxicated.

The U.S. Virgin Islands

ST. THOMAS

On St. Thomas most of the rental companies are within a few steps of one another in Red Hook harbor, making comparison shopping easy.

Advance reservations are a good idea, as the cheaper boats tend to rent first. However, there is usually enough competition to assure you a decent boat at a good price even on the spur of the moment.

Nauti Nymph (✉ 6501 Red Hook Plaza, Suite 201, 00802, ☎ FAX 809/775–5066, ☎ 800/714–7345) has 12 boats ranging from 21-ft, 150-hp craft to 29-ft, twin 200-hp speedsters. They range in price from $215 to $325 per day and include snorkel gear.

See and Ski (✉ 6501 Red Hook Plaza, Suite 201, 00802, ☎ 809/775–6265) specializes in 25-ft Makos with 250-hp Yamaha outboards and 28-ft Makos with small cuddy cabins and two 200-hp Yamaha outboards. These range from $265 to $345 per day.

ST. JOHN

Noah's Little Arks (☎ 809/693–9030) rents small inflatable boats with 15-hp outboards. A half-day rental goes for as little as $50.

Ocean Runner (✉ Cruz Bay, 00831, ☎ 809/693–8809) has a fleet of 20- to 27-ft open powercraft, which range in price from $195 to $350 per day. It also rents a 33-ft 500-hp Powerplay sportboat with a USCG-licensed captain for $700 per day. It is conveniently located on the downtown beach right next to the ferry dock. A deposit of $1,000 or a major credit card is required.

The British Virgin Islands

TORTOLA

Cane Garden Bay Pleasure Boat Rental (☎ 809/495–9660) has dozens of small watercraft for rent, including sailboards, kayaks, and beach cats—right up to 28-ft powercraft with 300-hp engines.

VIRGIN GORDA

Euphoric Cruises (✉ Virgin Gorda Yacht Harbour, ☎ 809/495–5542) has 24-ft Robalos with 200-hp outboards available for $250 per day or $1,500 per week.

Daysailing

Dozens of daysail boats operate out of the Virgins, varying from large multipassenger "cattle-marans" with live music, swinging dance floors, and crowded cockpit bars to quiet couple-only charters on small sailing vessels gently anchored in pristine, lonely coves. Take your pick.

Boats

The following vessels have been day chartering in the Virgins for many years and have a reputation for excellence.

On St. Thomas, the **Kon Tiki** (☎ 809/775–5055) is the wildest three-hour multipassenger "mini booze cruise" in the Caribbean. Be ready to bop till you drop, and watch out for those blender drinks.

In the Red Hook area on the east end of St. Thomas, Pat Stoken (☎ 809/775–1408 or 809/775–6547) of the clipper-bowed 44-ft ketch **Independence** is a favorite with local sailors. Cap'n Pat offers full- ($85) and half-day ($55) sails, and her complimentary lunch is nearly as tasty as her famous rum punch. (Ask her about sailing across the Pacific while raising a family.)

On St. John, Cruz Bay has been "snug harbor" for Bob Nose (☎ 809/776–6922) and his 32-ft double-ender **Alcyone** for many years. He's a fountain of island lore; ask him about diving for lobsters for Jimmy Carter.

On St. Croix, don't miss an exciting daysail to Buck Island on one of the fast trimarans for which St. Croix is famous. The wonderful, skilled

West Indian sailors known locally as Buck Island Captains gather daily on the seawall by the Chart House restaurant.

Charter Companies

Of course, daysail charter-boat companies tend to come and go with the trade winds. The best way to select one that fits your needs is to visit a large resort's activities desk or an independent booking agent.

The following businesses can book you on a submarine ride, a parasail boat, a kayak trip, a Jet Ski ride, a Hobie Cat sail, or a half-day, inshore, light-tackle fishing excursion. They get customer feedback on a daily basis and know exactly what type of boats and crew they are booking. They will be happy to answer your questions.

On St. Thomas, **Coconut Charters** (⊠ 6501 Red Hook Plaza, ☎ 809/775–2584) usually has a number of multihull vessels doing daysails. **The Charter Boat Center** (⊠ 6300 Estate Smith Bay 16-3, Charlotte Amalie, ☎ 809/775–7990 or 800/866–5714) at Red Hook books a number of local daysail boats, as well as bare-boat and crewed-charter vessels. The staff is especially knowledgeable about the sportfishing fleet.

On St. Croix, try one of the many tours run by **Mile-Mark Charters** (⊠ 59 King's Wharf, Christiansted, ☎ 809/773–2628 or 800/523–3483, FAX 809/773–7400). **Big Beard's Adventure Tours** (⊠ Pan Am Pavilion, Christiansted, ☎ 809/773–4482) runs trips to Buck Island and beach barbecues using two modern sailing catamarans. **Teroro Charters** (⊠ Green Cay Marina, Christiansted, ☎ 809/773–3161) features Captain Heinz's trimaran *Teroro II,* which departs for full- or half-day Buck Island trips from Green Cay Marina.

On St. John, **Connections** (☎ 809/776–6922, FAX 809/776–6902) represents a dozen of the finest local boats; many of the employees have actually worked on the boats they book.

Tortola daysail boats generally work out of **Village Cay Hotel and Marina** (⊠ Road Town, ☎ 809/494–2771).

Practical Information for Sailors

Moorings

Most of the public moorings in the U.S.V.I. are within National Park waters and are currently free. A dozen or so additional free public moorings have been placed at popular dive sites. All other moorings are private, and their unauthorized use is strictly prohibited.

In the B.V.I., public moorings (maintained by the Moor Seacure Company) are available for $15 per night at Cooper Island, Marina Cay, Anegada Reef Hotel, Rhymers at Cane Garden, Soper's Hole, Vixen Point, Drake's Anchorage, Biras Creek, Abe's by the Sea, and Harris at Little Harbour, Jost Van Dyke.

The National Park Trust of the B.V.I. has also installed moorings at various ecologically sensitive areas and heavily used dive sites at Norman, Peter, Cooper, Ginger, Dog, and Guana islands, as well as Virgin Gorda, Dead Chest, and RMS *Rhone,* and the Indians. There is a small fee for their use, and permits can be obtained through your charter company or from B.V.I. customs and immigration.

In the B.V.I., the red mooring buoys are for nondiving daylight use only. The yellow buoys are for commercial dive vessels. The white buoys are for recreational boats on a first-come, first-served basis, with a 90-minute time limit. The blue buoys are for dinghies only.

Prohibitions

Various bays and harbors within the Virgins are being set aside by their respective governments and national parks as "areas of particular concern." Anchoring, fishing, or diving is often not allowed at these ecologically sensitive areas. For instance, at press time the entire area of Horseshoe Reef (Anegada) was off-limits to all fishing and anchoring, and diving was actively discouraged, though not officially banned.

Since these restrictions are often temporary or seasonal in nature—and are designed and regulated by different government agencies—keeping up with recent changes can be difficult. Ask customs and immigration for the latest information on applicable rules and regulations. Also, be especially careful in park waters.

Jet Skis are legal in the U.S.V.I. but can be operated only at dead idle when near people or within harbors. They are banned in U.S. national-park waters. In the B.V.I., Jet Skis are not allowed, period. You can't even have one aboard your vessel. Heavy fines have been levied.

Fishing

Recreational fishing with a rod or hand line is permitted within Virgin Islands National Park waters without a permit, but spearfishing, even possessing a speargun, is strictly prohibited within the park's waters. All fishing is prohibited in Trunk Bay and in buoy-designated swimming areas. In the B.V.I., you need a special permit to fish, and in certain areas, such as Horseshoe Reef, it is prohibited.

Alcohol

Both countries take a dim view of drinking and diving on land and at sea. The U.S. Coast Guard in particular has recently been vigorously enforcing the law as it pertains to boating while intoxicated. The legal limit for recreational boaters is .10 blood alcohol content; it's .04 for USCG-licensed captains. (Also, USCG-licensed captains cannot drink *any* alcohol within four hours of stepping aboard their vessels.)

Important VHF Channels

VHF marine radio is standard equipment on all charter boats and many local shore operations. It's an ideal way to keep in touch with other vessels, the international marine operator, your charter company, or to make dinner reservations. However, please remember that a marine radio is also an important safety communication device, and there are strict international rules governing its operation. Channel 16 is for calling and distress ONLY. Immediately switch to another channel after making contact with your party. Always use your vessel's official radio call sign and name at the beginning and end of each contact. The U.S. Coast Guard and various other government agencies are monitoring Channel 16 (and 22A) at all times. Chatting on Channel 16 is simply not allowed.

Other important radio services include:

- Weather reports, Channel WX 03

- Port operators and harbor masters, Channel 12

- Ship to ship or to marinas, restaurants, dive shops, Channel 68

- Private ship to ship, Channel 70

- Ship to ship for safety only, Channel 6

- B.V.I. Tortola Radio (☎ 809/494–3111) and U.S. Virgin Islands Radio (WAH) (☎ 809/776–8282) on St. Thomas will place collect long-distance calls for you on your VHF marine radio. Contact them on Channel 16, and they will assign you a working channel to switch to. Your vessel can be reached by calling one of the above numbers—but only for a hefty charge. The traffic list is usually read hourly and announced on Channel 16. Private cellular phones can be rented through many charter companies, or directly from **VITEL Cellular** (☎ 809/777–8899) or **Cellular One** (☎ 809/777–7777).

Important Phone Numbers

Declaring an emergency at sea (on VHF Ch. 16) is a drastic move, reserved for boats in imminent danger—after asking help from the charter company's chase boat, nearby marinas, or other boats. The same restraint applies to calling out rescuers or reporting problems sighted from land. However, should you require emergency outside assistance because human life is potentially in serious danger, turn on your VHF radio to Channel 16, and while depressing the microphone switch on the side of the microphone, clearly repeat the words "MAYDAY! MAYDAY! MAYDAY!" and then your vessel's name and location. Then release the microphone switch and listen carefully. If possible, have someone monitor the radio throughout the emergency. Make sure when the emergency is over to announce repeatedly on Channel 16 that you no longer require assistance. Following are onshore contacts: **U.S. Coast Guard Marine Safety Division** (✉ St. Thomas, ☎ 809/776–3497) and **Virgin Islands Search and Rescue Ltd.** (✉ Tortola, ☎ 809/494–4357, FAX 809/494–5166). VISAR can usually be reached directly on Channel 16, or on Tortola Radio, which also monitors Channel 16.

Emergency Medical Services

When calling an ambulance while in either the British or United States Virgin Islands, make sure that you clearly state which island you are calling from.

IN THE U.S.V.I.

Ambulance/Emergency (☎ 911). **St. Thomas Hospital** (Charlotte Amalie, ☎ 809/776–8311). **St. John Clinic and Ambulance** (☎ 809/693–8900). **St. Croix Hospital** (Christiansted, ☎ 809/778–6311).

IN THE B.V.I.

Emergencies (Tortola, ☎ 999). **Tortola Hospital** (Road Town, ☎ 809/494–3497). There are two **clinics** on Virgin Gorda: Valley, ☎ 809/495–5337; Gorda Sound, ☎ 809/495–7310.

Marinas and Anchorages

Charter companies provide navigational charts and begin your vacation with a discussion of current weather conditions and favored anchorages. As you navigate between islands, clusters of masts will confirm you've found popular spots: You can join in—or avoid them and study the charts for more secluded spots. Some of the pertinent harbors for supplies and entertainment are listed below.

Islands with northern shores exposed to the Atlantic swell protect the rest of the islands from pounding surf, but they're not popular as anchorages. A few north-facing bays are interesting lunch stops or good for an overnight stay in rare summer periods when weather and surge are mild.

The U.S. Virgin Islands

ST. THOMAS'S SOUTHERN SHORE

St. Thomas at Charlotte Amalie is a bustling port, the busiest in the islands, that should be visited for its color and excitement. Charlotte Amalie can be toured on foot in half a day. You can shop the town for duty-free goodies or gather supplies, wines, and fresh produce at Market Square at the end of Main Street. Or check out open-air stands at the docks for island fruits and vegetables brought to town by boat.

U.S. Virgin Island Anchorages

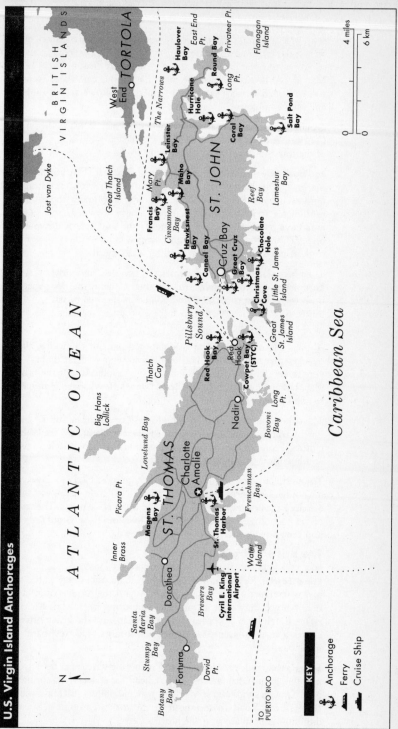

KEY

⚓ Anchorage

⛴ Ferry

🚢 Cruise Ship

N

4 miles

6 km

ATLANTIC OCEAN

Caribbean Sea

ST. THOMAS

ST. JOHN

TORTOLA

BRITISH VIRGIN ISLANDS

Jost van Dyke

West End

Great Thatch Island

Great Thatch Island

The Narrows

Mary Pt.

Leinster Bay

Maho Bay

Francis Bay

Cinnamon Bay

Hawksnest Bay

Caneel Bay

Cruz Bay

Great Cruz Bay

Christmas Cove

Chocolate Hole

Little St. James Island

Great St. James Island

St. James Island

Haulover Bay

East End Pt.

Round Bay

Long Pt.

Privateer Pt.

Flanagan Island

Hurricane Hole

Coral Bay

Reef Bay

Lameshur Bay

Salt Pond Bay

Pillsbury Sound

Red Hook Bay

Red Hook

Cowpet Bay (STYC)

Nadir

Bovoni Bay

Long Pt.

Thatch Cay

Big Hans Lollick

Inner Brass

Santa Maria Bay

Stumpy Bay

Fortuna

David Pt.

Botany Bay

Dorothea

Magens Bay

Picara Pt.

Loveland Bay

Charlotte Amalie

St. Thomas Harbor

Frenchman Bay

Water Island

Brewers Bay

Cyril E. King International Airport

TO PUERTO RICO

There's no quiet hideout for a boat close to town. The passage of large cruise ships, island ferries, and commercial traffic adds constant boat wake to the natural surge that reaches into the harbor. That surge makes anchoring stern-to at the waterfront pretty bumpy, even dangerous. For comfort, your best bet is to find anchoring space close to Yacht Haven Marina on the east side of the inner harbor. Or call ahead to rent a slip with such services as water, ice, fuel, and showers, plus cable TV and phone hookups.

Crown Bay Marina is in the Sub Base area, which is just to the west of Charlotte Amalie. It is a very modern, clean facility and is home to many of the finest megayachts in the Caribbean.

Red Hook Bay is usually a good, if busy, anchorage. There are numerous marinas to the west of the anchorage and an array of restaurants behind each dock. Red Hook is a convenient stop for eastbound boats heading for St. John or Tortola, but it's a busy, crowded harbor. **Christmas Cove** on nearby Great St. James Island and nearby **Cowpet Bay** on St. Thomas can be pleasant anchorages, but a southern slant to the trade winds at both can create rolling ocean swells.

The north side of St. Thomas is seldom traveled, and most of its harbors are not recommended for overnight anchoring. **Magens Bay**, however, is home to dozens of permanently moored boats, and many locals use it as an overnight anchorage in settled weather.

ST. JOHN'S HALO OF HARBORS

About 66% of St. John is a U.S. national park, with most of the 20 beaches protected by the National Park Service. That makes them very clean and attractive to most cruising sailors. Among the favored places to anchor overnight are **Cruz, Caneel, Hawksnest, Maho, Francis,** and **Leinster.**

The southeastern hook of St. John forms **Coral Harbor** and its several inner harbors, **Round Bay, Hurricane Hole,** and **Coral Bay,** arguably the cultural center of the island. The attractions here are people, artisans, and historical sites, not commerce.

The south coast of St. John is where you're most likely to have a solo anchorage and a private piece of beach. But isolation means you should also lock the boat against the '90s brand of pilfering pirate. The cruiser-tested anchorages are **Salt Pond Bay, Chocolate Hole, Great Cruz Bay,** and **Cruz Bay,** where you'll rejoin the crowd.

The British Virgin Islands

TORTOLA, JOST VAN DYKE, AND NEARBY ISLANDS

Cane Garden Bay is an interesting overnight anchorage in the summer when there's no northerly swell. Anchoring room is often scarce here, so you may want to pick up a mooring in front of Rhymer's beach hotel. It's a beautiful tropical setting, and the beach often becomes a carnival scene, with bars, restaurants, and steel-band-centered parties.

Soper's Hole is deep, with a limited anchoring space near the East End and numerous marina slips (radio ahead for space) or moorings for rent. Though shops and services are growing, sailors still taxi to nearby resorts or to Road Town (about 15 mi) for entertainment. Customs and immigration are near the north shore.

Road Harbour is protected from the swell, but holding ground in the anchorage close to town is imperfect, and a south wind makes it worse. Anchor in **Baughers Bay** and take a dinghy to town, or radio ahead for dock space at marinas along the outer or inner harbor. Road

Town, capital of the B.V.I., is historic, pretty, gently British, and worth a day's tour, whether you need the customs office, supplies, or a shore dinner.

From **Maya Cove** north and east to **Marina Cay** (both with good anchorages) are the dramatic cruising grounds that draw sailors to the area. Besides offering numerous fair-weather anchorages, **Trellis Bay** provides shelter in most blows. On shore, check out local artisans' works, quirky entertainment at the Last Resort, and reportedly excellent West Indian food at Conch Shell Point. Proximity to the airport makes it an unromantic anchorage, however.

Jost Van Dyke is the logical overnight anchorage after you've explored Tortola's northwest shore. **Little Harbour** is so popular it fills up early (4 PM is considered quitting time for cruisers who want the best overnight anchorages). There's always plenty of anchoring room in **Great Harbour,** but be sure to anchor well off the beach, as the water rapidly becomes shallow here. Farther south, **White Bay** is a lovely spot in settled weather, but enter only in good light: The entrance through the small barrier reef can be tricky.

ISLANDS ACROSS SIR FRANCIS DRAKE CHANNEL
Five smaller islands (**Norman, Peter, Salt, Cooper,** and **Ginger**) form the southern boundary of the cruising area, and anchored sailboats cluster in their harbors like sea urchins. Check the charts carefully, since some likely looking spots (**Salt Island Bay** and **Lee Bay**) aren't suitable for overnight stays because of poor holding ground, or because the coves are too deep.

VIRGIN GORDA'S WESTERN SHORES
Everyone visits the Baths on Virgin Gorda's southern tip, where volcanic debris has been eroded into a tumble of gargantuan boulders. The boulders are prized for the pools and grottoes they form, but the beach is unsheltered and hard to approach by dinghy (you WILL get wet). Anchoring nearby is challenging in too-deep, rock-filled water. The best bet is to pick up one of the numerous nearby moorings.

Since the docks at **Virgin Gorda Yacht Harbour** (room for 120 boats) are a good spot to take on fuel, ice, and supplies, many skippers park the boat there and take a taxi to the Baths or to explore the island.

From Virgin Gorda Yacht Harbour to **Gorda Sound** there are several day anchorages, but no solid overnight havens. The sound, though, is totally accommodating, with sheltered anchorages in every direction and a wealth of shoreside attractions. Just east of Gorda Sound, anchorages on **Necker Island, Eustatia Island** (days only), and **Saba Rock** put you close to snorkeler's heaven. Those same reefs complicate reaching **Deep Bay,** around the corner from Saba Rock, but it's a fine summer anchorage.

ANEGADA
The anchorage off the **Anegada Reef Hotel** is a good one but can be tricky to enter in poor light. Call Lowell Wheatley on VHF Channel 16 for help guiding you in. The holding ground is excellent, but two anchors are recommended—the wind often picks up at night. Note: This area is off-limits to many bare boats. Exercise caution at all times; many of the coral heads in this area are uncharted. Also, Horseshoe Reef, which extends southward from the island's eastern end, is an important spawning ground for sea life. At press time, anchoring and fishing in this area were prohibited, but check with your charter company for up-to-date information.

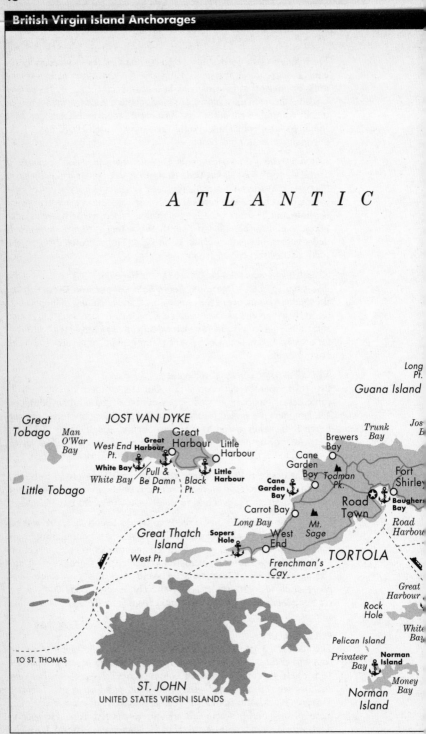

ATLANTIC

Long
Pt.
Guana Island

Great
Tobago

*Man
O'War
Bay*

JOST VAN DYKE

West End
Pt.

**Great
Harbour**

Great
Harbour

Little
Harbour

Trunk
Bay

Jos
B

Brewers
Bay

White Bay

White Bay

Pull &
Be Damn
Pt.

Black
Pt.

**Little
Harbour**

Cane
Garden
Bay

**Cane
Garden
Bay**

*Todman
Pk.*

Fort
Shirle

**Baughers
Bay**

Little Tobago

Carrot Bay

Road
Town

Great Thatch
Island

Long Bay

**Sopers
Hole**

West
End

*Mt.
Sage*

Road
Harbou

West Pt.

*Frenchman's
Cay*

TORTOLA

Great
Harbour

Rock
Hole

White
Bay

Pelican Island

TO ST. THOMAS

*Privateer
Bay*

**Norman
Island**

Money
Bay

ST. JOHN
UNITED STATES VIRGIN ISLANDS

Norman
Island

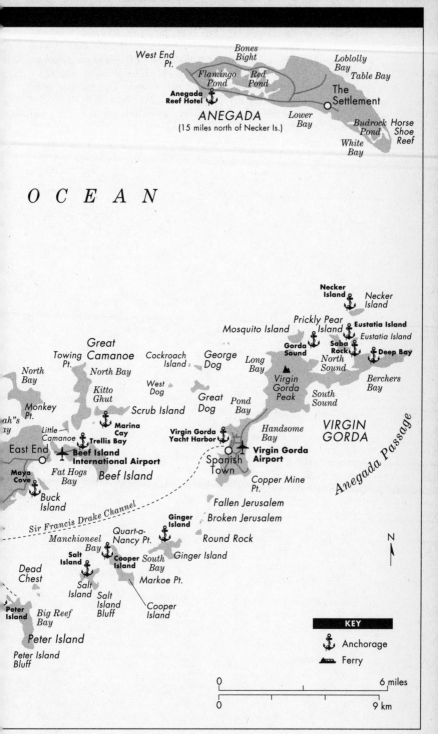

West End Pt.

Bones Bight

Flamingo Pond *Red Pond*

Loblolly Bay *Table Bay*

⚓ **Anegada Reef Hotel** ⚓

The Settlement ○

ANEGADA
(15 miles north of Necker Is.)

Lower Bay

Budrock Pond *Horse Shoe Reef*

White Bay

O C E A N

Necker Island ⚓ *Necker Island*

Prickly Pear Island ⚓ **Eustatia Island** *Eustatia Island*

Mosquito Island

Gorda Sound ⚓ **Saba Rock** ⚓ ⚓ **Deep Bay**

North Sound

Long Bay

Berchers Bay

Great Camanoe

Towing Pt.

Cockroach Island

George Dog

▲ *Virgin Gorda Peak*

South Sound

VIRGIN GORDA

North Bay

North Bay

West Dog

Kitto Ghut

Great Dog

Pond Bay

⚓ *Scrub Island*

Handsome Bay

Monkey Pt.

ah"s y

Little Camanoe ⚓ **Marina Cay**

⚓**Trellis Bay**

Virgin Gorda Yacht Harbor ⚓

East End ○

⚓ **Beef Island International Airport**

✈ **Virgin Gorda Airport**

○ **Spanish Town**

Maya Cove ⚓

Fat Hogs Bay

Beef Island

Copper Mine Pt.

⚓ *Buck Island*

Sir Francis Drake Channel

Fallen Jerusalem

Anegada Passage

Manchioneel Bay

Quart-a-Nancy Pt.

Ginger Island ⚓

Broken Jerusalem

Round Rock

Dead Chest

⚓ **Salt Island**

⚓**Cooper Island**

South Bay

Ginger Island

N ↑

Salt Island

Salt Island Bluff

Markoe Pt.

Peter Island

Big Reef Bay

Cooper Island

Peter Island

Peter Island Bluff

KEY

⚓ Anchorage

🚢 Ferry

0 ——————— 6 miles

0 ——————— 9 km

Further Reading

Cruising World magazine (✉ Box 3400, Newport, RI 02840-0992, ☎ 401/847–1588); *Sail* magazine (✉ 84 State St., 9th Fl., Boston, MA 02109-2202, ☎ 617/720–8600); *Yachtsman's Guide to the Virgin Islands* (✉ Box 610938, North Miami, FL 33261-0938, ☎ 305/893–4277); and *Cruising Guide to the Virgin Islands* (✉ Cruising Guide Publications, Inc., Box 1017, Dunedin, FL 34697-1017, ☎ 813/733–5322) are good, reliable publications that include useful information about boat chartering and navigation.

4 The United States Virgin Islands

St. Thomas, St. Croix, St. John

From St. Thomas's dazzling duty-free shops to St. Croix's historic sugar plantation ruins to the natural splendor of St. John's national parkland, the U.S. Virgin Islands offer three distinct ways to enjoy Caribbean ambience all under the American flag.

AT FIRST GLANCE, A TYPICAL MONDAY MORNING at the Squirrel Cage coffee shop on St. Thomas in the United States Virgin Islands might not seem much different from what you'd find back home in St. Paul, or Atlanta, or Steamboat Springs. A traffic cop strolls in to joke with the waitress and collect his first cup of coffee; a high-heeled secretary runs in from across the street for the morning paper and some toast; a store clerk lingers over a cup of tea to discuss the latest political controversy with the cook.

By Tricia
Cambron

Updated by
Carol
Bareuther and
Lynda Lohr

But is the coffee shop back home nestled in a bright pink hole-in-the-wall of a 19th-century building, only steps away from a park abloom with frangipani—in January? Are bush tea and johnnycake on the morning menu along with oatmeal and omelets?

Probably not.

It is the combination of the familiar and the exotic found in the U.S.V.I. that defines this "American Paradise" and explains much of its appeal. The effort to be all things to all people—while remaining true to the best of itself—has created a sometimes paradoxical blend of island serenity and American practicality in this U.S. territory 1,000 mi from the southern tip of the U.S. mainland.

The postcard images you'd expect from a tropical paradise are here: Stretches of beach arc into the distance, and white sails skim across water so blue and clear it stuns the senses; red-roof houses add their spot of color to the green hillsides' mosaic, along with the orange of the flamboyant tree, the red of the hibiscus, the magenta of the bougainvillea, and the blue stone ruins of old sugar mills; and towns of pastel-tone European-style villas, decorated by filigree wrought-iron terraces, line narrow streets climbing up from a harbor. Amid all the images can be found moments—sometimes whole days—of exquisite tranquillity: an egret standing in a pond at dawn, palm trees back-lit by a full moon, sunrises and sunsets that can send your spirit soaring with the frigate bird flying overhead.

The other part of the equation are all those things that make it so easy and appealing to visit this cluster of islands. The official language is English, the money is the dollar, and the U.S. government runs things. There's cable TV, Pizza Hut, and McDonald's. There's unfettered immigration to and from the mainland and investments are protected by the American flag. The American way has found success here—islanders have embraced American-style marketing and fast food, making the U.S.V.I.'s Radio Shack, Wendy's, and Kentucky Fried Chicken sales leaders for their franchises. Visitors to the U.S.V.I. have the opportunity to delve into a "foreign" culture while anchored by familiar language and landmarks. Surely not everything will suit your fancy, but chances are that among the three islands—St. Thomas, St. Croix, and St. John—you'll find your own idea of paradise. Park yourself on a bench under a bay rum tree and munch on a crispy, conch-filled pastry while observing the social scene. Rent a Jeep, stop for a bucket of take-out fried chicken, and head for the beach. Check into a beachfront condo on the East End of St. Thomas, eat burgers, and watch football at a beachfront bar and grill. Or check into an 18th-century plantation great house on St. Croix, dine on Danish delicacies, and go horseback riding at sunrise. Rent a tent or a cottage in the pristine national park on St. John, take a hike, kayak off the coast, read a book, or just listen to the sounds of the forest at night. Dance the night away on St. Thomas, watch turtles nest on St. Croix, or dive deep into "island time" and learn the art of "limin' " (hanging out, Caribbean-style) on all three.

Still, these idyllic bits of volcanic rock in the middle of the Caribbean Sea have not escaped the modern-day worries of overdevelopment, trash, crime, and traffic. The isolation and limited space of the islands have, in fact, even accentuated these problems. What, for example, do you do with 76 million cans and bottles imported annually when the nearest recycling plant is across 1,000 mi of ocean? Despite dilemmas such as this, wildlife has found refuge here. The brown pelican is on the endangered list worldwide but is a common sight in the U.S.V.I. The endangered native tree boa is protected, as is the hawksbill turtle, whose females lumber onto the beaches to lay their eggs.

Preserving its own culture while progressing as an Americanized tourist destination is another problem. The islands have been inhabited in turn by Arawak, Taino, and Carib Indians; Danish settlers and Spanish pirates; traders and invaders from all the European powers; Africans brought in as slaves; migrants from other Caribbean islands; and, finally, Americans, first as administrators, then as businesspeople and tourists. All of these influences are combining to create a more homogeneous culture, and with each passing year the U.S.V.I. loses more of its rich, predominantly black, spicy Caribbean personality.

Sailing into the Caribbean on his second voyage in 1493, Christopher Columbus came upon St. Croix before the group of islands including St. Thomas, St. John, and the British Virgin Islands. He named St. Croix "Santa Cruz" (called Ay Ay by the Carib Indians already living there) but moved on quickly after he encountered the fierce and inhospitable residents. As he approached St. Thomas and St. John he was impressed enough with the shapely silhouettes of the numerous islands and cays (including the B.V.I.) to name them after Ursula and her 11,000 virgins, but he found the islands barren and moved on to explore Puerto Rico.

Over the next century, as it became clear that Spain could not defend the entire Caribbean, other European powers began moving in and settling the islands. During the 1600s the French were joined by the Dutch and the English on St. Croix, and St. Thomas had a mixture of European residents in the early 1700s. By 1695 St. Croix was under the control of the French, but the colonists had moved on to what is today Haiti, and the island lay virtually dormant until 1733, when the Danish government bought it—along with St. Thomas and St. John—from the Danish West India Company. At that time settlers from St. Thomas and St. John moved to St. Croix to cultivate the island's gentler terrain. St. Croix grew into a plantation economy, but St. Thomas's soil and terrain were ill suited for agriculture. There the island's harbor became an internationally known seaport because of its size and ease of entry; it's still hailed as one of the most beautiful harbors in the world.

Plantations depended on slave labor, of which there was a plentiful supply in the Danish West Indies. As early as 1665 agreements between Brandenburger Company (which needed a base in the West Indies from which to ship the slaves it had imported from Africa) and the West India Company (which needed the kind of quick cash it could collect in duties, fees, and rents from the slave trade) established St. Thomas as a primary slave marketplace.

It is from the slaves who worked the plantations that the majority of Virgin Islanders find their ancestry. More than likely the sales clerk who sells you a watch and the waitress serving your rum punch trace their lineage back to ancestors captured in Africa some 300 years ago and brought to the West Indies, where they were sold on the block, priced according to their comeliness and strength. Most were captured along Africa's Gold Coast, from the tribes of Asante, Ibo, Mandika, Amina,

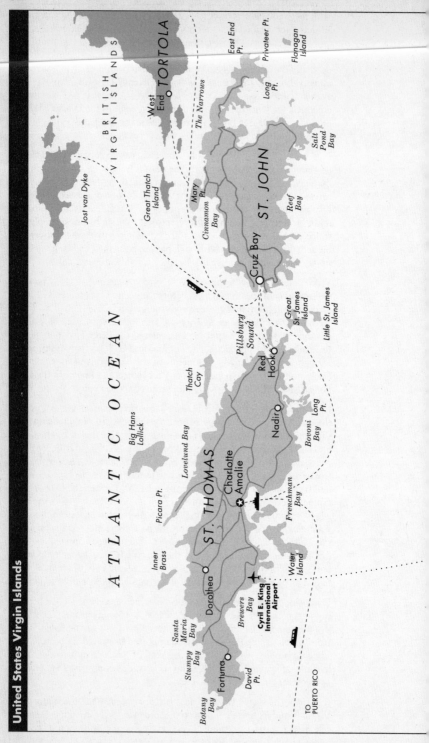

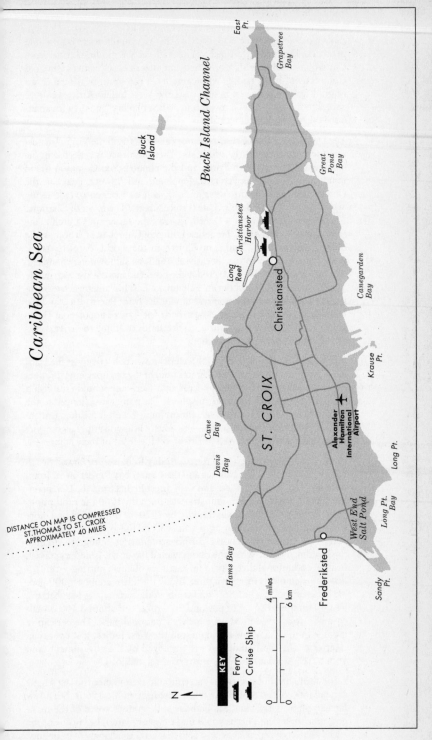

Caribbean Sea

Buck Island Channel

East Pt.

Grapetree Bay

Buck Island

Great Pond Bay

Christiansted Harbor

Long Reef

Canegarden Bay

Christiansted

ST. CROIX

Krause Pt.

Cane Bay

Alexander Hamilton International Airport

Davis Bay

Long Pt.

DISTANCE ON MAP IS COMPRESSED ST.THOMAS TO ST. CROIX APPROXIMATELY 40 MILES

Long Pt. Bay

West End Salt Pond

Hams Bay

Frederiksted

Sandy Pt.

4 miles

6 km

KEY

Ferry

Cruise Ship

N

0

0

and Woloff. They brought with them African rhythms in music and language, herbal medicine, and such crafts as basketry and wood carving. However, there is some evidence that the African influence began long before the Europeans traded slaves through the West Indies. Entries from Christopher Columbus's journal recount tales of island natives who told Columbus of black people who came from the south bearing a cargo of gold-tip metal spears. In any case, the West Indian/African culture comes to full bloom at Carnival time, when playing "mas" (with abandon) takes precedence over all else.

The Danes were among the first Europeans to settle in the Virgin Islands, and they ruled for nearly 200 years. Their influence is reflected in the language, architecture, religion, and the phone book: Common island family names, such as Petersen, Jeppesen, and Lawetz, bear out the Danish influence, as do street names, such as Kongen's Gade (King Street) and Kronprindsen's Gade (Prince Street). The town of Charlotte Amalie was named after a Danish queen. The Lutheran Church is the state church of Denmark; Frederick Lutheran Church in St. Thomas, the oldest predominately Lutheran Church in the world, dates to 1666. Jews came to the territory as early as 1665, as shipowners, chandlers, and brokers in the slave trade. Today their descendants coexist with nearly 1,500 Arabs—95% of whom are Palestinian. East Indians are active members of the business community. Immigrants from Puerto Rico and the Dominican Republic make up close to half of St. Croix's population. Transplants from Caribbean countries to the south continue to arrive, seeking better economic opportunities.

St. Thomas, St. Croix, and St. John were known collectively as the Danish West Indies until the United States bought the territory in 1917, during World War I, prompted by fears that Germany would establish a U-boat base in the Western Hemisphere. The name was changed to the United States Virgin Islands, and, almost immediately thereafter, British-held Tortola and Virgin Gorda—previously known simply as the Virgin Islands—hastily inserted "British" on the front of their name.

In the 1960s Pineapple Beach Resort (today Renaissance Grand Beach Resort) was built on St. Thomas and the Caneel Bay Resort on St. John, built in 1956, was expanded; and with direct flights from the U.S. mainland, the islands' tourism industry was born. In 1960 the total population of all three islands was 32,000. By 1970 the population had more than doubled, to 75,000, as workers from the B.V.I., Antigua, St. Kitts–Nevis, and other poorer Caribbean countries immigrated to man the building boom. When the boom waned the down-islanders stayed, bringing additional diversity to the territory but also putting a tremendous burden on its infrastructure. Today there are about 50,000 people living on the 32-sq-mi St. Thomas (about the same size as Manhattan), 51,000 on the 84 sq mi of pastoral St. Croix, and about 3,500 on 20-sq-mi St. John, two-thirds of which is a national park. The per capita income in the U.S.V.I. is the highest in the West Indies. Just over one-quarter of the total labor force is employed by the government, and about 10% work in tourism or tourism-related jobs.

Agriculture has not been a major economic factor since the last sugarcane plantation on St. Croix ceased operating in the 1960s, but a few farmers in St. Croix and St. Thomas still produce some of the mangos, pineapples, and herbs you'll find on your plate. The cuisine of the islands reflects a dependency on a land that gives grudgingly of its bounty. Root vegetables such as sweet potato, hardy vegetables such as okra, and stick-to-your-ribs breads and stuffings were staples 200 years ago, and their influence is still evident in the fungi (cornmeal and okra), johnnycake, and sweet-potato stuffings that are ever-present on menus today. The fruits are sweet (slaves got energy to cut sugarcane from a sugar-water drink made from sugar apples). Beverages include not only rum but coconut water, fruit juices, and *maubi*, made from tree bark and reputedly a virility enhancer.

The backbone of the V.I. economy is its tourism industry, but at the heart of the islands is an independent, separate being: a rollicking hodgepodge of West Indian culture with a sense of humor that puts sex and politics in almost every conversation. Lacking a major-league sports team, Virgin Islanders follow the activities and antics of their 15 elected senators with the rabidity of Washingtonians following their Redskins. Loyalty to country and faith in God are the rule in the Virgin Islands, not the exception. Prayer is a way of life, and ROTC is one of the most popular high-school extracurricular activities.

The struggle to preserve the predominantly black Caribbean–influenced culture is heating up in America's paradise. Native Virgin Islanders say they want access to more than just the beach when big money brings in big development. Senators in early 1996 agreed that majority own-ership of two of the casino hotels to be built in St. Croix will be re-served for natives. But the three islands are far from united as to exactly how they will balance continued economic growth and the pro-tection of their number-one resource—scenic beauty. The ongoing con-flict between progress and preservation here is no mere philosophical exercise, and attempts at resolutions display yet another aspect of the islands' unique blend of character.

ST. THOMAS

Updated by Carol Bareuther

The 32-sq-mi island of St. Thomas is a juxtaposition of congested water-front town—home to some of the best shopping in the Caribbean and the commercial center of the United States Virgin Islands—and white-sand beaches and green mountainsides whose loveliness can stand up against any in the Caribbean.

If you fly to St. Thomas, you'll land at the western end of the island; if you arrive by cruise ship, you'll come into one of the world's most beau-tiful harbors. Either way, one of your first sights of the island will be the town of Charlotte Amalie. From the harbor, you see an idyllic-look-ing village spreading up into the lower hills. Driving through on the way to your hotel, you'll find yourself in the heart of a bustling seaport. If you were expecting a quiet village, its inhabitants hanging out under palm trees, you've missed that era by about 300 years. While its sister islands in both the British and United States Virgin Islands developed rural, plantation economies, St. Thomas cultivated its harbor, and the island became a thriving commercial seaport very soon after it was set-tled by the Danes in the 1600s.

The success of the naturally perfect harbor was enhanced by the fact that the Danes—who ruled St. Thomas (with only a couple of short interruptions) from 1666 to 1917—managed to avoid getting involved in some 100 years' worth of European wars. Denmark was the only European country with colonies in the Caribbean to stay neutral dur-ing the war of the Spanish succession in the early 1700s. Thus, prod-ucts of the Dutch, English, and French islands—sugar, cotton, and indigo—were traded through Charlotte Amalie, along with the regu-lar shipments of slaves. When the Spanish wars ended, trade fell off, but by the end of the 1700s, Europe was at war again, Denmark again remained neutral, and St. Thomas continued to prosper. Even into the 1800s, while the economies of St. Croix and St. John foundered as the cultivation of sugarcane moved on to more easily tilled fields elsewhere,

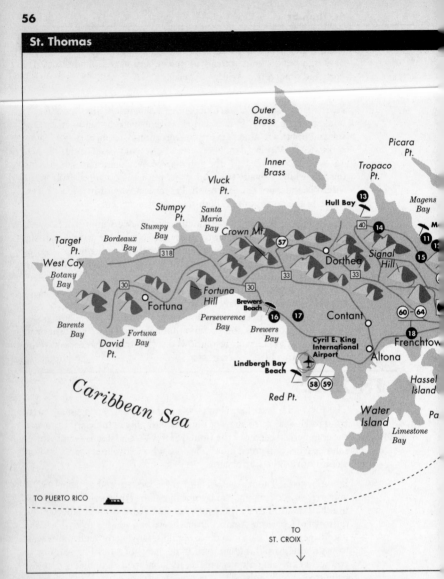

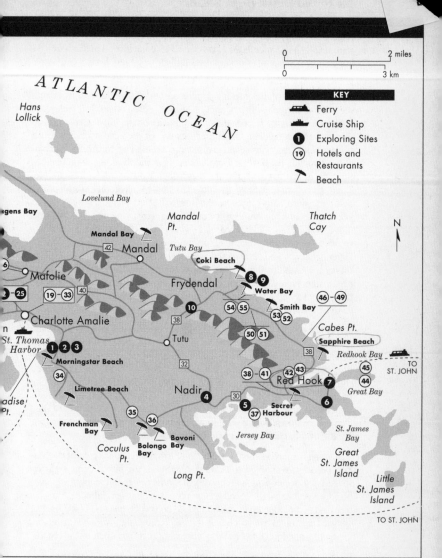

ATLANTIC OCEAN

Hans
Lollick

Lovelund Bay

gens Bay

Mandal Bay [42]

Mandal

Tutu Bay

Coki Beach

Mandal
Pt.

Thatch
Cay

Mafolie

[6]

[25]

[19]—[33] [40]

Charlotte Amalie

St. Thomas
Harbor

Morningstar Beach

1 2 3

34

Limetree Beach

adise
Pt.

Frenchman
Bay

Coculus
Pt.

35

36

Bolongo
Bay

Bovoni
Bay

Long Pt.

Frydendal

8 9

Water Bay

10

54 55

Smith Bay

53 52

46—**49**

Cabes Pt.

Sapphire Beach

[38]

Redhook Bay

TO
ST. JOHN

50 51

Tutu

[38]

[32]

Nadir

4

38 41

42 43

Red Hook

7

45

44

Great Bay

[30]

5

37

Secret
Harbour

6

Jersey Bay

St. James
Bay

Great
St. James
Island

Little
St. James
Island

TO ST. JOHN

KEY

🚢 Ferry

🚢 Cruise Ship

1 Exploring Sites

19 Hotels and
Restaurants

☂ Beach

0   2 miles
0   3 km

N

Romanos, **50**

Seagrape, **46**

Sib's Mountain Bar
and Restaurant, **56**

Tickles Dockside
Pub, **42**

Victor's New
Hide-Out, **60**

Virgilio's, **23**

Zorba's Cafe, **25**

Lodging

Admiral's Inn, **63**

The Anchorage, **40**

Best Western
Emerald Beach
Resort, **59**

Blackbeard's
Castle, **29**

Blazing Villas, **55**

Bluebeard's
Castle, **20**

Bolongo Bay Beach
Club & Villas, **36**

Colony Point Pleasant
Resort, **53**

Crystal Cove at
Sapphire Bay
West, **48**

Doubletree Sapphire
Beach Resort &
Marina, **46**

Elysian Beach
Resort, **44**

Hotel 1829, **21**

Island Beachcomber
Hotel, **58**

Island View Guest
House, **32**

Mafolie Hotel, **33**

Marriott's
Frenchman's Reef and
Morning Star Beach
Resorts, **34**

Pavilions & Pools, **49**

Renaissance Grand
Beach Resort, **54**

Ritz-Carlton St-
Thomas, **45**

Sapphire Village, **47**

Sea Horse
Cottages, **41**

Secret Harbour Beach
Resort, **38**

Secret Harbourview
Villas, **39**

Villa Blanca
Hotel, **30**

Villa Santana, **31**

Wyndham Sugar Bay
Beach Club &
Resort, **52**

St. Thomas's status remained strong. This prosperity led to the development of shipyards for repairing boats, a well-organized banking system, and a large merchant class. In 1845 Charlotte Amalie had 101 large importing houses owned by Englishmen, Frenchmen, Germans, Haitians, Spaniards, Americans, Sephardim, and Danes.

The Charlotte Amalie of today is still a harbor of superlatives, and you'll see a great variety of boats anchored in its blue waters, but today the trade is in tourists. Charlotte Amalie is one of the most active cruise-ship ports in the world. On almost any day of the year at least one and sometimes as many as seven cruise ships are tied up to the dock or anchored outside the harbor. Gently rocking in the shadows of these giant floating hotels are just about every other kind of vessel imaginable: There's a big three-masted schooner that will take you on a sunset cruise complete with rum punch and a Jimmy Buffett soundtrack; and that yacht that looks as though it could be straight out of a James Bond movie actually is—it starred in *Thunderball*. There is the 39-ft *Stars & Stripes*—sailed by Dennis Conner during the 1992 America's Cup Defender series and resurrected as the V.I. Challenge's first training vessel for the Cup 2000 in New Zealand—a Polynesian-style thatch-roof raft, and even a Chinese junk. Weaving around them all are ferries on their way to and from the B.V.I., and dinghies shuttling the boaties in to their landlubber jobs.

While the role of most of the above-mentioned boats is to re-create the romance of the tropics for the visitor, there are still working vessels to be found. Big container ships pull up in Sub Base, just west of the harbor, bringing in everything from cornflakes to tires, and anchored right along the waterfront are the picturesque down-island sloops like those that have plied the waters between the Leeward Islands for hundreds of years. They still deliver fruits and vegetables, but today they also return down-island with modern-day conveniences: refrigerators, VCRs, and carton after carton of disposable diapers.

The waterfront road through Charlotte Amalie was once part of the harbor. Before it was filled to build the highway, the beach came right up to the back door of the warehouses that now line the thoroughfare. Two hundred years ago, those warehouses contained indigo, tobacco, and cotton. Today the stone buildings house silk, crystal, linens, and Gucci leather. Exotic fragrances are still being traded, but by island beauty queens in air-conditioned perfume palaces instead of through open market stalls.

Pirates in the old days—the era of Blackbeard, Bluebeard, Captain Kidd, and any number of guys nicknamed Peg Leg—used St. Thomas as a base from which to raid merchant ships of any and every nation, though they were particularly fond of the gold- and silver-laden treasure ships heading from Mexico, Cuba, and Puerto Rico to Spain. There are still pirates around, but today's version use St. Thomas as a drop-off for their contraband: Illegal immigrants from neighboring Haiti and the Dominican Republic are smuggled in by boat to dark bays on the north side of the island, others use St. John to bring in Chinese people trying to make their way to the mainland, and planes drop water-proof bales of cocaine into Pillsbury Sound and off St. John.

Out of Charlotte Amalie, you'll probably go east if you're staying in a hotel. The western end of the island is the most undeveloped and, with the exception of some private homes, still relatively wild. If you're staying on the north side, you'll go up the mountain where the roads are lined with the dense greenery of giant ferns and philodendron, banana trees, and flamboyant trees that thrive in the cooler and wetter mountain climate. The quiet north side is where you get away from it all. The lush vegetation muffles the sound of all but the birds, and here you'll find many of the island's private villas for rent. In the drier areas to the south and to the east, the roads are lined with big cacti and succulents like giant aloes, punctuated with the bright colors of the hardy bougainvillea and hibiscus. The southeastern and far eastern ends of the island are flatter, and this is where you'll find the beachfront hotels and condominiums. At the eastern tip is Red Hook, a friendly little village anchored by the marine community nestled at Red Hook harbor.

Lodging

St. Thomas has the most rooms and the widest variety of accommodations in the U.S.V.I. You'll find everything here, from spartan motel rooms to lavish resorts that cater to your every need. In between there are hotels and inns to match just about every taste and price range.

If your visit to St. Thomas is a special occasion, or you've got money to burn, stay at a world-class luxury resort. You'll be pampered, albeit at a price of $300 to more than $900 per night, not including meals.

Those guests with more modest means will still find a tremendous variety from which to choose. Quite a number of fine hotels (many with rooms that feature kitchens and a living-room area) are scattered around the island in lovely settings, and there are several charming guest houses and inns with great views (if not always a beach at your door) and great service at about half the cost of the superluxe beachfront pleasure palaces. A good number of the inns and guest houses are in the hills above the historic district of Charlotte Amalie and are a good choice if you plan to get out and mingle in the local scene.

There are also inexpensive lodgings, perfect if you're here on the cheap and just want a clean room to come back to after a day of exploring or beach-bumming. Most of the less-expensive accommodations are right in town.

Families often choose to stay at one of the East End's condominium complexes, which offer full kitchens but have daily maid service, on-site restaurants, and many resort amenities. The East End area is convenient to St. John, is home to the boating crowd, and has a fair number of good restaurants within easy walking distance. Most of the condo complexes have swimming pools and tennis courts.

Although the condos are somewhat pricey (winter rates average $240 per night for a two-bedroom condominium, which will usually sleep six), the price of restaurant dining on St. Thomas is, too, so you may come out about even if you cook your own meals. If you're staying in a condominium and plan to cook, you might consider bringing some nonperishable foodstuffs with you. Because of shipping costs (virtually everything is imported), U.S.V.I. food prices are usually as high as or higher than those in the most expensive mainland U.S. cities.

Hotels and Inns
CHARLOTTE AMALIE

$$$–$$$$ ☒ **Best Western Emerald Beach Resort.** On a white-sand beach on Lindbergh Bay, just across from the airport, this miniresort has the feel of its much larger cousins on the East End. Each room in the four pink three-story buildings has its own terrace or balcony, palms, and colorful flowers that frame a view of the ocean. The rooms are decorated in modern tropical prints and rattan. A plus: The resort is popular with businesspeople, so the pool and beach are rarely crowded. A minus: The noise from nearby jets taking off and landing can be heard intermittently over a three-hour period each afternoon. ☒ *Box 340, 00804,*

☎ *809/777–8800 or 800/233–4936,* ℻ *809/776–3426. 90 rooms. Restaurant, pool, beach. AE, D, MC, V.*

\$\$\$ 🏨 **Blackbeard's Castle.** This small and very popular hillside inn is laid out around a tower from which, it's said, Blackbeard kept watch for invaders on the horizon. It's an elegantly informal kind of place, where guests while away Sunday morning with *The New York Times.* Stunning views (especially at sunset) of the harbor and Charlotte Amalie can be had from the gourmet restaurant Cafe LuLu's, the large freshwater pool, and the outdoor terraces, where locals come for cocktails. Charlotte Amalie is a short walk down the hill, and beaches are a short taxi ride away. Rates include Continental breakfast. ⊠ *Box 6041, 00804,* ☎ *809/776–1234 or 800/344–5771,* ℻ *809/776–4321. 24 rooms. Restaurant, bar, pool. AE, D, DC, MC, V.*

\$\$\$ 🏨 **Bluebeard's Castle.** Though not exactly a castle, this large red-roof complex offers kingly modern comforts on a steep hill overlooking the town, which from Bluebeard's glistens at night like a Christmas tree. All rooms are air-conditioned and have terraces. The hotel is a short ride away from the shops of Charlotte Amalie and Havensight Mall—there's free transportation to Magens Bay Beach and to town. ⊠ *Box 7480, 00801,* ☎ *809/774–1600 or 800/524–6599,* ℻ *809/774–5134. 184 rooms. 2 restaurants, bar, pool, 2 tennis courts. AE, D, DC, MC, V.*

\$\$–\$\$\$ 🏨 **Island Beachcomber Hotel.** This hotel is near the airport (just east of the Emerald Beach Resort) but is enclosed by a fence and landscaping so that, once inside, you are not aware of this—until a plane takes off. However, the hotel is also right on Lindbergh Beach, and the low rates reflect its otherwise less-than-ideal location. There's also a beach barbecue two times a week. ⊠ *Box 302579, 00803,* ☎ *809/774–5250 or 800/982–9898,* ℻ *809/774–5615. 47 rooms. Restaurant, beach. AE, D, DC, MC, V.*

\$\$ 🏨 **Villa Blanca Hotel.** Above Charlotte Amalie on Raphune Hill is this secluded hotel, surrounded by an attractive garden and with modern, balconied rooms with rattan furniture, kitchenettes, cable TVs, and ceiling fans (six have air-conditioning). All the rooms have views of Charlotte Amalie's harbor as well as partial views of Drake's Channel and the B.V.I. ⊠ *Box 7505, 00801,* ☎ *809/776–0749 or 800/231–0034,* ℻ *809/779–2661. 14 rooms. Pool. AE, D, DC, MC, V.*

\$–\$\$ 🏨 **Hotel 1829.** This historic Spanish-style inn is popular with visiting
★ government officials and people with business at Government House down the street. It's on Government Hill, just at the edge of Charlotte Amalie's shopping area. Rooms, on several levels (no elevator), range from elegant and roomy to quite small but are priced accordingly, so there's one for every budget. Author Graham Greene is said to have stayed here, and it's easy to imagine him musing over a drink in the small, dark bar. The gourmet terrace restaurant is a romantic spot for dinner. The rooms have refrigerators and TVs. There's a tiny, tiny pool for cooling off. ⊠ *Box 1567, 00801,* ☎ *809/776–1829 or 800/524–2002,* ℻ *809/776–4313. 15 rooms. Restaurant, pool. AE, D, MC, V.*

\$–\$\$ 🏨 **Villa Santana.** Built by General Santa Anna of Mexico circa 1857,
★ the villa still provides a panoramic view of the Charlotte Amalie harbor along with plenty of age-old West Indian charm. This St. Thomas landmark, close to town, has five villa-style rooms. Dark wicker furniture, white plaster and stone walls, shuttered windows, cathedral ceilings, and interesting nooks contribute to the feeling of romance and history. Villas La Torre and La Mansion are split level with spiral staircases, and all units have full kitchens and either four-poster or cradle beds. Rooms are kept cool by ceiling fans and natural trade winds and do not have telephones. ⊠ *2D Denmark Hill, 00802,* ☎ *809/776–1311,* ℻ *809/776–1311. 5 rooms. Pool, croquet. AE.*

$ ⊞ **Island View Guest House.** This clean, simply furnished guest house rests amid tropical foliage on the south face of 1,500-ft Crown Mountain, the highest point on St. Thomas. As a result it has one of the most sweeping views of Charlotte Amalie harbor available from its pool and shaded terrace, where complimentary breakfast is served. All rooms have some view, but on the balconies of the six newer rooms (all with a ceiling fan), perched on the very edge of the hill, you feel suspended in midair. ⊠ *Box 1903, 00801,* ☎ *809/774–4270 or 800/524–2023,* ℻ *809/774– 6167. 13 rooms with bath, 2 rooms share bath. Pool. AE, MC, V.*

$ ⊞ **Mafolie Hotel.** Perched high atop Charlotte Amalie on Mafolie Hill, where movie crews have filmed million-dollar sunsets, this pastel-yellow hotel has simply furnished rooms and a homey atmosphere that comes from being family-run for more than two decades. The pool bar is a favorite with locals, especially on Sunday afternoons. All rooms have TVs but no telephones. Rates include breakfast daily and free transportation to the beach. ⊠ *Box 1506, 00801,* ☎ *809/774–2790 or 800/225–7035,* ℻ *809/774–4091. 23 rooms. Restaurant, bar, pool. AE, MC, V.*

EAST END

$$$$ ⊞ **Elysian Beach Resort.** At this East End property, coral-color villas are stepped down the hillside to the edge of Cowpet Bay. Rooms are decorated in muted tropical floral prints. Activity centers on a kidney-shape pool complete with waterfall and thatch-roof pool bar. The Palm Court restaurant has gained a strong local following, a sure sign of success. All rooms have terraces, ceiling fans, TVs, and telephones; some have full kitchens. ⊠ *Box 51, Red Hook, 00802,* ☎ *809/775– 1000 or 800/753–2554,* ℻ *809/776–0910. 175 rooms. 2 restaurants, 2 bars, pool, tennis court, beach. AE, MC, V.*

$$$$ ⊞ **Renaissance Grand Beach Resort.** This resort's zigzag architectural ★ angles spell luxury, from the marble atrium lobby to the one-bedroom suites with private whirlpool baths. The beach is excellent, and there's a fitness center with Nautilus machines. The lobby is often populated by those lucky business types whose companies favor the resort as a convention-and-conference center. Daily organized activities for children include iguana hunts, T-shirt painting, and sand-castle building. This tends to be a very busy hotel, with lots of people in the restaurants and on the beach. ⊠ *Smith Bay Rd., Box 8267, 00801,* ☎ *809/775–1510 or 800/468–3571,* ℻ *809/775–2185. 290 rooms. 2 restaurants, snack bar, 2 pools, 6 tennis courts, beach. AE, D, DC, MC, V.*

$$$$ ⊞ **Ritz-Carlton St. Thomas.** Formerly named the Grand Palazzo, this ★ premier luxury resort, which opened in December 1996, resembles a villa in Venice and offers stunning ocean views through the lobby's glass doors. Guest rooms, in six buildings that fan out from the main villa, are spacious and tropically furnished—they just might tempt you to stay inside. When you do venture out, you'll find elegance everywhere, from the beautiful pool to the gourmet restaurant and the casual alfresco lunch area. A multilingual staff, a variety of music from classical to calypso, and 24-hour room service enhance the sophisticated atmosphere. ⊠ *Great Bay Estate, 00802,* ☎ *809/775–3333 or 800/241– 3333,* ℻ *809/775–4444. 152 rooms. 3 restaurants, 3 bars, pool, 3 tennis courts, health club, beach. AE, D, DC, MC, V.*

$$$$ ⊞ **Wyndham Sugar Bay Beach Club & Resort.** From afar, this large cluster of bulky white buildings looks rather overwhelming, but the hotel has a lot to offer. Most rooms overlook water and some have great views of the British Virgin Islands. All units have balconies and are spacious and comfortable, and all come with such amenities as hair dryers and coffeemakers. The beach is small, but there's a giant pool with waterfalls. Rates are all-inclusive, covering meals, beverages, use of the fitness center and tennis courts, a daily activity pro-

gram, and many water sports. ⊠ *6500 Estate Smith Bay, 00802,* ☎ *809/777–7100 or 800/927–7100,* ℻ *809/777–7200. 300 rooms. Restaurant, bar, 3 pools, 2 tennis courts, health club, beach, snorkeling. AE, D, DC, MC, V.*

$$$–$$$$ 🏨 **Colony Point Pleasant Resort.** Stretching up a steep, tree-filled hill
★ from Smith Bay, affording a great view of St. John and Drake's Channel to the east and north, this resort offers a range of accommodations, from simple bedrooms to multiroom suites. Units are in a number of buildings hidden among the trees, all have striking views, balconies, and kitchens. Three appealing, nice-size pools surrounded by decks are placed at different levels on the hillside. Although there are water sports here, the "beach" is almost nonexistent; guests are granted beach privileges next door at the Renaissance Grand Beach Resort, a one-minute walk away. Every guest gets four hours free use of a car daily. (You need only pay the $9.50 per day insurance cost.) ⊠ *6600 Estate Smith Bay, No. 4, 00802,* ☎ *809/775–7200 or 800/524–2300,* ℻ *809/776–5694. 134 rooms. 2 restaurants, bar, 3 pools, tennis court, exercise room, beach. AE, D, MC, V.*

$$$–$$$$ 🏨 **Doubletree Sapphire Beach Resort & Marina.** On a clear day the lush
★ green mountains of the neighboring B.V.I. seem close enough to touch from this resort on one of St. Thomas's prettiest beaches. There's excellent snorkeling on the reefs to each side of the beach. This is a quiet retreat where you can nap while swinging in one of the hammocks strung between the palm trees in your front yard; but on Sunday the place rocks with a beach party. All units have fully equipped kitchens, telephones, and satellite TV, and they come with a complimentary can of Doubletree's famous chocolate-chip cookies. Children are welcome and may join the Kids Klub. Children under age 12 sleep in their parents' accommodations at no extra charge and eat free (when dining with their parents) at the Seagrape Restaurant. ⊠ *Box 8088, 00801,* ☎ *809/775–6100 or 800/524–2090,* ℻ *809/775–2403. 171 rooms. 3 restaurants, 2 bars, 4 tennis courts, beach. AE, MC, V.*

$$$–$$$$ 🏨 **Pavilions & Pools.** You'll find simple, tropical-cool decor and privacy at this small hotel, where each island-style room has its own very private 22-by-14-ft or 18-by-16-ft pool and a small sunning deck. The unpretentious accommodations include telephones, full kitchens, and VCRs. Water sports are available at Sapphire Beach on the adjacent property. Snorkel gear is provided. ⊠ *6400 Estate Smith Bay, 00802,* ☎ *809/775–6110 or 800/524–2001,* ℻ *809/775–6110. 25 rooms. Restaurant. AE, MC, V.*

$$$–$$$$ 🏨 **Secret Harbour Beach Resort.** The beige buildings, containing lowrise studios and suites, are nestled around an inviting, perfectly framed sandy cove on Nazareth Bay, where you can watch the marvelous sunsets. From early April to the end of December, children under age 12 stay free, making this a family-friendly resort all summer. ⊠ *6280 Estate Nazareth, 00802-1104,* ☎ *809/775–6550 or 800/524–2250,* ℻ *809/775–1501. 60 suite-style rooms and 7 studios. 2 restaurants, bar, 2 tennis courts, beach. AE, MC, V.*

FRENCHTOWN

$ 🏨 **Admiral's Inn.** This charming inn stretches down a hillside on the
★ point of land known as Frenchtown, just west of Charlotte Amalie. All rooms have wonderful views of either the town and the harbor or the ocean; the four ocean-view rooms have private balconies and refrigerators. All units have rattan furniture; cream- or teal-color bedspreads; vertical blinds; coral, teal, and cream carpeting; and large, tiled vanity areas. The rocky shoreline is perfect for snorkeling. The inn's freshwater pool is surrounded by a large wooden deck ideal for sunning. There's bar service at the pool, and a Continental breakfast is

included in the room rate. ⊠ *Villa Olga, 00802,* ☎ *809/774–1376 or 800/544–0493,* FAX *809/774–8010. 14 rooms. Restaurant, bar, pool. AE, D, MC, V.*

$$$$ 🏨 **Bolongo Bay Beach Club & Villas.** This 75-room beachfront resort also includes the 20-room Bolongo Villas next door and the 6-room Bolongo Bayside Inn across the street. All resort rooms have efficiency kitchens and balconies and are just steps from a strand of white beach. The oceanfront villas feature minisuites, and one-, two-, and three-bedroom units with full kitchens and large balconies, right on the ocean with beautiful views. The resort offers a choice of all-inclusive or semi-inclusive plans, which means you'll pay less if you want fewer activities. The all-inclusive room rate covers all meals, use of tennis courts, snorkel gear, canoes, Sunfish sailboats, Windsurfers, paddleboats, a scuba lesson, and an all-day sail and a half-day snorkel tour on one of the resort's yachts. There's a three-night minimum for the all-inclusive plan, and over holiday periods. ⊠ *50 Estate Bolongo, 00802,* ☎ *809/775–1800 or 800/524–4746,* FAX *809/775–3208. 101 units. 2 restaurants, 3 pools, 2 tennis courts, health club, volleyball, beach. AE, D, DC, MC, V.*

$$$$ 🏨 **Marriott's Frenchman's Reef and Morning Star Beach Resorts.** Sprawl-
★ ing, luxurious, and on a prime harbor promontory east of Charlotte Amalie like a permanently anchored cruise ship, these two resorts are St. Thomas's full-service American superhotels. All rooms are spacious and furnished with contemporary furniture in soft pastels. Many Frenchman's Reef rooms have glorious ocean and harbor views, but a few look out over the parking lot. Morning Star rooms are more luxurious, in buildings tucked among the foliage that stretches along the fine white sand of Morning Star Beach; the sound of the surf can lull you to sleep. In addition to enjoying various snack and sandwich stops and a raw bar, you can dine alfresco on American or gourmet Caribbean fare, or oceanfront on the Tavern on the Beach; there's also a lavish buffet served, overlooking the sparkling lights of Charlotte Amalie and the harbor. Live entertainment and disco, scheduled activities for all ages, and a shuttle boat to town make having fun easy. This is a property you won't ever have to leave. ⊠ *Box 7100, 00801,* ☎ *809/776–8500 or 800/524–2000,* FAX *809/776–3054. 517 rooms, 18 suites. 6 restaurants, 6 bars, snack bar, 2 pools, 4 tennis courts, beach. AE, D, DC, MC, V.*

Cottages and Condominiums

$$$–$$$$ 🏨 **The Anchorage.** Next door to the St. Thomas Yacht Club and facing Cowpet Bay, these two- and three-bedroom villas are right on the beach. They have washing machines and dryers, and the complex has two lighted tennis courts, a freshwater pool, and an informal dining room. ⊠ *Ocean Property Management, Box 8529, 00801,* ☎ *809/775–2600 or 800/874–7897,* FAX *809/775–5901. 30 rooms. Restaurant, pool, 2 tennis courts. AE, D, MC, V.*

$$$–$$$$ 🏨 **Crystal Cove at Sapphire Bay West.** One of the older condominium complexes on the island, Crystal Cove was built as part of a Harvard University–sponsored architectural competition. The unassuming buildings blend into the Sapphire Beach setting so well that egrets and ducks are right at home in the pond in the center of the property. There are studio, one-, and two-bedroom units, each with a porch or balcony. There's also good snorkeling. ⊠ *Ocean Property Management, Box 8529, 00801,* ☎ *809/775–2600 or 800/874–7897,* FAX *809/775–5901. 56 units. Pool, 2 tennis courts. AE, D, DC, MC, V.*

$$$–$$$$ 🏨 **Secret Harbourview Villas.** These units rest on a gentle hill just behind Secret Harbour Resort and the beach and share all the resort's facilities. All units have air-conditioning and maid service. ⊠ *Ocean Property Management, Box 8529 (office in Bldg. No. 5), 00801,* ☎

809/775–2600 *or* 800/874–7897, ⍁ 809/775–5901. 26 *units. 2 restaurants, pool, 3 tennis courts, exercise room. AE, D, DC, MC, V.*

$$$ ⬚ **Blazing Villas.** On the Renaissance Grand Beach Resort property,
★ these cool pastel yellow, pink, green, and blue villas each have their
own private garden patio and can be combined with other villas to create a 4-bedroom, 4-bath unit. All rooms have a refrigerator, microwave, and telephone. Guests can use all the adjoining resort's facilities. ⊠ *Box 502697, 00805,* ☏ *809/776–0760 or 800/382–2002,* ⍁ *809/776–3603. 19 rooms. 2 restaurants, snack bar, 2 pools, 6 tennis courts, beach. AE, MC, V.*

$$–$$$ ⬚ **Sapphire Village.** A stay in these high-rise units may take you back
• to the swinging-singles days of apartment-house living, since many of
the units are rented out long-term to refugees from northern winters working down here for the season. The best units overlook the marina and St. John; the beach is in sight and just a short walk down the hill. ⊠ *Ocean Property Management, Box 8529, 00801,* ☏ *809/775–2600 or 800/874–7897,* ⍁ *809/775–5901. 35 units. Restaurant, pub, 2 pools. AE, D, MC, V.*

$–$$$ ⬚ **Sea Horse Cottages.** These simple cottages, at the eastern end of the
island on Nazareth Bay, look across to St. Croix, 40 mi south. Although there's no beach, steps go directly into the sea from a swimming platform. All rooms have kitchens and ceiling fans. ⊠ *Box 302312, 00803,* ☏ *809/775–9231. 15 units, from studios to 2-bedrooms. Pool. No credit cards.*

Private Homes and Villas

Private-home rentals may be arranged through various agents, including **McLaughlin-Anderson Vacations** (⊠ 100 Blackbeard's Hill, Suite 3, 00802, ☏ 809/776–0635 or 800/537–6246) and **Calypso Realty** (⊠ Box 12178, 00801, ☏ 809/774–1620 or 800/747–4858), which both specialize in luxury-end villas. Write for their brochures containing photographs of the properties they represent.

Dining

Dining on St. Thomas is relaxed and informal. Very few restaurants on the island demand a jacket and tie. Still, at dinner in the snazzier restaurants, shorts and T-shirts are highly inappropriate, and you would do well to wear slacks and a shirt with buttons. Dress codes on St. Thomas almost never call for women to wear skirts, but you'll never go wrong with something flowy. The fancier restaurants on St. Thomas advise or require that you make reservations; for the places reviewed below, reservations are not necessary unless otherwise mentioned.

If you're up for some fast food, you'll find **Kentucky Fried Chicken** at four locations—Buccaneer Mall, Sub Base, Ft. Mylner, and Tutu Park Mall. **McDonald's** is open at Wheatley Center, in Frenchtown, and near Tutu Park Mall, where there is a kiddie playground. **Pizza Hut** is on the Charlotte Amalie waterfront.

In addition to the restaurants reviewed here, hotel restaurants are mentioned in Lodging, *above.*

Charlotte Amalie

$$$$ ✕ **Entre Nous.** The view here, from high over Charlotte Amalie's harbor, is as exhilarating as the dining is elegant. Enjoy the candlelit ambience while deciding between such main dinner courses as rack of lamb, Caribbean lobster, veal, and Chateaubriand, as you watch the light-bedecked cruise ships pull slowly out of the harbor. ⊠ *Bluebeard's Castle,* ☏ *809/776–4050. AE, MC, V. No lunch.*

$$$$ ✕ **Hotel 1829.** You'll dine by candlelight flickering over stone walls
★ and pink table linens at this restaurant on the terrace of the hotel. The
menu and wine list are extensive, from Caribbean rock lobster to rack
of lamb. Many items, including a warm spinach salad, are prepared
table-side; and the restaurant is justly famous for its dessert soufflés,
made of chocolate, Grand Marnier, raspberry, or coconut, to name a
few. ⊠ *Government Hill near Main St.,* ☎ *809/776–1829. Reservations essential. AE, D, MC, V. No lunch.*

$$$$ ✕ **Virgilio's.** For the best northern Italian cuisine on the island, don't
★ miss this intimate, elegant hideaway. Eclectic art covers the two-story-
high brick walls. Come here for more than 40 homemade pastas com-
plemented by superb sauces, including *capellini* (very thin spaghetti) with
fresh tomatoes and garlic, and spaghetti peasant-style (in a rich tomato
sauce with mushrooms and prosciutto). Try Virgilio's own mango flambé
with crepes or a steaming cup of cappuccino for dessert. Maître d' Regis
is on hand day and night, welcoming customers and helping the gracious
staff. ⊠ *18 Main St.,* ☎ *809/776–4920. AE, MC, V. Closed Sun.*

$$$–$$$$ ✕ **Cafesito.** Eat in the cool comfort of air-conditioning or sit outside
under the umbrellas and people-watch along the bustling Charlotte
Amalie waterfront while digging into a family-size serving of this
eatery's signature paella. The atmosphere is informal, and the Mediter-
ranean/Spanish menu is brimming with tapas and seafood selections.
Order sangria or choose from the extensive wine list. Don't forget to
ask about the dessert of the day. ⊠ *Waterfront Hwy. at Guttet's Gade,*
☎ *809/774–9574. AE, MC, V.*

$$$–$$$$ ✕ **La Scala.** Old-world elegance comes to life in this open-air restau-
★ rant set in the beautifully restored brick and stone interior of Palm
Passage. For lunch, try a yellowfin tuna burger with black olive,
tomato, and basil salsa. At dinner, don't miss the farfel pasta with roast
chicken, spinach, and mushrooms. Dinnertime is definitely more ro-
mantic, missing the daytime shoppers roaming around nearby stores.
⊠ *Palm Passage at the Waterfront,* ☎ *809/774–2206. AE, MC, V.
Closed Sun.*

$$–$$$ ✕ **Greenhouse Bar and Restaurant.** Watch the waterfront wake up at
this large and bustling open-air restaurant, whose wait staff looks like
a bunch of all-American college kids on spring break. Breakfast and
lunch (burgers, salads, and sandwiches) are good values. Dinner spe-
cials include peel 'n' eat shrimp, Maine lobster, and prime rib. You can
work it all off dancing to the Wednesday night band, which plays until
the crowd clears. ⊠ *Waterfront Hwy. at Storetvaer Gade,* ☎ *809/774–
7998. AE, D, MC, V.*

$$ ✕ **Zorba's Cafe.** Tired of shopping? Summon up one last ounce of en-
★ ergy and head up Government Hill to Zorba's. President Clinton and
his family did on a New Year's 1997 visit to St. Thomas. Sit and have
a cold, cold beer or bracing iced tea in the 19th-century stone-paved
courtyard surrounded by banana trees. Greek salads and appetizers,
moussaka, and an excellent vegetarian plate top the menu. ⊠ *Government Hill,* ☎ *809/776–0444. AE, MC, V.*

$–$$ ✕ **Hard Rock Cafe.** A hot spot from the day it opened, this waterfront
restaurant is pretty much like its namesakes around the world. Rock-
and-roll memorabilia abounds, and the menu offers hamburgers, sandwiches, salads, and great desserts. Doors are open from 11 AM until 2
AM; there's always a wait for a table during prime meal times. ⊠ *International Plaza on the Waterfront,* ☎ *809/777–5555. AE, MC, V.*

$ ✕ **Beni Iguana's.** Sushi is served as "edible art" in a charming Danish
courtyard setting. Among the offerings are cucumber and avocado or
scallop with scallion rolls, specialty big rolls like the Kung Fooee (shi-
itake, cucumber, daikon, and flying fish roe), and tuna or salmon
sashimi. A pictorial menu board makes ordering by the piece, plate,

or combination platter much easier. ⊠ *Grand Hotel Court,* ☎ *809/777–8744. No credit cards.*

$ ✕ **Gladys' Cafe.** Even if the great local specialties such as conch in but-
★ ter sauce, salt fish and dumplings, and hearty red bean soup didn't make this a recommended café, it would be worth going to for Gladys' smile. While you're there, pick up some of Gladys' special hot sauce for $6 per bottle. ⊠ *Royal Dane Mall,* ☎ *809/774–6604. AE. No dinner.*

East End

$$$$ ✕ **Romanos.** Inside this huge old stucco house in Smith Bay is a de-
★ lightful surprise: a spare, elegant setting and superb northern Italian cuisine. Owner Tony hasn't advertised since the restaurant opened in 1988, and it is always packed. Try the pastas, either with a classic sauce or one of Tony's unique creations, such as a cream sauce with mush-rooms, prosciutto, pine nuts, and Parmesan. ⊠ *97 Smith Bay,* ☎ *809/775–0045. MC, V. Closed Sun. No lunch.*

$$$–$$$$ ✕ **Agave Terrace.** Seafood is the specialty at this dimly lit, open-air pavil-ion restaurant, where fresh fish is served as steaks or fillets and the catch of the day is listed on the blackboard nightly. Come early and have a drink at the Lookout Lounge, which has breathtaking views of the British Virgins. The food enjoys as good a reputation as the view. ⊠ *Colony Point Pleasant Resort at Smith Bay,* ☎ *809/775–4142. AE, MC, V. No lunch.*

$$$ ✕ **The Blue Marlin.** Dockside dining at its friendliest is the trademark of this open-air restaurant close to the St. John ferry dock at Red Hook. The fish is so fresh you may see it coming in from one of the boats docked just steps away. For starters, try the medallion of yellowfin tuna seviche marinated in lime, onion, and white wine. Entrées include a grilled fillet of wahoo with pineapple and cucumber sauce and sea bass poached in spiced carrot essence and topped with caviar. Steak, poul-try, and pasta lovers will find something to please on the menu, too. ⊠ *Piccola Marina, Red Hook,* ☎ *809/775–6350. AE, MC, V.*

$$$ ✕ **Seagrape.** This hotel-restaurant has an all-star location right on Sap-phire Beach. The ocean laps gently at the shore, not far from your table. The menu is gourmet Continental, with steak, seafood (including lob-ster scampi), and veal marsala. The food is well prepared, the setting is lovely, and the staff is attentive and friendly. Some nights a band plays at the adjoining outdoor cocktail lounge. ⊠ *Doubletree Sapphire Beach Resort & Marina,* ☎ *809/775–6100. AE, MC, V.*

$$–$$$ ✕ **Mim's Seaside Bistro.** Walk straight from the beach into this open-air eatery, where you can sip a Beach Bar Bomber while listening to the lapping waves. Try a ham and baked Brie open-face sandwich for lunch; for dinner, indulge in fish—served grilled, sautéed, blackened, broiled, or island-style. Thursday is all-you-can-eat shrimp night. ⊠ *Watergate Villas,* ☎ *809/775–2081. AE, MC, V.*

$$–$$$ ✕ **Raffles.** In the comfort of a homelike dining room, set seaside in a
★ quaint marina, owner/chef Sandra Englesburger puts on a one-woman culinary show. Her all-from-scratch creations include an English shep-herd's pie, mahimahi in a rich lobster sauce, and a two-day Peking duck. The dessert special is named Peter's Paradise—a dark choco-late sphere filled with white chocolate mousse and tropical fruit. Raf-fles is definitely a find. ⊠ *41-6-1 Compass Point Marina,* ☎ *809/775–6004. AE, MC, V.*

$$ ✕ **Tickles Dockside Pub.** The Crown Bay location has been a locals' choice for years, but this branch of the casual, alfresco restaurant, just off the docks, is new to East End. Enjoy sandwiches, ribs, and chicken (served with sweet potato French fries) while you watch the iguanas beg for table scraps—and bring your camera. ⊠ *American Yacht Har-bor, Red Hook, Bldg. D,* ☎ *809/775–9425. MC, V.*

$–$$ ✕ **Eunice's Terrace.** This excellent West Indian cook is justly famous for introducing President Clinton to native-style cuisine. Her roomy, two-story restaurant has a bar and a menu of native dishes, including callaloo, conch fritters, fried fish, local sweet potato, fungi, and green banana. ⊠ *Rte. 38 near Renaissance Grand Beach Resort and Coral World, Smith Bay,* ☎ *809/775–3975. AE, MC, V.*

Frenchtown

$$$–$$$$ ✕ **Craig & Sally's.** In the heart of Frenchtown, Sally Darash whips up
★ such eclectic starters as grilled shrimp and melon kabobs and entrées such as polenta-crusted yellowtail snapper with artichoke and olive sauce. Save room for dessert—the white chocolate cheesecake is truly special. Husband Craig makes sure more than a dozen wines are available by the glass and many more by the bottle. ⊠ *22 Honduras,* ☎ *809/777–9949. AE, MC, V.*

$$$ ✕ **The Chart House.** In an old great house on the tip of the Frenchtown peninsula, this restaurant offers superb views along with fresh fish and teriyaki dishes, lobster, Hawaiian chicken, and a large salad bar. ⊠ *Villa Olga,* ☎ *809/774–4262. AE, D, DC, MC, V.*

$$–$$$ ✕ **Alexander's Cafe.** This charming restaurant is a favorite with the
★ people in the restaurant business on St. Thomas—always a sign of quality. Alexander is Austrian, and the schnitzels are delicious and reasonably priced; pasta specials are fresh and tasty. Save room for strudel. Next door is **Alexander's Bar & Grill,** serving food from the same kitchen but in a more casual setting and at slightly lower prices. ⊠ *24A Honduras,* ☎ *809/776–4211. AE, D, MC, V. Closed Sun.*

$–$$ ✕ **Victor's New Hide-Out.** This landmark restaurant is a little hard to find—it's up the hill between the Nisky Shopping Center and the airport—but the search is worth it. Native food—steamed fish, marinated pork chops, and local lobster—and native music are offered in a casual, friendly West Indian atmosphere. ⊠ *Sub Base,* ☎ *809/776–9379. AE, MC, V.*

Northside

$$–$$$ ✕ **Ferrari's.** St. Thomas residents have consistently voted this the "best
★ value" restaurant in the *U.S.V.I. Daily News* poll. The menu features such traditional Italian staples as antipasto, veal marsala, lasagna, manicotti, pizzas, and garlic bread. Sit at a table or have a seat at the bar from 4:30 until 11. ⊠ *33 Crown Mountain Rd.,* ☎ *809/774–6800. AE, MC, V. No lunch.*

$–$$ ✕ **Sib's Mountain Bar and Restaurant.** Here you'll find live music, football, burgers, barbecued ribs and chicken, and beers. This friendly two-fisted drinking bar, with a restaurant on the back porch, is a good place for a casual dinner after a day at the beach. Kids of all ages can doodle on the paper tablecloths with the colorful crayons left on every table. ⊠ *Mafolie Hill,* ☎ *809/774–8967. AE, MC, V.*

Beaches

All beaches on St. Thomas are open to the public, but often you have to walk through a resort to reach them. Resort guests frequently have access to lounge chairs and floats that are off- limits to nonguests; for this reason, you may feel more comfortable at one of the beaches not associated with a resort, such as Magens or Coki. Whichever one you choose, remember to remove your valuables from the car and keep them out of sight when you go swimming.

Coki Beach, next to Coral World, is a popular snorkeling spot for cruise-ship passengers; it's common to find a group of them among the reefs on the east and west ends of the beach.

The beach at **Hull Bay,** on the north shore, faces Inner and Outer Brass cays and attracts fishermen and beachcombers. It's open to rough Atlantic waves, making it the only place to surf on the island.

Magens Bay is usually lively because of its spectacular loop of white sand, more than a half-mile long, and its calm waters, which are protected by two peninsulas. The bottom is flat and sandy, so this is a place for sunning and swimming rather than snorkeling. Food, changing facilities, and rest rooms are available.

At **Morning Star Beach,** close to Charlotte Amalie, many young residents show up for body surfing or volleyball. The pretty curve of beach fronts the Morning Star section of Marriott's Frenchman's Reef Hotel. Snorkeling is good near the rocks when the current doesn't affect visibility.

From **Sapphire Beach** there is a fine view of St. John and other islands. Snorkeling is excellent at the reef to the right or east, near Pettyklip Point. Sapphire Beach Resort rents water-sports gear.

The condo resort at **Secret Harbour** doesn't at all detract from the attractiveness of this covelike East End beach. Not only is it pretty, it is also superb for snorkeling—go out to the left, near the rocks.

Outdoor Activities and Sports

Fishing

In the past quarter-century, some 20 world records, many for blue marlin, have been set in the waters surrounding the Virgin Islands, most notably at St. Thomas's famed North Drop. To book a boat, call the **Charter Boat Center** (☎ 809/775–7990 or 800/866–5714), **American Yacht Harbor** (☎ 809/775–6454), or **Sapphire Beach Marina** (☎ 809/775–6100). Or, to find the trip that will best suit you, walk down the docks at either American Yacht Harbor or Sapphire Beach Marina and chat with the captains as they come in from fishing.

Golf

Mahogany Run Golf Course. Designed by Tom Fazio, the scenic par-70, 18-hole golf course overlooks the Caribbean sea with a view of the B.V.I. It features the "Devil's Triangle," a three-hole challenge that often stumps even the best golfers. The road to the golf course was once bordered by centuries-old mahogany trees cleared to build the golf course. ⊠ *Rte. 42,* ☎ *809/777–5000.*

Hiking

Colony Point Pleasant Resort. There's a free self-guided nature walk at this resort (☎ 809/775–7200); just stop by the front desk for the map and brochure. In addition, there's an ecowalk at **Magens Bay.**

Kayaking

Virgin Islands Ecotours. Paddle through a marine sanctuary on sit-atop two-man ocean kayaks. These 2½-hour tours include stops for swimming and snorkeling. ⊠ *2 Estate Nadir, on Rte. 32, 00802* ☎ *809/779–2155.*

Mountain Biking

St. Thomas Mountain Bike Adventure. Take a 1½-hour cycle out past Magens Bay to Peterborg Point on Trek 830 21-speed mountain bikes. Lots of photo opportunities for fiora, fauna, and a lesser seen side of Magens' picturesque half-moon beach. Helmets, water, and guide provided. ⊠ *Box 7037, 00801,* ☎ *809/776–1727.*

Parasailing

Parasailers sit in a harness attached to a parachute that lifts off from the boat deck until they're sailing high in the air. **Caribbean Parasail**

and Watersports (☎ 809/775–9360) operates out of several locations, including the Charlotte Amalie waterfront and major hotels.

Sailing

☞ Chapter 3, Sailing in the Virgin Islands.

Snorkeling/Diving

☞ Chapter 2, Diving and Snorkeling in the Virgin Islands.

Stargazing

Star Charters Astronomy Adventures. Scan the heavens with the Caribbean's largest optical telescope—an 18-inch Newtonian Reflector—and learn both the science and lore of the stars. ⊠ *Nisky Mail Center #693, 00802,* ☎ *809/774–9211.*

Tennis

Just because you're staying in a guest house without courts doesn't mean you can't indulge in a set or two. Most hotels rent time to nonguests. For reservations call **Bluebeard's Castle Hotel** (☎ 809/774–1600, ext. 196), **Mahogany Run Tennis Club** (☎ 809/775–5000), **Marriott Frenchman's Reef Tennis Courts** (☎ 809/776–8500, ext. 444), **Sapphire Beach Resort** (☎ 809/775–6100, ext. 2131), **Renaissance Grand Beach Resort** (☎ 809/775–1510), **Ritz-Carlton** (☎ 809/775–3333); or **Wyndham Sugar Bay** (☎ 809/777–7100). All of the above courts have lights and are open into the evening. **Bolongo Bay Beach Club** (☎ 809/775–1800) has courts for the use of guests only. There are two public courts at **Sub Base** (next to the Water and Power Authority), open on a first-come, first-served basis. The lights are on here until 8 PM.

Shopping

St. Thomas has always been a commercial center, and the old stone buildings that once stored indigo, rum, and molasses bound for the European market now house perfumes from France, cameras from Japan, clothing from France and Italy, and silks and linens from China, sure to entice cruise-ship passengers on a shore-leave shopping spree.

Most people would agree that St. Thomas lives up to its self-described billing as a shopper's paradise. Even if shopping isn't your idea of how to spend a vacation, you still may want to slip in on a quiet day (check the cruise-ship listings—Monday and Saturday are usually the least crowded) to check out the prices. Among the best buys are liquor, linens, imported china, crystal (most stores ship), and jewelry. The sheer volume of jewelry available makes this one of the few items for which comparison shopping is worth the effort.

Most stores take major credit cards. There is no sales tax in the U.S.V.I., and shoppers can take advantage of the $1,200 duty-free allowance per family member. Remember to save your receipts.

Although you'll find the occasional salesclerk who'll make a deal, bartering is not the norm here, so don't go into a store expecting to haggle over prices.

If you buy a plant, be sure to stop at the **Department of Agriculture** (⊠ Rte. 40) to get the plant's roots sprayed for diseases and to get a certificate to present to U.S. customs when you leave the territory.

Shopping Districts

The prime shopping area in **Charlotte Amalie** is between Post Office and Market squares and consists of three parallel streets running east to west (Waterfront Highway, Main Street, and Back Street) and the alleyways connecting them. Particularly attractive are **Royal Dane Mall**

Charlotte Amalie Shopping

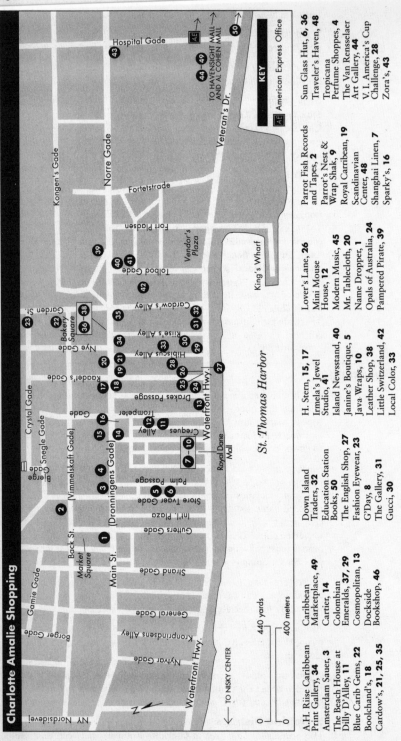

St. Thomas Harbor

KEY

AE American Express Office

A.H. Riise Caribbean Print Gallery, **34**
Amsterdam Sauer, **3**
The Beach House at Dilly D'Alley, **11**
Blue Carib Gems, **22**
Boolchand's, **18**
Cardow's, **21, 25, 35**

Caribbean Marketplace, **49**
Cartier, **14**
Colombian Emeralds, **37, 29**
Cosmopolitan, **13**
Dockside Bookshop, **46**

Down Island Traders, **32**
Education Station Books, **50**
The English Shop, **27**
Fashion Eyewear, **23**
G'Day, **8**
The Gallery, **31**
Gucci, **30**

H. Stern, **15, 17**
Irmela's Jewel Studio, **41**
Island Newsstand, **40**
Janine's Boutique, **5**
Java Wraps, **10**
Leather Shop, **38**
Little Switzerland, **42**
Local Color, **33**

Lover's Lane, **26**
Mini Mouse House, **12**
Modern Music, **45**
Mr. Tablecloth, **20**
Name Dropper, **1**
Opals of Australia, **24**
Pampered Pirate, **39**

Parrot Fish Records and Tapes, **2**
Parrot's Nest & Wrap Shak, **9**
Royal Carribean, **19**
Scandinavian Center, **48**
Shanghai Linen, **7**
Sparky's, **16**

Sun Glass Hut, **6, 36**
Traveler's Haven, **48**
Tropicana Perfume Shoppes, **4**
The Van Rensselaer Art Gallery, **44**
V.I. America's Cup Challenge, **28**
Zora's, **43**

and **A. H. Riise Alley,** quaint alleys between Main Street and the Waterfront, and **Bakery Square** on Back Street.

Vendors Plaza, on the waterfront side of Emancipation Gardens, is a central location for outdoor vendors who sell handmade earrings, necklaces, and bracelets; straw baskets and handbags; T-shirts; fabrics; African artifacts; local foods; and freshly blended tropical fruit smoothies.

West of town, the pink-stucco **Nisky Center** is more of a hometown shopping center than a tourist area, but there's a bank, pharmacy, clothing stores, and a Radio Shack.

Havensight Mall, next to the cruise-ship dock, may not be as charming as Charlotte Amalie, but it does have more than 60 shops. You'll find an excellent bookstore, bank, pharmacy, gourmet grocery, and smaller branches of many downtown stores. Next door, the dozen-plus **Port** of Sale shops offer factory-outlet prices on brand-name clothing and accessories.

East of town, **Tillett Gardens** (⊠ Estate Tutu, ☎ 809/775–1405) is an oasis of artistic endeavor on the highway across from Four Winds Shopping Center. The late Jim Tillett and then-wife Rhoda converted this old Danish farm into an artist's retreat in 1959. Today you can watch craftspeople and artisans produce silk-screen fabrics, pottery, candles, watercolors, gold jewelry, stained glass, and other handicrafts. There's usually something special happening in the gardens as well: the Classics in the Gardens program is a classical music series presented under the stars, and Arts Alive is a visual arts and crafts festival held four times yearly.

Tutu Park Shopping Center, behind the Four Winds Shopping Center, is the island's one and only enclosed mall. The 47 stores and food court are anchored by a Kmart and the Plaza Extra grocery store. Archaeologists have discovered evidence that ancient Arawak Indians once lived near the mall grounds.

Red Hook now has **American Yacht Harbor,** a waterfront shopping area that includes smaller branches of a number of Charlotte Amalie stores, restaurants, and a few bars.

Don't forget **St. John** (☞ Shopping *in* St. John, *below*). A ferry ride (an hour from Charlotte Amalie or 20 minutes from Red Hook) will take you to the charming shops of **Mongoose Junction** and **Wharfside Village,** which specialize in unique, often island-made items.

Art Galleries
A. H. Riise Caribbean Print Gallery. Haitian and Virgin Islands art are displayed and sold here, along with art books, exquisite botanical prints, and historic photo note cards from MAPes MONDe. ⊠ *37 Main St., at Riise's Alley,* ☎ *809/776–2303.*

The Gallery. Inside the waterfront branch of Down Island Traders (and owned by the same people), the Gallery carries Haitian art along with works by a number of Virgin Islands artists. Items on display include metal sculpture, wood carvings, painted screens and boxes, figures carved from stone, and oversize papier-mâché figures. Prices range from $50 to $5,000. ⊠ *Waterfront Hwy. at Post Office Alley,* ☎ *809/ 776–4641.*

The Van Rensselaer Art Gallery. Owner Corrine Van Rensselaer features her own artwork plus the best from the island's many artists. Look for watercolors, batik, paintings, ceramics, and oils. ⊠ *Al Cohen Mall, Rte. 30,* ☎ *809/774–4598.*

Books and Magazines

Dockside Bookshop. This place is packed with books for children, travelers, cooks, and historians, as well as a good selection of paperback mysteries, best-sellers, art books, calendars, and art prints. It carries a selection of books written in and about the Caribbean and the Virgin Islands, from literature to chartering guides to books on seashells and tropical flowers. There's no markup here. ⊠ *Havensight Mall, Bldg. IV,* ☎ *809/774–4937.*

Education Station Books. There is no markup at this full-service bookstore that concentrates on Caribbean literature and black American and African history. There's also a large cookbook selection, a music section featuring jazz and "world beat" tapes from Africa, and prints by local artists. In addition, you can buy and sell used books of all types here. Visit Education Station Ltd., just next door, for children's books. ⊠ *Wheatley Center, intersection of Rte. 35 and Rte.38,* ☎ *809/776–3008.*

Two shops that have the largest selection of **magazines and newspapers** on St. Thomas are **Island Newsstand** (⊠ Grand Hotel in Charlotte Amalie) and **Magazines** (⊠ Fort Mylner Shopping Center near Tillett Gardens). Expect to pay about 20% above stateside prices.

Cameras and Electronics

Boolchand's. A variety of brand-name cameras, audio and video equipment, and binoculars are sold here. ⊠ *31 Main St.,* ☎ *809/776–0794; and Havensight Mall,* ☎ *809/776–0302.*

Royal Caribbean. Shop here for cameras, camcorders, stereos, watches, and clocks. ⊠ *33 Main St.,* ☎ *809/776–4110; and Havensight Mall,* ☎ *809/776–8890.*

China and Crystal

A. H. Riise Gift Shops. A. H. Riise carries Waterford, Royal Crown, and Royal Doulton at good prices. A five-piece place setting of Royal Crown Derby's Old Imari goes for less than $500. ⊠ *37 Main St., at Riise's Alley,* ☎ *809/776–2303; and Havensight Mall,* ☎ *809/776–2303.*

The English Shop. This store offers figurines, cutlery, and china and crystal from major European and Japanese manufacturers. Spode, Limoges, Royal Doulton, Portmeirion, Noritaki, and Wedgwood are featured. You can choose what you like from the catalogs here, and shopkeepers will order and factory-ship it for you. ⊠ *Waterfront Hwy.,* ☎ *809/ 776–5399; and Havensight Mall,* ☎ *809/776–3776.*

Little Switzerland. All of this establishment's shops carry crystal from Baccarat, Waterford, Orrefors, and Riedel; china from Villeroy & Boch and Wedgwood among others; and fine Swiss watches, including the best Rolex selection. There is also an assortment of cut-crystal animals, china and porcelain figurines, and many other affordable collectibles. ⊠ *Emancipation Garden, 5 Main Street, inside the A. H. Riise Gift Mart; and dockside at Havensight Mall,* ☎ *809/776–2010.*

Scandinavian Center. Look for a variety of handmade products from Scandinavia, including Royal Copenhagen porcelain and crystal and Georg Jensen jewelry and flatware. ⊠ *Havensight Mall,* ☎ *809/774–6642.*

Clothing

FOR WOMEN

The Beach House at Dilly D'Alley. Downstairs is the place for fancy T-shirts, sundresses, linen pants, and accessories; upstairs you'll find a giant selection of the latest swimwear. ⊠ *Trompeter Gade,* ☎ *809/776–5006.*

G'Day. Everything in this tiny shop is drenched in the bright colors of Australian artist Ken Done, Scandinavian artist Sigrid Olsen, and items by Cotton Fields—swimwear, resortwear, accessories, and umbrellas. ⊠ *Waterfront Hwy. at Royal Dane Mall,* ☎ *809/774–8855.*

Janine's Boutique. Here you'll find women's and men's dressy and casual apparel from European designers and manufacturers, including the Louis Feraud collection, and select finds from Valentino, Christian Dior, YSL, and Pierre Cardin. ⊠ *A–2 Palm Passage,* ☎ *809/774–8243.*

Java Wraps. Wear the snazzy Indonesian batik creations the U.S. Virgin Islands' female athletes modeled at the opening ceremonies of the 1996 Summer Olympic Games in Atlanta. Find a full range of beach cover-ups, swimwear, and leisurewear for women, men, and children. ⊠ *Waterfront Hwy. at Royal Dane Mall,* ☎ *809/774–3700.*

Local Color. St. John artist Sloop Jones exhibits colorful island designs on cool hand-painted dresses, T-shirts, and sweaters. Also for sale is wearable art by other local artists; unique jewelry; sundresses, shorts, and shirts in bright prints; and big-brim straw hats dipped in fuchsia, turquoise, and other tropical colors. ⊠ *Hibiscus Alley,* ☎ *809/774–3727.*

Lover's Lane. With the motto "couples that play together, stay together," this romantic shop sells sensuous lingerie, sexy menswear, and provocative swimwear. ⊠ *Waterfront Hwy. at Raadets Gade,* ☎ *809/ 777–9616).*

Name Dropper. You'll get 25% off stateside prices at this boutique. Look for Jones New York, Christian Dior, Evan-Picone, and Chaus. The store also carries a full line of accessories. ⊠ *83 Main St.,* ☎ *809/ 774–0577.*

FOR MEN

Cosmopolitan. Look for the top lines in menswear at this sophisticated shopping emporium. The store carries lines like Paul and Shark, Bally, Timberland, Sperry Topsider, Testoni, Burma Bibas, Givenchy, Nautica, Fila, Hom, Lachco, and Gottex. ⊠ *Drake's Passage at the Waterfront,* ☎ *809/776–2040.*

V.I. America's Cup Challenge. Support the V.I.'s bid to win the 2000 Cup from New Zealand by wearing official team clothing—T-shirts, polo shirts, hats, caps, visors, and more. ⊠ *Hibiscus Alley,* ☎ *809/774–9090.*

Crafts and Gifts

Caribbean Marketplace. This is the place to look for handicrafts from around the world, including the Caribbean and Asia. Look for Sunny Caribee spices, soaps, coffee and teas from Tortola, and coffee from Trinidad. ⊠ *Havensight Mall,* ☎ *809/776–5400.*

Down Island Traders. These traders deal in hand-painted calabash bowls; finely printed Caribbean note cards; jams, jellies, spices, and herbs; herbal teas made of rum, passion fruit, and mango; high-mountain coffee from Jamaica; and a variety of handicrafts from throughout the Caribbean. ⊠ *Waterfront Hwy. at Post Office Alley,* ☎ *809/776–4641.*

Pampered Pirate. This busy store carries island-made dolls, Christmas ornaments, prints, and paintings along with its other gift items. ⊠ *4 Norre Gade,* ☎ *809/775–5450.*

Parrot's Nest & Wrap Shak. Here you'll find handcrafted cloth dolls, wood figurines, African artwork, shell art, and jewelry from the Far East, South America, and the Caribbean. Cool cotton wraps make great resortwear. ⊠ *Royal Dane Mall,* ☎ *809/774–9211.*

Food

Cost-U-Less. This store sells everything from soup to nuts, but in giant sizes and case lots. The fresh meat and seafood department does offer smaller family-sized portions. ⊠ *Four Winds Plaza,* ☎ *809/777–3588.*

Fruit Bowl. For fruits and vegetables, this is the place. ⊠ *Wheatley Center,* ☎ *809/774–8565.*

Gourmet Gallery. Visiting millionaires buy their caviar here. There's also an excellent and reasonably priced wine selection, as well as condiments, cheeses, and specialty ingredients for everything from tacos to curries to chow mein. ⊠ *Crown Bay Marina,* ☎ *809/776–8555.*

Havensight Market. A full-time French chef makes a mouthwatering assortment of salads and freshly baked breads. There are also specialty produce, ethnic ingredients, and a full complement of wines. ⊠ *Havensight Mall,* ☎ *809/774–4948.*

Marina Market. There's no better fresh meat and seafood department on the island. ⊠ *Across from Red Hook ferry,* ☎ *809/779–2411.*

Plaza Extra. This mainland-type supermarket has a large selection of Middle Eastern foods. ⊠ *Tutu Park Mall,* ☎ *809/775–5646.*

Pueblo Supermarket (⊠ Four Winds Plaza, ☎ 809/775–4655; Sub Base, ☎ 809/774–4200; and Estate Thomas, ☎ 809/774–2695) sells stateside brands but at higher prices because of the cost of shipping.

Jewelry

A. H. Riise Gift Shops. This is St. Thomas's oldest and largest shop for luxury items, with jewelry, pearls, ceramics, china, crystal, flatware, perfumes, and watches. ⊠ *37 Main St., at Riise's Alley,* ☎ *89/776–2303; and Havensight Mall,* ☎ *809/776–2303.*

Amsterdam Sauer. Many fine one-of-a-kind designs are displayed and available for sale here. ⊠ *14 Main St.,* ☎ *809/774–2222; and Havensight Mall,* ☎ *809/776–3828.*

Blue Carib Gems. At family-owned and -run Blue Carib Gems, watch Alan O'Hara Sr. polish Caribbean amber and larimar, black coral, agate, and other gems and fashion them into gold and silver settings. Visit son Alan Jr. at the Wharfside Village branch on St. John. ⊠ *2-3 Back St.,* ☎ *809/774–8525.*

Cardow's (⊠ Three stores on Main St., ☎ 809/776–1140; two at Havensight Mall, ☎ 809/774–0530 or 809/774–5905) offers an enormous "chain bar" more than 100 ft long, where you're guaranteed 30%–50% savings off U.S. retail prices or your money will be refunded within 30 days of purchase.

Cartier. In addition to the fantastically beautiful and fantastically priced items, there are a surprising number of affordable ones, including Cartier silk scarves, which are cheaper than Hermés, and quite lush. ⊠ *31 Main St.,* ☎ *809/774–1590.*

Colombian Emeralds. Well known in the Caribbean, this store offers set and unset gems of every description, including high-quality emeralds. There are additional locations on the Waterfront and at Havensight Mall. ⊠ *30 Main St.,* ☎ *809/774–3400.*

H. Stern (⊠ 12 Main St., ☎ 809/776–1939; 32 AB Main St., ☎ 809/776–1146; and Havensight Mall, ☎ 809/776–1223) is one of the most respected names in gems.

Irmela's Jewel Studio. For 26 years Irmela has been offering some of the Caribbean's most exquisite jewelry designs inside the historic stone walls of the Grand Hotel. She will design or create any custom piece of jewelry and specializes in unusual gems and pearls. ⊠ *Grand Hotel Court, Tolbod Gade entrance,* ☎ *809/774–5875.*

Little Switzerland. The sole U.S.V.I. distributor for Rolex watches, the store also does a booming mail-order business; ask for a catalog. ⊠ *Emancipation Gardens, 5 Main St., inside the A. H. Riise Gift Mart, and dockside at Havensight Mall,* ☎ *809/776–2010.*

Opals of Australia. The name says it all. Here you will find the best opal selection on the island. ⊠ *Drake's Passage,* ☎ *809/774–8244.*

Leather Goods

Leather Shop. You'll find mostly big names at big prices here (Fendi and Bottega Veneta are prevalent), but there are also some reasonably priced, high-quality purses, wallets, and briefcases. ⊠ *24 Main St.,* ☎ *809/776–3995; and Havensight Mall,* ☎ *809/776–0040.*

Traveler's Haven. This store sells leather bags, backpacks, vests, and money belts. ⊠ *Havensight Mall,* ☎ *809/775–1798.*

Zora's. Fine leather sandals made to order are the specialty here, as well as a selection of made-only-in-the-Virgin-Islands backpacks, briefcases, and "fish" purses in durable, brightly colored canvas. ⊠ *Norre Gade across from Roosevelt Park,* ☎ *809/774–2559.*

Linens

Mr. Tablecloth. The friendly staff here will help you choose among the floor-to-ceiling array of linens, from Tuscany lace tablecloths to Irish linen pillowcases. You'll be pleasantly amazed at the prices. ⊠ *6-7 Main St.,* ☎ *809/774–4343.*

Shanghai Linen. The trade is brisk here, and bargains can easily be found. ⊠ *Waterfront Hwy.,* ☎ *809/776–2828.*

Liquor and Wine

A. H. Riise Liquors. This Riise venture offers a large selection of liquors, cordials, wines, and tobacco, including rare vintage cognacs, Armagnacs, ports, and Madeiras. It also stocks imported cigars, fruits in brandy, and barware from England. ⊠ *Main St. and Riise's Alley,* ☎ *809/776–2303; Havensight Mall,* ☎ *809/776–7713.*

Al Cohen's Discount Liquor. This warehouse-style store has a large wine department. ⊠ *Across from Havensight Mall, Long Bay Rd.,* ☎ *809/774–3690.*

Gourmet Gallery. This aromatic grocery store (there's a bakery in the back) caters to the yachting crowd by offering one of the best wine selections on St. Thomas. ⊠ *Crown Bay Marina,* ☎ *809/776–8555.*

Music

Modern Music. Shop for the latest stateside and Caribbean CD and cassette releases, plus oldies, classical, and New Age music. ⊠ *Across from Havensight Mall,* ☎ *809/774–3100; Nisky Center,* ☎ *809/777–8787.*

Parrot Fish Records and Tapes. A stock of standard stateside tapes and compact discs, plus a good selection of Caribbean artists, including local groups, can be found here. For a catalog of calypso, soca, steel band, and reggae music, write to Parrot Fish, Box 9206, St. Thomas 00801. ⊠ *Back St.,* ☎ *809/776–4514.*

Perfumes

Where you buy perfume hardly matters, because prices are about the same in all stores.

Sparky's. Spiffy enough to match its neighbor, Cartier, Sparky's has a wide range of perfumes and cosmetics. The impeccably turned out salesclerks can also give you a facial and makeup lesson. ✉ *30 Main St.,* ☎ *809/776–7510.*

Tropicana Perfume Shoppes. Tropicana has the largest selection of fragrances for men and women in all of the Virgin Islands. ✉ *2 Main St.,* ☎ *809/774–0010.*

Sunglasses

Fashion Eyewear. Tucked into a tiny building is this even tinier sunglass shop. ✉ *20A Garden St.,* ☎ *809/776–9075.*

Sun Glass Hut. Take your pick from among such name-brand eyewear as Biagiotti, Serengetti, Carrera, and others. ✉ *15 Main Street,* ☎ *809/777–5585; 37 Main Street,* ☎ *809/774–9030; 24 Palm Passage,* ☎ *809/777–5593; and Havensight Mall,* ☎ *809/777–8765.*

Toys

Mini Mouse House. Birds sing, dogs bark, and fish swim in this animated toyland. Adults have as much fun trying out the wares as do kids. ✉ *3A Trompeter Gade,* ☎ *809/776–4242.*

Nightlife

Check out the variety of nightlife on St. Thomas: On any given night, especially in season, you'll find steel-pan orchestras, rock-and-roll bands, piano music, jazz, broken-bottle dancing, disco, and karaoke. Pick up a copy of the bright-yellow *St. Thomas This Week* magazine when you arrive (you'll see it at the airport, in stores, and in hotel lobbies); the back pages list who's playing where. The *Daily News* Thursday edition carries complete listings for the upcoming weekend.

Nightspots

Barnacle Bill's. Bill Grogan has turned this Crown Bay landmark into a musicians' home away from home. David Bromberg, Bonnie Raitt, Maria Muldaur, and Ry Cooder have performed in this small room with a parachute-covered ceiling. All Mondays are Limelight Mondays, when local or visiting entertainers take their turn at the mike before an audience composed mostly of fellow performers. Live bands from all over the Caribbean play on other nights. ✉ *8136 Sub Base,* ☎ *809/774–7444.*

The Greenhouse. This place is slowly making a transition from a waterfront bar to something like the Caribbean equivalent of the T.G.I. Friday's chain in the United States. It strives to meet all tastes, starting with a breakfast that's popular with locals before work; burgers and taco salad for lunch; and then prime rib and lobster specials for dinner. Once the Greenhouse puts away the salt-and-pepper shakers at 10 PM, it becomes a rock-and-roll club with a DJ or live reggae bands rousting the weary to their feet six days a week. ✉ *Waterfront Hwy. at Storetvaer Gade,* ☎ *809/774–7998.*

Old Mill Complex. In—you guessed it—an old mill, this is a rock-till-you-drop late-night spot Thursday through Sunday. Whatever the tunes, the place is lively. There's a small dance floor and good sound system. ✉ *193 Contant,* ☎ *809/776–3004.*

Stixx On The Water. Old friends from anchorages around the world rendezvous at this Yacht Haven Marina bar and restaurant, and there's always room for a new friend or two. Stixx features rock, country, and reggae music nightly. There's a dance floor for those who feel like kicking up their heels. ✉ *At Ramada Yacht Haven Marina,* ☎ *809/774–4480.*

Jazz/Piano Bars

You'll find piano bars at **Entre Nous** at Bluebeard's Castle Hotel (☎ 809/776–4050) and **Randy's Bistro** at Al Cohen Mall on Raphune Hill (☎ 809/777–3199). "Gray, Gray, Gray" plays piano at both. An island favorite, he's been around for years and shouldn't be missed.

Exploring St. Thomas

St. Thomas is only 13 mi long and less than 4 mi wide, but it's an extremely hilly island, and even an 8- or 10-mi trip could take several hours. Don't let that discourage you, though, because the ridge of mountains that runs from east to west through the middle, and separates the Caribbean and Atlantic sides of the island, offers spectacular vistas and is a lot of fun to explore.

Charlotte Amalie

When exploring **Charlotte Amalie,** look beyond the pricey shops, T-shirt vendors, and bustling crowds for a glimpse of the island's history. The city served as the capital of Denmark's outpost in the Caribbean until 1917, an aspect of the island often lost in the glitter and glitz of the shopping district. If you're driving, park in the public parking lot next to Fort Christian. You can easily walk around this historic town, although it will sometimes be hilly. Don't worry, there are plenty of places along the way to rest your feet and sample some of the fine local island cuisine.

A note about the street names: In deference to the island's heritage, the streets downtown are labeled by their Danish names. Locals will use both the Danish name and the English name (such as Dronningens Gade and Norre Gade for Main Street), but most people refer to things by where they are located (a block toward the Waterfront off Main Street, or next to the Little Switzerland Shop). It's best to ask for directions by shop names or landmarks.

Numbers in the text correspond to numbers in the margin and on the Charlotte Amalie map.

A GOOD WALK

Start a walking tour of historic Charlotte Amalie at **Fort Christian** ①, the rust-colored fortress facing the Waterfront, which bears the distinction of being St. Thomas's oldest standing structure. On the second story roof, get a bird's-eye view of the **Legislature Building** ② and a sea of multicolored umbrellas that mark **Vendors Plaza** ③. Look across the red-roofed houses in town and up the hillside to the regal white facade of the **Danish Consulate Building** ④, home of the island's governor.

Once back outside the fort, stroll through **Emancipation Garden** ⑤, where several benches make a great place to rendezvous with friends after shopping. To mail a postcard back home, head across the street to the **U.S. Post Office** ⑥. Cross Main Street, or Norre Gade, to see statues of three famous St. Thomians in **Educators Park** ⑦. The street that separates Emancipation Garden and the Post Office is called Tolbod Gade. The **V.I. Visitor's Information Center** ⑧ is on the waterfront side of Tolbod Gade, next to the Little Switzerland Shop, and is a must for picking up an island map and brochures on restaurants and attractions.

Go back across Norre Gade and cross Tolbod Gade to the **Grand Hotel Court** ⑨, where you'll find shops and Beni Iguana's sushi bar. Cross Norre Gade again and head east to see **Frederick Lutheran Church** ⑩, the second oldest Lutheran church in the Western Hemisphere. Continue east on Norre Gade 1½ blocks to **Roosevelt Park** ⑪. Just one block farther east, across Hospital Gade, is the **Memorial Moravian Church** ⑫.

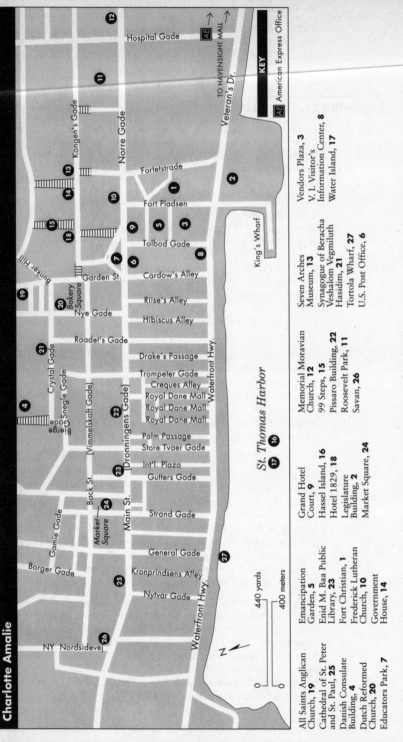

Charlotte Amalie

St. Thomas Harbor

King's Wharf

Hospital Gade

Norre Gade

Kongen's Gade

Fortetstrade

Fort Pladsen

Tolbod Gade

Cardow's Alley

Garden St.

Bakery Square

Riise's Alley

Nye Gade

Hibiscus Alley

Raadet's Gade

Drake's Passage

Crystal Gade

Trompeter Gade

Creques Alley

Snegle Gade

Royal Dane Mall

Royal Dane Mall

Royal Dane Mall

Bjerge Gade

Palm Passage

Store Tvaer Gade

Int'l. Plaza

Gutters Gade

Back St.

Strand Gade

Main St.

Market Square

General Gade

Gamle Gade

Kronprindsens Alley

Borger Gade

Nytvar Gade

NY Nordsidevej

Waterfront Hwy.

Bunker Hill

(Vimmelskaft Gade)

(Dronningens Gade)

TO HAVENSIGHT MALL

Veteran's Dr.

KEY

AE American Express Office

AE V.I. Visitor's

N

0 | 440 yards
0 | 400 meters

All Saints Anglican Church, **19**
Cathedral of St. Peter and St. Paul, **25**
Danish Consulate Building, **4**
Dutch Reformed Church, **20**
Educators Park, **7**

Emancipation Garden, **5**
Enid M. Baa Public Library, **23**
Fort Christian, **1**
Frederick Lutheran Church, **10**
Government House, **14**

Grand Hotel Court, **9**
Hassel Island, **16**
Hotel 1829, **18**
Legislature Building, **2**
Market Square, **24**

Memorial Moravian Church, **12**
99 Steps, **15**
Pissaro Building, **11**
Roosevelt Park, **26**
Savan, **26**

Seven Arches Museum, **13**
Synagogue of Beracha Veshalom Vegmiluth Hasidim, **21**
Tortola Wharf, **27**
U.S. Post Office, **6**

Vendors Plaza, **3**
V.I. Visitor's Information Center, **8**
Water Island, **17**

Turn north on Hospital Gade one block to Kongen's Gade, also called Government Hill.

Walking west on Kongen's Gade, back in a narrow alley on your right, you'll find the **Seven Arches Museum** ⑬, an attraction that takes you back to 1800, when this former home was built. You can relax here with a cooling island drink. Walk west up the hill on Kongen's Gade to **Government House** ⑭, all white except for the red carpet rolled down the front steps and black protective canons in front. A few yards farther west, hike up the **99 steps** ⑮. The climb is worth the effort since you'll be rewarded with a picture postcard view of town and the harbor. The two land masses in the harbor are **Hassel Island** ⑯ to the east and **Water Island** ⑰ to the west. Back down the steps, pass by **Hotel 1829** ⑱, a local landmark for fine dining.

Continue walking west on Kongen's Gade past Hotel 1829 and Zorba's, the Greek taverna two doors down and continue straight ahead to Garden Street. Church history buffs will love looking at two impressive structures within the next two square blocks. North on Garden Street, find the **All Saints Anglican Church** ⑲. Backtrack on Garden Street and turn west on Crystal Gade to reach the **Dutch Reformed Church** ⑳, recognizable by its imposing columns. One block farther west on Crystal Gade is the **Synagogue of Beracha Veshalom Vegmiluth Hasidim** ㉑ and the neighboring Weibel Museum.

Walk two blocks south, back to Main Street. The most concentrated shopping area is the less-than-mile-long stretch from the bottom of Kongen's Gade west to Market Square. Shops holding designer clothes, electronics, and gemstones were once warehouses, with narrow alleyways just wide enough to carry cargo to and from the many trading ships that docked in the Charlotte Amalie harbor. Today, Royal Dane Mall—scattered with bronze plaques telling of past perils and buried riches—Drake's Passage, and Palm Passage are just a few of the cobblestoned alleyways that have been remodeled to house quaint cafés and the glamorous duty-free shops for which St. Thomas is known. On Main Street, opposite Royal Dane Mall, you'll find the **Pissarro Building** ㉒, birthplace of the famed French impressionist and now home of an art gallery. Farther west on Main Street is the pink-painted **Enid M. Baa Public Library** ㉓ and then **Market Square** ㉔. Past the square is the **Cathedral of St. Peter and St. Paul** ㉕ and the **Savan** ㉖ district.

Walking east again on Main Street, turn right on General Gade and out to the Waterfront to the **Tortola Wharf** ㉗, where ferries ply the waters between the U.S. and B.V.I. From here, "Good Day" is the only passport you'll need to continue your day shopping in historic Charlotte Amalie.

TIMING

A quick jaunt around town takes about an hour. If you really want to immerse yourself in history, plan to spend at least half a day. Most cruise-ship passengers head to town in the morning, so afternoons are often quieter unless there are several ships in port. Wednesdays are the busiest cruise-ship days, while Sundays are lightest. Some shops open on Sundays, but public buildings are closed. If you get hot while walking, there are plenty of places to get a cold drink. Most of the shops along Main Street keep their doors propped open wide, letting air-conditioning waft out and creating a wonderfully cooling effect on the sidewalks. Whether spending a morning or the afternoon in town, plan to spend the other half of your day at a beach. Charlotte Amalie may be small, but the hubbub makes some "limin' " time a must.

SIGHTS TO SEE

⑲ All Saints Anglican Church. Built in 1848 from stone quarried on the island, the church has thick, arched window frames lined with the yellow brick that came to the islands as ballast aboard merchant ships. The merchants left the brick on the waterfront when they filled their boats with molasses, sugar, mahogany, and rum for the return voyage. The church was built in celebration of the end of slavery in the Virgin Islands in 1848. ⊠ *Domini Gade,* ☎ *809/774–0217.* ☾ *Mon.–Sat. 6–3.*

㉕ Cathedral of St. Peter and St. Paul. This building was consecrated as a parish church in 1848 and serves as the seat of the territory's Roman Catholic diocese. The ceiling and walls of the church are covered in the soft tones of murals painted in 1899 by two Belgian artists, Father Leo Servais and Brother Ildephonsus. The San Juan–marble altar and side walls were added in the 1960s. ⊠ *Lower Main St.,* ☎ *809/774–0201.* ☾ *Mon.–Sat. 8–5.*

❹ Danish Consulate Building. Built in 1830, it housed the Danish Consulate until the Danish West India Co. sold its properties to the local government in 1992. It now serves as home to the territory's governor. ⊠ *Take the stairs north at corner of Bjerge Gade and Crystal Gade to Denmark Hill.*

⑳ Dutch Reformed Church. Founded in 1744, burned down in 1804 and rebuilt in 1844, and then blown down by Hurricane Marilyn in 1995 and rebuilt in 1997, this structure has an austere loveliness. The unembellished cream-color hall gives visitors a sense of peace—albeit monochromatically. The only touches of another color are the forest green shutters and carpet. ⊠ *Nye Gade and Crystal Gade,* ☎ *809/776–8255.* ☾ *Weekdays 9–5. Call ahead; doors are sometimes locked.*

❼ Educators Park. A peaceful place amid the town's hustle and bustle, the park has memorials to three famous Virgin Islanders: educator Edith Williams, J. Antonio Jarvis (a founder of the V.I. *Daily News*), and educator and author Rothchild Francis, for whom Market Square is named. The last gave many speeches from this location. ⊠ *Main St. across from U.S. Post Office.*

❺ Emancipation Garden. Built to honor the freeing of slaves in 1848, today the gazebo's smooth floor is used for official ceremonies. There are two monuments here that accent the island's Danish-American tie—a bust of Danish King Christian and a scaled down model of the U.S. Liberty Bell. ⊠ *Between Tolbod Gade and Ft. Christian.*

㉓ Enid M. Baa Public Library. This large pink building is typical of the 18th-century town houses common to the north side of Main Street. The merchants' homes were built across from the brick warehouses, with their stores downstairs and living quarters upstairs. The library was the home of St. Thomas merchant and landowner Baron von Bretton. It's the first recorded fireproof building. Its high-ceiling, cool, stone-floor interior is perfect for an afternoon of browsing through the historic-papers collection or just sitting in the breeze by an open window reading the daily paper. ⊠ *Main St.,* ☎ *809/774–0630.* ☾ *Weekdays 9–5, Sat. 9–3.*

❶ Fort Christian. St. Thomas's oldest standing structure, this monument anchors the shopping district. It was built 1672–80, and now has U.S. national landmark status. The clock tower was added in the 19th century. This remarkable redoubt has, over time, been used as a jail, governor's residence, town hall, courthouse, and church. It now houses a museum featuring artifacts of U.S.V.I. history, natural history, and turn-of-the-century furnishings. ⊠ *Waterfront Hwy. just east of the shopping district,* ☎ *809/776–4566.* ☾ *Weekdays 9–4.*

❿ Frederick Lutheran Church. This historic church features a massive mahogany altar. The pews, each with its own door, were once rented to families of the congregation. Lutheranism is the state religion of Denmark, and, when the territory was without a minister, the governor—who had his own elevated pew—would fill in. ✉ *Norre Gade,* ☎ *809/776–1315.* ⊙ *Mon.–Sat. 9–4.*

⓮ Government House. Built as an elegant home in 1867, it serves as the governor's office with the first floor open to the public. The staircases are of native mahogany, as are the plaques hand-lettered in gold with the names of the governors appointed and, since 1970, elected. Brochures detailing the history of Government House are available, but you may have to search for them. Look behind or under the guest book to the left of the entrance.

The three murals at the back of the lobby were painted by Pepino Mangravatti in the 1930s as part of the U.S. government's Works Projects Administration (WPA). The murals depict Columbus's landing on St. Croix during his second voyage in 1493; the transfer of the islands from Denmark to the United States in 1917; and a sugar plantation on St. John.

To tour the second floor you will have to be accompanied by the deputy administrator. You can call ahead to make an appointment, or you can take a chance that the officials will be in. It's worth the extra effort it takes to visit the second floor if for no reason other than the view from the terrace. Imagine the affairs of state of a colonial time being conducted in the hush of the high-ceiling, chandeliered ballroom. In the reception room are four small paintings by Camille Pissarro, but unfortunately they are hard to appreciate because they are enclosed in frosted-glass cases. More interesting, and visible, is the large painting by an unknown artist that was found in Denmark and depicts a romanticized version of St. Croix; the painting was purchased by former governor Ralph M. Paiewonsky, who then gave it to Government House. ✉ *Government Hill,* ☎ *809/774–0001.* ⊙ *Weekdays 8–5.*

❾ Grand Hotel Court. This imposing building stands at the head of Main Street. Once the island's premier hotel, it has been converted into offices and shops. ✉ *Tolbod Gade at Norre Gade.*

⓰ Hassel Island. East of Water Island in Charlotte Amalie harbor, it is part of the Virgin Islands National Park due in part to its ruins of the British military garrison (built during a brief British occupation of the U.S.V.I. during the 1800s) and the remains of a marine railway (where ships were hoisted onto land to the ship repair yard). Also on Hassel Island is the shell of the hotel that writer Herman Wouk's fictitious character Norman Paperman tried to turn into his own paradise in the book *Don't Stop the Carnival.* Presently there is no transportation to the island.

⓲ Hotel 1829. Dating from the same year, it was originally the residence of a prominent merchant named Lavalette. The hotel's bright coral-colored exterior walls are accented with fancy black wrought iron, and the interior is paneled in a dark wood, which makes it feel delightfully cool. From the dining terrace, where gourmet food is served, see an exquisite view of the harbor framed by tangerine-colored bougainvillea. ✉ *Government Hill,* ☎ *809/776–1829.*

❷ Legislature Building. Its pastoral-looking lime green exterior conceals the vociferous political wrangling of the Virgin Islands Senate going on inside. Built originally by the Danish as a police barracks, the building was later used to billet U.S. Marines, and much later it housed a public school. Visitors are welcome to sit in on sessions in the upstairs chambers. ⊠ *Waterfront Hwy. across from Ft. Christian,* ☎ *809/774–0880.* ◌ *Daily 8–5.*

㉔ Market Square. Formally called Rothchild Francis Square, it's a good place to stop for a fresh fruit snack. A cadre of old-timers sell papaya, tannia roots, and herbs; and sidewalk vendors offer a variety of African fabrics and artifacts, tie-dyed cotton clothes at good prices, and fresh-squeezed fruit juices. ⊠ *North off Main St. at Strand Gade.*

⑫ Memorial Moravian Church. Built in 1884, it was named to commemorate the 150th anniversary of the Moravian Church in the Virgin Islands. ⊠ *17 Norre Gade,* ☎ *809/776–0066.* ◌ *Weekdays 8–5.*

⊙ ⑮ 99 Steps. A staircase "street" built by the Danes in the 1700s leads to the residential area above Charlotte Amalie and Blackbeard's Castle. The castle's tower, built in 1679, was once used by the notorious pirate Edward Teach. Today, this lookout is at the center of a small hotel. If you count the stairs as you go up, you'll discover, as have thousands before you, that there are more than 99. ⊠ *Look for the steps heading north from Government Hill.*

㉒ Pissarro Building. Home to several shops and an art gallery, it was the birthplace of French impressionist painter Camille Pissarro. ⊠ *38 Main St.*

⊙ ⑪ Roosevelt Park. A good spot to people watch, you'll see members of the local legal community head to the nearby court buildings while you rest on the park benches. The small monument on the south side of the park is dedicated to U.S.V.I. war veterans. School kids enjoy playing on the wood-and-tire playground. ⊠ *Norre Gade.*

㉖ Savan. A neighborhood of small streets and small houses, it was first laid out in the 1700s as the residential area for a growing class of "free coloreds," a middle class of artisans, clerks, and shopkeepers. You'll find a row of Rastafarian shops along the first block and a restaurant that sells pâté, and a delicious turnover-type pastry stuffed with meat or vegetables. ⊠ *Turn north off lower Main St. onto General Gade.*

⑬ Seven Arches Museum. In a restored West Indian home built about 1800, you'll find historic furnishings, cannon balls, and gas lamps. Behind the house is a quaint West Indian cottage. ☎ *809/774–9295.* ▨ *$5 donation suggested.* ◌ *Tues.–Sun. 10–3 or by appointment.*

NEED A BREAK?
Stop for a refreshing glass of bush—the local lingo for herb—tea in the charming courtyard of Seven Arches Museum. Sitting amidst the yellow ballast brick arches and welcoming arms staircase, you'll feel like you've traveled back in time to when schooners sailed the harbor, rum shops lined the waterfront, and hitching posts dotted the streets for those who rode their donkeys into town.

㉑ Synagogue of Beracha Veshalom Vegmiluth Hasidim. The synagogue's Hebrew name translates as the Congregation of Blessing, Peace, and Loving Deeds. The small building's white pillars contrast with rough stone walls, as does the rich mahogany of the pews and altar. The sand on the floor symbolizes the exodus from Egypt. Since the synagogue first opened its doors in 1833, it has held a weekly Sabbath service, making it the oldest synagogue building in continuous use under the American flag and the second oldest (after the one on Curaçao) in the Western Hemisphere. Next door, the **Weibel Museum** showcases the 300-year-old history of the Jews on St. Thomas. ⊠ *15 Crystal Gade,* ☎ *809/774–4312.* ◌ *Weekdays 9–4.*

㉗ **Tortola Wharf.** Catch the *Native Son* and other ferries to the B.V.I. There's an upstairs restaurant where you can watch the Charlotte Amalie harbor traffic as you enjoy an iced tea. ⊠ *Waterfront Hwy.*

❻ **U.S. Post Office.** While you buy your postcard stamps, contemplate the murals of waterfront scenes by *Saturday Evening Post* artist Stephen Dohanos. His art was commissioned as part of the Works Projects Administration (WPA) in the 1930s. ⊠ *Tolbod Gade and Main St.*

❸ **Vendors Plaza.** Merchants sell everything from T-shirts to African attire to leather goods. Look for local art among the ever-changing selections at this busy market. ⊠ *West of Ft. Christian at the Waterfront.*

❽ **V.I. Visitor's Information Center.** This hospitality lounge comes complete with bathrooms and a place to stash your luggage if you want to shop on your way to the airport. ⊠ *Tolbod Gade across from Emancipation Garden,* ☎ *800/372–8784.* ⊙ *Weekdays 8–6, Sun. 9–1.*

⑰ **Water Island.** Look about a quarter of a mile out in Charlotte Amalie harbor for a view of this island. It was once a peninsula of St. Thomas, but a channel was cut through so U.S. submarines could get to their base in a bay just to the west, known as Sub Base. On December 12, 1996, the U.S. Department of the Interior transferred 50-acres of the island, which included beaches and roads, to the territorial government, making it the fourth largest of the U.S. Virgin Islands. A ferry goes between Sub Base and the island several times daily at a cost of $3.

Around the Island

The rest of St. Thomas is best visited by car or taxi. Your rental car should come with a good map; if not, ask for one. The roads are marked with route numbers, but they're confusing and seem to switch numbers suddenly. If you stop to ask for directions, it's best to have your map in hand because the locals probably know the road you're looking for by another name. And remember to drive on the left.

As you head up into the hills, you may feel like you're driving on a roller coaster (made all the more scary because the roads have no shoulders), but you'll be rewarded with spectacular vistas, the best of which come on the North Side, although the others are all something to write home about. Look for glimpses of St. Croix some 40 mi to the south, and watch out for wandering cows and goats. Don't hesitate to take an unexpected turn off the main road—after all, discovery is what vacations are all about.

You'll find plenty of restaurants and watering holes spread out around the island, so food and drink won't be far no matter where you travel.

A GOOD DRIVE

Charlotte Amalie is the jumping off and landing spot for this island tour. Heading east out of town along the Waterfront Highway, you'll see what looks like a ski lift cutting an upward line into the hills from behind the main cruise-ship dock. Actually, it's the **Paradise Point Tramway** ①, a Swiss-built gondola that takes you to Paradise Point and a bird's-eye view of Charlotte Amalie harbor. To get to the tramway terminal, take a right turn at the Nelson Mandela Circle onto Route 30 and keep the Wendy's on your right. A few yards farther on the right is the **Havensight Mall** ②, where you'll find many of the same stores found in Charlotte Amalie. Also at the mall are the offices for the **Atlantis Submarine** ③, from which you can visit the underwater life of the islands without getting wet.

Past Havensight, Route 30 narrows as it winds along St. Thomas's southeast shore. Look for southerly vistas of the Caribbean Sea, and on a clear day, you may even spot St. Croix some 40 mi away. Marriott's Frenchman's Reef Beach Resort, Bolongo Bay Beach Club & Villas, and Mim's Seaside Bistro are along this stretch of Route 30, although you can't see them from the road because they're nestled by the beach.

Just before Route 30 intersects Route 32, you'll pass the **Clinton Phipps Racetrack** ④, where haphazard scheduled races turn into community celebrations. Take a right turn onto Route 32 and head east toward Red Hook. Less than 30 years ago, this was a dirt road that meandered out to a few scattered houses. Today the East End is growing fast, becoming home to most of the island's boating and resort communities. V.I. Ecotours conducts kayak paddles through the mangrove swamps that line the right side of the road. About a mile farther east of V.I. Ecotours, take a right turn for a detour to **Compass Point** ⑤, home to a fair-size marina, several shops, and restaurants. Just before entering Red Hook, Route 32 makes a three-way fork. To the right, you'll find a number of resorts—Secret Harbour Beach Resort and Secret Harbourview Villas, the Sea Horse Cottages, the Anchorage condominiums, Elysian Beach Resort, and the Ritz-Carlton. Straight ahead is the entrance to **Virgin Islands National Park Headquarters** ⑥, a good place for a picnic lunch. Red Hook itself is to the left.

Red Hook ⑦ has grown from a sleepy little town to an increasingly self-sustaining village. Park your car in the public lot or the private lot across the street—about $5 for the entire day—for a ferry trip to St. John, only 20 minutes by boat, but light years away in ambience. The ferry leaves at 6:30 AM, 7:30 AM, and on the hour until midnight.

North of Red Hook, and past the Sapphire Beach Resort & Marina, the road turns into Route 38. If you're on St. Thomas at full moon, grab the champagne (and the bug spray) and head out to **Sapphire Beach** where the moon rising out of the sea illuminates the beach in a most romantic light. Continuing along Route 38, you'll pass the Colony Point Pleasant Resort, Wyndham Sugar Bay Beach Club & Resort, and Renaissance Grand Beach Resort, before coming to the right turn in Smith Bay that will take you past Romano's restaurant and out to **Coki Point** ⑧ and the **Coral World Marine Park** ⑨. A few yards north of the beach entrance, on Route 38, pick up a sampling of juicy mangoes, ripe papayas, and super-sweet midget finger bananas from the open-air tropical fruit stands.

Once past Smith Bay, you'll climb Cassi Hill, where spectacular views of the neighboring B.V.I. are out the back window. If you continue straight ahead on Route 38, you'll enter the Tutu Valley, where **Tillett Gardens** ⑩, Four Winds Shopping Plaza, and the Tutu Park Mall are located. To continue on a driving tour around the island, take a sharp right turn on Route 42.

Because the north shore receives more rain than the Caribbean side of the island, the vegetation here is much more lush. Route 42 passes by the Mahogany Run Golf Course, then at a T-intersection, a right turn on Route 35 leads to **Magens Bay Beach** ⑪. Following Route 35 back up from the beach, turn right at the intersection and onto Route 40. **Drake's Seat** ⑫ is ahead on the right. From this crow's nest spot, see Magens Bay and Mahogany Run to the north, the B.V.I. and Drake's Passage to the east, and, off to the west, Mountain Top, Hull Bay, and such smaller islands as the Inner and Outer Brass islands. Continue west, following Route 40 as it makes a hairpin zig to the left (straight ahead is Route 37, which detours to **Hull Bay** ⑬), then zag to the right to the **Estate St. Peter Greathouse Botanical Gardens** ⑭. Follow Route 40 to a four-way intersection, turn left on Route 33 and see St. Thomas's most spectacular view from **Mountain Top** ⑮.

Coming back to the four-way intersection, take Route 33 and continue along the lush green residential districts of the north side. The attractions are natural here—breathtaking views and junglelike foliage sometimes so big and dense that it would make a perfect set for Disney's movie *Honey I Shrunk the Kids*. Green thumbers may want to stop at one of the nurseries along the way; try Bryan's. Food lovers should stop at Ferrari's restaurant to take note of the nightly dinner specials.

Continuing west, turning onto Route 301 then Route 30, you'll come to **Brewer's Beach** ⑯, a popular spot with students at the nearby University of the Virgin Islands. Across from Brewer's is the entrance to the **Reichhold Center for the Arts** ⑰, an amphitheater offering everything from Ray Charles to the Puerto Rican Symphony, local beauty pageants, and the yearly Agricultural Fair in November. Route 30 past the University will take you to Veterans Drive, which skirts the Cyril E. King International Airport and Lindberg Bay Beach, where the Emerald Beach and Island Beachcomber resorts are located.

End your island tour by turning into the delightfully quaint **Frenchtown** ⑱. Reward yourself for braving the hairpin turns and stop in at Betsy's Bar. You'll find imaginative mixed drinks, such as the Cruzan rum–based Native Virgin Islander or Passion Fruit Margarita, fresh seafood from Lisa's kitchen, and enough good conversation to make you want to stay in the islands forever.

TIMING

Allow yourself a full day to explore St. Thomas by car, especially if you want to stop for picture taking or to enjoy a light bite or refreshing swim along the way. Most of the cruise-ship passengers head out on island tours during the morning, so this is the time when north-side attractions such as Mountain Top and Drake's Seat tend to be jammed. Drive out east first and you'll be more likely to have the north side to yourself come afternoon. Both Coki Point and Magens Bay beaches have changing facilities, so there's no need to wear your swimsuit all day. Remember that most of the gas stations are on the more populated east end of the island, so fill up before heading to the north side.

SIGHTS TO SEE

☝ ❸ ***Atlantis* Submarine.** Probably the only way any of us are going to go 150 ft underwater, this submarine carries 46 passengers on a two-hour ride; it's air-conditioned, and there's a surface vessel that maintains constant radio contact. While submerged, you may see sting-rays, turtles, colorful coral, and more fish than any aquarium ever imagined. Watch for the remains of the *Michelle,* and an occasional lemon shark. Children's admission is significantly lower than adults'. ⊠ *Havensight Mall,* ☎ *800/253–0493.* ☞ *$72.*

☝ ⑯ **Brewer's Beach.** If you're hungry, trucks selling lunch, snacks, and drinks often park along the road bordering this long strand of powdery white beach. ⊠ *Rte. 30 near the airport.*

❹ **Clinton Phipps Racetrack.** Scheduled races are held here, especially on local holidays, with sanctioned betting. Be prepared for large crowds; it's a popular sport. ⊠ *Rte. 30 at Nadir,* ☎ *809/775–4555.*

☝ ❽ **Coki Point.** Snorkel the reefs at its eastern and western ends. You may want to dash in for a swim or just do some people-watching while nibbling on a meat pâté snack (a fried meat- or conch-filled pie), which you can buy from one of the vendors. Don't leave valuables unattended in your car or on the beach at Coki Point. ⊠ *Turn north off Rte. 38.*

⑤ Compass Point. It's fun to park your car and walk around here. The boaters—many of whom have sailed here from points around the globe—are easy to engage in conversation. ⊠ *Turn south off Red Hook Rd. at well-marked entrance road just east of Independent Boat Yard.*

⑨ Coral World Marine Park. Coral World, at Coki Point, is home to a three-level underwater observatory (call ahead for shark-feeding times), the world's largest reef tank, and an aquarium with more than 20 TV-size tanks providing capsulated views of life in the waters of the Virgin Islands and around the world. Coral World's staff will answer your questions about the turtles, iguanas, parrots, and flamingos that inhabit the park, and there's a restaurant, souvenir shop, and the world's only underwater mailbox, from which you can send postcards. ⊠ *Turn north off Smith Bay Rd. at sign,* ☎ *809/775–1555.*

⑫ Drake's Seat. Sir Francis Drake was supposed to have kept watch over his fleet and looked for enemy ships of the Spanish fleet from this vantage point. The panoramic vista is especially breathtaking (and romantic) at dusk, and if you arrive late in the day you'll miss the hordes of day-trippers on taxi tours who stop at Drake's Seat to take a picture and buy a T-shirt from one of the many vendors. By afternoon the crowd thins and most of the vendors are gone. ⊠ *Rte. 40.*

⑭ Estate St. Peter Greathouse Botanical Gardens. Perched on a mountainside 1,000 ft above sea level, with views of more than 20 other islands and islets, is this unusual spot where you can wander through a gallery displaying local art, sip a complimentary rum or virgin punch while looking out at the view, or follow a nature trail that leads through nearly 200 varieties of tropical trees and plants, including an orchid jungle. ⊠ *Rte. 40, St. Peter Mountain Rd.,* ☎ *809/774–4999.* ☞ *$8.* ☉ *Mon.–Sat. 9–4:30.*

⑱ Frenchtown. Popular with tourists for its several bars and restaurants, Frenchtown also serves as home to the descendants of immigrants from St. Barthélemy (St. Barts). You can watch them pull up their boats and display their catch of the day along the Waterfront. Frenchtown's harbor has an abundance of yellowtail, parrot fish, and oldwife nearly as colorful as the fishermen's small boats. If you want to get a feel for the residential district of Frenchtown, walk west to some of the town's winding streets, where the tiny wood houses have been passed down from generation to generation. ⊠ *Turn south off Waterfront Hwy. at the U.S. Post Office.*

② Havensight Mall. If you're not up for the crowds on Charlotte Amalie's Main Street, do your shopping here. Just about all the major stores have branches to cater to cruise-ship passengers who disembark nearby. You'll find the Dockside Book Shop, Havensight Market, and offices for *Atlantis* submarine here, too. ⊠ *Rte. 30 at Havensight.*

⑬ Hull Bay. You may come across the fishing boats and homes of the descendants of settlers from the French West Indies who fled to St. Thomas more than 200 years ago. If you have the opportunity to engage them in conversation, you will hear speech patterns slightly different from those of other St. Thomians. Hull Bay, with its rougher Atlantic surf and relative isolation, is one of the best surfing spots on St. Thomas. Take a break from the rigors of sightseeing at the **Hull Bay Hideaway,** a laid-back beach bar where a local band plays rock and roll on Sunday afternoons. ⊠ *Rte. 37.*

⑪ Magens Bay Beach. Popular with tourists and locals, it is the island's busiest beach. It's often listed among the world's most beautiful beaches, and on weekends and holidays it hops with groups partying under the sheds. There's also an outdoor bar, bathhouses, a nature trail, and a snack bar. ⊠ *Take Rte. 35 until it ends at admission booth.* 🎟 *$1.*

NEED A
BREAK? Do as the locals do and stop in for an afternoon delight at **Udder Delight,** after a vigorous swim at Magens Bay. This one-room shop next to St. Thomas Dairies serves up a Virgin Islands' tradition—a milk shake enlivened with a splash of Cruzan rum. Kids can enjoy virgin shakes, with a touch of soursop, mango, or banana flavoring.

🐾 ⓯ **Mountain Top.** Don't forget to stop for a banana daiquiri and spectacular views from the observation deck more than 1,500 ft above sea level. There are also a number of shops selling everything from Caribbean art to nautical antiques, ship models, and T-shirts. Kids will like talking to the tropical parrots—and hearing them answer back. ⊠ *Head north off Rte. 33; look for signs.*

🐾 ❶ **Paradise Point Tramway.** Fly skyward in a gondola straight up the hill to Paradise Point, a scenic overlook with breathtaking views of Charlotte Amalie and the harbor. There are several shops, a bar, and a restaurant. ⊠ *Rte. 30 at Havensight,* ☎ *809/774–9809.* 🎟 *$10.* ☉ *Daily 7:30–4:30.*

❼ **Red Hook.** This busy shopping village has several small branches of some Charlotte Amalie shops, including Little Switzerland, at the newly expanded American Yacht Harbor. There are also a deli and candy store, Tickles Dockside Pub, and Mackenzie's Restaurant. Both pub and restaurant serve burgers, salads, and sandwiches. There are more restaurants (try the Blue Marlin), two small grocery stores (including the Marina Market), and a few shops spread up and down the busy road. Visit with the fishing and sailing charter crews tending their boats along the docks.

NEED A
BREAK? Walk up to the second floor of the American Yacht Harbor building and cross to the marina side. From this large open-air deck, you'll see a sea of sailboat masts during the winter charter season and sky-high flybridges on million-dollar sportfishing rigs when summer marlin mania peaks. A rising moon at dusk adds just the right romantic slant to launch a wonderful evening at nearby restaurants.

⓱ **Reichhold Center for the Arts.** This open-air amphitheater has its more expensive seats covered by a roof. Schedules vary so check the local paper to see what's on when you're in town. ⊠ *Rte. 30 across from Brewers Beach,* ☎ *809/693–1559.*

⓾ **Tillett Gardens.** Clustered in a booming local shopping area, you'll find a colony where local artisans craft stained glass, pottery, gold jewelry, and ceramics. Tillett's paintings and silk-screened fabrics are also on display and for sale. The gardens encircle a shaded courtyard with fountains and Polli's, an outdoor Mexican restaurant. ⊠ *Rte. 38 across from Four Winds Shopping Center.*

❻ **Virgin Islands National Park Headquarters.** This park facility consists of a dock, a small grassy area with picnic tables, and a visitor center where maps and brochures are available. Iguanas are common here. If you see one, hold out a hibiscus flower, which is this prehistoric-looking creature's favorite food. ⊠ *Turn east off Rte. 32 at sign,* ☎ *809/775–6238.* ☉ *Weekdays 8–5.*

While feeding the iguanas, take time out for a picnic on the national park grounds. There's nothing better than paper-bagged veggie fare from the Grateful Deli in Red Hook. Try the Speedway Boogie Burrito, a combination of fresh vegetables topped with hummus and wrapped up in a flour tortilla or pita, or a U.F.O. Tofu, celestially seasoned baked tofu topped with lettuce, tomato, and avocado on whole wheat bread. Fresh salads, breads, and juices add to the perfect picnic meal.

St. Thomas A to Z

Emergencies
Police: ☎ 911.

Hospital: The emergency room of the **Roy L. Schneider Hospital & Community Health Center** (☎ 809/776–8311) in Sugar Estate, Charlotte Amalie, is open 24 hours a day.

Air Ambulance: Bohlke International Airways (☎ 809/778–9177) operates out of the airport in St. Croix; **Medical Air Services** (☎ 809/777–8580 or 800/966–6272) has its Caribbean headquarters in St. Thomas; and **Air Ambulance Network** (☎ 800/327–1966) also serves the area from Florida.

Coast Guard: For emergencies call the **Marine Safety Detachment** (☎ 809/776–3497) from 7 to 3:30 weekdays. If there is no answer, call the **Rescue Coordination Center** (☎ 809/729–6770) in San Juan, open 24 hours a day.

Pharmacies: Sunrise Pharmacy is open at Red Hook (☎ 809/775–6600). **Havensight Pharmacy** is in the Havensight Mall (☎ 809/776–1235). **Kmart** operates a pharmacy inside its Tutu Park Mall (☎ 809/777–3854).

Getting Around
BY BUS
Public transportation is a viable alternative to taxis. Service runs from town to the eastern and western ends of the island. There is no service to the north. Buses run about every 20 minutes from clearly marked VITRAN bus stops. Fares are $1 between outlying areas and town and 75¢ in town. Ask the bus driver for a schedule.

BY CAR
Some words of warning about driving in St. Thomas: Driving is on the left side of the road, and everybody here is in a hurry—though it's hard to imagine what the big rush is. Just drive defensively and don't let the person on your tail bother you.

Traffic can get pretty bad, but it needn't get in your way. Avoid driving in town at rush hour (7–9 AM and 4:30–6 PM), and don't drive along the Waterfront any more than you have to, because traffic there is frequently bumper-to-bumper. Instead, find the routes (starting from the East End, Route 38 to 42 to 40 to 33) that go up and over the mountain and then drop you back onto the Veteran's Highway.

If you are going to drive, be sure to get one of the new maps that include both the route number and the name of the road that is used by locals. The standard U.S.V.I. map does a pretty good job, but the "Island Map of St. Thomas" (✉ Earle Publishing, Box 1859, St. Thomas 00801, ☎ 809/777–6557) gives even more detailed names as well as landmarks. It's generally available anywhere you find tourist maps and guidebooks.

Car Rentals: You can rent a car from **ABC Rentals** (☎ 809/776–1222 or 800/524–2080), **Anchorage E-Z Car** (☎ 809/775–6255 or 800/524–2027), **Avis** (☎ 809/774–1468 or 800/331–1084), **Budget** (☎ 809/776–5774 or 800/527–0700), **Cowpet Rent-a-Car** (☎ 809/775–7376 or 800/524–2072), **Dependable Car Rental** (☎ 809/774–2253 or 800/522–3076), **Discount** (☎ 809/776–4858), **Hertz** (☎ 809/774–1879 or 800/654–3131), or **Thrifty** (☎ 809/775–7282).

BY TAXI

In town, taxi stands are across from **Emancipation Garden** (in front of Little Switzerland, behind the post office) and along the Waterfront. But you probably won't have to look for a stand, as taxis are plentiful and routinely cruise the streets. Walking down Main Street, you'll be asked "Back to ship?" often enough to make you never want to carry another shopping bag.

Away from Charlotte Amalie, you'll find taxis available at all major hotels and at such public beaches as Magens Bay and Coki Point. Calling taxis will work, too, but allow plenty of time.

Like cabbies the world over, St. Thomas drivers run the gamut from the friendly to the rude. Nine times out of 10 you'll be treated well, but if you are cheated or treated rudely, take the license number and report the driver to the **V.I. Taxi Commission** (☎ 809/774–4550).

Guided Tours

V.I. Taxi Association City-Island Tour (☎ 809/774–4550) gives a two-hour $20 tour for two people in an open-air safari bus or enclosed van; aimed at cruise-ship passengers, this tour includes stops at Drake's Seat and Mountain Top. For just a bit more money (about $30 for two) you can hire a taxi and ask the driver to take the opposite route so you'll avoid the crowds. But do see Mountain Top: The view is wonderful.

Tropic Tours (☎ 809/774–1855 or 800/524–4334) offers half-day shopping and sightseeing tours of St. Thomas by bus six days a week ($20 per person). The full-day St. John tour ($60 per person) includes snorkeling and lunch and is offered every day. Tropic picks up at all the major hotels.

The **St. Thomas–St. John Vacation Handbook,** available free at hotels and the two tourist centers (☞ Visitor Information, *below*), has an excellent self-guided walking tour of Charlotte Amalie. Bird-watching, whale-watching, and a chance to wait hidden on a beach while the magnificent hawksbill turtles come ashore to lay their eggs are all open to visitors. Write the **St. Croix Environmental Association** (✉ Arawak Bldg. #3, Gallows Bay, St. Croix, 00820 ☎ 809/773–1989) or **EAST** (✉ Environmental Association of St. Thomas–St. John, Box 12379, St. Thomas 00801, ☎ 809/776–1976) for more information on hikes and special programs, or check the community calendar in the *Daily News* for up-to-date information.

Seaborne Seaplane Adventures (✉ 5305 Long Bay Rd., ☎ 809/777–4491) offers narrated "flightseeing" tours of the U.S. and British Virgin Islands. Extra-large windows give exceptional views. The 40-minute 'round-the-island tour is $89 per person. Service to St. Croix is $100 per person round-trip, and flights between St. Thomas and either West End, Tortola, or Leverick Bay, Virgin Gorda, range from $59 to $89 per person one-way.

The **Kon Tiki** party boat (✉ Gregorie Channel East dock, ☎ 809/775–5055) is a kick. Put your sophistication aside, climb on this big palm-thatch raft, and dip into bottomless barrels of rum punch along with a couple hundred of your soon-to-be closest friends. Dance to the steel-drum band, sun on the roof (watch out; you'll fry), and join the limbo dancing on the way home from an afternoon of swimming and beachcombing at Honeymoon Beach on Water Island. This popular three-hour afternoon excursion, with a mixture of cruise-ship passengers and hotel visitors, costs $29 for adults, $15 for children under 13 (although few come to this party).

Visitor Information

The **U.S. Virgin Islands Division of Tourism** has an office in St. Thomas (⌧ Box 6400, Charlotte Amalie, 00804, ☎ 809/774–8784 or 800/372–8784, ℻ 809/774–4390). There is a **Visitor's Center** in downtown Charlotte Amalie (☞ *see* Exploring), and a **Welcome Center** for cruise-ship passengers at Havensight Mall.

The **National Park Service** has a visitor center across the harbor from the ferry dock at Red Hook. There is an **American Express** office on St. Thomas (⌧ Guardian Bldg., across from Havensight Mall, ☎ 809/774–1855).

ST. CROIX

By Fredreka Schouten

Updated by Lynda Lohr

St. Croix, the largest of the three U.S.V.I. with 84 sq mi, lies 40 mi to the south of St. Thomas. But unlike the bustling island-city of St. Thomas, its harbor teeming with cruise ships and its shopping district crowded with bargain hunters, St. Croix lives at a slower pace and with a more diverse economy, mixing tourism with light and heavy industry on rolling land that was once covered with waving carpets of sugarcane.

St. Croix's population has grown dramatically over the last 30 years, and its diversity reflects the island's varied history. The cultivation of sugarcane was more important here than on St. Thomas or St. John and continued as an economic force into the 1960s. After the end of slavery in 1848, the need for workers brought waves of immigrants from other Caribbean islands, particularly nearby Vieques, Puerto Rico. St. Croix was divided into plantation estates, and the ruins of plantation great houses and more than 100 sugar mills that dot the island's landscape are evidence of an era when St. Croix rivaled Barbados as the greatest producer of sugar in the West Indies.

Tourism began and boomed in the 1960s, bringing visitors—as well as migrants—from the mainland United States (referred to by locals as Continentals). In the late 1960s and early 1970s industrial development brought St. Croix yet another wave of immigrants. This time they came mostly from Trinidad and St. Lucia, to seek work at the Hess oil refinery or at the aluminum-processing plants that dominate the South Shore.

St. Croix is a study of contrasting beauty. The island is not as hilly as St. Thomas or St. John. A lush rain forest envelops the northwest, the East End is dry and barren, and palm-lined beaches with startlingly clear aquamarine water ring the island. The island's capital, Christiansted, is a restored Danish port on a coral-bound bay on the northeastern shore. The tin-roofed, 18th-century buildings in both Christiansted and Frederiksted, on the western end of the island, are either pale yellow, pink, or ocher, resplendent with bright blazes of bougainvillea and hibiscus. The prosperous Danes built well (and more than once—both towns were devastated by fire in the 19th century), using imported bricks or blocks cut from coral, fashioning covered sidewalks (called galleries here) and stately colonnades, and leaving an enduring cosmopolitan air as their legacy.

Lodging

From plush resorts to simple beachfront digs, St. Croix's variety of accommodations is bound to suit every type of traveler. Room rates on St. Croix are competitive with those on other islands, and those who travel off-season will enjoy substantial price reductions. Many properties offer honeymoon and dive packages that are also big money savers.

All hotels have air-conditioning and cable television, unless otherwise noted.

Christiansted

$$–$$$ 🏨 **Hilty House.** Tucked away on a hilltop above Christiansted, this small bed-and-breakfast is a tranquil alternative to beach and in-town accommodations. Unless you want to spend your entire vacation reading or sunning at the large tiled pool, you'll need a rental car for trips to the beach, dining out, and shopping. Built on the ruins of an 18th-century rum factory, this property has the feel of a Florentine villa. Look forward to patios perfect for whiling away an afternoon in the sun or shade, and an immense, high-ceilinged great room to gather with other guests. It has four charming guest rooms and three cozy efficiency cottages next to the main house. Affable owners Jacqueline and Hugh Hoare-Ward live on the property. A prix-fixe dinner is served in the great room on Monday only to guests and locals alike (reservations essential). ✉ *Box 26077, Gallows Bay 00824,* ☎ ℻ *809/773–2594. 4 rooms with bath, 3 cottages. Dining room, pool. No credit cards.*

$$–$$$ 🏨 **King's Alley Hotel.** Right in the center of Christiansted's hustle and
★   bustle, this small hotel provides convenience and charm. It puts you within walking distance of many of the island's best restaurants and finest shops. The 12 premium rooms in the just-completed section across the courtyard feature mahogany four-poster beds, Mexican tile floors, and Indonesian print fabrics. French doors open onto balconies with a view of the waterfront and the shopping arcade below. The 23 standard rooms in the hotel's older section are a tad less interesting but still attractive. The staff can arrange all watersports, tours, golf, and tennis. The hotel is part of the recently reconstructed Kings Alley Complex. ✉ *57 King St., Box 4120, 00822,* ☎ *809/773–0103 or 800/ 843–3574,* ℻ *809/773–4431. 35 rooms. Pool. AE, D, DC, MC, V.*

$$ 🏨 **Hotel Caravelle.** The charming three-story Caravelle is an excellent bet for moderately priced lodging in Christiansted. All rooms have refrigerators, television with free HBO, and telephones. They're decorated in tasteful dusky blues and whites, with floral-print bedspreads and curtains, and have vaulted ceilings. Baths are clean and new, though the unique tile in the showers is a holdover from when the hotel was built in 1968. Superior rooms overlook the harbor, but most rooms do have some sort of ocean view. Owners Sid and Amy Kalmans are friendly and helpful. The Seaport Grille, a casual terrace eatery, serves seafood and Continental cuisine. ✉ *44A Queen Cross St., 00820,* ☎ *809/773– 0687 or 800/524–0410,* ℻ *809/778–7004. 43 rooms, 1 2-bedroom suite. Restaurant, bar, pool, meeting room. AE, D, DC, MC, V.*

$–$$ 🏨 **King Christian Hotel.** This central Christiansted inn, a bright yellow, 250-year-old former warehouse, houses a row of shops and restaurants on the first floor, with guest rooms occupying the second and third floors. Pass through the small, nondescript lobby to reach a freshwater swimming pool ringed with teal-and-white patio furniture. The sun deck overlooks the pool on one side and the harbor on the other. White wicker furniture and bright pastels strike a pleasant note in the guest rooms, equipped with coffeemakers and refrigerators. Rooms on the south side overlook a noisy main street, but those facing the water are quiet and have balconies (for the best view, request Room 201, 202, 301, or 302).

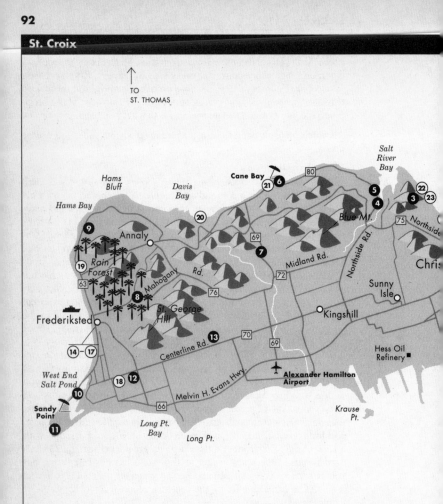

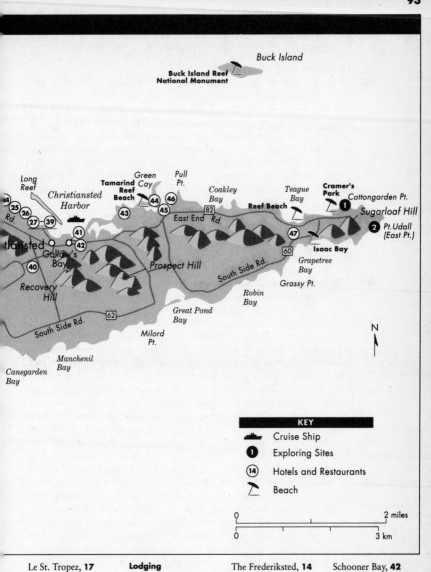

Le St. Tropez, **17**
Tivoli Gardens **34**
Top Hat, **35**
Tutto Bene, **36**
Villa Morales, **18**

Lodging
Buccaneer, **43**
Chenay Bay Beach
Resort, **46**
Club St. Croix, **26**
Colony Cove, **24**
Cormorant Beach
Club and Villas, **23**

The Frederiksted, **14**
Hibiscus Beach
Hotel, **22**
Hilty House, **40**
Hotel Caravelle, **37**
King Christian
Hotel, **38**
King's Alley
Hotel, **39**

Schooner Bay, **42**
Sprat Hall, **19**
Sugar Beach, **25**
Tamarind
Reef Hotel, **44**
Villa Madeleine, **47**
Waves at Cane
Bay, **21**
Westin Carambola
Beach Resort, **20**

⌧ *59 Kings Wharf, Box 3619, 00822-3619,* ☎ *809/773–2285 or 800/524–2012,* FAX *809/773–9411. 39 rooms. Pool. AE, D, DC, MC, V.*

The East End

$$$$ ⊞ **The Buccaneer.** This self-contained hotel on the grounds of an old 300-acre sugar plantation has it all. Look for palm-fringed sandy beaches, swimming pools, golf, all water sports, tennis, a nature and jogging trail, shopping arcade, health spa, and four restaurants. A palm tree–lined main drive leads to the large pink hotel at the top of a hill, and a number of smaller guest cottages, shops, and restaurants are scattered throughout the property's rolling, manicured lawns. The ambience is Mediterranean rather than tropical, with marble or colorful tile floors, four-poster beds and massive wardrobes of pale wood, pastel fabrics, and locally produced artwork. All rooms have such modern conveniences as hair dryers, refrigerators, and cable TV. Spacious bathrooms are noteworthy for their marble bench showers and double sinks. ⌧ *Box 25200, Gallows Bay 00824,* ☎ *809/773–2100 or 800/225–3881,* FAX *809/778–8215. 150 rooms. 4 restaurants, in-room safes, 2 pools, spa, 8 tennis courts, jogging, 3 beaches. AE, D, DC, MC, V.*

$$$$ ⊞ **Villa Madeleine.** A West Indian plantation great house is the centerpiece
★ of this exquisite hotel, one of St. Croix's most attractive. Richly upholstered furniture, Oriental rugs, teal walls, and whimsically painted driftwood set the mood in the billiards room, the austere library, and the sitting room. The great house sits atop a hill, and private guest villas are scattered in both directions, with a spectacular view of both the north and south shores. The villa decor is modern tropical: rattan and plush cushions, rocking chairs, and in many villas, bamboo four-poster beds. Each villa has a full kitchen and a private swimming pool. Special touches in the rooms include pink-marble showers and, in many cottages, hand-painted floral borders along the walls, done in splashy tropical colors. Enjoy fine dining on the terrace at Cafe Madeleine or steak at the Turf Club. ⌧ *Box 26160, Teague Bay, 00824,* ☎ *809/778–8782 or 800/496–7379,* FAX *809/773–2150. 43 villas. 2 restaurants, bar, tennis court, billiards, library, concierge. AE, D, DC, MC, V.*

$$$–$$$$ ⊞ **Chenay Bay Beach Resort.** Although the rooms here are rather basic, the beachfront location and complimentary tennis and water-sports equipment (including kayaks) make this resort a good value for families and active folks. Rooms have ceramic-tile floors, bright-peach or yellow walls, and rattan furnishings. Kitchenettes and front porches add versatility to each room. Gravel paths connect the terraced gray-and-white wood cottages with the shore, where you'll find a large L-shape pool, a protected beach, a picnic area with barbecues, and a casual restaurant. The all-you-can eat pasta night is a bargain. In the summer months the hotel offers a free morning camp for children 3–12. In the spring and fall, parents get two free hours of babysitting per day. ⌧ *Box 24600, 00824,* ☎ *809/773–2918 or 800/548–4457. 50 rooms. Restaurant, bar, picnic area, pool, 2 tennis courts. AE, MC, V.*

$$$ ⊞ **Tamarind Reef Hotel.** A casual, seaside place, this small motel-like property provides good snorkeling as well as excellent sunning at its large pool and sandy beach, but serious swimmers won't be happy because the reef comes right to the shore, making it hard to even get in the water and too shallow for swimming. The spacious, modern rooms have rattan furniture and tropical-print drapes and bedspreads, and all have either a terrace or deck with views of the sea and St. Croix's sister islands to the north. Many of the rooms come with basic kitchenettes, making this a good spot for those who like to prepare light meals. Three rooms have handicapped facilities. There's a bar and snack bar just off the beach and a restaurant at the adjacent Green Cay Marina. ⊠ *5001 Tamarind Reef, 00820,* ☎ *809/773–4455,* FAX *809/773–3989 or 800/619–0014. 46 rooms. Snack bar, pool. AE, MC, V.*

Frederiksted

$–$$ 🏨 **The Frederiksted.** Don't be put off by the neat but unprepossessing exterior. This modern four-story inn is your best bet for lodging in Frederiksted. In the inviting, outdoor tile courtyard, the glass tables and yellow chairs of the hotel's bar and restaurant crowd around a small freshwater swimming pool. Yellow-striped awnings and tropical greenery create a sunny, welcoming atmosphere. Steps at one side of the courtyard lead to the second floor's main desk and sun deck. The bright, pleasant guest rooms are outfitted with bar refrigerators and microwaves and are decorated with light-color rattan furniture and print bedspreads. Bathrooms are on the small side but are bright and clean. The nicest rooms are those with an ocean view; these are also the only rooms that have a bathtub in addition to a shower. ⊠ *20 Strand St., 00840,* ☎ *809/772–0500 or 800/595–9519,* FAX *809/772–0500, ext. 399. 40 rooms. Restaurant, bar, pool. AE, D, DC, MC, V.*

The North Shore

$$$$ 🏨 **Cormorant Beach Club and Villas.** Breeze-bent palm trees, hammocks, the thrum of North Shore waves, and a blissful sense of respected privacy rule here. The open-air public spaces are filled with tropical plants and comfy wicker furniture in cool peach and mint-green shades. Ceiling fans and tile floors add to the atmosphere at this resort, which resembles a series of connected Moorish villas. The beachfront rooms are lovely, with dark wicker furniture, pale-peach walls, white-tile floors, and floral-print spreads and curtains; all rooms have a patio or balcony and telephone, cable TV, and electronic safes. Bathrooms stand out for their coral rock–wall showers, marble-top double sinks, and brass fixtures. Morning coffee and afternoon tea are set out daily in the building breezeways; the airy, high-ceiling restaurant is one of St. Croix's best. The hotel offers partial and all-inclusive meal plans that include all drinks. ⊠ *4126 La Grande Princesse, Christiansted 00820,* ☎ *809/778–8920 or 800/548–4460,* FAX *809/778–9218. 34 rooms, 4 suites, 14 2- and 3-bedroom villas. Restaurant, bar, pool, 2 tennis courts, croquet, beach, snorkeling. AE, DC, MC, V.*

$$$$ 🏨 **Westin Carambola Beach Resort.** The 26 quaint, two-story red-★ roofed villas, including one that's wheelchair-accessible, are connected by lovely arcades that seem hacked from the luxuriant undergrowth. The rooms are identical; the only difference is the view—ocean or garden. Decor is Laura Ashley–style English country house, with rocking chairs and sofas upholstered in soothing floral patterns, terra-cotta floors, rough-textured ceramic lamps, and mahogany ceilings and furnishings. All have private patios and huge baths (showers only). The two-bedroom suite, with its 3-ft-thick plantation walls and large patio, is the *perfect* Caribbean family dwelling. There are two fine restaurants (the Sunday buffet brunch is legendary for its munificent table), an exquisite ecru beach, and lots of quiet nooks for a secluded drink. ⊠ *Box 3031, Kingshill 00851,* ☎ *809/778–3800 or 800/228–3000,* FAX *809/778–1682. 150 rooms, 1 2-bedroom cottage. 2 restaurants, deli, pool, 4 tennis courts, library. AE, D, DC, MC, V.*

$$$–$$$$ 🏨 **Hibiscus Beach Hotel.** This affordable, appealing property is set on the same stretch of palm tree–lined beach as its sister hotel, the Cormorant. Guest rooms at the Hibiscus Beach are divided among five two-story pink buildings, each named for a tropical flower. Most have views of the oceanfront, thanks to the staggered placement of the buildings at strategic angles, but request a room in the Hibiscus building—it's closest to the water. Rooms have welcome amenities such as cable TV, safe, and minibar, and are tastefully furnished: White tiled floors and

white walls are brightened with pink-striped curtains; bright, flowered bedspreads; and fresh-cut hibiscus blossoms. Bathrooms are clean but nondescript—both the shower stalls and the vanity mirrors are on the small side. Every unit has a roomy balcony that faces the sea. The staff is friendly and helpful, and the manager's party in the open-air bar-restaurant is a pleasant gathering. ⊠ *4131 Estate La Grande Princesse, Christiansted 00820-4441,* ☎ *809/773–4042 or 800/442–0121,* ℻ *809/773–7668. 37 rooms. Restaurant, minibar, in-room safes, pool, snorkeling. AE, D, MC, V.*

$$–$$$ ⊡ **Waves at Cane Bay.** The sound of crashing waves will lull you to sleep at this 12-room inn perched at the water's edge. It caters to couples as well as divers who take advantage of the world-famous Cane Bay Wall just 100 yards offshore. The hotel is rather isolated, and its beachfront is rocky, but Cane Bay Beach is right next door and there is a small patch of sand at poolside for sunbathing. The unusual pool was carved from the coral along the shore. The floor and one wall are concrete, but the seaside wall is made of natural coral, and the pool water is circulated as the waves crash dramatically over the side, creating a foamy whirlpool on blustery days. The two peach and mint-green buildings house enormous, balconied guest rooms done in cream and soft pastel prints, all with kitchens or kitchenettes. ⊠ *Box 1749, Kingshill 00851,* ☎ *809/778–1805 or 800/545–0603. 12 rooms, 8 with air-conditioning, 1 suite. Restaurant, bar, in-room safes, pool, snorkeling. AE, MC, V.*

The West End

$$–$$$ ⊡ **Sprat Hall.** This 20-acre seaside property more than a mile north of Frederiksted appeals to a special sort of guest, one who enjoys the vagaries of a visit to someone's home. Joyce Hurd presides over the slightly ramshackle 17th-century plantation where she was born. Some of the guest rooms in the rather cluttered antiques-filled great house have four-poster beds and planter's chairs. More modern rooms and cottages are spread out all over the estate. Only one of the great-house rooms has air-conditioning. The glorious strand of beach that runs north from Frederiksted sits a good hike down a gentle hill. Hurd conjures up dinner for guests and visitors, but you'll have to make your choice for dinner when she delivers your complimentary Continental breakfast. A rental car will give you more flexibility. The Hurd family also operates extensive horseback riding facilities here. ⊠ *Box 695, Frederiksted 00841,* ☎ *809/772–0305 or 800/843–3584. 9 rooms, 8 suites, 1 1-bedroom cottage, 2 2-bedroom cottages. Restaurant, beach, horseback riding. AE.*

Cottages and Condominiums

$$$–$$$$ ⊡ **Club St. Croix.** Popular with honeymooners, this condominium resort's studio, one-, and two-bedroom apartments are spacious and bright. Indian-print throw rugs and cushions complement the bamboo furniture and rough, white-tile floors; the modern decor is further highlighted by glass-top tables and mirrored closet doors. Penthouses have loft bedrooms reached by spiral staircases, and studios have Murphy beds in the sitting rooms. Every room has a full kitchen and a sun deck, with waterfront views of Christiansted and Buck Island. On the beach you'll find a poolside restaurant and bar and a dock. Although the rooms are well kept, the grounds could use a bit more attention. ⊠ *Estate Golden Rock, Christiansted 00820,* ☎ *809/773–4800 or 800/524–2025,* ℻ *809/778–4009. 54 suites. Restaurant, pool, 3 tennis courts, beach, meeting room. AE, D, MC, V.*

$$–$$$$ ⊡ **Sugar Beach.** On the beach on the north side of the island, Sugar Beach is just five minutes outside Christiansted. The apartments here, which range from studios to four bedrooms, are immaculate and breezy. Each has a large patio or balcony, all with good views of the ocean. The larger apartments have washer and dryer units, and all have full kitchens with microwaves. Though the exteriors of these condos are done in an ordinary beige stucco, the white interiors, all with cool, tropical furnishings, are lovely. The pool is built around the ruins of a 250-year-old sugar mill. ⊠ *Estate Golden Rock, Christiansted 00820,* ☎ *809/773–5345 or 800/524–2049,* FAX *809/773–1359. 46 apartments. Pool, beach, 2 tennis courts, meeting room. AE, D, MC, V.*

$$$ ☷ **Colony Cove.** Next door to Sugar Beach, Colony Cove offers a condominium-style resort alternative. Apartments here are sunny, tropical retreats done in pastel prints, rattan, and white tile. Each has two bedrooms, two baths, a balcony, full kitchen (so complete, it even has lasagna pans), and a washer and dryer. You'll find a large pool, watersports center, and tennis courts on the grounds, and you can walk along the beach to reach the restaurant next door. The most compelling reason to stay here, though, is manager Susan Ivey, a dedicated naturalist who grows herbal gardens throughout the grounds and often leads nature walks and informal ecology seminars. ⊠ *3221 Golden Rock, Christiansted 00820,* ☎ *809/773–1965 or 800/828–0746,* FAX *809/773–5397. 59 apartments. Snack bar, pool, 2 tennis courts. AE, MC, V.*

$$$ ☷ **Schooner Bay.** This red-roof condominium village climbs the hillside above Gallows Bay, just outside Christiansted. The modern apartments have balconies, full kitchens, and two or three bedrooms. The decor features floral fabrics and rattan, and the floors are covered in beige tile. All apartments have ceiling fans, air-conditioning in the bedrooms, washer and dryer, microwave oven, and dishwasher. The three-bedroom units have spiral staircases. Sun worshipers might be disappointed that the nearest beach is east, at the Buccaneer, but those with a yen to explore historic Christiansted will find this location ideal—within walking distance, yet away from the bustle of downtown. ⊠ *Schooner Bay, Gallows Bay, Christiansted 00820,* ☎ *809/773–4800, ext. 407, or 800/524–2025,* FAX *809/778-4009. 40 apartments. 2 pools, tennis court, snorkeling. AE, D, MC, V.*

Private Homes and Villas

Renting a private house gives you the convenience of home plus top-notch amenities. Many houses come with private pools, hot tubs, and deluxe furnishings. Most companies meet you at the airport, arrange for a rental car, and provide useful information to make your vacation more interesting. Call **The Collection** (☎ 609/751–2413), **Petan Corp./Rent A Villa** (☎ 800/533–6863), **Island Villas** (☎ 809/773–8821), **Teague Bay Properties** (☎ 809/773–4850), or **Richards & Ayer** (☎ 809/772–0420).

Dining

Seven flags have flown over St. Croix, and each has left its legacy in the island's cuisine. Visitors can feast on Italian, French, Danish, and American dishes; there are even Chinese and Mexican restaurants in Christiansted. Seafood, taken fresh from the waters around the island, is plentiful and always good; wahoo, mahimahi, and conch are popular. For a true island experience, stop in a local Cruzan restaurant to feast on goat stew, curry chicken, or fried pork chops. Regardless of where you eat, your meal will be an informal affair. Note that several hotels offer worthwhile all-inclusive packages with dine-around options at top island restaurants.

Christiansted

$$$$ ✕ **Top Hat.** Owned by a delightful Danish couple, this restaurant has
★ been in business since 1970 serving international cuisine with an em-

phasis on Danish specialties—roast duck stuffed with apples and prunes, *frikadeller* (savory meatballs in a tangy cocktail sauce), fried Camembert with lingonberries, and smoked eel. The old West Indian structure, complete with gingerbread trim, is nicely accented in gray, white, and pink. The salad bar features such Danish delights as herring in sour cream and duck liver pâté. ⊠ *52 Company St.,* ☎ *809/ 773–2346. AE, D, MC, V. Closed May–Aug. No lunch.*

$$$ ✕ **Antoine's.** Watch the seaplanes to St. Thomas take off and land while you enjoy your meal in this charming, open-air restaurant upstairs at the Anchor Inn. Chef Antoine Doos, a Swiss native, conjures up Austrian and German fare. If you like sauerbraten, knockwurst, or bratwurst, for instance, this is the place to go. Seafood lovers will also enjoy the selection: snapper, tuna, dolphin, and shrimp. ⊠ *58 King St.,* ☎ *809/773–0263. AE, MC, V.*

$$$ ✕ **Indies.** A historic courtyard, with cool green columns and handmade
★ floral-print tablecloths, is the setting for a wonderful experience: owner-chef Catherine Plav-Drigger's gourmet, island-inspired dishes. The menu changes each day to take advantage of the island's freshest bounties. Indulge in the crab cakes or the spicy Caribbean spring rolls to start, then the spice-rubbed chicken (every bite reveals a new, subtle flavor), or the dolphin rub down baked in coconut milk, ginger, tomato, and spicy peppers. Enjoy live jazz Saturday evenings. ⊠ *55– 56 Company St.,* ☎ *809/692–9440. AE, MC, V. No lunch weekends.*

$$$ ✕ **Kendricks.** This restaurant, a longtime favorite with locals, moved
★ its great food and tranquil ambience to Gallows Bay, and didn't miss a beat. At the upstairs restaurant, waiters in bow ties dote on customers seated at tables laid with crisp linens and fine china. The menu is stylish Continental, and dishes are lovingly presented. Try the lobster spring rolls with warm ginger and soy butter to start, or the silken cream of shiitake soup. Move on to the house specialty, roasted pecan-crusted pork loin with ginger mayonnaise. At the downstairs café, enjoy the nightly jazz band while you dine on lighter fare, such as fettucini with grilled Portobello mushrooms. ⊠ *12 Chandlers Wharf, Gallows Bay,* ☎ *809/773–9199. AE, MC, V. Closed Sun.*

$$ ✕ **Bombay Club.** This dimly lit boîte plastered with bright local artwork is in a historic pub. The bar, with its cool, exposed stone walls, is a favored haven for expatriates. The typical pub grub includes fine salads, nachos, scrumptious buffalo wings, pastas, and simple chicken and steak dishes. Don't pass up the heavenly stuffed crabs with roast garlic herb sauce. ⊠ *5A King St.,* ☎ *809/773–1838. MC, V. No lunch weekends.*

$$ ✕ **Camille's.** This tiny, lively spot, whose warm, exposed brick walls are splashed with colorful island prints, is perfect for lunch or a light supper. Sandwiches and burgers are the big draw here, though the daily seafood special, often wahoo or mahimahi, is also popular. ⊠ *Company and Queen Cross Sts.,* ☎ *809/773–2985. MC, V. Closed Sun.*

$$ ✕ **Club Comanche.** The atmosphere is very friendly and casual at this upstairs terrace restaurant, where the decor includes an outrigger canoe hanging from the ceiling. The curry of beef fillet is a popular dish, as are the stuffed shrimp Savannah and such reliable old standbys as shrimp Louis and filet mignon béarnaise. There are also about 15 appetizers on the varied menu. ⊠ *Strand St.,* ☎ *809/773–2665. AE, MC, V. Closed Sun.*

$$ ✕ **Harvey's.** The plain, even dowdy room contains just 12 tables, and plastic, flowered tablecloths constitute the sole attempt at decor. But who cares? The delicious local food ranks among the island's best. Daily specials such as mouth-watering goat stew and melting whelks in butter, served with heaping helpings of rice, fungi, and vegetables, are listed on the blackboard. Genial owner Sarah Harvey takes great pride in her kitchen, bustling out from behind the stove to chat and urge you to eat up. ⊠ *11B Company St.,* ☎ *809/773–3433. No credit cards. Closed Sun. No dinner Mon.–Wed.*

$$ ✕ **Tivoli Gardens.** Alfresco dining, fresh breezes, and bowers of hang-
★ ing plants make this restaurant in the heart of Christiansted into a true garden. Its Continental menu features steak and lobster, and more lob-ster. Start with fresh lobster in cream sauce with hints of garlic and herbs stuffed into mushrooms. To make lobster eating easy, the chef takes all the succulent meat from a whole lobster, puts it all into half the lobster's shell, and drips butter over top. For dessert, try the bittersweet choco-late velvet—a chocoholic's dream that's closer to candy than cake. ⊠ *39 Strand St.,* ☎ *809/773–6782. AE, MC, V. No lunch weekends.*

$$ ✕ **Tutto Bene.** Its yellow walls, brightly striped cushions, and painted trompe l'oeil tables make Tutto Bene look more like a sophisticated Mex-ican cantina than an Italian cucina. A quick inspection of the menu, how-ever, will clear up any confusion. Written on hanging mirrors is the daily menu, which includes such inventive creations as veal chop with sun-dried tomatoes, crab-meat ravioli, and zuppa di mare, a combination of clams, shrimp, and mussels poached in white wine served over capellini. Desserts, prepared by one of the island's finest pastry chefs, are top-notch. ⊠ *2 Company St.,* ☎ *809/773–5229. AE, D, MC, V.*

$ ✕ **Java Mon.** The new in-spot for quick meals, Java Mon has a 1950s decor that mimics the Norman Rockwell magazine covers on the wall. As soon as owner Todd Phillips opened this hole-in-the wall on the Chris-tiansted waterfront in July 1996, it attracted a varied following of folks looking for take-out or eat-in dreadlox and bagels, roast pork Cubano sandwiches, black cherry cheesecake, and cups of espresso and cap-puccino. Sun-dried-tomato cream cheese provides an interesting addition to a pedestrian bagel. ⊠ *59 Kings Wharf,* ☎ *809/773–2285, ext. 119. No credit cards. No dinner.*

East End

$$$$ ✕ **The Galleon.** A popular spot with residents and visitors to the East End, this dockside restaurant offers something for everyone. Start with the Caesar salad or gravlox (fresh salmon with dill and pepper). Pasta lovers should sample the eggplant ravioli, an interesting combination of homemade pasta filled with grilled eggplant, Parmesan, ricotta, and mozzarella cheese. The osso buco and rack of lamb are legendary. ⊠ *Teague Bay, (take Rte.82 out of Christiansted and turn left at sign for Green Cay Marina),* ☎ *809/773–9949. AE, V. Dinner only.*

$$$$ ✕ **Great House at Villa Madeleine.** This elegant restaurant, part of the Villa Madeleine resort nestled in the hills on St. Croix's East End, serves such diverse cuisine as chicken alla Bolognese, swordfish medallions sautéed with green tomato and asparagus, and a number of fine beef dishes. The wine list is extensive. ⊠ *19A Teague Bay (take Rte. 82 out of Christiansted and turn right at Reef Condominiums),* ☎ *809/778–7377. AE, D, DC, MC, V.*

Frederiksted

$$$ ✕ **Blue Moon.** This terrific little bistro, popular for its live jazz on Fri-day night, has an eclectic, often-changing menu that draws heavily on Asian, Cajun, and French influences. Try the delicious seafood chow-der or luna pie (veggies and cheese baked in phyllo dough) as an ap-petizer; the sweet-potato ravioli in mushroom sauce as an entrée; for dessert, the chocolate mint napoleon is heavenly. ⊠ *17 Strand St.,* ☎ *809/772–2222. AE. Closed July–Sept. and Mon.*

$$$ ✕ **Café du Soleil.** This upstairs terrace eatery bills itself as "the per-fect place to watch the sun set," and it's no exaggeration. Even the mauve walls and maroon and salmon napery cleverly duplicate the sun's pyrotechnics. The food understandably takes a back seat to the main event, but you won't go wrong with the stuffed Portobello mushrooms. For dinner, try the fresh fish and accompanying sauces, which vary with the catch of the day. ⊠ *625 Strand St.,* ☏ *809/772–5400. AE, MC, V. Closed Mon. and Tues. Dinner and Sun. brunch only.*

$$$ ✕ **Le St. Tropez.** A ceramic-tile bar and soft lighting add to the Mediterranean atmosphere at this pleasant bistro, tucked into a courtyard off Frederiksted's main thoroughfare. Diners, seated either inside or on the adjoining patio, enjoy French fare such as salads, brochettes, and grilled meats in delicate sauces. The menu changes daily, often taking advantage of fresh local seafood. The fresh basil, tomato, and mozzarella salad is heavenly. ⊠ *67 King St.,* ☏ *809/772–3000. AE, MC, V. Closed Sun.*

$$ ✕ **Villa Morales.** This simple family-run eatery is a popular spot for locals, with dancing in the cavernous back room. The kitchen turns out well-prepared Cruzan and Spanish dishes like goat stew and baked chicken, all served with heaping helpings of fungi, rice, and vegetables. ⊠ *Plot 82C, off Rte. 70, Estate Whim,* ☏ *809/772–0556. Reservations essential. AE, MC, V. Closed Sun.–Mon. No dinner Tues.–Wed.*

Beaches

Buck Island and its reef, part of the U.S. National Park system, can be reached only by boat; nonetheless, a visit here is a must on any trip to St. Croix. Its beach is beautiful, but its finest treasures are those you can see when you plop off the boat and adjust your face mask, snorkel, and flippers. Get there with one of the island's many charter-boat companies (☞ Daysailing *in* Chapter 3).

The waters are not always gentle at **Cane Bay,** a breezy north-shore beach, but the scuba diving and snorkeling are wondrous, and there are never many people around. Just swim straight out to see elkhorn and brain corals. Less than 200 yards out is the drop-off or so-called Cane Bay Wall.

Isaac Bay, at St. Croix's East End, is almost impossible to reach without a four-wheel-drive vehicle but worth it if you want some seclusion and calm swimming, plus a barrier reef for snorkeling. You can get here via footpaths from Jacks Bay.

South of Frederiksted, try the beach at **On the Beach Resort,** where palm trees can provide plenty of shade for those who need it and there is a fine beachside restaurant for a casual lunch on weekends.

Tamarind Reef Beach is a small but attractive beach east of Christiansted. Both Green Cay and Buck Island seem smack in front of you and make the view arresting. Snorkeling is good.

There are several popular West End beaches along the coast north of Frederiksted. The beach at the **Rainbow Beach Club** has a bar, casual restaurant, water sports, and volleyball.

Outdoor Activities and Sports

Fishing

In the past quarter-century, some 20 world records—many for blue marlin—have been set in these waters. Sailfish, skipjack, bonito, tuna (allison, blackfin, and yellowfin), and wahoo are abundant.

Ruffian Enterprises (⊠ St. Croix Marina, Christiansted, ☏ 809/773–6011 day, or 809/773–0917 night) will take you out on a 42-ft Ocean, *Shenanigans.* Half- or full-day charters are also available on **Cruzan Diver's Afternoon Delight** (☏ 809/772–3701) and **Captain Bunny's Catch 22** (☏ 809/778–6987).

Golf

The Buccaneer's (☎ 809/773–2100) 18-hole course is conveniently close to (east of) Christiansted. Yet more spectacular is the course at **Westin Carambola Beach Resort** (☎ 809/778–5638) in the valleyed northwestern part of the island, designed by Robert Trent Jones. **The Reef Golf Course** (☎ 809/773–8844), in the northeastern part of the island, has nine holes.

Horseback Riding

At Sprat Hall, near Frederiksted, Jill Hurd runs **Paul and Jill's Equestrian Stables** (☎ 809/772–2880 or 809/772–2627) and will take you clip-clopping through the rain forest (explaining the flora, fauna, and ruins along the way), along the coast, or on moonlit rides. Costs range from $50 to $75 for the three-hour rides.

Sailing

☞ Chapter 3, Sailing in the Virgin Islands.

Snorkeling/Diving

☞ Chapter 2, Diving and Snorkeling in the Virgin Islands.

Tennis

The public courts found in Frederiksted and out east at Cramer Park are in pretty questionable shape: It's better to pay the fees to play at the many hotel courts around the island.

There are a pro, a full tennis pro shop, and eight courts (two lighted) at the **Buccaneer Hotel** (☎ 809/773–2100); four courts (two lighted) at the **Westin Carambola Beach Resort** (☎ 809/778–3800); three lighted courts at **Club St. Croix** (☎ 809/773–4800); and two courts at the **Chenay Bay Beach Resort** (☎ 809/773–2918).

Windsurfing

Most hotels rent Windsurfers and other water sports equipment to nonguests.

Tradewindsurfing Inc. (✉ Hotel on the Cay, ☎ 809/773–7060) offers Windsurfer rentals, sales, and rides; parasailing; and a wide range of water-sports equipment, such as Jet Skis and kayaks.

Shopping

Although St. Croix doesn't offer as many shopping opportunities as St. Thomas, the island does provide an array of smaller stores with unique merchandise. In Christiansted, the best shopping areas are the **Pan Am Pavilion** and **Caravelle Arcade** off Strand Street, and along King and Company streets. These streets give way to arcades filled with small stores and boutiques. Stores are often closed on Sunday.

Books

The Bookie. This shop carries paperback novels as well as a line of stationery, newspapers, and greeting cards. Stop in for the latest local gossip and to find out about upcoming events. ✉ *1111 Strand St., Christiansted,* ☎ 809/773–2592.

Trader Bob's Dockside Book Store. If you're looking for Caribbean books or the latest good read, try this bookstore across from the post office in the Gallows Bay shopping area. ✉ *5030 Anchor Way,* ☎ 809/ 773–6001.

China and Crystal

Little Switzerland. The St. Croix branch of this Virgin Islands institution features a variety of Rosenthal flatware, Lladro figurines, Waterford and Baccarat crystal, Lalique figurines, and Wedgwood and Royal

Doulton china. ⊠ *Hamilton House, 1108 King St., Christiansted,* ☎ *809/773–1976.*

Clothing

Caribbean Clothing Company. This fashionable store features contemporary sportswear by top American designers as well as Bally shoes for men. ⊠ *41 Queen Cross St., Christiansted,* ☎ *809/773–5012.*

Cruzan Carib. From work clothes to playwear, you'll find it all at this St. Croix store open since 1968. Look for interesting hats and accessories. ⊠ *Pan Am Pavilion,* ☎ *809/773–3210.*

From the Gecko. Come here for the hippest clothes on St. Croix, from superb batik sarongs to hand-painted silk scarves. ⊠ *1233 Queen Cross St.,* ☎ *809/778–9433.*

Gold Coast. Fashionable swimsuits and casual sports clothes for both men and women fill the shelves at this pleasant shop. ⊠ *2220 Queen Cross St., Christiansted,* ☎ *809/773–2006.*

Java Wraps. Indonesian batik cover-ups and resortwear for men, women, and children are featured here. They also have fine home furnishings from around the world. ⊠ *51 Company St., Christiansted,* ☎ *809/773–2920; Pan Am Pavilion,* ☎ *809/773–3770.*

Skirt Tails. Look for hand-painted batik and washable silk clothing in a rainbow of colors, perfect for vacations in the tropics. The store carries swimwear, sarongs, pant and short sets, and flowy dresses. ⊠ *Pan Am Pavilion, Christiansted,* ☎ *809/773–1991.*

Urban Threadz. Urban islandwear by Karl Kani, No Fear, and many other popular lines for contemporary men and women are available here. Check the **Urban Kidz** store three doors down for Guess, Calvin Klein, Boss, Nautica, and Fila children's clothes. ⊠ *52C Company St., Christiansted,* ☎ *809/773–2883.*

The White House. This contemporary store sells clothes in all-white and natural colors. Look for exquisite lingerie, elegant evening wear, and unusual casual clothing. ⊠ *8B Kings Alley Walk, Christiansted,* ☎ *809/773–9222.*

Crafts and Gifts

Folk Art Traders. Owners Patty and Charles Eitzen travel to Haiti, Jamaica, Guyana, and throughout the Caribbean to find treasures to sell in their shop. The baskets, ceramic masks, pottery, jewelry, and sculpture found here are unique examples of folk-art traditions from around the world. ⊠ *1B Queen Cross St., at Strand St., Christiansted,* ☎ *809/773–1900.*

Green Papaya. This store sells handcrafted furniture and accessories for the home, with attention to the unusual. Oriental baskets, lovely wrought-iron lamps, and hurricanes with hand-blown teardrop lanterns are among its selection of goods from all over the world. ⊠ *Caravelle Arcade No. 15,* ☎ *809/773–8848.*

Only in Paradise Gifts. This place has something for everyone. It features fine jewelry in pearls, sterling silver, and art glass. It has wall hangings, tapestries, ceramic vases, and leather goods including sandals and purses. There is a lingerie and leather-handbag shop behind the store. ⊠ *5 Company St., Christiansted,* ☎ *809/773–0331.*

The Royal Poinciana. This attractively designed store carries island seasonings and hot sauces, West Indian crafts, bath gels, and herbal teas. ⊠ *1111 Strand St., Christiansted,* ☎ *809/773–9892.*

Jewelry

Colombian Emeralds. Specializing—of course—in emeralds, this store also carries diamonds, rubies, sapphires, and gold. A branch store, **Jewelers' Warehouse** (1 Queen Cross St., Christainsted, ☎ 809/773–5590), is across the street. The chain, the Caribbean's largest jeweler, offers certified appraisal and international guarantees. ⊠ *43 Queen Cross St., Christiansted,* ☎ *809/773–1928 or 809/773–9189.*

Crucian Gold. This store, in a small courtyard in a West Indian–style cottage, carries the unique gold creations of St. Croix native Brian Bishop. His trademark piece is the Turk's Head ring, made of an interwoven gold strand. ⊠ *59 King St., Christiansted,* ☎ *809/773–5241.*

Diamonds Direct. Look for factory outlet prices on diamonds and gold jewelry, as well as Citizen, Seiko, and Benrus watches. ⊠ *53B Company St., Christiansted,* ☎ *809/773–7325.*

Karavan West Indies. This shop is just east of downtown Christiansted, in the residential Gallows Bay neighborhood, which retains traces of its 200-year-old fishing village heritage. The owner designs her own jewelry and also sells an assortment of tchotchkes, including handmade Christmas ornaments and magical beads, from amber to amethyst. ⊠ *5030 Anchor Way, Gallows Bay Market Place,* ☎ *809/773–9999.*

Sonya's. Sonya Hough started her jewelry store in 1964 to feature her own jewelry creations, and now runs it with her daughter, Diana. Hough invented the hook bracelet, popular among locals. Hurricane Marilyn's visit to the island in 1995 inspired a "hurricane" bracelet. Its unique clasp features a gold strand shaped like the storm's swirling winds as they hit St. Croix, St. John, and St. Thomas. ⊠ *1 Company St., Christiansted,* ☎ *809/778–8605.*

Leather Goods

Kicks. This upscale shop carries a good, if small, selection of shoes and leather goods. ⊠ *57 Company St., Christiansted,* ☎ *809/773–7801.*

Liquor

Cruzan Rum Distillery. A tour of the company's rebuilt factory culminates in a tasting of its products, all sold here at bargain prices. ⊠ *West Airport Rd.,* ☎ *809/692–2280.*

Harborside Market and Spirits. A good selection of liquor at duty-free prices is available at this conveniently located shop. ⊠ *59 Kings Wharf, Christiansted,* ☎ *809/773–8899.*

Woolworth. This department store carries a huge line of discount, duty-free liquor. ⊠ *Sunny Isle Shopping Center, Centerline Rd.,* ☎ *809/778–5466.*

Perfumes

St. Croix Perfume Center. An extensive array of fragrances, including all the major brands, is available here. ⊠ *1114 King St., Christiansted,* ☎ *809/773–7604.*

Violette Boutique. Perfume, skin-care, and makeup products are the draw here. ⊠ *Caravelle Arcade, 38 Strand St., Christiansted,* ☎ *809/773–2148.*

Nightlife and the Arts

Christiansted

Island Center for the Performing Arts (☎ 809/778–5272), mid-island, hosts St. Croix's major concerts, plays, and performances by visiting entertainers.

Christiansted has a lively and eminently casual club scene near the waterfront. At **Mango Grove** (⊠ 53 King St., ☎ 809/773–0200) on Fridays, Saturdays, and Sundays, you'll hear live guitar and vocals in an open-air courtyard with a bar and Cinzano umbrella–covered tables. Easy jazz can be heard in the courtyard bar at **Indies** (⊠ 55–56 Company St., ☎ 809/692–9440) Saturday evenings. To party under the stars in a very, very informal setting, head to the **Wreck Bar** (☎ 809/773–6092), on Christiansted's Hospital Street, for crab races as well as rock and roll. **Hotel on the Cay** (⊠ Protestant Cay, ☎ 809/773–2035) has a West Indian buffet on Tuesday night that features a broken bottle dancer and Mocko Jumbie. On Thursday night, the **Cormorant** (⊠ 4126 La Grande Princesse, ☎ 809/778–8920) throws a similar event. The **2 Plus 2 Disco** (⊠ 17 La Grande Princesse, ☎ 809/773–3710) spins a great mix of calypso, soul, disco, and reggae, with live music on weekends.

Frederiksted

Although less hopping than Christiansted, Frederiksted restaurants and clubs have a variety of weekend entertainment. **Blue Moon** (⊠ 17 Strand St., ☎ 809/772–2222), a waterfront restaurant, is the place to be for live jazz on Friday 9 PM–1 AM. **Pier 69** (⊠ 69 King St., ☎ 809/772–0069) has blues, jazz, and reggae every Friday and Saturday at 9:30 PM.

Exploring St. Croix

St. Croix is a big island, as the Virgin Islands go, with two towns, Christiansted and Frederiksted, both named after Danish kings. There are lots of interesting spots spread out between the towns and to the east of Christiansted. They're all just right for exploring, but make sure you have a map in hand. Many secondary roads remain unmarked; if you get confused, don't hesitate to ask for help.

Christiansted

Christiansted is an historic, Danish-style town that always served as St. Croix's commercial center. Trade here in the 1700s and 1800s was in sugar, rum, and molasses. Today the town is home to law offices, tourist shops, and restaurants, but many of the buildings, built from the harbor up into the gentle hillsides, date from the 18th century.

Your best bet is to spend the morning, when it's still cool, exploring the historic sites. This two-hour endeavor won't tax your walking shoes and will leave you with lots of energy for poking around the town's eclectic shops. Break for lunch at an open-air restaurant before spending as much time as you like shopping.

Numbers in the text correspond to numbers in the margin and on the St. Croix map.

A GOOD WALK

St. Croix's main town is an easy walk. History remains the focus, and if you have a bit of an imagination, you can transport yourself back to the 1800s when sugar ruled and the streets were filled with planters attending to their town business.

Pick up a map at the **Visitor's Center** on Queen Cross Street to get your bearings, and then walk two blocks down Company Street to the waterfront to begin your tour. Start at **Fort Christianvaern,** where National Park Service rangers will be glad to answer your every question about the island's history. You'll enjoy a panoramic view from the ramparts. The big island off to the east is **Buck Island Reef National Monument.**

Leaving the fort, cross the shady **D. Hamilton Jackson Park** to the **Scale House,** where goods coming into the port were once weighed and inspected. In front of the fort sits the **Danish Custom's House,** closed to visitors but interesting to see from the outside if you're a history buff. Built in 1830 on foundations that date to 1751, the building served as a Customs House until 1926, when it became the Christiansted Library. It has served as the National Park Service headquarters since 1972.

Head across the parking lot to Company Street. On your right, at Hospital Street, you'll find the old **Post Office Building.** On your left, between Hospital and Church streets, the **Steeple Building** and its museum sit waiting to be explored. If you're visiting on Wednesday or Saturday, head up Company Street until you see the **Market** on your left. This is a great place to browse for a fresh fruit snack—banana, papaya, mango, and more. Backtrack down Company Street to Queen Cross Street. Turn left and go one block to King Street. Turn right and walk until you reach the yellow **Government House** on your right.

With a few history chapters under your Panama hat, it's time to explore the town's alleys and arcades, chock full of interesting merchandise, cozy restaurants, and seaside views. Go up King Street until you meet Queen Cross Street. Turn right and you're in the heart of the shopping district. One block toward the water and in Caravelle Arcade to your left, you'll find the **St. Croix Aquarium.**

You can't get lost. All roads lead downhill to the water, and from Kings Alley eastward, a walkway runs along the wharf to Fort Christianvaern.

SIGHTS TO SEE

Buck Island Reef National Monument. Off the northeast coast and reached only by boat, this is a must-see on any visit to St. Croix. The island's pristine beaches are just right for sunbathing, but there's enough shade for those who don't want to fry. The spectacular snorkeling trail set in the reef allows visitors the opportunity for a close-up study of coral formations and tropical fish. The crew members give special attention to novice snorkelers and children. A hiking trail to Buck Island's highest point offers spectacular views of the reef below and St. John to the north. Charter boat trips leave daily from the Christiansted Waterfront or from Green Cay Marina, about 2 mi east of Christiansted. Check with your hotel for recommendations. ⊠ *Northshore,* ☎ *809/773–1460.*

Danish Customs House. Built in 1830 on foundations that date to 1734, this building originally served as a Customs House, where officers collected duties on arriving merchandise. The Post Office was on the second floor. In 1926 it became the Christiansted Library. It has been the National Park Service headquarters since 1972. ⊠ *King St.* ☉ *Weekdays 8–5.*

D. Hamilton Jackson Park. When you're tired of sightseeing, stop here for a rest. It's named for a famed labor leader, judge, and journalist who started the first newspaper not under the thumb of the Danish crown. ⊠ *Between Ft. Christiansvaern and the Danish Customs House.*

Fort Christiansvaern. This large yellow structure dominates the harbor front. In 1749 the Danish built the fort to protect the harbor, but the structure was repeatedly damaged by hurricane-force winds and was partially rebuilt in 1771. It is now a National Historic Site and the best preserved of the five remaining Danish-built forts in the Virgin Islands. ⊠ *Hospital St.,* ☎ *809/773–1460.* 🖃 *$2 (includes admission to Steeple Building,* ☞ *below).* ☉ *Weekdays 8–5, weekends and holidays 9–5.*

Government House. One of the town's most elegant buildings, it was built as a home for a Danish merchant in 1747. The building today houses U.S.V.I. government offices. Slip into the peaceful inner courtyard to admire the still pools and gardens. A sweeping staircase leads visitors to a second-story ballroom, still the site of official government functions. ⊠ *King St.,* ☎ *809/773–1404. Closed for renovations.*

The Market. Built in 1735 as a slave market, this wood-and-galvanized-aluminum structure is where today's farmers and others sell their goods every Wednesday and Saturday from 8 to 5. ⊠ *Company St.*

Post Office Building. Built in 1749, it once housed the Danish West India & Guinea Company warehouse. The Danish Customs House and the post office building were once one structure. ⊠ *Church St.*

Ⓒ **St. Croix Aquarium.** The tanks are home to an ever-changing variety of local sea creatures. Children are invited to explore the discovery room, with its microscopes, interactive displays, and educational videos. ⊠ *Caravelle Arcade,* ☎ *809/773–8995.* ⊠ *$4.50.* ☉ *Tues.–Sat. 11–4.*

Scale House. Closed for renovation at press time, it should open under National Park Service authority by 1998. The building was constructed in 1856. It once served as a scale house, where goods passing through the port were weighed and inspected. ⊠ *King St.*

Steeple Building. Built by the Danes in 1753, it was the first Danish Lutheran church on St. Croix. It is now a national park museum and contains exhibits documenting the island's Indian habitation. There is also an extensive array of archaeological artifacts, a handful of displays concerning the plantation experience, and exhibits on the architectural development of Christiansted, the early history of the church, and Alexander Hamilton, the first secretary of the U.S. Treasury, who grew up in St. Croix. ⊠ *Church St.,* ☎ *809/773–1460.* ⊠ *$2 (includes admission to fort,* ☞ *above).* ☉ *When staffing permits. Check at Fort Christiansvaern.*

Visitor's Center. You'll find maps, brochures, and friendly advice at this local government–operated location. ⊠ *41A and B Queen Cross St., Box 4538, Christiansted 00822,* ☎ *809/773–0495.* ☉ *Weekdays 8–5.*

Outside Christiansted and Points East

An easy drive to the East End takes you through some of the island's choicest real estate. The roads are flat and well marked. Ruins of old sugar estates dot the landscape. You can make the entire loop in about an hour, a good way to end the day.

A GOOD DRIVE

Head east out of Christiansted on Route 75, also called Hospital Street. The road turns into Route 82. You'll pass the big pink Buccaneer Hotel on your left just outside of town. Continue east until the road ends at **Cramer's Park** ①, a nice spot for an afternoon swim. Just beyond, the dirt road takes you to **Point Udall** ②. Backtrack until you come to Route 60. Follow this road around the desolate south shore to experience an undeveloped St. Croix. Route 60 returns you to Route 82.

SIGHTS TO SEE

❶ **Cramer's Park.** This U.S.V.I. territorial beach on the northeast coast is very popular with locals. It's a spot for beach picnics and camping on long weekends. ⊠ *Rte. 82.*

❷ **Point Udall.** This rocky promontory, the easternmost point in the United States, juts into the Caribbean Sea. The climb to this point, by a rutted dirt road, may be slow, but it's worth the effort. On the way back, look for "The Castle," an enormous mansion atop the cliffs that resembles a cross between a Moorish mosque and the Taj Mahal. It was built by an extravagant recluse known only as the Contessa. ⊠ *Rte. 82.*

Between Christiansted and Frederiksted

A drive through St. Croix's countryside will take you past ruins of old plantations, many bearing whimsical names bestowed by early owners. The traffic moves quickly—by island standards—on the main roads, but you can pause and poke around if you head down some side lanes to see what's around. It's easy to find your way west, but driving from the north to the south requires good navigation. Don't leave your hotel without your map. Allow an entire day for this trip so you'll have enough time for a swim.

A GOOD DRIVE

Head west out of Christiansted on Route 75. At Route 751, turn right for a look at the upscale homes and sweeping sea views of **Judith's Fancy** ③. There's a gate at the entrance, but if you'd like to drive through, smile nicely at the gatekeeper and you won't have any problems. Follow Route 751, which turns into Hamilton Drive. At your second right, turn onto Caribe Road for a ride past the ruins of an estate built by the Knights of Malta in the 1600s. When Caribe Road ends at Jefferson Way, turn right to return to the gatehouse. Return to Route 75 and travel west until you reach Route 80. Turn right, traveling just a few minutes down Route 80, to reach **Salt River Marina** ④, where you'll see lots of boats. At the marina, turn right for **Salt River Bay National Historical Park and Ecological Preserve** ⑤. There's not much to see here now, but a park is planned for the distant future. Return to Route 80, where a left turn will bring you back to Route 75. Turn right to continue along the north shore past **Cane Bay** ⑥ and its inviting sandy beach to Davis Bay and the Westin Carambola Beach Resort. The hotel has a parking lot for visitors who wish to enjoy the beach.

Leaving Carambola, backtrack to Route 69 for the trip up **Mount Eagle** ⑦. Look for the paw prints on the road at the base of the hill, known locally as the Beast. Turn right on Route 705, at a developed spot in the road called Grove Place on your map. This is not well marked, so follow your map carefully. Turn right again onto Route 76, also called Mahogany Road, for a drive west through what islanders call their rain forest. It's not a true rain forest; technically it's a semimoist tropical forest. In some places, a thick tangle of turpentine and mahogany trees forms a canopy over the road. Stop in at **St. Croix Leap** ⑧ to shop for locally produced wood works.

When you reach Route 63, you'll see the sea in front of you. Turn right for **Estate Mount Washington Plantation** ⑨, at Hams Bluff, a drive with spectacular views. Turn around and head south on Route 63 toward Frederiksted.

SIGHTS TO SEE

⑥ **Cane Bay.** This is one of St. Croix's best launches for scuba diving, and you may see a few wet-suited, tank-backed figures near the small stone jetty making their way out to the drop-off (a bit farther out there is a steeper drop-off to 12,000 ft). ✉ *Rte. 80.*

NEED A BREAK?

Just past Cane Bay, on the sea side of the road, is the popular **Picnic in Paradise** (✉ Rte. 80, ☎ 809/778–1212), a gourmet delicatessen, restaurant, and beach club. Pick up quiche, pasta, or salad to take to the beach for lunch, or dine alfresco at one of the outdoor tables.

⑨ **Estate Mount Washington Plantation.** Several years ago, while surveying the property, the owners discovered the ruins of a historic sugar plantation buried beneath the rain-forest brush. The grounds have since been cleared and opened to the public. There is a free, self-guided walking tour of the animal-powered mill, rum factory, and other ruins, and an antiques shop is located in the old stables. ⊠ *Rte. 63 (watch for antiques shop sign),* ☎ *809/772–1026.* ⊙ *Ruins open daily; antiques shop, Sat. 10–4.*

❸ Judith's Fancy. This upscale neighborhood is home to the ruins of an old great house and the tower of the same name left from a 17th-century château that was once home to the governor of the Knights of Malta. The "Judith" comes from the first name of a woman buried on the property. From the guardhouse at the neighborhood entrance, follow Hamilton Drive past some of St. Croix's loveliest homes. At the end of Hamilton Drive, the road overlooks Salt River Bay, where Christopher Columbus anchored in 1493. A skirmish between members of Columbus's crew and a group of Arawak-speaking Indians resulted in the first bloody encounter between Europeans and West Indians. The peninsula on the east side of the bay is named for the event: Cabo de las Flechas (Cape of the Arrows). On the way back, make a detour left off Hamilton Drive onto Caribe Road, for a close look at the ruins. ⊠ *Turn north onto Rte. 751 off Rte. 75.*

❼ Mount Eagle. This is St. Croix's highest peak, at 1,165 ft. Leaving Cane Bay and passing North Star Beach, follow the beautiful coastal road that dips briefly into the forest, then turn left on Rte. 69. Just after you make the turn, the pavement is marked with the words "The Beast" and a set of giant paw prints. The hill you're about to climb is the location of the infamous Beast of the America's Paradise Triathlon, an annual St. Croix event in which participants must bike up this intimidating slope. ⊠ *Rte. 69.*

❽ St. Croix Leap. In the heart of the rain forest, this is a workshop where you can purchase a wide range of articles including mirrors, tables, bread boards, and mahogany jewelry boxes crafted by local artisans. ⊠ *Rte. 76,* ☎ *809/772–0421.*

❺ Salt River Bay National Historical Park and Ecological Preserve. This joint national and local park was dedicated in November 1993. In addition to such sites of cultural significance as a prehistoric ceremonial ball court and burial site, it encompasses a bio-diverse coastal estuary that hosts the largest remaining mangrove forest in the U.S.V.I., a submarine canyon, and several endangered species, including the hawksbill turtle and roseate tern. At present, few sites are of more than archaeological interest to laypeople, but plans call for a museum, interpretive walking trails, and a replica of a Carib village. ⊠ *Rte. 75 to Rte. 80.*

❹ Salt River Marina. This lush lagoon is home to the Anchor Dive Shop, a shipbuilding company, and a couple of casual eateries catering to yachties. The road that veers to the left behind the marina leads to the beach where Columbus landed. ⊠ *Tradewinds Rd. at Rte. 80,* ☎ *809/778–1522.*

Frederiksted

Frederiksted, St. Croix's second largest town, was founded in 1751. It's noted less for its Danish than for its Victorian architecture, which dates from after the uprising of former slaves and the great fire of 1878. A single long cruise-ship pier juts into the sparkling sea. A stroll around will take you no more than an hour.

A GOOD WALK

Pick up a map at the **Visitor's Center** located at the pier. Head inland for a stop at the redbrick **Fort Frederik.** There are benches in front if you like to people watch. Across the street sits the **Customs House.** Wander up Customs House Street to Queen Street for a visit to the **Market**—a good spot to find a fresh banana or mango if you're there early in the morning. Turn inland on Market Street to Prince Street, where you'll turn left for a stroll past **St. Patrick's Church.** Turn around, but continue on Prince Street until you reach **St. Paul's Anglican Church.** Continue to King Cross Street. Turn toward the water and past **Apothecary Hall** on your left. After you've enjoyed the historic sites, stop for lunch at one of the town's attractive restaurants before continuing your tour.

SIGHTS TO SEE

Apothecary Hall. Built in 1839, this is a good example of 19th-century architecture. ⊠ *King Cross St.*

Fort Frederik. In 1848 the slaves of the Danish West Indies were freed by Governor General Peter van Scholten as he stood on the fort's ramparts. The fort, completed in 1760, houses a number of interesting historical exhibits as well as an art gallery. ⊠ *Waterfront,* ☎ *809/ 772–2021.* 🎫 *Free.* ⊙ *Weekdays 8:30–4:30.*

The Market. Stop here for fresh fruits and vegetables sold early in the morning, just as they have been for more than 200 years. ⊠ *Queen St.*

St. Patrick's Church. This Roman Catholic church, complete with three turrets, was built in 1843 of coral. Wander inside and you'll find woodwork handcrafted by Frederiksted artisans. The churchyard is filled with 18th-century gravestones. ⊠ *Prince St.*

St. Paul's Anglican Church. This church is a mixture of classic and Gothic Revival architecture, built in 1812. ⊠ *Prince St.*

Visitor's Center. Right on the pier, this structure once served as a Customs House. Built at the end of the 1700s, the two-story gallery was added in the 1800s. This is a great place to pick up brochures or view the exhibits to learn everything you need to know about St. Croix. ⊠ *Waterfront,* ☎ *809/772–0357.* ⊙ *Weekdays 8–5.*

Frederiksted to Christiansted Along the Southern Route

This trip takes you from the ends of the earth at Sandy Point to shopping center row. It's a good way to see both sides of this rapidly developing island.

A GOOD DRIVE

Leave Frederiksted on Veteran's Shore Drive. To find this unmarked route, turn left at the boat ramp along the water, past a fairly attractive public housing community, Marley Homes. Continue past two small resorts on your right until you come to **West End Salt Pond** ⑩ on your left. Salt ponds are formed when seawater washes over and through the berm. Salt crystals sometimes form on the edge. In old days, natives used the salt as a seasoning. This salt pond is a great spot for bird-watchers.

Turn around and drive back to the boat ramp in Frederiksted. Head inland until you meet Route 70. Continue on 70 until it runs into Route 661. Near where Route 661 meets Route 66 turn right until you reach **Sandy Point Beach** ⑪, where between March and June the majestic leatherback turtles come ashore to lay their eggs. Retrace your drive back to Route 70. Turn right and follow this major road to the **Estate Whim Plantation Museum** ⑫, a must-see on your tour. Continue east until you see the signs for **St. George Village Botanical Gardens** ⑬. Route 70 continues back to Christiansted past old sugar estates with names like Die Liefde, Body Slob (a slob is a low spot in the ground), and Barren Spot.

SIGHTS TO SEE

🐚 ⑫ **Estate Whim Plantation Museum.** The lovingly restored estate, with a windmill, cook house, and other buildings, will give you a true sense of what life was like on St. Croix's sugar plantations in the 1800s. The oval-shape great house has high ceilings and antique furniture, decor, and utensils well worth seeing. Notice its fresh and airy atmosphere—the waterless stone moat around the great house was used not for defense but for gathering cooling air. The apothecary exhibit is the largest in all the West Indies. You will also find a museum gift shop. This is a great place for your kids to stretch their legs on the spacious grounds. ⊠ *Rte. 70, Box 2855, Frederiksted 00841,* ☎ *809/772–0598.* ⊠ *$5.* ☉ *Mon.–Sat. 10–4.*

⑬ St. George Village Botanical Gardens. At this 17-acre estate you'll find lush and fragrant flora amid the ruins of a 19th-century sugarcane plantation village. There are miniature versions of each ecosystem on St. Croix, from a semi-arid cactus grove to a verdant rain forest. ⊠ *Turn north off Rte. 70 at sign. Box 3011, Kingshill 00851-3011,* ☎ *809/ 692–2874.* ⊠ *$5.* ☉ *Daily 9–4. Closed holidays.*

⑩ West End Salt Pond. A bird-watcher's delight, this salt pond attracts a vast variety of birds, including flamingos. ⊠ *Veteran's Shore Dr.,* ⊠ *Free.*

NEED A BREAK?   If you're hungry as you head south of Frederiksted, stop at the seaside **On the Beach** (⊠ Veteran's Shore Dr., ☎ 809/772-4242) for yummy salads and sandwiches, and then enjoy a swim at the beach. The adjacent hotel attracts gay and lesbian guests, but residents and visitors of all persuasions enjoy the restaurant.

⑪ Sandy Point Beach. A ritual that began millions of years ago is played out annually in spring. That's when the majestic leatherback turtles come ashore to lay their eggs. These creatures, which can weigh up to 800 pounds and are of an older species than the dinosaurs, are oblivious to onlookers when they lay their eggs in the sand. With only the moonlight to guide them, Earthwatch volunteers patrol the beach nightly during the turtles' nesting season to protect the eggs from predators and poachers. The beach is a federal wildlife preserve. ⊠ *Rte. 66, west on unpaved road,* ☎ *809/773–1989.* ☉ *Spring turtle-watching, days and hours vary.*

St. Croix A to Z

Emergencies

Police and Ambulance: ☎ 911. **Hospitals:** Outside Christiansted there is the **Gov. Juan F. Luis Hospital and Health Center** (⊠ 6 Diamond Ruby, north of Sunny Isle Shopping Center, on Rte. 79, ☎ 809/778–6311) or the **Frederiksted Health Center** (⊠ 516 Strand St., ☎ 809/772–1992).

Air Ambulance: Bohlke International Airways (☎ 809/778–9177) operates out of the St. Croix airport. **Air Ambulance Network** (☎ 800/ 327–1966) also serves the area from Florida.

Pharmacies: People's Drug Store, Inc. has two branches on St. Croix: on the Christiansted Wharf (☎ 809/778–7355) and at the Sunny Isle Shopping Center (☎ 809/778–5537), just a few miles west of Christiansted on Centerline Road. In Frederiksted, try **D&D Apothecary Hall** at 50 Queen Street (☎ 809/772–1890).

Coast Guard: To reach the Coast Guard in St. Croix, dial 809/778–8185. The **Rescue Coordination Center in San Juan, Puerto Rico,** is at 809/729–6770.

Getting Around

BY CAR

Unlike St. Thomas and St. John, where narrow roads wind through hillsides, St. Croix is relatively flat, and it even has a four-lane highway. The speed limit on the Melvin H. Evans Highway is 55 mph and ranges from 35 to 40 mph elsewhere on the island. Seat belts are mandatory. Roads are often unmarked, so be patient as you explore the island, and remember that getting lost is often half the fun.

Car Rentals: For some unexplained reason, all the car rental companies occasionally have no cars to rent. To avoid disappointment, make your reservations early. Call **Atlas** (☎ 809/773–2886 or 800/426–6009), **Avis** (☎ 809/778–9355 or 800/331–1084), **Budget** (☎ 809/778–9636 or 800/527–0700), **Midwest** (☎ 809/772–0438), **Caribbean Jeep & Car** (☎ 809/773–4399), **Fair Auto Rental** (☎ 809/773–5031), **Olympic** (☎ 809/773–2208 or 800/344–5776), and **Thrifty** (☎ 809/773–7200).

BY PUBLIC TRANSPORTATION

Privately owned **taxi-vans** crisscross St. Croix regularly, providing reliable service between Frederiksted and Christiansted along Centerline Road. This inexpensive ($1.50) mode of transportation is favored by local residents. Because of the many stops on the 20-mile drive between the two main towns, the taxi-vans offer a slower—albeit more interesting—ride.

Because service is minimal, **public buses** are also not the quickest way to get around on the island, but the new deluxe mainland-size buses make this means of transportation comfortable and the price very reasonable. Fares are $1 between outlying areas and town, 75¢ in town.

BY TAXI

Taxis, generally station wagons or minivans, are a phone call away from most hotels and are available in downtown Christiansted, at the Alexander Hamilton Airport, and at the Frederiksted pier during cruise-ship arrivals. Rates, set by law, are prominently displayed at the airport, and drivers are required to show a rate sheet to passengers on request. Try the **St. Croix Taxi Association** (☎ 809/778–1088) at the airport, and **Antilles Taxi Service** (☎ 809/773–5020) or **Cruzan Taxi and Tours** (☎ 809/773–6388) in Christiansted.

Guided Tours

Van tours of St. Croix are offered by **St. Croix Safari Tours** (☎ 809/773–6700) and **St. Croix Transit** (☎ 809/772–3333). The tours, which depart from Christiansted and last about three hours, cost from $25 per person.

Visitor Information

The **U.S. Virgin Islands Division of Tourism** has offices on St. Croix at 41A and B Queen Cross Street in Christiansted (⊠ Box 4538, 00822, ☎ 809/773–0495) and on the pier in Frederiksted (⊠ Strand St., 00840, ☎ 809/772–0357).

ST. JOHN

By Margaret Enos Kearns and Janet E. Bigham

Updated by Lynda Lohr

About 20 minutes by ferry, 3 mi east of St. Thomas across Pillsbury Sound from Red Hook, the island of St. John comes close to realizing that travel-folder dream of "an unspoiled tropical paradise." Beautiful and largely undisturbed, St. John is covered with tropical vegetation, including a bay-tree forest that once supplied St. Thomas with the raw material for its fragrant bay rum. Clean, gleaming, white-sand beaches fringe the many bays scalloped out along the northern shore,

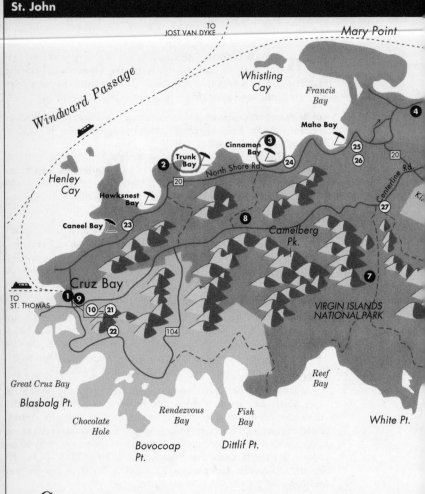

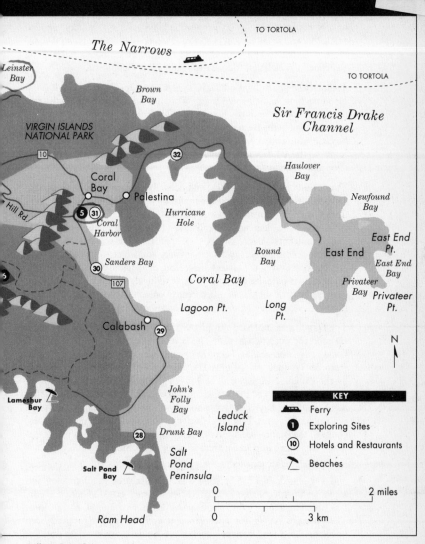

TO TORTOLA

The Narrows

Leinster
Bay

Brown
Bay

*Sir Francis Drake
Channel*

TO TORTOLA

VIRGIN ISLANDS
NATIONAL PARK

10

Coral
Bay

Palestina

*Hurricane
Hole*

Haulover
Bay

Newfound
Bay

Hill Rd.

5 31

Coral
Harbor

Round
Bay

East End

East End
Pt.

East End
Bay

Sanders Bay

30

107

Coral Bay

Lagoon Pt.

Long
Pt.

Privateer
Bay

Privateer
Pt.

Calabash

29

N

John's
Folly
Bay

Leduck
Island

Lameshur
Bay

28

Drunk Bay

Salt
Pond
Peninsula

Salt Pond
Bay

KEY
Ferry
Exploring Sites
Hotels and Restaurants
Beaches

0 ———— 2 miles
0 ———— 3 km

Ram Head

Gallows Point Suite
Resort, **11**
Harmony, **26**
Jadan Cottages, **20**
Maho Bay Camp, **25**
Serendip, **22**

and the iridescent water is perfect for swimming, fishing, snorkeling, diving, and underwater photography. There are two campgrounds, one luxury resort, two eco-resorts, and plenty of guest houses, condominiums, and small inns in between. Two-thirds of St. John's 20 sq mi were donated to the United States as a national park in 1956 by Laurance Rockefeller, founder of Caneel Bay Plantation.

Today there are only about 3,500 permanent residents on St. John, a bit more than half of them black West Indians either born in the territory or elsewhere in the Caribbean. The rest are people who moved here to work in the tourist and construction businesses or to retire. Cruz Bay, the administrative capital, is still a small West Indian village. It is home to the V.I. National Park Visitor's Center and a coterie of small shopping centers.

The activity level in Cruz Bay, and actually all over the island, has increased, and when cruise ships make their regularly scheduled visits during the winter months, Cruz Bay can get busy. Cruz Bay has a serious noise problem when bands play in any one of the town's bars and restaurants. A few places stay open into the wee hours, so take that into account when you decide where you'll sleep. While Coral Bay and the east end of the island are feeling the pressure of development, for the most part the island still has a natural, undeveloped feel to it. Perhaps because there is so much beauty preserved on St. John, the community is active in curbing excesses on private land, as well.

The Danes acquired St. John in 1675, when Governor Jorgen Iverson claimed the unsettled island. The British residents of nearby Tortola, however, considered St. John theirs, and when a small party of Danes from St. Thomas moved onto the island they were "invited" to leave by the British, and they did. In 1717 a group of Danish planters took formal possession of the island and formed the first permanent settlement, at Coral Bay. The question of who owned St. John wasn't settled until 1762, when Britain—which had continued to dispute the Danes' claim to the island—decided that keeping up good relations with Denmark was more important than keeping St. John.

By 1728 St. John had 87 plantations and a population of 123 whites and 677 blacks. In 1733 St. John was hit by a drought, hurricanes, and a plague of insects that destroyed the summer crops. There were by this time more than 1,000 slaves working more than 100 plantations. The Africans on St. John were recent arrivals, and many had been noblemen and landowners—even slave holders—themselves and felt threatened now with famine. Conditions for slaves on the island were already unusually severe, and the white population, sensing the slaves' growing desperation, enacted even harsher measures to keep them in line. On November 23 the slaves revolted, surprising the Danes with their military prowess, and captured the fort at Coral Bay. They controlled the island for six months, during which time nearly a quarter of the island's population—black and white—was killed. The rebellion was finally put down by 100 Danish militia and 220 Creole troops brought in from Martinique.

St. John today is perhaps the most racially integrated of the three U.S.V.I.; the people here, black and white, share a stronger sense of community than is found on St. Thomas or St. Croix. This may be due to St. John's small size and to the consensus among residents that the island's beauty is sacrosanct and must be protected. Recently residents joined forces to successfully fight the government's plan to install the island's first traffic light in Cruz Bay. The residents claimed it would make traffic worse and change the character of the island.

Sightseeing is best done by car, with or without a driver or guide. St. John may be small, but the roads are narrow and wind up and down steep hills, so don't expect to get anywhere in a hurry. Except for at cozy Cruz Bay, places to go and things to do are spread across the island, and, if you plan to do a lot of touring, renting a car will be cheaper, give you more freedom, and be a lot more fun than depending on taxis, which are reluctant to go anywhere until they have a full load of passengers. Although you may be tempted by an open-air Suzuki or Jeep, a conventional car goes just about everywhere and you'll be able to lock up your valuables. If you'd like a tour, a taxi driver can guide you to scenic mountain trails, secret coves, and eerie bush-covered ruins of old forts and palatial plantation houses.

Secure in its protection as a national park, St. John offers respite and refuge to the traveler who wants to escape from the pressures of 20th-century life for a day, a week, or perhaps forever.

Lodging

You're not going to find a lot of beachfront hotel properties on St. John; that's why you've got all those pristine beaches and tranquil roads through forest and greenery. Two-thirds of the island cannot be developed because it is part of the national park, and the steep terrain discourages development elsewhere. However, the island's one luxury hotel—Caneel Bay Resort—is world-class and expensive. Its rates do include most water sports and endless privacy, so you may find it best suits your needs.

If you don't opt for Caneel, your choice of accommodations includes two campgrounds, both at the edge of beautiful beaches (bring bug repellent); in-town inns; two eco-resorts; condominium complexes and cottages near town; and luxurious villas, almost always with stunning views, and often with pools.

Many of the accommodations have kitchens. In recent years, St. John's handful of grocery stores have improved their stock. It's now possible to buy everything from sun-dried tomatoes to green chilies, as well as the basics, but prices will take your breath away. If you're on a budget, bring staples such as pasta, canned goods, and paper products from home.

Hotels and Inns

$$$$ ☆ **Caneel Bay Resort.** This incredibly lush 170-acre peninsula resort
★ was originally part of the Durloo plantation owned by the Danish West India Company. It opened as a resort in 1936, was bought by Laurance S. Rockefeller in 1952, and joined Rosewood Resorts in 1991. While there are no crowds and no glitz, the grand dame of the island's tourism industry has begun to shake out her skirts a bit with the development of a children's program. There are still no room phones, but management will loan you a cellular at no charge except for the phone bill. You'll find tasteful tropical furnishing in spacious open-to-the-breezes rooms. There are seven beaches, one more gorgeous than the next, peace and quiet, and a luxurious air. Guests come here to enjoy the ambience and the pampering. Jackets are requested for men (during winter season) in two of the restaurants after 6 PM. Peter Burwash International runs the tennis program here. ✉ *Box 720, Cruz Bay 00830,* ☎ *809/776–6111 or 800/223–7637. 166 rooms. 3 restaurants, 11 tennis courts, beaches, meeting rooms. AE, MC, V.*

$$$$ ☆ **Gallows Point Suite Resort.** These soft-gray buildings with peaked roofs and shuttered windows are clustered on the peninsula south of the Cruz Bay ferry dock. The garden apartments have kitchens and sky-lighted, plant-filled showers big enough to frolic in. The upper-level apartments have loft bedrooms and better views. There's no air-conditioning; the harborside villas get better trade winds, but they're also noisier. Daily maid service is included. The entranceway is bridged by Ellington's restaurant. ⊠ *Box 58, Cruz Bay 00831,* ☎ *809/776–6434 or 800/323–7229,* FAX *809/776–6520. 60 rooms. Pool, beach, snorkeling. AE, DC, MC, V.*

$–$$$ 🄃 **Estate Concordia.** The latest brainchild of Stanley Selengut, the developer of Maho Bay Campgrounds, these environmentally correct studios and duplexes are on 51 oceanfront acres on remote Salt Pond Bay. The spacious units are constructed from recycled materials, and energy is wind- and solar-generated (even the ice maker is solar-powered). Next door you'll find the resort's five eco-tents, upscale camping structures made of environmentally friendly materials and with solar power and composting toilets. ⊠ *Box 310, Cruz Bay 00830,* ☎ *800/392–9004 or 212/472–9453,* FAX *212/861–6210. 14 units. Pool, beach. MC, V.*

$$ 🄃 **Harmony.** Nestled in the tree-covered hills adjacent to the Maho Bay Campground is a Stanley Selengut eco-tourism resort. The spacious two-story units here have your Caribbean basics—decks, sliding glass doors, living-dining areas, and great views—but staying here is definitely a learning experience. As at Estate Concordia, buildings, including walls and floors, are made from recycled materials. You'd never know the carpeting came from milk cartons and ketchup bottles, the doormat from recycled tires, and the pristine white walls from old newspapers. Energy for the low-wattage appliances comes entirely from wind and sun. In some units you can use the laptop computer to explore environmental preservation and monitor the unit's energy consumption. Tile floors, undyed organic cotton linens, and South American handicrafts create a look to match the ideals. There's a water sports concession on the beach. ⊠ *Box 310, Cruz Bay 00830,* ☎ *212/472–9453 or 800/392–9004,* FAX *212/861–6210. 12 units. Restaurant, beach, snorkeling, windsurfing. MC, V.*

Villas, Condominiums, and Cottages

The island has about 350 villas, condominiums, and cottages tucked here and there between Cruz Bay and Coral Bay. Many villas come with pools; most have hot tubs; a few have private beaches. The condominiums are in complexes with pools and modern amenities. Cottages tend to be more modest. Although most of the condominiums are within walking distance of Cruz Bay, you'll need a rental car to get from your home to the beach, dinner out, and shopping if you rent a villa or cottage. Many on-island managers pick you up at the ferry dock, answer all your questions, and are available during your stay to solve problems and provide advice. Prices range from $ to $$$$.

For luxury villas, try **Caribbean Villas and Resorts** (⊠ Box 48, 00830, ☎ 809/776–6152 or 800/338–0987, FAX 809/779–4044), **Catered To, Inc.** (⊠ Box 704, 00830, ☎ 809/776–6641, FAX 809/693–8191), **Destination St. John** (⊠ Box 8306, 00831, ☎ FAX 809/776–6969 or ☎ 800/562–1901), **Private Homes for Private Vacations** (⊠ Mamey Peak, 00830, ☎ 809/776–6876), **Vacation Homes** (⊠ Box 272, 00830, ☎ 809/776–6094, FAX 809/693–8455), **Vacation Vistas** (⊠ Box 476, 00831, ☎ FAX 809/776–6462), **Windspree** (⊠ 6-2-1A Estate Carolina, 00830, ☎ FAX 809/693–5423).

For condominiums, call **Caribbean Villas and Resorts** (⊠ Box 48, 00830, ☎ 809/776–6152 or 800/338–0987, FAX 809/779–4044). It manages Cruz Views, Cruz Bay Villas, and Pastory Estates. **Coconut Coast** (⊠ Box 618, 00831 (☎ FAX 809/693–9100 or ☎ 800/858–7989) has on-the-water condominiums. **Destination St. John** (⊠ Box 8306, 00831, ☎ 809/776–6969 or 800/562–1901) handles Lavender Hill.

Park Isle Villas (⊠ Box 1263, 00831, ☎ FAX 809/693-8261 or ☎ 800/416–1205) manages Battery Hill and Villa Caribe. **Star Villa** (⊠ Box 999, 00830, ☎ 809/776–6704, FAX 809/776–6183) has 11 lovely units. The **Virgin Grand Villas** (⊠ Great Cruz Bay 00830, ☎ 809/693–8856, FAX 809/693–8878) sits across the road from what used to be the Hyatt Regency St. John Hotel. At press time, that hotel was slated to reopen as The Westin Resort, St. John, in the fourth quarter of 1997, at which time the villas will become Westin Vacation Club Resort at St. John. Until then, villa guests can use the pool, public beach, and tennis courts at the hotel, but no other hotel facilities. When the hotel reopens, all facilities will be available.

For more modest accommodations try **Jadan Cottages** (⊠ Box 84, 00831, ☎ 809/776–6423, FAX 809/779–4323). A five-minute walk from Cruz Bay, the studio and two-bedroom cottages sit in an attractive garden. Affordable **Serendip** (⊠ Box 273, Cruz Bay 00831, ☎ FAX 809/776–6646) features lovely views, but you need a car since it's about a mile up a killer hill out of Cruz Bay. **Estate Zootenvaal,** (⊠ Hurricane Hole, 00830, ☎ FAX 809/776–6321) is at the far reaches of the island past Coral Bay at Hurricane Hole. It has basic cottages and a small private beach.

Bed and Breakfast

$$ ✕ **Frank Bay Bed and Breakfast** (⊠ Box 408, 00831, ☎ 809/693–8617 or 800/561–7290) is right across from the water and a five-minute walk from Cruz Bay. Owner Josh Crosley dishes up island hospitality with homemade muffins. The rooms are modest, with batik fabrics, ceiling fans, and rocking chairs. Named Bougainvillea, Shade, and Garden, the three rooms are open to the tropical breezes. In winter season, there's a three-day minimum.

Campgrounds

$ ⚠ **Cinnamon Bay Campground.** Very basic concrete "cottages," tents, and bare sites are available at this National Park Service location surrounded by jungle and set at the edge of big, beautiful Cinnamon Bay Beach. The tents and cottages both come with outdoor propane camping stoves, coolers, cooking gear, and sheets and towels. You'll read by electric lights in the cottages and propane lanterns in the tents. Bring your own tent and supplies for the bare sites. All have grills and picnic tables. There are no locks on doors. You'll have to trek down the path for cool showers and flush toilets. Hiking, snorkeling, swimming, and evening environmental or history programs are free and at your doorstep. Spaces for the winter months often fill up far in advance, so call for reservations (a maximum of one year ahead). If you're willing to schlep your tent and all your gear, the $17 a night bare sights are St. John's biggest bargain. The T'Ree Lizards Restaurant serves very good dinners that attract more than just campers. ⊠ *Box 720, Cruz Bay 00830-0720, ☎ 809/776–6330 or 800/539–9998, FAX 809/776–6458. 44 tents, 38 cottages, 26 bare sites. Restaurant, beach, snorkeling, windsurfing. AE, MC, V.*

$ ⚠ **Maho Bay Camp.** Eight miles from Cruz Bay, this private eco-campground is a lush hillside community of rustic tent cottages of canvas and screen linked by environmentally protective elevated wooden walkways, boardwalks, stairs, and ramps, which also lead down to the beach. The 16-by-16-ft shelters have beds, dining table and chairs, electric lamps with outlets, propane stove, ice cooler, kitchenware, and cutlery. All units are nestled among the trees, some hidden in the tropical greenery and others with spectacular views of the Caribbean. The camp has the chummy feel of a retreat and is very popular, so book well in advance. ⊠ *Box 310, Cruz Bay 00830, ☎ 212/472–9453 or*

800/392–9004, FAX *212/861–6210. 113 tent cottages. Restaurant, beach, snorkeling, windsurfing. MC, V.*

Dining

It used to be that you didn't come to St. John for the cuisine, but you'll find that now it's surprisingly good. There are restaurants to suit every taste, from the elegant restaurants at Caneel Bay Resort to casual eateries in Cruz Bay.

If you're renting a house or condo and doing your own cooking, the best places to shop are **Starfish Market** (☎ 809/779–4949) in the Boulon Center, **Marina Market** (☎ 809/779–4401) on Rte. 104, and **Tropicale** (☎ 809/693–7474) in Palm Plaza on Rte. 104. Prices are much higher than what you'd pay at home.

Bordeaux Mountain

$$$$ ✕ **Le Chateau de Bordeaux.** One of the best views you're going to find
★ to dine by anywhere is on the terrace here or in the air-conditioned dining room. The rustic cabin is practically a glorified tree house, magically transformed into an elegant, ultraromantic aerie by wrought-iron chandeliers, lace tablecloths, and antiques. The innovative preparations appeal equally to the eye and the palate. You might start with velvety carrot soup, perfectly contrasted with roasted chilies. Segue into rosemary-perfumed rack of lamb with a honey-Dijon-nut crust in a shallot-and-port-wine sauce, or salmon with mustard and maple glaze served on a bed of pasta. Don't miss the whelks, done to perfection. The comprehensive, moderately priced wine list is predictably strong on Bordeaux reds. ⊠ *Rte. 10, just east of Centerline Rd.,* ☎ *809/776–6611. AE, MC, V.*

Coral Bay

$$ ✕ **Shipwreck Landing.** Start with one of the house drinks, perhaps a fresh-squeezed concoction of lime, coconut, and rum, then move on to hearty taco salads, fried shrimp, teriyaki chicken, and conch fritters. The birds keep up a lively chatter in the bougainvillea that surrounds the open-air restaurant, and there's live music on Sunday night in season. ⊠ *Coral Bay,* ☎ *809/693–5640. MC, V.*

$ ✕ **Skinny Legs Bar and Restaurant.** Sailors who live aboard their boats anchored just off shore and an eclectic coterie of residents gather for lunch and dinner at this funky, inexpensive spot. If owners Doug Sica and Mo Chabuz are around, take a gander at their gams; you'll see where the restaurant got its name. It's a great place for burgers, fish sandwiches, and watching whatever sports event is on cable TV. ⊠ *Coral Bay,* ☎ *809/779–4982. No credit cards.*

Cruz Bay

$$$$ ✕ **Asolare.** Eclectic Asian cuisine dominates the menu at this elegant open-air eatery in an old St. John house overlooking the harbor. Come early and relax over drinks while you enjoy the sunset. Start with an appetizer, say, crayfish summer roll, a new twist on the usual spring roll, with tamarind peanut sauce. Dinners include such delights as rice noodles with shrimp, chicken, and chilies. If you still have room for dessert, try the chocolate pyramid, a luscious chocolate cake with homemade ice cream. ⊠ *Caneel Hill,* ☎ *809/779–4747. AE, MC, V. No lunch.*

$$$$ ✕ **Paradiso.** This popular spot is on the upper level of Mongoose
★ Junction, the island's largest shopping area. The menu is an eclectic mix, including everything from the slightly Italian wahoo *Putanesca*

(a local fish with a black olive sauce) to grilled New York strip steak to roasted rack of lamb. One can dine indoors, in the comfort of air-conditioning, or outdoors on a small terrace overlooking the street. ✉ *Mongoose Junction,* ☏ *809/693–8899. AE, MC, V. No lunch.*

$$$ ✕ Ellington's. This peaceful, appealing spot extends out onto the second-story veranda of the Gallows Point Suite Resort's central building. The outside tables are particularly quiet and romantic. The menu is Continental, with dishes of chicken, fish, and steak. You might start with the jumbo shrimp cooked in sweet coconut and served with mango sauce, or the seafood chowder. Entrées include sea scallops and pesto, swordfish scampi, filet mignon, and fresh lobster. Save room for dessert, though, perhaps the banana–chocolate-chip cake or the white-chocolate brownie. ✉ *Gallows Point Suite Resort,* ☏ *809/693–8490. AE, MC, V. No lunch.*

$$$ ✕ Fish Trap. There are several rooms and terraces here, all open to the breezes and buzzing with truly happy diners. Chef Aaron Willis conjures tasty appetizers such as conch fritters and Fish Trap chowder. The menu also includes an interesting pasta of the day, steak, chicken, and hamburgers. ✉ *Downtown,* ☏ *809/693–9994. AE, D, MC, V. Closed Mon.*

$$$ ✕ Lime Inn. This busy, roofed, open-air restaurant has an ornamental garden and beach-furniture chairs. There are several shrimp and steak dishes and such specials as sautéed chicken with artichoke hearts in lemon sauce. On Wednesday night there's an all-you-can-eat shrimp feast, and prime rib is the specialty every Saturday night. ✉ *Downtown, east of the Chase Manhattan Bank,* ☏ *809/776–6425. AE, MC, V. Closed Sun.*

$$$ ✕ Mongoose Restaurant. Choose either the cozy but open-air dining room or the bar and dining area; the dramatically high ceiling and walls of the latter are basically open arches welcoming the breezes. Hamburgers, sandwiches, and salads compose the lunch menu. Dinner offerings include grilled local tuna, wahoo, or other fresh fish; grilled sirloin steak; and daily pasta specials. ✉ *Mongoose Junction,* ☏ *809/693–8687. AE, MC, V.*

$$$ ✕ Pusser's. With dark paneling and brass rails, the decor is very like that of any good old British pub, but diners and drinkers here won't be fooled for a minute—tropical temperatures, lazily rotating ceiling fans, and menu items with Caribbean twists are quick reminders that this is Cruz Bay, not Cambridge. Step outside the bar area to the covered deck, take a seat, soak in the view, and order up some terrific conch chowder or a lobster club sandwich. The rum Painkillers pack a punch. ✉ *Wharfside Village,* ☏ *809/693–8489. AE, MC, V.*

$$$ ✕ Saychelles. Nestled at the water's edge in downtown Cruz Bay is this
★ cozy spot with intimate indoor and terrace dining. The house specialty here is Saychelles Bouillabaisse, served with aioli toasts. Other tempting items include grilled fresh fish, shrimp flambéed in gin, marinated pork tenderloin with pineapple black bean salsa, and pasta with a choice of six different sauces, including basil-pesto and primavera. There is also an extensive tapas menu—the marinated mussels, salmon carpaccio, and conch fritters are superb—if you feel like snacking the evening away. ✉ *Wharfside Village,* ☏ *809/693–7030. AE, MC, V. No lunch.*

$$ ✕ Cafe Roma. This casual, but very popular second-floor restaurant is right in the heart of Cruz Bay and the place to come if you want well-prepared traditional Italian cuisine: lasagna, spaghetti and meatballs, manicotti, chicken Parmesan. There are also a variety of excellent pizzas. Polenta cake with raspberry sauce is the dessert specialty here. ⊠ *Downtown on Vesta Gade,* ☎ *809/776–6524. MC, V. No lunch.*

$ ✕ **Luscious Licks.** This funky hole-in-the-wall serves up mostly healthy foods such as all-natural fruit smoothies, veggie pita sandwiches, and homemade muffins. Try the barbecue tofu in sweet-and-sour-sauce or the spinach and olive fettuccine. It also sells Ben & Jerry's ice cream and, with a nod to the yuppies, specialty coffees. Ask for the local's platter, a bit of this and that—whatever owner Bonny Corbeil conjured up in her kitchen that day. ⊠ *Next door to Mongoose Junction,* ☎ *809/693–8400. No credit cards.*

Friis Bay

$–$$ ✕ **Miss Lucy's.** This delightful local eatery is in the middle of nowhere;
★   taxi rates are prohibitive, so drive here in a rental car—it's worth the trip. The lilac and maroon trellised restaurant, adorned with local artwork, is swept by cooling sea breezes; you can also eat outside on a tiny beach anchored by sea-grape trees. Dinners are served with complimentary johnnycakes and soup (try the superlative fish chowder or spicy black bean), not to mention mounds of rice, potatoes, fungi, plantains, yams, and carrots. Have the meltingly tender conch fritters to start, then curried goat stew or steamed kingfish Creole. Wash it all down with one of the addictive fresh-fruit drinks (ask for the passion-fruit daiquiri). ⊠ *Calabash, Friis Bay,* ☎ *809/779–4404. AE, MC, V. Call for summer hrs.*

Beaches

Unlike most islands, where there is a good-better-best scale in rating beaches, St. John is blessed with so many great beaches that the scale is good, great, and why-tell-anyone-else-about-this-place? Most of the good beaches, popular with locals and day-trippers from St. Thomas, are along the north shore of the island, within the boundaries of the national park. Although some are more developed than others, all are under park-service supervision. They can get crowded on weekends, holidays, and during high season, but by and large the beaches retain a pristine quality. Those along the south shore and the eastern half of the island are still quiet and isolated.

Caneel Bay. Caneel Bay is actually the general name for seven white-sand beaches on the north shore, six of which can be reached only by water if you are not a hotel guest. The seventh beach, **Caneel Beach** is easily reachable from the main entrance of the resort (just follow the signs). (Public access to beaches is a civil right in the U.S.V.I., but public access across the land to the beach is not.) The main beach (ask for directions) is open to the public. Visitors are welcome, and nonguests can dine at the hotels' two restaurants that are open to the public (jacket required at dinner during winter season), and cruise the inviting two-level gift shop.

Cinnamon Bay. A long, sandy beach facing beautiful cays serves the adjoining national-park campground. Facilities (showers, toilets, commissary, restaurant, beach shop, gift shop, small museum, as well as kayak, windsurfing, and snorkeling-equipment rentals) are open to all. There's good snorkeling off the point to the right—look for the big angelfish and the swarms of purple triggerfish that live here. Afternoons on Cinnamon Bay can be windy, so you may want to come here early, before the wind picks up. Across the road from the beach parking lot is the beginning of the Cinnamon Bay hiking trail: Look for the ruins of a sugar mill that mark the trailhead. There are actually two paths here: a nature trail that takes you on a flat circle through the woods with signs identifying the flora, and a steep trail that heads all the way up to Centerline Road.

Hawksnest Beach. This narrow, sea-grape-tree–lined beach is becoming more popular every day. There are rest rooms, cooking grills, and a covered shed for picnicking. It's popular for group outings and is the closest beach to town, so it is often fairly crowded.

Maho Bay. This is a popular beach and the Maho Bay Campground is here, too—a wonderful mélange of open-air, rustic tent cottages nestled in the hillside above. The campground offers informal talks and slide and film presentations. In spring, jazz and jungle harmonize when Maho sponsors a series of jazz and classical music in its outdoor pavilion. Maho Bay is also the site of Harmony, an environmentally correct hotel.

Trunk Bay. Probably St. John's most-photographed beach, this is also the preferred spot for beginning snorkelers, because of its underwater trail. It's the St. John stop for cruise-ship passengers who choose a snorkeling tour for the day, so if you're looking for seclusion, check cruise-ship listings in *St. Thomas This Week* to find out what days the highest number are in port. Crowded or not (and crowded is a relative term here), it's a stunning beach and sure to please. There are changing rooms, a snack bar, picnic tables, a gift shop, telephones, small lockers, and snorkeling equipment for rent.

Salt Pond Bay. On the scenic southeastern coast of St. John, next to Coral Bay and rugged Drunk Bay, if you're adventurous this beach is worth exploring. It's a short hike down a hill from the parking lot, and the only facility is an outhouse, although a few picnic tables are scattered about. The beach is a little rockier here, but there are interesting tidal pools and the snorkeling is good. Take special care to leave nothing valuable in the car, as reports of thefts are numerous.

Outdoor Activities and Sports

Fishing

Sportfishing trips can be arranged by calling the **Charterboat Center** (☎ 809/775–7990), at Red Hook on St. Thomas. **American Yacht Harbor** (☎ 809/775–6454) offers sportfishing trips. They are in Red Hook on St. Thomas but will come and pick you up on St. John. **St. John World Class Anglers** (☎ 809/779–4281) offers light-tackle shore and offshore fishing and half- and full-day trips.

Hiking

The Virgin Islands National Park (☎ 809/776–6201) maintains more than 20 trails on the north and south shores. They vary in difficulty and length, but there is something for almost everyone. These trails are not garden paths, however, and the park service recommends that you wear long pants to protect yourself against insects and thorny vegetation; sturdy and comfortable walking shoes, rather than sandals or flip-flops (even if the trail ends up at the beach); and a head covering. The park service publishes a trail map, detailing the points of interest, dangers, trail lengths, and estimated hiking times. Check in at the visitor center in Cruz Bay on St. John.

Horseback Riding

Carolina Corral (☎ 809/693–5161) is the place to head if you want to ride horseback along a picturesque trail. You can take horse rides and donkey rides as well as horseback riding lessons and rides in donkey carts. Look for Dana Romo and her animals along the road in Coral Bay near the Coral Bay Cafe.

Sailing

☞ Chapter 3, Sailing in the Virgin Islands.

Sea Kayaking

Trips are led by professional guides and use traditional kayaks to ply coastal waters. They are run by **Arawak Expeditions** (☎ 809/693–8312 or 800/238–8687). Prices start at $40 for a half-day trip.

Snorkeling/Diving

☞ Chapter 2, Diving and Snorkeling in the Virgin Islands.

Tennis

Caneel Bay Resort (☎ 809/776–6111) has 11 courts (none lighted) for guests only and a pro shop. The **Public Courts,** near the fire station in Cruz Bay, are lighted until 10 PM and are available on a first-come, first-served basis.

Windsurfing

Try **Cinnamon Bay Campground** (☎ 809/776–6330), where rentals are available for $12–$15 per day.

Shopping

With so much natural beauty to offer, the pleasures of shopping on St. John are all but overlooked in travel literature, but the blend of luxury items and handicrafts found in the shops on St. John makes for excellent shopping opportunities. Most shops carry a little of this and a bit of that, so it pays to poke around. The Cruz Bay shopping district runs from **Wharfside Village** just around the corner from the ferry dock, through the streets of the town to **Mongoose Junction** on North Shore Road. At Mongoose Junction, so named because it's where those furry island creatures used to gather at a garbage can, you'll find an inviting shopping center with stonework walls. Steps connect the two sections. The shops are upscale and original. Out on Rte. 104, stop in at **Palm Plaza** to explore its few gift and crafts shops. At the island's other end, you'll find a shop here and there strung out from the village of **Coral Bay** to the small complex at **Shipwreck Landing.** Look for an eclectic collection of clothes, jewelry, and artwork.

ARTS AND CRAFTS

Bamboula. Owner Jo Sterling travels the Caribbean and the world to bring back unusual clothing items for men and women, shoes, accessories, and housewares, including rugs and bedspreads, for this multicultural boutique. ✉ *Mongoose Junction,* ☎ *809/693–8699.*

The Canvas Factory. If you're a true shopper, you may need an extra bag to carry all your treasures home; this shop offers every kind of tote and carrier imaginable, from a simple bag to a suitcase with numerous zippered compartments, all made of canvas, naturally. It also sells great canvas hats in assorted styles and colors. ✉ *Mongoose Junction,* ☎ *809/776–6196.*

Donald Schnell Pottery. Choose from the unique hand-blown glass, pottery, and dinnerware made from crushed coral. Whether you opt for wind chimes, kaleidoscopes, or fanciful water fountains, your selection can be shipped worldwide. ✉ *Mongoose Junction,* ☎ *809/776–6420.*

Fabric Mill. Shop here for handmade island animals and dolls, as well as place mats, napkins, cookbooks, and batik wraps. Or take home a bolt of tropical brights from the upholstery-fabric selection. ✉ *Mongoose Junction,* ☎ *809/776–6194.*

Pink Papaya. This store is home of St. John native M. L. Etre's well-known artwork plus a huge collection of one-of-a-kind gift items, from bright tablecloths to unusual trays, dinnerware, and unique tropical jewelry. ✉ *Lemon Tree Mall, Cruz Bay,* ☎ *809/693–8535.*

BOOKS

MAPes MONDe. Stop here for a huge variety of books on the Caribbean, including the exquisite-looking publications that are the hallmark of Virgin Island publisher MAPes MONDe. You'll also find many reproductions of old maps, prints, and greeting cards. ⊠ *Mongoose Junction,* ☎ *809/779–4545.*

National Park Headquarters. Here you'll find several good histories of St. John, including *St. John Back Time,* by Ruth Hull Low and Rafael Valls, and for linguists, *What a Pistarckle!,* by Lito Valls. ⊠ *At the Creek,* ☎ *809/776–6201.*

St. John Books. This is the place to come for current newspapers and magazines, a variety of books, and a good cup of coffee. ⊠ *Mongoose Junction,* ☎ *809/779–4260.*

CLOTHING

Big Planet Adventure Outfitters. You knew when you got off the boat that someplace on St. John would sell Birkenstock sandals. This outdoor-clothing store is where you'll find them, as well as colorful and durable cotton clothing and accessories, including designs by Patagonia, the North Face, and Sierra Designs. The adjacent **Little Planet** section sells children's clothes, often recycled from such unlikely materials as plastic bottles. ⊠ *Mongoose Junction,* ☎ *809/776–6638 or 800/238–8687.*

Bougainvillea Boutique. If you'd like to look like you stepped out of the pages of the resort-wear spread in some upscale travel magazine, try this store. Owner Susan Stair carries very chic men's and women's resort wear, straw hats, leather handbags, and fine gift items. ⊠ *Mongoose Junction,* ☎ *809/693–7190.*

The Clothing Studio. Several talented artists hand-paint original designs on clothing for all members of the family. You'll find T-shirts, beach cover-ups, pants, shorts, and even bathing suits with beautiful hand-painted creations. ⊠ *Mongoose Junction,* ☎ *809/776–6585.*

Let's Go Bananas. This shop is packed with racks and racks of bathing suits and casual islandwear in cool 100% cotton. ⊠ *Wharfside Village,* ☎ *809/693–8380.*

Mumbo Jumbo. You'll find great prices on tropical women's wear plus an eclectic selection of interesting housewares and children's toys. ⊠ *Coral Bay,* ☎ *809/779–4227.*

Pusser's Company Store. Pusser's stores originated in the B.V.I., and this branch carries all the items these stores are famous for: nautical memorabilia, casual sportswear for the whole family, books, and, of course, famous Pusser's Rum. ⊠ *Wharfside Village Shopping Center, Cruz Bay,* ☎ *809/693–8489.*

JEWELRY

Blue Carib Gems. Custom-made jewelry, loose gemstones, and old coins are for sale here. There is also a small art gallery. ⊠ *Wharfside Village,* ☎ *809/693–8299.*

Caravan Gallery. This shop is a great spot to browse—the more you look the more you see. Interesting and exotic jewelry, folk art, tribal art, and masks cover the walls and tables. Owner Radha Speer creates much of the unusual jewelry you'll find here. ⊠ *Mongoose Junction,* ☎ *809/693–8550.*

Colombian Emeralds (⊠ Mongoose Junction, ☎ 809/776–6007) and its sister store, **Jeweler's Warehouse** (⊠ Wharfside Village, ☎ 809/693–7490), sell high-quality emeralds, rubies, and diamonds, as well as a treasure chest of other jewels set in attractive gold and silver settings. The stores also carry perfume, the only place to shop for the latest fragrances in St. John.

Free Bird Creations. Unique handcrafted jewelry—earrings, bracelets, pendants and chains—are sold here. The store also has a good selection of practical waterproof watches great for your excursions to the beach. ⊠ *Wharfside Village,* ☎ *809/693–8625.*

Heads Up. This tiny store carries the unique St. John watch for men and women. Nautical flags in place of numbers on the watch face spell St. John, U.S.V.I. Look also for the best selection of hats and top-drawer sunglasses at less than mainland prices. ⊠ *Veste Gade, Cruz Bay,* ☎ *809/693–8840.*

R&I Patton Goldsmiths. Rudy and Irene Patton design most of the unique silver and gold jewelry in this shop. The rest comes from various jeweler friends of theirs. Sea fans (those large, lacy plants that sway with the ocean's currents) in filigreed silver, lapis set in long drops of gold, and starfish and hibiscus pendants in silver or gold, and gold sand dollar–shaped charms and earrings are tempting choices. To commemorate your Reef Bay hike (or your stay at Caneel), there are petroglyphs of every size and metal. ⊠ *Mongoose Junction,* ☎ *809/776–6548.*

Nightlife

St. John is not the place to go for glitter and all-night partying. Still, after-hours Cruz Bay can be a lively little village in which to dine, drink, dance, chat, or flirt. Notices posted across from the **U.S. Post Office** and at **Connections** telephone center (and on telephone poles) will keep you apprised of special events: comedy nights, movies, and the like.

After a sunset drink at **Ellington's** (⊠ Gallows Point Suite Resort, ☎ 809/693–8490) up the hill from Cruz Bay, you can stroll here and there in town, where everything is clustered around the small waterfront park. Many of the young people from the U.S. mainland who live and work on St. John will be out sipping and socializing, too.

Some friendly hubbub can be found at the rough-and-ready **Backyard** (☎ 809/776–8553), *the* place for sports-watching as well as grooving to Bonnie Raitt et al.

Young folks like to gather at **Woody's** (☎ 809/779–4625) in Cruz Bay. The sidewalk tables provide a close-up view of Cruz Bay's action.

There's calypso and reggae on Wednesday and Friday at **Fred's** (☎ 809/776–6363).

The Inn at Tamarind Court (☎ 809/776–6378) serves up a blend of jazz and rock on Friday and reggae on Saturday.

Outside of town, **Caneel Bay** (☎ 809/776–6111) usually has entertainment several nights a week in season. Caneel's offerings run toward quiet calypso.

At Coral Bay, on the far side of the island, check out the action at **Skinny Legs** (☎ 809/779–4982).

Exploring St. John

St. John is an easy place to explore. One road goes along the north shore, another across the center of the mountains. There are a few roads branching off here and there, but it's hard to get lost. Pick up a map at the Visitor's Center before you start out, and you'll have no problems. Few residents remember the route numbers, so if you ask for directions, make sure you have your map in hand. Because so much of St. John is national park and therefore undeveloped, its natural scenery and vistas are outstanding. Bring along your swimsuit for stops at some of the most beautiful beaches in the world. You can spend all day or just a couple of hours exploring. There are lunch spots at Cinnamon Bay and in Coral Bay, or do what the residents do: shop for a picnic lunch in Cruz Bay. The grocery stores even sell Styrofoam coolers just for this purpose.

Numbers in the text correspond to numbers in the margin and on the St. John map.

A Good Drive

Start your exploration in **Cruz Bay** ①, at the ferry dock. Just across the street, locals and visitors take a break on the park benches. Near Sparky's, go through the wrought iron gate to the Visitor's Center. There are few historic or tourist sites in Cruz Bay. The most fun comes from people watching and poking around the small shops. At an area called the Creek, where North Shore Road (Route 20) starts, you'll find the V.I. National Park Visitor's Center. Rangers here can answer all your questions.

Drive north out of Cruz Bay on North Shore Road to four of the most beautiful beaches in all of the Caribbean. Hawksnest, the first beach you will come to, is quite narrow but has a fine reef close to shore. This is where Alan Alda shot scenes for his film *Four Seasons.* Just as you've recovered from the beautiful views over Hawksnest, a dirt road heads to the left. Stop here for a worthwhile 10-minute hike up **Peace Hill** ②. Trunk Bay is next. This is a long curve of shimmering white sand. It's a popular beach and can be quite crowded. You'll find the famous underwater snorkeling trail here. Next comes **Cinnamon Bay Beach** ③, where there is also a campground and a small museum. Finally you'll come to Maho Bay, a gentle curve of beach nestled against a steep hill. Continue on this one-way road and bear left and then right when you get to the sea for a stop at **Annaberg Plantation** ④. The ruins of an old Danish school are near the junction by the sea.

Retrace your route, passing the one-way road and eventually a sign on your right that points toward Cruz Bay. Go up a very steep hill until you meet Centerline Road (Route 10). Turn left toward **Coral Bay** ⑤, a quiet, very laid-back village.

For stunning views of neighboring islands, head back to Cruz Bay on hilly Centerline Drive (Route 10), camera in hand, to watch for the many scenic stops along the road. At **Bordeaux Mountain** ⑥ overlook, you can see forever; well, at least to the British Virgin Islands. As you continue west, you'll see the trailhead for **Reef Bay Trail** ⑦ on your left. Continuing west toward Cruz Bay, make a right on a dirt road that's marked V.I. National Park. You're coming the other way, so watch carefully for the sign. This road leads you to the stabilized **Catherineberg Ruins** ⑧, a great spot to wander around for a bit.

When you reach Cruz Bay, make the u-turn around the Texaco gas station. Travel about two blocks until you see a slightly paved road on your left. The big white house on a small rise houses the **Elaine Ione Sprauve Library and Museum** ⑨.

Sights to See

❹ **Annaberg Plantation.** In the 18th century, sugar plantations dotted the steep hills of the U.S.V.I., and slaves, Danes, and Dutchmen toiled to harvest the sugarcane that produced sugar, molasses, and rum for export. Built in the 1780s, the partially restored plantation at Leinster Bay was once an important sugar mill. There are no official visiting hours and no admission charge. The National Park Service has regular tours, and some well-informed taxi drivers will show you around. Occasionally you'll find what the park calls a living history demonstration—someone making johnnycake or weaving baskets. For information on tours and cultural demonstrations, call the St. John National Park Service Visitor's Center (☎ 809/776–6201). ⊠ *Leinster Bay Rd.*

⑥ Bordeaux Mountain. St. John's highest peak rises to 1,277 ft. Centerline Road passes near enough to the top to offer breathtaking views before the road plunges down to Coral Bay. Drive nearly to the end of the dirt road for spectacular views at Picture Point, and for the trailhead for the hike downhill to Lameshur. Get a National Park Trail Map, available from the National Park Service, before you start. ⊠ *Centerline Rd.*

⑧ Catherineberg Ruins. At this fine example of an 18th-century sugar and rum factory there is a storage vault underneath the windmill. Across the road, look for the round mill, which was later used to hold water. In the 1733 rebellion by the slaves against the planters, Catherineberg served as headquarters for Amina warriors, a tribe of Africans captured into slavery. It's now part of the V.I. National Park. ⊠ *Centerline Rd.*

❸ Cinnamon Bay Beach. There are more than 20 mi of hiking trails in the St. John National Park. Two good trails begin at Cinnamon Bay. Both start across the road from the beach. The ruins of a sugar mill mark the trailhead to an easy nature trail. It takes you on a flat circle through the woods, past an old Danish cemetery and signs that identify the flora. The other trail, which starts where the road bends past the ruins, heads all the way up to Centerline Road. The National Park campground is here, and history buffs will enjoy the little, self-guided **Cinnamon Bay Museum.** Snorkelers will find good snorkeling around the point to the right, although watch out if the waves are up. Look for the big angelfish and the schools of blue tangs that live here. ⊠ *North Shore Rd.*

❺ Coral Bay. This laid-back community at the dry, eastern end of the island is named for its shape rather than for its underwater life—the word *coral* comes from *krawl,* Danish for *corral.* It's a quiet, neighborhoody, local, and quite small settlement; a place to get away from it all. You'll need a Jeep if you plan to stay at this end of the island, as some of the roads are on the rough side. ⊠ *Rte. 10.*

NEED A BREAK?

Just south of Coral Bay village sits **Coral Bay Cafe.** For burgers, West Indian dishes, and cold drinks, stop in at this tiny eatery just past the gas station. Much of Coral Bay's tiny population will drive by with a wave while you enjoy your lunch or dinner at umbrella-shaded picnic tables. ⊠ *Rte. 107,* ☎ 809/693–5161.

---

❶ Cruz Bay. St. John's hub is compact and only covers several blocks, but it's where the ferries arrive from St. Thomas and the British Virgin Islands, and it's where you can get taxis or rent a car to travel around the island. There are plenty of shops through which to browse, along with a number of watering holes where you can stop to take a breather. There are also many restaurants plus a grassy square with benches where you can sit back and take everything in. Look for the current edition of the "St. John Map" featuring Max the Mongoose. It's a handy and amusing guide to where everything is.

You'll find one of the most inviting shopping experiences in the Caribbean at **Mongoose Junction.** Its West Indian–style architecture and native stone blend into the surrounding woods, making it a widely touted example of good development in a community grappling with growth problems. There's a deli-bakery with great pastries and a vast array of picnic supplies here, as well as several restaurants and numerous one-of-a-kind shops.

To pick up a handy guide to St. John's hiking trails, see various large maps of the island, and check out current park-service programs and program schedules, including guided walks and cultural demonstrations, stop by the **V.I. National Park Visitor's Center.** There's also an 18-minute video tour you can watch and a 90-gallon aquarium. ⊠ *Cruz Bay, 00831,* ☎ *809/776–6201.* ☒ *Free.* ☉ *Daily 8–4:30.*

❾ **Elaine Ione Sprauve Library and Museum.** On the hill just above Cruz Bay is the **Enighed Estate Great House,** built in 1757. *Enighed* is the Danish word for "concord," meaning unity or peace. The great house and its surrounding buildings (a sugar-production factory and horse-driven mill) were destroyed by fire and hurricanes, and the house sat in ruins until it was restored in 1982. Today it is home to the library and museum and houses a small collection of Indian pottery, colonial artifacts, and contemporary craft work by local artisans. The library hosts occasional crafts demonstrations and classes. ⊠ *Rte. 104, make a right past the Texaco station,* ☎ *809/776–6359.* ☒ *Free.* ☉ *Weekdays 9–5.*

❷ **Peace Hill.** It's worth a stop at this unmarked spot just past the Hawksnest Bay overlook for breathtaking views of St. John, St. Thomas, and the nearby British Virgin Islands. The flat promontory features an old sugar mill. The pile of white stones you'll see is what remains of *Christ of the Caribbean,* a statue honoring world peace erected in 1953 by Col. Julius Wadsworth. The statue fell to Hurricane Marilyn's winds in 1995, and the National Park Service decided not to rebuild it. From the parking lot, the statue is about 100 yards up a rocky path. ⊠ *Off North Shore Rd.*

❼ **Reef Bay Trail.** Although one of the most interesting hikes on St. John, unless you are a rugged individualist who wants a physical challenge (and that describes a lot of people who stay on St. John), you'll probably get the most out of the trip if you join a hike led by a National Park Service ranger, who can identify the trees and plants on the hike down, fill you in on the history of the Reef Bay Plantation, and tell you about the carvings you'll find in the rocks at the bottom of the trail. The National Park Service provides a boat ($10) to take you back to Cruz Bay, saving you the uphill return climb. The **Reef Bay Plantation,** according to architectural historian Frederik C. Gjessing, is the most architecturally ambitious plantation structure on St. John. The great house is largely intact, though gutted, and its classical beauty is still visible from what remains. You'll also see the remnants of a cook house, servants' quarters, stable, and outhouse. Reef Bay was the last working plantation on St. John when it stopped production in 1920. ⊠ *Rte. 10 between Cruz Bay and Coral Bay. There's a parking area on the left. Trail is off to the right.*

St. John A to Z

Emergencies
Police or ambulance (☎ 911).

Hospitals: For medical emergencies, visit the **Myrah Keating Smith Community Health Center** (⊠ Rte. 10 about 7 min east of Cruz Bay, ☎ 809/693–8900).

Air Ambulance: The only U.S.V.I.-based air ambulance service is **Bohlke International Airways** (☎ 809/778–9177), which operates out of the airport on St. Croix. **Air Medical Services** (☎ 800/443–0013) and **Air Ambulance Network** (☎ 800/327–1966) also serve the area from Florida.

Coast Guard: The **Marine Safety Detachment** (☎ 809/776–3497) on St. Thomas can be reached from 7 AM to 3:30 PM weekdays. If there is no answer, call the **Rescue Coordination Center** (☎ 809/722–2943) in San Juan, open 24 hours a day.

Pharmacy: The **St. John Drug Center** (☎ 809/776–6353) is in the Boulon shopping center, up Centerline Road in Cruz Bay.

Getting Around

BY BUS AND TAXI

On St. John buses and taxis are the same thing: open-air safari buses. Technically the safari buses are private taxis, but everyone uses them as an informal bus system. You'll find them congregated at the Cruz Bay Dock, ready to take you to any of the beaches or other island destinations, but you can also pick them up anywhere on the road by signaling. You're likely to travel with other tourists en route to their destinations. Typical rates from Cruz Bay (for two people) are $3.75 each to Trunk Bay, $4 each to Cinnamon Bay Campground, and $6.25 each to either Annaberg Plantation or Coral Bay.

BY CAR

Use caution when driving on St. John. The terrain is very hilly, the roads winding, and the blind curves numerous. You may suddenly come upon a huge safari bus careening around a corner, or a couple of hikers strolling along the side of the road. Major roads are well paved, but once you get off a specific route, dirt roads filled with potholes are common. For such driving, a four-wheel-drive vehicle is your best bet.

At the height of the winter season, you may find it tough to find a car, so reserve ahead of time to ensure you'll get the vehicle of your choice. **Car Rentals:** Call **Avis** (☎ 809/776–6374 or 800/331–1084), **Best** (☎ 809/693–8177), **Cool Breeze** (☎ 809/776–6588), **Delbert Hill Taxi Rental Service** (☎ 809/776–6637), **Denzil Clyne** (☎ 809/776–6715), **O'Connor Jeep** (☎ 809/776–6343), **St. John Car Rental** (☎ 809/776–6103), or **Spencer's Jeep** (☎ 809/693–8784 or 888/776–6628).

Guided Tours

Along with providing trail maps and brochures about St. John National Park, the park service also gives a variety of guided tours on- and off-shore. For more information or to arrange a tour contact the **V.I. National Park Visitor's Center** (✉ Cruz Bay, ☎ 809/776–6201; ✉ Cinnamon Bay, ☎ 809/776–6330). Fees charged cover the cost of transportation. The availability of the tours listed below varies depending on the time of year, so check with the visitor center.

The following tours require that you make reservations:

Reef Bay Hike. After you bus from the Visitor's Center to the trailhead, this vigorous hike at Reef Bay visits petroglyph carvings and an old sugar-mill factory. You'll need your serious walking shoes, and it's up to you to bring food and drink. An optional return-trip by boat ($10) saves you a hike back up the hill (making this a walk of only average difficulty) and will have you back in Cruz Bay by 3:30 PM. ☞ *$4.50 for the bus ride.*

Around-the-Island Snorkel Tour. A motorboat makes a six-hour trip around the island with three stops for snorkeling. You provide your own snorkeling gear and lunch. ☞ *$40.*

Bird Walks. Birders are bused to Francis Bay for a two-hour trail walk with a park-ranger guide. ☞ *$10 round-trip.*

The following tours do not require that you make reservations, but you will need to check in advance to verify the times and days tours are given:

Annaberg Ruins Tour. Park rangers tell all about this fascinating plantation. They'll tell you how slaves converted sugarcane to sugar and molasses, and that the red bricks came from Denmark and the yellow, from Holland. And they'll point out the jail where misbehaving slaves were sent to await their fate. Meet at the plantation. ✉ *Free.*

Water's Edge Walk. This one-hour walk along the coral flats and mangrove lagoon meets at the shoreline below the Annaberg Plantation parking lot. You'll need wading shoes. ✉ *Free.*

Snorkel Trips. Easy 1½-hour trips start at the Trunk Bay Beach. Bring your own snorkeling gear and a T-shirt for protection from the sun. ✉ *Free.*

During the evenings two to three days a week at **Cinnamon Bay,** rangers hold informal talks on park history, marine research, and other topics. Confirm times, because schedules change often in the islands.

Visitor Information

Information about the U.S.V.I. is available on St. John through the U.S. **Virgin Islands Government Tourist Office** (✉ Box 200, Cruz Bay, St. John 00830, in the compound between Sparky's and the U.S. Post Office, ☎ 809/776–6450). The **National Park Service** (✉ Box 710, Cruz Bay, St. John 00831, ☎ 809/776–6201) also has a visitor center at the Creek in Cruz Bay.

U.S. VIRGIN ISLANDS A TO Z

Arriving and Departing

From the U.S. by Plane

AIRPORTS AND AIRLINES

One advantage of visiting the U.S.V.I. is the abundance of nonstop and connecting flights that can have you at the beach in three to four hours from most East Coast departures. You may fly into the U.S.V.I. direct on **Delta** (☎ 800/221–1212) from Atlanta and on **US Airways** (☎ 800/428–4322) from Baltimore. **American** (☎ 800/474–4884) flies direct from Miami, New York, and San Juan, and **Prestige Airways** (☎ 800/299–8784) comes in direct from Washington, D.C., via Miami. Another option is to pick up a local flight from San Juan on **American Eagle** (☎ 800/474–4884).

BETWEEN THE AIRPORTS AND HOTELS

If you bought a package from a travel agency, your airport transfers *may* be included. Otherwise, you may be able to arrange for a pick-up by your hotel. Most hotels on **St. Thomas** don't have airport shuttles, but taxivans at the airport are plentiful. Per-person fees, set by the Virgin Island Taxi Commission, are from the airport to Marriott's Frenchman's Reef, $7.50; to Point Pleasant, $9; to Bluebeard's Castle, $5; and to the Ritz-Carlton, $12. Expect to pay a higher rate if you're alone and to be charged 50¢ per bag. During rush hour the trip to East End resorts can take up to 40 minutes, but a half hour is typical. Driving time from the airport to Charlotte Amalie is 15 minutes. Getting from the airport to **St. Croix** hotels by taxi costs about $10–$13. **St. John**'s Caneel Bay Resort has a private ferry that meets guests on the Charlotte Amalie waterfront. If you're not staying at Caneel, you can take a ferry to Cruz Bay from Charlotte Amalie or Red Hook and then walk or take a cab.

From the U.S. by Ship

Virtually every type of ship and major cruise line calls at St. Thomas; only a few call at St. Croix. One or both of these ports is usually included as part of a ship's eastern Caribbean itinerary. Many of the ships that call at St. Thomas also call in St. John or offer an excursion to that island. For a sailing aboard an ocean liner, contact **Cunard Line** (✉ 555 5th Ave., New York, NY 10017, ☎ 800/528–6273), **Dolphin Cruise Lines**

(✉ 901 South America Way, Miami, FL 33132, ☎ 800/222–1003), **Holland America Line** (✉ 300 Elliot Ave. W, Seattle, WA 98119, ☎ 800/426–0327), **Norwegian Cruise Lines** (✉ Box 025403, Miami, FL 33102, ☎ 800/327–7030), **Princess Cruises** (✉ 10100 Santa Monica Blvd., Los Angeles, CA 90067, ☎ 800/421–0522), **Royal Caribbean Cruise Line** (✉ 1050 Caribbean Way, Miami, FL 33132, ☎ 800/327–6700), or **Royal Cruise Lines** (✉ 1 Maritime Plaza, San Francisco, CA 94111, ☎ 800/622–0538). For a cruise aboard a luxury yacht, contact **Renaissance Cruises** (✉ 1800 Eller Dr., Suite 300, Box 350307, Fort Lauderdale, FL 33335-0307, ☎ 800/525–2450) or **Seabourn Cruise Line** (✉ 55 Francisco St., San Francisco, CA 94133, ☎ 800/929–9595). To travel aboard a real wind-powered sailing ship, contact **Windstar Cruises** (✉ 300 Elliot Ave. W, Seattle, WA 98119, ☎ 800/258–7245). Itineraries and ship deployments change frequently, so contact your cruise line or travel agent for the latest scheduled sailings.

For more information on cruises, see *Fodor's Caribbean Ports of Call 1998* (available in bookstores, or ☎ 800/533–6478).

Dining

Just about every kind of cuisine you can imagine is available in the U.S.V.I. The beauty and freedom of the islands have attracted a cadre of professionally trained chefs who know their way around fresh fish and local fruits. And locals are beginning to realize how attractive their cuisine is to tourists. As a result you can dine on everything from terrific, cheap local dishes, such as goat water and johnnycakes, to imports such as hot pastrami sandwiches and raspberries in crème fraîche.

A word of warning about the cost of eating and drinking in the U.S.V.I.: If you are staying in a large hotel you will pay prices similar to those in New York City or Paris—in other words, dining out is usually expensive. Fancy restaurants may have a token chicken dish under $20, but otherwise, main courses are in the high range. You can, however, find good inexpensive Caribbean restaurants, and the familiar fast-food franchises are plentiful on St. Thomas and St. Croix.

As for drinking, outside the hotels a beer in a bar will cost between $2 and $3 and a piña colada $4 or more.

St. Thomas is the most cosmopolitan of the islands and has the most visitors, so it is not surprising that the island also has the largest number and greatest variety of restaurants. St. Croix restaurants are both more relaxed and, in some ways, more elegant. Dining on St. John ranges from casual open-air eateries to upscale fine dining at a handful of sophisticated spots.

If you have a kitchen and plan to cook, you'll be able to find good variety in typical mainland-style supermarkets on both St. Thomas and St. Croix. St. John has several small markets scattered throughout the town of Cruz Bay, including the Starfish Market, Marina Market, and Tropicale. Prices on all three islands are higher than on the mainland.

CATEGORY	COST*
$$$$	over $35
$$$	$25–$35
$$	$15–$25
$	under $15

Average cost of a three-course dinner, per person, excluding drinks and service; there is no sales tax in the U.S.V.I.

Getting Around

By Bus

Although public buses are not the quickest way to get around on the islands, they are a fun and inexpensive mode of transportation to parts of St. Thomas and St. Croix. St. Thomas's 20 deluxe mainland-size buses make public transportation a very reasonable and comfortable way to get from east and west to town and back (there is no service north, however). Fifteen buses serve the island of St. Croix. St. John has no public bus system, so residents rely on taxi vans and safari buses for mass transportation.

By Car

Any U.S. driver's license is good for 90 days here; the minimum age for drivers is 18, although many agencies won't rent to anyone under the age of 25.

Driving is on the left side of the road (although your steering wheel will be on the left side of the car). The law requires drivers and passengers to wear seat belts: Many of the roads are narrow and the islands are dotted with hills, so there is ample reason to drive carefully. Even at a sedate speed of 20 mi per hour, driving can be an adventure—for example, you may find yourself in a stick-shift Jeep slogging behind a slow tourist-packed safari bus at a steep hairpin turn on St. John. Give a little beep at blind turns. Note that the general speed limit on these islands is only 25–35 mph, which will seem fast enough for you on most roads. If you don't think you'll need to lock up your valuables, a Jeep or open-air Suzuki with four-wheel drive will make it easier to navigate pot-holed dirt side roads and to get up slick hills when it rains. All main roads are paved.

By Ferry

Ferries are a great way to travel around the islands. There is ferry service between St. Thomas and St. John and their neighbors, the B.V.I. A hydrofoil also runs the 40-mi route between St. Thomas and St. Croix. There's something special about spending a day on St. John and then joining your fellow passengers—a mix of tourists, local families headed home after a day with relatives, and restaurant workers on the way to work—for a peaceful, sundown ride back to St. Thomas.

Ferries to St. John leave from either the Charlotte Amalie waterfront west of the U.S. Coast Guard dock or Red Hook.

From Charlotte Amalie, they depart at 9 and 11 AM and 1, 3, 4, and 5:30 PM. To Charlotte Amalie from Cruz Bay, they leave at 7:15, 9:15, and 11:15 AM and at 1:15, 2:15, and 3:45 PM. The fare for the 45-minute rides runs $7 for adults, $3 for children, and $5 for seniors with identification.

From Red Hook, the ferries to Cruz Bay leave at 6:30 and 7:30 AM. Starting at 8 AM, they leave hourly until midnight. Returning from Cruz Bay, they leave hourly starting at 6 AM until 10 PM. The last ferry heads back to Red Hook at 11:15 PM. The 15- to 20-minute ferry ride is $3 one way for adults, $1 for children under 12, and $1.25 for seniors with identification.

Reefer (☎ 809/776–8500, ext. 445) is the name of both brightly colored 26-passenger skiffs that run between the Charlotte Amalie waterfront and Marriott's Frenchman's Reef hotel every hour from 9 to 4, returning from the Reef from 9:30 until 4:30. It's a good way to beat the traffic (and is about the same price as a taxi) to Morning Star Beach, which adjoins the Reef. And you get a great view of the harbor as you bob along in the shadow of the giant cruise ships anchored in the harbor. The captain of the *Reefer* may also be persuaded to drop you at Yacht Haven, but check first. The fare is $4 one way, and the trip takes about 15 minutes. It runs every day.

A hydrofoil, the **Katrun II,** runs between St. Thomas and St. Croix daily. The boat leaves from the Charlotte Amalie waterfront on St. Thomas at 7:15 AM and 3:15 PM and departs from Gallows Bay outside of Christiansted, St. Croix, at 9:15 AM and 5:00 PM. The 1-hour-and-15-minute trip costs $37 one-way and $70 round-trip.

Regular ferry service is also available between the U.S.V.I. and the B.V.I., making a day trip or an overnight trip easy. It's a beautiful ride, especially if you arrive early enough to get to a topside seat. Don't be surprised when seagulls ride along with you. You'll need to present proof of citizenship upon entering the B.V.I.; a passport is best, but a birth certificate or voter's registration card will suffice.

There's daily service between either Charlotte Amalie or Red Hook and West End or Road Town, Tortola, by either **Smiths Ferry** (☎ 809/775–7292) or **Native Son, Inc.** (☎ 809/774–8685), and to Virgin Gorda by Smiths Ferry. The times and days the ferries run change, so it's best to call for schedules once you're in the islands.

Fare is $19 one-way or $35 round-trip, and the trip from Charlotte Amalie takes 45 minutes to an hour to West End, up to 1½ hours to Road Town; from Red Hook, the trip is only a half hour.

There's also daily service between Cruz Bay, St. John, and West End, Tortola, aboard the **Sundance** (☎ 809/776–6597). The half-hour one-way trip is $18.

By Plane
Leeward Islands Air Transport (LIAT, ☎ 809/774–2313) has service from St. Thomas, St. Croix, and San Juan to Caribbean islands to the south. **American Eagle** (☎ 800/474–4844) offers frequent flights daily between San Juan and St. Thomas, and between St. Thomas and St. Croix. **Seaborne Seaplane** (☎ 809/777–4491) flies between St. Thomas and St. Croix several times daily.

By Taxi
Taxis of all shapes and sizes are available at various ferry, shopping, resort, and airport areas on St. Thomas and St. Croix and respond quickly to a call. U.S.V.I. taxis do not have meters, but you need not worry about fare-gouging if you check a list of standard rates to popular destinations (required by law to be carried by each driver, and often posted in hotel and airport lobbies and printed in free tourist periodicals, such as *St. Thomas This Week*) and settle on the final bill before you start out. Fares are per person, not per destination, but drivers taking multiple fares (which often happens, especially coming in from the airport) will charge you a lower rate than if you're in the cab by yourself.

Lodging

The U.S.V.I. has myriad lodging options to suit any style, from luxury five-star resorts to casual condominiums and national campgrounds.

On all three islands you can opt for a big luxury hotel, where you never need leave the premises. Instead, you may simply glide from air-conditioned splendor to hotel beach to windsurfing to pool bar to gourmet restaurant and end the night at the in-house disco. Advantages: They're opulent and obvious. Disadvantages: They are very expensive, and the value provided does not always coincide with the expense incurred.

On St. Thomas, guest houses and smaller hotels are not typically on the beach, but they offer pools and shuttle service to nearby beaches

(St. Thomas is not a walking island)—and some have breathtaking views. A handful of historic hotels and inns above town have a pleasing island ambience. The only drawback is that you have to take taxis at night to get around.

In keeping with its small-town atmosphere and more relaxed pace, St. Croix offers a good variety of more moderately priced small hotels and guest houses, which are either on the beach or in a rural setting where a walk to the beach is easy.

Accommodations on St. John defy easy categorization. People come here expressly to experience the unspoiled tropical setting, and the island's better-known lodging choices are keyed to this fact. The national park campground offerings start with bare campsites (about as far back to nature as you could hope for, short of some deserted cay) and progress through tents and small cottages. There is also a privately owned Swiss Family Robinson–style community of tent shelters on wood decks, connected by elevated boardwalks and separated by vegetation.

At the other end of the spectrum are luxury retreats of understated elegance that offer rest and relaxation of a high—and pricey—order while taking care to fit into and not detract from their natural surroundings.

Between accommodations for the campers, the rich and powerful at rest, and environmentally conscious sybarites, there are moderately priced condominiums and inexpensive cottages throughout St. John—mostly in and around Cruz Bay—and plenty of private homes available for rent.

An especially appealing choice for the family or group of friends who want an affordable casual beach vacation is to rent a condominium or private home. All three islands have good variety in style and price range. Most condos are on or near a beach or on a hillside with a spectacular view; they generally have fully equipped kitchens, laundry facilities, and swimming pools. Many have a restaurant and bar on the property, and some offer daily maid service (vital if you don't want to spend all your time washing beach towels).

The prices below reflect rates during high season, which generally runs from December 15 to April 15. Rates are 25% to 50% lower the rest of the year.

CATEGORY	COST*
$$$$	over $200
$$$	$150–$200
$$	$100–$150
$	under $100

All prices are for a standard double room, excluding 8% accommodations tax.

Mail

The main U.S. Post Office on St. Thomas is near the hospital, with branches in Charlotte Amalie, Frenchtown, and Tutu Mall; there's a post office at Christiansted, Frederiksted, Gallows Bay, and Sunny Isle on St. Croix, and at Cruz Bay on St. John. **The U.S. Postal Service** (St. Thomas, ☎ 809/774–1950; St. Croix, ☎ 809/773–1505; St. John, ☎ 809/779–4227) offers Express Mail, one-day service to major cities if you mail before noon; outlying areas may take two days. Postal rates are the same as elsewhere in the United States: 32¢ for a letter, 20¢ for a postcard to anywhere in the United States, 50¢ for a ½-ounce letter mailed to a foreign country. Bring stamps. As they are everywhere else, post office lines can be excruciatingly slow.

Got to get it there fast? **Federal Express** (☎ 809/774–3393) is alive and well, but get your package to the office at the Havensight Mall (☎ 809/777–4140) in Charlotte Amalie on St. Thomas before 5 PM or to the St. Croix office in the Villa La Reine Shopping Center (☎ 809/778–8180) before 4 PM if you want overnight service. In St. John, **Sprint Courier Service** (☎ 809/693–8130) connects to all major couriers.

Opening and Closing Times

Shops on Charlotte Amalie's Main Street on St. Thomas are open weekdays and Saturday 9–5. Havensight Mall shops' (next to the cruise-ships dock) hours are the same, though some shops sometimes stay open until 9 on Friday, depending on how many cruise ships are staying late at the dock. You may also find some shops open on Sunday if a lot of cruise ships are in port. At the American Yacht Harbor in Red Hook, shops are generally open Monday through Saturday 9–6. Hotel shops are usually open evenings, as well.

St. Croix store hours are usually weekdays 9–5, but you will definitely find some shops in Christiansted open in the evening. Many stores are closed on Sunday.

On St. John, store hours are reliably similar to those on the other two islands, and Wharfside Village and Mongoose Junction shops in Cruz Bay are often open into the evening.

Precautions

Vacationers tend to assume that normal precautions aren't necessary in paradise. They are. Crime exists here, but not to the same degree that it does in larger cities on the U.S. mainland. Still, it's best to stick to well-lighted streets at night and use the same kind of street sense (don't wander the back alleys of Charlotte Amalie after five rum punches, for example) that you would in any unfamiliar territory. If you intend to carry things around, rent a car, not a Jeep, and lock possessions in the trunk. Keep your rental car locked wherever you park. Don't leave cameras, purses, and other valuables lying on the beach while you snorkel for an hour (or even for a minute), whether you're on the deserted beaches of St. John or the more crowded Magens and Coki beaches on St. Thomas.

Telephones

The area code for all of the U.S.V.I. is 809, and there is direct dialing to the mainland. Local calls from a public phone cost 25¢ for each five minutes.

On St. John the place to go for any telephone or message needs is **Connections** (Cruz Bay, ☎ 809/776–6922; Coral Bay, ☎ 809/779–4994). On St. Thomas, it's **Islander Services** (☎ 809/774–8128) at 5302 Store Tvaer Gade, behind the Greenhouse Restaurant in Charlotte Amalie; or **East End Secretarial Services** (☎ 809/775–5262, FAX 809/775–3590), upstairs at the Red Hook Plaza. **AT&T** has a state-of-the-art telecommunications center complete with 15 desk booths, fax and copy services, video phone, TDD equipment (for people with hearing impairments), across from the Havensight Mall on St. Thomas.

On St. Croix, visit **AnswerPLUS** (✉ 5005B Chandler's Wharf, Gallows Bay, ☎ 809/773–4444) or **Worldwide Calling** (✉ head of the pier in Frederiksted, ☎ 809/772–2490). The above businesses also provide copying and fax services, mail boxes, and long-distance dialing.

Visitor Information

Information about the United States Virgin Islands is available through the following **U.S.V.I. Government Tourist Offices:** ⊠ 225 Peachtree St., Suite 760, Atlanta, GA 30303, ☎ 404/688–0906, FAX 404/525–1102; ⊠ 500 N. Michigan Ave., Suite 2030, Chicago, IL 60611, ☎ 312/670–8784, FAX 312/670–8789; ⊠ 3460 Wilshire Blvd., Suite 412, Los Angeles, CA 90010, ☎ 213/739–0138, FAX 213/739–2005; ⊠ 2655 Le Jeune Rd., Suite 907, Coral Gables, FL 33134, ☎ 305/442–7200, FAX 305/445–9044; ⊠ 1270 Ave. of the Americas, Room 2108, New York, NY 10020, ☎ 212/332–2222, FAX 212/332–2223; ⊠ 900 17th Ave. NW, Suite 500, Washington, DC 20006, ☎ 202/293–3707, FAX 202/785–2542; ⊠ 1300 Ashford Ave., Condado, Santurce, Puerto Rico 00907, ☎ 809/724–3816, FAX 809/724–7223; ⊠ 3300 Bloor St., Suite 3120, Center Tower, Toronto, Ontario, Can. M8X 2X3, ☎ 416/233–1414, FAX 416/233–9367; and ⊠ 2 Cinnamon Row, Plantation Wharf, York Place, London SW11 3TW, ☎ 071/978–5262, telex 27231, FAX 071/924–3171.

5 The British Virgin Islands

Tortola, Virgin Gorda, Jost Van Dyke, Peter Island, Anegada, Other British Virgin Islands

The British Virgin Islands are a spectacular cluster of mountainous islands, and although they are now regularly visited by cruise ships, they retain their quiet, laid-back, and friendly atmosphere.

Updated by
Pamela
Acheson

THE BRITISH VIRGIN ISLANDS consist of about 50 islands, islets, and cays that are serene, seductive, and spectacularly beautiful. At some points they lie only a mile or so from the U.S. Virgin Islands, but they remain unique and have managed to retain their quiet, friendly, and very laid-back character. Although the past five years have seen a huge increase in the number of automobiles and the construction of a cruise-ship dock, for the most part the B.V.I. still remain happily free of the runaway development that has detracted from the charm of so many West Indian islands.

The pleasures found here are understated: sailing around the multitude of tiny, nearby islands; diving to the wreck of the RMS *Rhone,* sunk off Salt Island in 1867; snorkeling in one of hundreds of wonderful spots; walking along deserted beaches; taking in spectacular views from the islands' peaks; and settling down on some breeze-swept terrace to admire the sunset.

Tortola and Virgin Gorda are the only two B.V.I. with road systems, and they are dramatic, with dizzying roller-coaster dips and climbs and glorious views. Distractions are the real danger here, from the glittering mosaic of azure sea, white skies, and emerald islets to the ambling cattle and grazing goats peppered along the roadside. The natural beauty is overwhelming.

Much of the credit for this blissful simplicity must go to the B.V.I.'s sensitive tourism policies. No building can rise higher than the surrounding palms—two stories is the limit. The lack of direct air flights from the mainland United States also helps the British islands retain the endearing qualities of yesteryear's Caribbean. To fly in, you first have to go to Puerto Rico, 60 mi to the west, or to nearby St. Thomas in the U.S.V.I. and catch a small plane to the little airports on Beef Island/Tortola or Virgin Gorda. The B.V.I. government recently approved a major expansion of the Beef Island airport, which is scheduled for completion in 2003. For some this is a mixed blessing: access to the B.V.I. will be much easier, but at the same time the number of tourists will be on the rise. Even now, the number of day visitors from cruise ships is sometimes problematic. Road Town, which opened a new cruise-ship dock several years ago, can be simply overrun with debarkers on cruise-ship days. The Baths, on Virgin Gorda, also gets overloaded with cruise-ship visitors.

Many of the travelers who return year after year arrive by water, either aboard their own ketches and yawls or on one of the convenient ferryboats that cross the turquoise waters between St. Thomas and Tortola. No doubt the passage provides a fine prelude to a stay in these unhurried tropical havens. Departing from the clamor of St. Thomas's brash and bumptious Charlotte Amalie, ferry passengers find their cares vanishing with the ship's wake. From the upper deck of the *Native Son,* one of the ferries that make the one-hour St. Thomas–Tortola crossing, passengers can view the hilly little islands as they slip past, some velvety green, others rocky and wild. Thickets of swaying masts mark favored moorings on some islands, serving as reminders of the superb sailing to be found hereabouts.

Tortola, about 10 sq mi, is the largest of the islands; Virgin Gorda, with 8 sq mi, ranks second. The islands scattered around them include Jost Van Dyke, Great Camanoe, Norman, Peter, Salt, Cooper, Ginger, Dead Chest, and Anegada, among others.

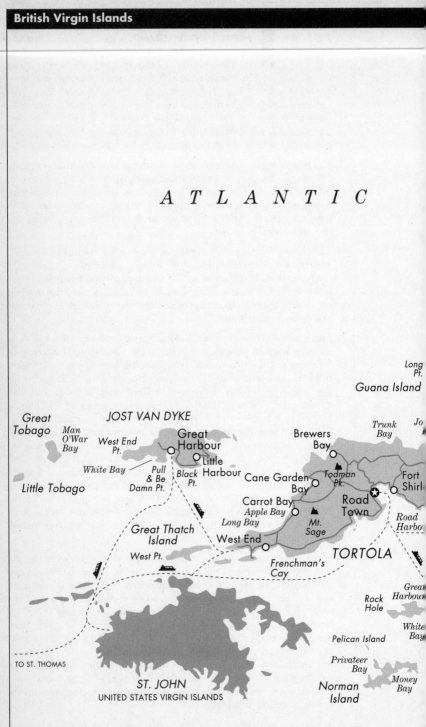

A T L A N T I C

Great
Tobago

Man
O'War
Bay

Little Tobago

JOST VAN DYKE

West End
Pt.

White Bay

Pull
& Be
Damn Pt.

Great
Harbour

Little
Harbour

Black
Pt.

Cane Garden
Bay

Carrot Bay

Apple Bay

Long Bay

West End

Frenchman's
Cay

Great Thatch
Island

West Pt.

Brewers
Bay

Todman
Pk.

Mt.
Sage

Road
Town

TORTOLA

Rock
Hole

Great
Harbour

Pelican Island

Privateer
Bay

Norman
Island

Money
Bay

White
Bay

Road
Harbo

Fort
Shirl

Trunk
Bay

Jo

Long
Pt.

Guana Island

TO ST. THOMAS

ST. JOHN
UNITED STATES VIRGIN ISLANDS

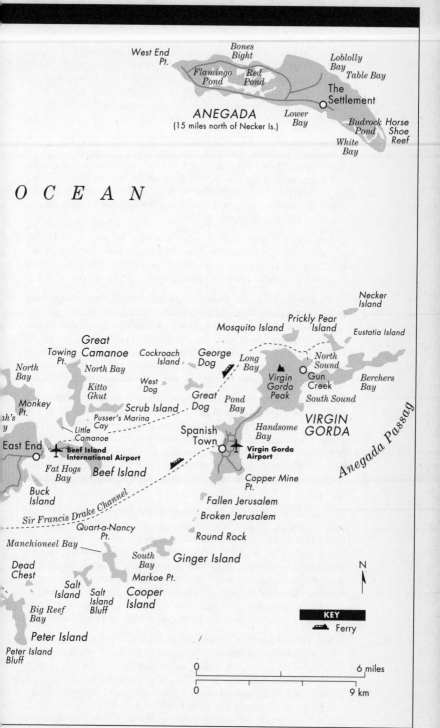

West End
Pt.

Bones
Bight

Loblolly
Bay

Table Bay

Flamingo
Pond

Red
Pond

The
Settlement

ANEGADA
(15 miles north of Necker Is.)

Lower
Bay

Budrock
Pond

Horse
Shoe
Reef

White
Bay

O C E A N

Necker
Island

Prickly Pear
Island

Mosquito Island

Eustatia Island

**Great
Camanoe**

Towing
Pt.

Cockroach
Island

**George
Dog**

Long
Bay

North
Sound

*North
Bay*

North Bay

West
Dog

Virgin
Gorda
Peak

Gun
Creek

Berchers
Bay

*Monkey
Pt.*

Kitto
Ghut

**Great
Dog**

Pond
Bay

South Sound

*uh's
y*

Scrub Island

Pusser's Marina
Cay

Spanish
Town

Handsome
Bay

**VIRGIN
GORDA**

Little
Camanoe

East End

**Beef Island
International Airport**

**Virgin Gorda
Airport**

Anegada Passag

Fat Hogs
Bay

Beef Island

Copper Mine
Pt.

Buck
Island

Fallen Jerusalem

Sir Francis Drake Channel

Broken Jerusalem

Quart-a-Nancy
Pt.

Round Rock

Manchioneel Bay

South
Bay

Ginger Island

Dead
Chest

Markoe Pt.

Salt
Island

Salt
Island
Bluff

**Cooper
Island**

Big Reef
Bay

N

Peter Island

Peter Island
Bluff

KEY

Ferry

0   6 miles

0   9 km

Tortola is the most populated of the B.V.I. and has the most hotels, restaurants, and shops. Virgin Gorda offers a limited number of restaurants and shops, and many of the resorts on the island are self-contained. Jost Van Dyke is a major charter boat anchorage, and while little bars now line the beach at Great Harbour, there are few places to stay overnight on the island. The other islands are either uninhabited or have a single hotel or resort. But many of these, such as Peter Island, offer excellent anchorages, and their bays and harbors are extremely popular with overnighting boaters.

Sailing has always been a popular activity in the B.V.I. The first arrivals here were a romantic seafaring tribe, the Siboney Indians, who wandered among these islands living off the indigenous plant and marine life. Then, around the year 900, the peaceable Arawak Indians sailed from South America, established settlements here, and farmed and fished. Eventually they were overwhelmed by the warlike Caribs, who slaughtered and ate their enemies.

Christopher Columbus was the first European to visit, in 1493. Impressed by the number of islands dotting the horizon, he named them *Las Once Mil Virgines*—The 11,000 Virgins—in honor of the 11,000 virgin-companions of Saint Ursula, martyred in the 4th century.

In the ensuing years, the Spaniards passed through these waters fruitlessly seeking gold. Then came the pirates, who found the islands' hidden coves and treacherous reefs an ideal base from which to prey on passing galleons crammed with Mexican and Peruvian gold, silver, and spices. Among the most notorious of these predatory men were Blackbeard Teach, Bluebeard, Captain Kidd, and Sir Francis Drake, who lent his name to the channel that sweeps through the two main clusters of the B.V.I.

In the 17th century, these colorful cutthroats were replaced by the Dutch who, in turn, were soon sent packing by the British. It was the British who established a plantation economy, and for the next 150 years developed the sugar industry. African slaves were brought in to work the cane fields while the plantation owners and their families reaped the benefits. When slavery was abolished in 1838, the plantation economy quickly faltered, and the majority of the white population returned to Europe.

The islands dozed, a forgotten corner of the British empire, until the early 1960s. In 1966, a new constitution granting greater autonomy to the islands was approved. While the governor is still appointed by the Queen of England, his or her limited powers concentrate on external affairs and local security. The Legislative Council, which consists of representatives from nine island districts, administers other matters. General elections are held every four years. The arrangement seems to suit the British Virgin Islanders just fine: The political mood is serene, with none of the occasional turmoil found on other islands.

In the 1960s Laurance Rockefeller and American-expatriate Charlie Cary brought the beginnings of tourism to the B.V.I. when they both became convinced that the islands' balmy weather, powder-soft beaches, and splendid sailing would make them an ideal holiday destination. Attempts at building a small tourist industry began in 1965, when Rockefeller set about creating the Little Dix resort on Virgin Gorda. Dedicated to preserving the natural beauty of the island while providing its guests with unpretentious yet elegant surroundings, Little Dix set the standard that still prevails in the B.V.I. A few years later, Cary and his wife, Ginny, established the Moorings marina complex on Tortola, and sailing in the area burgeoned.

For a long time, tourism accounted for most of the B.V.I.'s income, but now offshore banking is the number-one industry. Still, the majority of jobs on the islands are tourism-related; light industry is practically nonexistent and, for the present, is unlikely to appear. British Virgin Islanders love their unspoiled tropical home and are determined to maintain its easygoing charms, for both themselves and the travelers who are their guests.

TORTOLA

Unwinding can easily become a full-time occupation on Tortola, where the leisurely pace of the island's inhabitants has made traffic lights unnecessary (although, with the recent increase in traffic in Road Town, a traffic light might be a good idea). Even the scenery seems to have been created with the idea of inspiring the poet in us. Though Tortola offers a wealth of things to see and do, many visitors prefer just to loll about on a deserted beach or linger over lunch at one of the island's many delightful restaurants. Beaches are never more than a few minutes away, and the steeply sloping green hills that form Tortola's spine are continuously fanned by gentle trade winds. The neighboring islands glimmer like emeralds in a sea of sapphire. It's a world far removed from the hustle of modern life.

Lodging

Luxury on Tortola is more a state of mind—serenity, seclusion, gentility—than state-of-the-art amenities and facilities. Except for Prospect Reef, hotels in Road Town don't have beaches but do have pools and are within walking distance of restaurants, nightlife, and shopping. Accommodations outside Road Town are relatively isolated but are on beaches, some of which are exquisite, while others are small or artificial.

Hotels and Inns

ROAD TOWN

$$–$$$$ ⊞ **Moorings-Mariner Inn.** Headquarters for the Moorings Charter operation and popular with yachting folk who find its full-service facilities convenient and the companionship of fellow "boaties" congenial, this is also a good choice for those who want to be within easy walking distance of town. The atmosphere is a combination of laid-back and lively, and the rooms, including four full-size suites, are large and comfortable. The rooms' pale-peach decor is picked up in the peach tiles on the floors, and bright, tropical-print bedspreads and curtains add color. All rooms have a small kitchenette—with sink, refrigerator, and two-burner stove—and a balcony, and most rooms face the water, except for eight that overlook the pool or the tennis court. ⊠ *Box 139,* ☎ *284/494–2331,* 𝖥𝖠𝖷 *284/494–2226. 40 rooms. Restaurant, bar, pool, tennis court, volleyball, dive shop. AE, MC, V.*

$$–$$$$ ⊞ **Prospect Reef Resort.** This 7-acre waterside resort is near town and overlooks Sir Francis Drake Channel. Brightly painted buildings sit on sprawling grounds amidst creative rock paths and a network of lagoons. The 11 different housing units include small rooms, larger rooms with kitchenettes, and two-story, two-bedroom apartments with private interior courtyards. All have a balcony or patio. In addition to the hotel's 25-meter swimming pool and separate diving pool, there are two adjoining saltwater swimming areas created at the edge of a narrow, artificial beach. The resort also boasts its own harbor with sailboats available for day trips or longer excursions. Lighted tennis courts and a rather rustic pitch-and-putt golf course are among the pleasures on the grounds. You may even see one of the local goats moseying around. A bonus at the largest resort in the B.V.I.: splendid views of sunrise

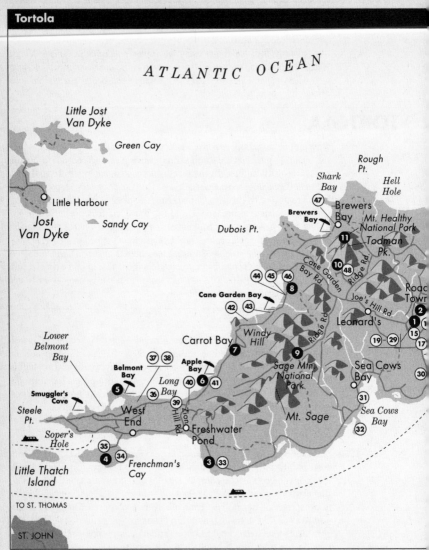

ATLANTIC OCEAN

Little Jost
Van Dyke

Green Cay

Little Harbour

Jost
Van Dyke

Sandy Cay

Dubois Pt.

Shark
Bay

Rough
Pt.

Hell
Hole

Brewers
Bay

Mt. Healthy
National Park

Todman
Pk.

Cane Garden
Bay Rd

Ridge Rd

Joe's Hill Rd.

Road
Town

Leonard's

Cane Garden Bay

Carrot Bay

Windy
Hill

Sage Mtn
National
Park

Sea Cows
Bay

Sea Cows
Bay

Mt. Sage

Lower
Belmont
Bay

Belmont
Bay

Smuggler's
Cove

Steele
Pt.

Soper's
Hole

Little Thatch
Island

West
End

Apple
Bay

Long
Bay

Zion Hill Rd

Freshwater
Pond

Frenchman's
Cay

TO ST. THOMAS

ST. JOHN

Exploring
Belmont Point, **5**
Bomba's Surfside
Shack, **6**
Cane Garden Bay, **8**
Fort Burt, **2**
Fort Recovery, **3**
Frenchman's Cay, **4**
Mount Healthy
National Park, **11**
North Shore Shell
Museum, **7**

Queen Elizabeth II
Bridge, **12**
RMS *Rhone*, **13**
Road Town, **1**
Sage Mountain
National Park, **9**
Skyworld, **10**

Dining
The Apple, **40**
Brandywine Bay, **52**
C and F
Restaurant, **22**
Capriccio di Mare, **18**
Conch Shell Point, **50**
Fishtrap, **14**
Fort Wine
Gourmet, **23**
Garden
Restaurant, **31**

The Last Resort
(Bellamy Cay), **51**
The Lime
'n Mango, **27**
Mrs. Scatliffe's, **43**
Myett's, **44**
The Pub, **24**
Pusser's Landing, **35**
Pusser's Pub, **17**
Quito's Gazebo, **46**
Skyworld, **48**
Spaghetti
Junction, **20**

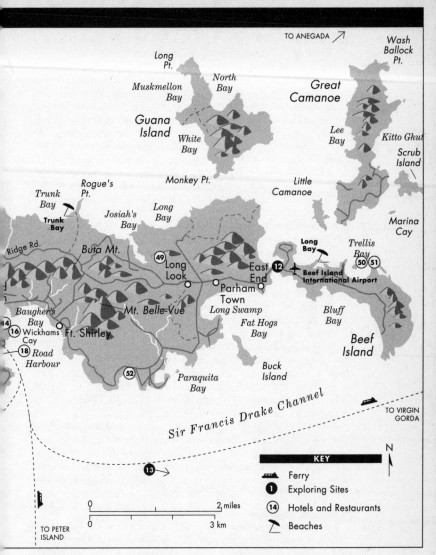

TO ANEGADA ↗

Wash
Ballock
Pt.

Long
Pt.

*Muskmellon
Bay*

*North
Bay*

Great
Camanoe

Guana
Island

*White
Bay*

*Lee
Bay*

Kitto Ghut

*Scrub
Island*

Monkey Pt.

*Little
Camanoe*

*Trunk
Bay*

*Rogue's
Pt.*

*Marina
Cay*

**Trunk
Bay**

*Josiah's
Bay*

*Long
Bay*

*Long
Bay*

*Trellis
Bay*

(50)(51)

Ridge Rd.

Buta Mt.

(49)

Long
Look

East
End

(12)

Beef Island
International Airport

Parham
Town

Baugher's
Bay

(4)
(16) Wickhams
Cay
(18) *Road
Harbour*

Mt. Belle-Vue

Ft. Shirley

Long Swamp

*Fat Hogs
Bay*

*Bluff
Bay*

Beef
Island

(52)

*Paraquita
Bay*

*Buck
Island*

Sir Francis Drake Channel

TO VIRGIN
GORDA

(13) →

KEY

N

⛴ Ferry

① Exploring Sites

⑭ Hotels and Restaurants

☂ Beaches

0 ——— 2 miles
0 ——— 3 km

TO PETER
ISLAND

The Struggling
Man, **31**

Sugar Mill
Restaurant, **41**

Tavern in the
Town, **21**

Virgin Queen, **15**

Lodging

Brewers Bay
Campground, **47**

Equinox House, **38**

Frenchman's Cay
Hotel, **34**

Heritage Villas, **42**

Hotel Castle
Maria, **25**

Long Bay Beach
Resort, **36**

Maria's Resort
by the Sea, **19**

Moorings-Mariner
Inn, **26**

Mount Sage Villas, **28**

Nanny Cay Resort
and Marina, **32**

Ole Works Inn, **45**

Prospect Reef
Resort, **30**

Rockview Holiday
Homes, **29**

Sebastian's on the
Beach, **39**

Sugar Mill Hotel, **41**

Sunset House and
Villas, **37**

Tamarind Club
Hotel and Villas, **49**

Treasure Isle
Hotel, **27**

Village Cay
Resort, **16**

The Villas at Fort
Recovery Estates, **33**

over Drake's Channel. The resort also offers a superb camp for kids. ⊠ *Box 104,* ☎ *284/494–3311,* ℻ *284/494–5595. 130 rooms. 2 restaurants, 2 bars, snack bar, 2 pools, saltwater pool, wading pool, 6 tennis courts, beauty salon, convention center. AE, MC, V.*

$$–$$$$ ★ 🏨 **Treasure Isle Hotel.** Owned by the Moorings, this hillside hotel, painted in bright shades of lemon, violet, and mango pink, is one of the prettiest properties on the island. The rooms are simply decorated but spacious and accented with fabrics sporting prints in the manner of Matisse. Set on a hillside overlooking the harbor, Treasure Isle is a handy base for in-town shopping and visits to nearby marinas. The comfortable lounge of the Spy Glass Bar, which is open to the breezes and the heady aroma of tropical flowers, is the perfect place to relax and study the stunning view of the harbor and distant islands. There is daily transportation to Cane Garden Bay and Brewers Bay. ⊠ *Box 68,* ☎ *284/494–2501,* ℻ *284/494–2507. 40 rooms. Restaurant, 2 bars, pool. AE, MC, V.*

$$–$$$ 🏨 **Maria's Resort by the Sea.** Perched on the edge of Road Harbour, next to the large government building and the cruise-ship dock, this simple hotel is an easy walk from restaurants in town. The small rooms are minimally decorated with white rattan furniture, floral-print bedspreads, and murals painted by local artists. All rooms have kitchenettes and balconies, some of which offer harbor views. A freshwater pool is available for cooling dips. ⊠ *Box 206,* ☎ *284/494–2595. 20 rooms. Restaurant, bar, pool. AE, MC, V.*

$$–$$$ 🏨 **Village Cay Resort.** This pleasant, compact hotel looks out on Road Harbour and several marinas. It is popular with yachters and those who want to be within easy walking distance of Road Town restaurants and shops. Rooms are nicely decorated in tropical prints. Some units have cathedral ceilings, while others are quite small. There is a small pool. ⊠ *Box 145, Wickham's Cay,* ☎ *284/494–2771,* ℻ *284/494–2773. 18 rooms. Restaurant, bar, pool. AE, MC, V.*

$–$$ 🏨 **Hotel Castle Maria.** These very simple accommodations, which are just outside of town, are ideal for those who are on a budget. Some rooms have kitchenettes, balconies, and air-conditioning. All have refrigerators and cable TV. Close to in-town diversions, Castle Maria also has its own freshwater pool and a bar. ⊠ *Box 206, Road Town,* ☎ *284/ 494–2553. 30 rooms. Bar, pool. AE, MC, V.*

OUTSIDE ROAD TOWN

$$$–$$$$ 🏨 **Frenchman's Cay Hotel.** This casual collection of condos also functions as a resort—it has one- and two-bedroom villas that overlook Drake's Channel. Each unit includes a full kitchen, dining area, and sitting room—ideal for families or couples. Rooms are done in neutral colors, with cream-color curtains and bedspreads and tile floors. Ceiling fans and pleasant breezes keep the rooms cool. There is a small pool and a modest-size artificial beach that is sandy to the water's edge but rocky offshore. It's not good for wading without shoes but does offer good snorkeling. Snorkelers will particularly enjoy the offshore reef here. The alfresco bar and dining room are breeze-swept and offer simple fare. ⊠ *Box 1054, West End,* ☎ *284/495–4844,* ℻ *284/495–4056. 9 units. Restaurant, bar, pool, tennis court, beach. AE, D, MC, V.*

$$$–$$$$ ★ 🏨 **Long Bay Beach Resort.** Spectacularly set on a gentle mile-long arc of white sand, this appealing hotel is the best on Tortola. There is a wide variety of accommodations to choose from, including 32 deluxe beachfront rooms, with two queen-size beds or one king-size four-poster bed, marble-top wet bars, showers with Italian tiles, and balconies. There are also smaller beach cabanas, 10 tropical hideaways set on stilts at the water's edge. Hillside choices all have balconies and lovely views and range from small but adequate rooms to studios with a comfortable seating area to roomy one- and two-bedroom villas. The use of floral prints and rattan furniture sets a tropical mood throughout. The Beach restaurant, which has a charming upper-level deck, offers all-day dining, and the Garden restaurant serves gourmet dinners in a romantic, candlelit setting. There's a new fitness center. Peter Burwash runs the tennis program. A pool and a nine-hole, par-3, pitch-and-putt golf course complete the complex. ⊠ *Box 433, Road Town,* ☎ *284/495–4252 or 800/729–9599,* FAX *284/495–4677. 62 rooms, 20 villas. 2 restaurants, 2 bars, pool, tennis court, beach. AE, MC, V.*

$$$–$$$$ 🏨 **Nanny Cay Resort and Marina.** With its pastel-painted, gingerbread-trimmed buildings clustered amid overgrown gardens, this hotel exudes the ambience of a small village, albeit one in need of sprucing up. The rooms, each with its own patio or balcony, have kitchenettes, air-conditioning, ceiling fans, telephones, and cable TV. Typically tropical decor includes cane furniture, floral bedspreads, shuttered windows, and a pastel color scheme. There is a nice-size swimming pool, a saltwater pool made out of large boulders at the water's edge, and an artificial beach. ⊠ *Box 281, Road Town,* ☎ *284/494–2512,* FAX *284/494–3288. 42 rooms. 2 restaurants, 2 bars, 1 pool, saltwater pool. AE, MC, V.*

$$$–$$$$ 🏨 **Sugar Mill Hotel.** The owners of this small, out-of-the-way hotel know what they're doing—they were well-established food and travel writers before they settled down and opened the Sugar Mill more than two decades ago. The reception area, bar, and restaurant are in the ruins of a centuries-old sugar mill that gives the place its name, and the walls are hung with bright Haitian artwork. Guest houses are scattered up a hill. The rooms are simply furnished in soft pastels and rattan, with ceiling fans. Some units have air-conditioning. This is a popular spot, with some visitors returning year after year. Light sleepers might want to request air-conditioning, to block out the noise of the roosters, who start crowing long before dawn. There's a small circular swimming pool set into the hillside and a tiny beach where lunch is served on a shady terrace. The dinner restaurant is well known on the island (☞ Dining, *below*). ⊠ *Box 425, Road Town,* ☎ *284/495–4355,* FAX *284/495–4696. 21 rooms. 2 restaurants, 2 bars, pool, beach. AE, MC, V.*

$$–$$$$ 🏨 **The Villas at Fort Recovery Estates.** This appealing, somewhat remote ★ group of one- to four-bedroom cottages, built around the remnants of a Dutch fort, stretches along a little beach facing the Sir Francis Drake Channel. A tasteful new second-story has been added, with seven penthouse villas. All units have excellent views, with sliding glass doors that open onto patios or balconies facing the ocean, and fully equipped kitchens. Bedrooms are air-conditioned; living rooms (not air-conditioned) are suitable as an additional bedroom for one child. The grounds are bright with tropical flowers. Management here is exceptionally helpful and friendly. A gourmet kitchen provides excellent room-service meals which are served, course by course, by candlelight. There's a pool, a recently expanded beach, exercise and yoga classes, massages, VCRs and videos for rent, and baby-sitting services, and arrangements can be made for car rental, guided land and water tours, and more. ⊠ *Box 239, Road Town,* ☎ *284/495–4467,* FAX *284/495–4036. 17 units. Room service, pool, beach, baby-sitting. AE, MC, V.*

$$–$$$ 🏨 **Sebastian's on the Beach.** The best rooms here are the eight small rooms that open right onto the beach. They're airy and white, simply decorated with floral-print curtains and bedspreads, and have either terraces or balconies and great ocean breezes and views. Bathrooms have only stall showers. There is no air-conditioning, but ceiling fans and louvered windows keep the rooms cool, and you are lulled to sleep by the sound of the ocean. The 18 rooms that don't face the beach are very simple, lack views, and can be noisy. Some of these are across the street and are quite a bit cheaper than the beach rooms. The restaurant here is casual but excellent. ⊠ *Box 441, Road Town,* ☎ *284/495–4212,* FAX *284/495–4466. 26 rooms. Restaurant, bar, snack bar, beach. AE.*

$$–$$$ ⊞ **Tamarind Club Hotel and Villas.** This out-of-the-way small hotel on the north side of the island has opened and closed several times over the years. Recently under new management, it has been overhauled and is quite charming. It's tucked into a valley not too far from East End and about a half-mile inland from the beach at Josiah's Bay. The 10 rooms are built around a courtyard and pool. All have ceiling fans; some are air-conditioned. There are also three two-bedroom villas. ⊠ *Box 441, Road Town,* ☎ *284/495–2477,* FAX *284/495–2858. 10 rooms, 3 2-bedroom villas. Restaurant, bar, pool. MC, V.*

$–$$ ⊞ **Ole Works Inn.** Nestled in the hillside across the road from one of Tortola's most beautiful beaches is this rustic but appealing inn—owned by local recording star Quito Rhymer. A steeply pitched roof, wood, and island stonework add a contemporary flair to what was once an old sugar mill. Simply decorated rooms have ceiling fans, air-conditioning, and refrigerators. The Honeymoon Suite has an indoor swing for two. ⊠ *Box 560, Cane Garden Bay,* ☎ *284/495–4837,* FAX *284/495–9618. 18 rooms. MC, V.*

Private Homes and Villas

Rockview Holiday Homes (⊠ Box 263, Road Town, ☎ 284/494–2550) represents the island's top-of-the-line properties. Homes offer accommodations for 2 to 10 people in one- to five-bedroom villas, decorated in soothing pastels. Many have swimming pools, Jacuzzis, and glazed terra-cotta courtyards. Standouts, both on Long Bay, are **Sunset House and Villas,** an exquisite hideaway whose first guest was Britain's Princess Alexandra (but you needn't be royalty to receive the royal treatment here), and **Equinox House,** a handsome three-bedroom estate set among lavish tumbling gardens. Rates vary but range from expensive ($$$) to very expensive ($$$$) in season. **Mount Sage Villas** (⊠ Box 821, Road Town, ☎ 284/495–9567), near the highest peak on Tortola, is a bit of a drive down to the beaches, but views and breezes are spectacular.

Campgrounds

$ 🛆 **Brewers Bay Campground.** Both prepared and bare sites are on Brewers Bay, one of Tortola's prime snorkeling spots. Check out the ruins of the distillery that gave the bay its name. There are public bathrooms but no showers. ⊠ *Box 185, Road Town,* ☎ *284/494–3463. 10 prepared and 18 bare sites. Restaurant, bar, beach, windsurfing, baby-sitting. No credit cards.*

Dining

There's no lack of dining options on Tortola. Seafood is plentiful, and although other fresh ingredients are scarce, the island's chefs are an adaptable lot who apply creative genius to whatever the weekly supply boat delivers.

Road Town

$$–$$$ ✕ **Lime 'n' Mango.** A long open-air veranda is the romantic setting for this popular restaurant at the Treasure Isle Hotel. The menu features both local specialties and, surprisingly, authentic Mexican cuisine. Try the conch fritters, salt fish cakes, or Jamaican calamari for an appetizer. The fajitas—chicken, beef, or vegetarian—are without a doubt the best Mexican entrée, arriving at your table sizzling in a hot iron frying pan along with a basket of warm tortillas. The coconut shrimp is also popular, and the Anegada lobster is always fresh. ⊠ *Treasure Isle Hotel, Road Town,* ☎ *284/494–2501. AE, MC, V.*

$$ ✕ **C and F Restaurant.** Crowds head here for the best barbecue in town (chicken, fish, and ribs), fresh local fish prepared your way, and excellent curries. Sometimes there's a wait for a table, but it is worth it. The restaurant is just outside Road Town, on a side street past the Moorings and just past Riteway. ⊠ *Purcell Estate,* ☎ *284/494–4941. Reservations not accepted. AE, MC, V. No lunch.*

$$ ✗ **The Fishtrap.** Dine alfresco at this restaurant, which serves grilled local fish, steaks, and chicken, plus Mexican and Oriental selections. Friday and Saturday there's a barbecue with a terrific salad bar; Sunday prime rib is the special. The lunch menu includes burgers and salads. ⊠ *Columbus Centre, Wickham's Cay, Road Town,* ☎ *284/494–3626. AE, MC, V. No lunch Sun.*

$$ ✗ **The Pub.** At this lively waterfront spot, tables are arranged along a terrace facing a small marina and Road Town harbor. Hamburgers, salads, and sandwiches are typical lunch offerings. In the evenings you can also choose grilled fish, steak, or chicken, or barbecued ribs. There's entertainment here weekends and almost always a spirited dart game. ⊠ *Waterfront Dr., Road Town,* ☎ *284/494–2608. Reservations not accepted. AE, MC, V. Closed Sun.*

$$ ✗ **Pusser's Pub.** Almost everyone who visits Tortola stops here at least once to have a bite to eat and to sample the famous Pusser's Rum Painkiller. The menu includes such English Pub fare as shepherd's pie, local specialties like Road Town Rice and chicken rotis, and cheezy pizzas. ⊠ *Waterfront Dr., Road Town,* ☎ *284/494–3897. AE, MC, V.*

$$ ✗ **Spaghetti Junction.** This cozy spot is popular with the boating crowd. Penne with a spicy tomato sauce, spinach-mushroom lasagna, and capellini with shellfish are house specialties here, but the menu also includes more traditional Italian fare (veal or chicken parmigiana, pastas, etc.). The sun-dried tomatoes in the Caesar salad are a nice twist. Check out the gorilla in the rest room. ⊠ *Waterfront Dr., Road Town,* ☎ *284/494–4880. No credit cards. Closed Sept. and holidays. No lunch.*

$$ ✗ **Tavern in the Town.** Birds and bougainvillea brighten the garden setting of this English-style pub. Mixed grills and fish-and-chips are in the British tradition, though you can also order such entrées as duck in orange and rum sauce and garlic shrimp, as well as hamburgers. ⊠ *Waterfront Dr., Road Town,* ☎ *284/494–2790. No credit cards. Closed Sat.*

$–$$ ✗ **Capriccio di Mare.** The owners of the well-known Brandywine Bay
★ restaurant also run this authentic Italian café. People stop by in the morning for an espresso and a fresh pastry, and all day long for a cappuccino or a tiramisu, delicious toast Italiano (grilled ham and Swiss-cheese sandwiches), fresh salads, bowls of perfectly cooked linguine or penne with a variety of sauces, and crispy tomato and mozzarella pizzas topped with hot Italian sausage or fresh grilled eggplant. Drink specialties include the Mango Bellini, an adaptation of the famous Bellini cocktail served by Harry's Bar in Venice. ⊠ *Waterfront Dr., Road Town,* ☎ *284/494–5369. Reservations not accepted. No credit cards. Closed Sun. Closes at 9 PM Mon.–Sat.*

$–$$ ✗ **Fort Wine Gourmet.** Tables look out through French doors at this charming spot, which doubles as a gourmet deli. It's open all day and is a great place for an espresso or a cappuccino, a fresh pastry, or a tasty salad or sandwich. ⊠ *Main St., Road Town,* ☎ *284/494–3036. Reservations not accepted. AE, MC, V. Closed Sun.*

$–$$ ✗ **Virgin Queen.** The sailing and rugby crowd and locals gather here to play darts, drink beer, and eat Queen's Pizza, which some patrons say is the best pizza in the Caribbean. Also on the menu is excellent West Indian and English fare: Choose from salt fish, barbecued ribs with beans and rice, bangers and mash, shepherd's pie, and chili, to name only a selection of delicious menu items. ⊠ *Fleming St., Road Town,* ☎ *284/494–2310. Reservations not accepted. No credit cards. Closed Sun.*

Outside Road Town

$$$ ✕ **Brandywine Bay.** For the best in romantic dining, don't miss this
★ hillside gem. Candlelit, outdoor tables look out on a sweeping view of
neighboring islands. Italian owner-chef Davide Pugliese prepares foods
the Tuscan way, grilled with lots of fresh herbs. The remarkable menu,
which hostess Cele Pugliese describes table-side, can include homemade
mozzarella, foie gras, grilled local wahoo, and grilled veal chop with
ricotta and sun-dried tomatoes and always includes duck with an ex-
otic sauce—maybe berry, mango, orange and ginger, or passion fruit.
The lemon tart and the tiramisu are irresistible. The wine list is excel-
lent. ⊠ *Sir Francis Drake Hwy., east of Road Town,* ☏ *284/495–2301.
Reservations essential. AE, MC, V. Closed Sun. No lunch.*

$$$ ✕ **Skyworld.** The longtime owner-chef of the well-known Upstairs
★ restaurant recently took over this mountaintop aerie, bringing his superb
menu with him. Come at sunset and watch the western horizon go
ablaze with color, then settle back in the casually elegant dining room to
feast on some delectable cuisine. The superbly cooked filet mignon with
peaches and an outstanding port wine sauce is truly exceptional. Other
house specialties include a delicious lobster au gratin appetizer, grilled
local fish, roast duck, and key lime pie. This is also a special place for
lunch. Be sure to walk up to the **Skyworld Observatory** for a terrific view
of neighboring islands. ⊠ *Ridge Rd.,* ☏ *284/494–3567. AE, MC, V.*

$$$ ✕ **Sugar Mill Restaurant.** Candles gleam, and the background music is
peaceful in this well-known restaurant. Owners Jeff and Jinx Morgan
never disappoint. Well-prepared selections on the à la carte menu in-
clude pasta and vegetarian entrées. Oysters Caribe or wild mushroom
bisque are good choices for starters. House favorite entrées include the
Jamaican jerk pork roast with pineapple chipotle sauce, spicy Caribbean
sausage with Creole sauce, mahogany glazed duck, and fresh local fish
with herb butter. Although the setting is romantic, service here can be
a bit on the speedy side. ⊠ *Apple Bay,* ☏ *284/495–4355. AE, MC, V.*

$$–$$$ ✕ **Conch Shell Point.** This peaceful restaurant is on a point overlook-
★ ing boat-studded Trellis Bay. The French chef specializes in excellent
sauces; duck breast served with plum sauce is outstanding. The menu
includes grilled mahimahi flamed with pernod anise butter, fresh local
lobster, and filet mignon. ⊠ *Beef Island, just past airport,* ☏ *284/495–
2285. AE, MC, V. Closed Mon.*

$$–$$$ ✕ **Garden Restaurant.** Relax over dinner in this dimly lit, intimate, open-
air restaurant at Long Bay Beach Resort. The relatively extensive menu
changes daily to accommodate resort guests. Appetizers might include
spinach Caesar salad or conch chowder, and entrées, baked local
wahoo in ginger butter, beef tenderloin in wine sauce, or fettuccine with
scallops. ⊠ *West End at Long Bay Beach Resort,* ☏ *284/495–4252.
AE, MC, V.*

$$–$$$ ✕ **The Last Resort.** Actually on Bellamy Cay just off Beef Island (free
ferry service provided to and from Trellis Bay/Beef Island), this spot
features an English buffet, complete with pumpkin soup, prime rib and
Yorkshire pudding, and vegetarian selections—as well as the inimitable
cabaret humor and ribald ditties of owner Tony Snell, the B.V.I.'s an-
swer to Benny Hill. ⊠ *Bellamy Cay,* ☏ *284/495–2520. AE, MC, V.*

$$–$$$ ✕ **Pusser's Landing.** Yachters flock to the two-story home of this pop-
ular waterfront restaurant. Downstairs belly up to the large, outdoor
mahogany bar or choose a waterside table for drinks, sandwiches, and
light dinners. Head upstairs for quieter alfresco dining and a delight-
fully eclectic menu that includes homemade black bean soup, freshly
grilled local fish, pasta, and such pub favorites as shepherd's pie. The
air-conditioned Dinner Theater, with its 15-ft movie screen, features a
prix-fixe, three-course meal and movie combos, and sports events.
⊠ *Soper's Hole,* ☏ *284/495–4554. AE, MC, V.*

$$ ✕ **The Apple.** This small, inviting restaurant is in a West Indian house. Soft candlelight creates a relaxed atmosphere for diners as they sample fish steamed in lime butter, conch or whelks in garlic sauce, and other local seafood dishes. There is a traditional West Indian barbecue and buffet every Sunday evening from 7 until 9, and coconut chips and conch fritters are served at Happy Hour weekdays from 5 until 7. The excellent lunch menu includes a variety of sandwiches, meat and vegetarian lasagna, lobster quiche, seafood crepes, and croissants with ham and Swiss or spinach and feta. ⊠ *Little Apple Bay,* ☎ *284/495–4437. AE, MC, V.*

$$ ✕ **Mrs. Scatliffe's.** The best West Indian cooking on the island is here, according to many knowledgeable Tortolans (though some bemoan, "She gone Continental"). Meals are served on the upstairs terrace of Mrs. Scatliffe's home. The food is freshly prepared—vegetables come from the family garden; the baked chicken in coconut is meltingly tender. After dinner, live entertainment is provided by family members. ⊠ *Carrot Bay,* ☎ *284/495–4556. Reservations essential. No credit cards.*

$$ ✕ **Myett's.** Right in the middle of Cane Garden Bay Beach, this two-
★ level restaurant and bar is hopping day and night. Lobster chowder made from fresh Anegada lobsters is the house specialty. The menu includes everything from hamburgers to fruit platters and vegetarian dishes to grilled shrimp, lobster, steak, and tuna. Sunday there is an all-day barbecue buffet and a live reggae band. ⊠ *Cane Garden Bay,* ☎ *284/495–9543. Reservations not accepted. MC, V.*

$ ✕ **Quito's Gazebo.** This rustic beachside bar and restaurant is owned and operated by Quito Rhymer, a multitalented B.V.I. recording star who plays the guitar and sings Calypso ballads and love songs Tuesday, Thursday, Friday, and Sunday; a reggae band performs Saturday. The menu is Caribbean with an emphasis on fresh fish. Try the conch stew or the curried chicken. A Caribbean buffet is featured on Sunday night, and Friday is Fish Fry Night. The atmosphere is so convivial that by the time you finish dinner here you are likely to find yourself swapping yarns with some colorful local personalities. ⊠ *Cane Garden Bay,* ☎ *284/495–4837. MC, V. Closed Mon.*

$ ✕ **The Struggling Man.** Barely more than a roadside shack, this pleasant waterfront place with raffish candy-cane decor offers striking views of Drake's Channel and simple, tasty West Indian specialties. ⊠ *Sea Cows Bay,* ☎ *284/494–4163. Reservations not accepted. No credit cards.*

Beaches

Beaches in the B.V.I. have less development than those on St. Thomas or St. Croix—and fewer people. Try to get out on a boat at least one day during your stay, whether a dive-snorkeling boat or a day-trip sailing vessel. This is often the best way to get to the most virgin Virgin beaches on the less-populated islands, some of which have no road access.

Tortola's north side has a number of postcard-perfect, palm-fringed white sand beaches that curl luxuriantly around turquoise bays and coves. Nearly all are accessible by car (preferably four-wheel-drive), albeit down bumpy roads that corkscrew precipitously. Facilities run the gamut, from absolutely none to a number of beachside bars and restaurants plus water-sports rentals.

If you want to surf, the area of **Apple Bay** (⊠ North Shore Rd), which includes **Little Apple Bay** and **Capoon's Bay,** is the spot—although the beach itself is pretty narrow. Sebastian's, the very casual hotel here, caters especially to those in search of the perfect wave. Good waves are never a sure thing, but January and February are usually high times here.

The water at **Brewers Bay** (✉ Brewers Bay Rd. W or Brewers Bay Rd. E.) is good for snorkeling. There's a campground here, but in the summer you'll find almost nobody around. The beach and its old sugar mill and rum-distillery ruins are just north of Cane Garden Bay (up and over a steep hill), just past Luck Hill.

Cane Garden Bay (✉ Cane Garden Bay Rd.) rivals St. Thomas's Magens Bay in beauty and is Tortola's most popular beach. It's the closest one to Road Town—one steep uphill and downhill drive—and is also one of the B.V.I.'s best-known anchorages. It's a grand beach for jogging if you can resist staying out of that translucent water. You can rent sailboards and such, and for noshing or sipping you have a choice of going to Myett's, Stanley's Welcome Bar, Rhymer's, the Wedding, and Quito's Gazebo, where local recording star Quito Rhymer sings island ballads four nights a week. For true romance, nothing beats an evening of stargazing from the bow of a boat, listening to Quito's love songs drift across the bay.

Elizabeth Beach (✉ Ridge Rd.) is a wide beach lined with palm trees, accessible by walking down a private road. The undertow can be severe here in winter.

Josiah's Bay (✉ Ridge Rd.) is another favored place to hang-10, although in winter the undertow can be strong. The wide and very often deserted beach is a nice place for a quiet picnic.

The scenery at **Long Bay East** (✉ Beef Island Rd.) on Beef Island draws superlatives: a view of Little Camanoe and Great Camanoe islands, and if you walk around the bend to the right, you can see little Marina Cay and Scrub Island. Long Bay is also a good spot for interesting seashell finds. Take the Queen Elizabeth II Bridge to Beef Island and watch for a small dirt turnoff on the left before the airport. Follow the road that curves along the east side of the dried-up marsh flat, but don't drive directly across the flat.

Long Bay West (✉ Long Bay Rd.) is a stunning mile-long stretch of white sand. Have your camera ready for snapping the breathtaking approach. Although Long Bay Hotel sits along part of it, the entire beach is open to the public. The water is not as calm here as at Cane Garden or Brewers Bay, but it's still quite swimmable.

After bouncing your way to the beautiful **Smuggler's Cove** (✉ Belmont Rd.) you'll really feel as if you've found a hidden piece of the island, although you probably won't be alone on weekends. Have a beer or a toasted cheese sandwich (the only item on the menu) at the extremely casual snack bar. There is a fine view of the island of Jost Van Dyke. The snorkeling is good.

About the only thing you'll find moving at **Trunk Bay** (✉ Ridge Rd.) is the surf. It's directly north of Road Town, midway between Cane Garden Bay and Beef Island, and to get to it you'll have to hike down a *ghut* (gully) from the high Ridge Road.

Outdoor Activities and Sports

Horseback Riding

Equestrians should get in touch with **Shadow Stables** (✉ Ridge Rd., ☎ 284/494–2262), which offers small group rides down to the beaches or up in the hills. The **Ellis Thomas Riding School** (✉ Sea Cows Bay, ☎ 284/494–4442) teaches riding but also has trips into Tortola's hills and along the beaches.

Sailboarding

One of the best spots for sailboarding is at Trellis Bay on Beef Island. **Boardsailing B.V.I.** (✉ Trellis Bay, Beef Island, ☎ 284/495–2447) offers private and group lessons, and hourly and daily rentals.

Sailing

☞ Chapter 3, Sailing in the Virgin Islands.

Snorkeling/Diving

☞ Chapter 2, Diving and Snorkeling in the Virgin Islands.

Spectator Sports

Numerous local **softball** teams play on weekend evenings at the Old Recreation Grounds between Long Bush Road and Lower Estate Road. The season runs from February through August.

Cricket matches are held at the New Recreation Grounds next to the J. R. O'Neal Botanic Gardens on weekends from February through April.

Basketball fans can catch games at the New Recreation Grounds on any Monday, Wednesday, Friday, or Saturday between May and August. For further information, contact the B.V.I. Tourist Board (☎ 284/494–3134).

Sportfishing

A number of companies can transport and outfit you for a few hours of reel fun; try **Pelican Charters Ltd.** (✉ Prospect Reef, ☎ 284/496–7386).

Tennis

Tortola's tennis facilities range from simple untended concrete courts to professionally maintained surfaces where organized tournaments and socials are hosted. Listed below are facilities available to the public; some have restrictions for nonguests.

Frenchman's Cay. One artificial grass court with a pretty view of Sir Francis Drake Channel. Available to hotel and restaurant guests free, others at an hourly charge. Lighted. No pro. ✉ *West End,* ☎ *284/495–4844.*

Moorings-Mariner Inn. One all-weather hard court. Available to hotel and marina guests and Treasure Isle Hotel guests only. No lights. No pro. ✉ *Road Town,* ☎ *284/494–2331.*

Prospect Reef Resort. Six hard-surface courts. Available to hotel guests free (charge for lights) and to nonguests for an hourly charge. Lighted. Pro Mike Adamson, the island's most famous tennis pro, is available if requested in advance. ✉ *Road Town,* ☎ *284/494–3311.*

Shopping

The B.V.I. are not known as a shopper's delight, but you can find some interesting items, particularly artwork. Don't be put off by an informal shop entrance. Some of the best finds in the B.V.I. lie behind shopworn doors.

Shopping Districts

Most of the shops and boutiques on Tortola are clustered on and off Road Town's Main Street and at **Wickham's Cay** shopping area adjacent to the marina. There is also an ever-growing group of art and clothing stores at **Soper's Hole** on Tortola's West End.

Specialty Stores

ART

Caribbean Fine Arts Ltd. (✉ Main St., Road Town, ☎ 284/494–4240) has a wide range of Caribbean art, including original watercolors, oils, and acrylics, as well as signed prints, limited-edition serigraphs, and turn-of-the-century sepia photographs.

Collector's Corner (⊠ Columbus Centre, Wickham's Cay, ☎ 284/494–3550) carries antique maps, watercolors by local artists, gold and silver jewelry, coral, and Larimar—a pale blue Caribbean gemstone.

Islands Treasures (⊠ Soper's Hole Marina, ☎ 284/495–4787) is the place to find model ships, coffee-table books on the Caribbean, Caribbean maps and prints, and watercolors, paintings, pottery, and sculpture by island artists.

Sunny Caribbee Art Gallery (⊠ Main St., Road Town, ☎ 284/494–2178) has one of the largest displays in the Caribbean of paintings, prints, and watercolors by artists from virtually all of the Caribbean islands.

CLOTHING

Arawak (⊠ On the dock at Nanny Cay, ☎ 284/494–5240) carries gifts, sportswear and resortwear for men and women, accessories, and children's clothing.

Domino (⊠ Main St., Road Town, ☎ 284/494–5879) sells a colorful array of comfortable, light cotton clothing, including selections from Indonesia, plus island jewelry and gift items.

The Pusser's Company Store (⊠ Main St. and Waterfront Rd., Road Town, ☎ 284/494–2467; ⊠ Soper's Hole Marina, ☎ 284/495–4603) features nautical memorabilia, ship models, marine paintings, an entire line of clothes and gift items bearing the Pusser's logo, and handsome decorator bottles of Pusser's rum.

Sea Urchin (⊠ Columbus Centre, Road Town, ☎ 284/494–3129 or 284/494–2044; ⊠ Soper's Hole Marina, ☎ 284/495–4850) has a good selection of island-living designs: print shirts and shorts, slinky swimsuits, sandals, and T-shirts.

Turtle Dove Boutique (⊠ Flemming St., Road Town, ☎ 284/494–3611) is among the best in the B.V.I. for French perfume, international swimwear, and silk dresses, as well as gifts and accessories for the home.

Violet's (⊠ Wickham's Cay I, ☎ 284/494–6398) has a collection of beautiful silk lingerie and a small line of designer dresses.

FOOD AND DRINK

Ample Hamper (⊠ Village Cay Marina, Wickham's Cay, ☎ 284/494–2494; ⊠ Soper's Hole Marina, ☎ 284/495–4684) has a good selection of cheeses, wines, fresh fruits, and canned goods from the United Kingdom and the United States. You can have the management here provision your yacht or rental villa.

Fort Wine Gourmet (⊠ Main St., Road Town, ☎ 284/494–3036), a café-cum-store, carries a remarkably sophisticated selection of gourmet items and fine wines, including Petrossian caviar and Hediard goods from France.

Gourmet Galley (⊠ Wickham's Cay II, Road Town, ☎ 284/494–6999) sells wines, cheeses, fresh fruits and vegetables, and provides full provisioning for yachtspeople and villa renters.

GIFTS

Buccaneer's Bounty (⊠ Main St., Road Town, ☎ 284/494–7510) is a brand-new gift shop that carries a delightful assortment of greeting cards, nautical and tropical artwork, books on seashells, and books on the islands.

Caribbean Corner Spice House (⊠ Main St., Road Town, ☎ 284/494–5564; ⊠ Soper's Hole, ☎ 284/495–4498) makes and sells exotic herbs and spices, jams, jellies, hot sauces, and natural soaps. It also carries Cuban cigars.

J. R. O'Neal, Ltd. (✉ Main St., Road Town, ☎ 284/494–2292) stocks the shelves of its somewhat hidden shop with fine crystal, Royal Worcester china, a wonderful selection of hand-painted Italian dishes, hand-blown Mexican glassware, ceramic housewares from Spain, and woven rugs and tablecloths from India.

Pink Pineapple (✉ Prospect Reef Resort, ☎ 809/494–3311) has a remarkable array of gift items, from wearable artwork and hand-painted jewelry to watercolors and batik fabric.

The Sunny Caribbee Herb and Spice Company (✉ Main St., Road Town, ☎ 284/494–2178), in a brightly painted West Indian house, packages its own herbs, teas, coffees, herb vinegars, hot sauces, natural soaps, skin and suntan lotions, and exotic concoctions—Arawak Love Potion and Island Hangover Cure, for example. You'll also find a selection of Caribbean books and art and hand-painted decorative accessories. A small branch of this store is at the Skyworld restaurant (☞ Dining, *above*).

JEWELRY

Felix Gold and Silver Ltd. (✉ Main St., Road Town, ☎ 284/494–2406) hand crafts exceptionally fine jewelry in its on-site workshop at this unimpressive site. Choose from island or nautical themes or have something custom-made.

Samarkand (✉ Main St., Road Town, ☎ 284/494–6415) features handmade gold and silver pendants, earrings, bracelets, and pins, many with an island theme, plus genuine Spanish Pieces of Eight (coins commonly found in sunken Spanish galleons).

PERFUME

Flamboyance (✉ Main St., Road Town, ☎ 284/494–4099; ✉ Soper's Hole Marina, ☎ 284/495–5946) carries a wide selection of designer fragrances and upscale cosmetics.

TEXTILES

Caribbean Handprints (✉ Main St., Road Town, ☎ 284/494–3717) creates silk-screened fabric and sells it by the yard or in the form of dresses, shirts, pants, bathrobes, beach cover-ups, and beach bags.

Zenaida's of West End (✉ Frenchman's Cay, ☎ 284/495–4867) displays the fabric finds of Argentinean Vivian Jenik Helm, who travels through South America, Africa, and India in search of batiks, hand-painted and hand-blocked fabrics, and interesting weaves that can be made into pareos (women's wraps) or wall hangings. The shop also offers a selection of unusual bags, belts, sarongs, scarves, and ethnic jewelry.

Nightlife

Though the B.V.I. are not noted for swinging, Tortola now has a number of watering holes, many of which are especially popular with yachties. Check the weekly *Limin' Times* for current schedules of entertainment.

Bing's Drop In Bar. This is a rollicking local hangout with a DJ nightly in season. ✉ *Fat Hog's Bay, East End,* ☎ *284/495–2627.*

Bomba's Surfside Shack. This unusually decorated little shack looks like a pile of junk during the day but is actually one of Tortola's liveliest night spots. Sunday at 4 PM there's always some sort of live music, and Wednesday at 8 PM the Blue Haze Combo shows up. Also, every evening of the full moon, nearly everyone on Tortola surfaces to party through the night and dance to local bands. ✉ *Apple Bay,* ☎ *284/495–4148.*

Jolly Roger. An ever-changing array of local, American, and down-island bands play everything from rhythm and blues to reggae to country to good old rock and roll Friday and Saturday at 8 PM. ⊠ *West End,* ☎ *284/495–4559.*

Myett's. Bands play here Friday and Saturday evenings and Sunday afternoons, and there is usually a lively dance crowd. ⊠ *Cane Garden Bay,* ☎ *284/495–9543.*

The Pub. You'll find an all-day Friday Happy Hour, guitarist Reuben Chinnery on Friday and Saturday, and late-night entertainment by local bands on occasion. ⊠ *Waterfront St., Road Town,* ☎ *284/494–2608.*

The Pusser's Deli. Thursday is "nickel beer night," and crowds gather here for pints of John Courage. Other nights try Pusser's famous mixed drink—"Painkillers"—and snack on the excellent pizza. ⊠ *Waterfront St., Road Town,* ☎ *284/494–4199.*

Pusser's Landing. The schedule at Pusser's varies nightly, but you can usually count on some kind of live music (it could be reggae, rock, or a steel band) on Friday and Saturday evenings and Sunday afternoon. ⊠ *Soper's Hole, West End,* ☎ *284/495–4554.*

Quito's Gazebo. B.V.I. recording star Quito Rhymer sings island ballads and love songs (including many he has written himself), accompanied by the guitar and the gentle lapping of the surf, at this rustic beachside bar-restaurant on Cane Garden Bay. Solo shows are on Sunday, Tuesday, and Thursday nights at 8:30. Friday and Saturday, Quito and the band The Edge pump out a variety of tunes. ⊠ *Cane Garden Bay,* ☎ *284/495–4837.*

Sebastian's. There is often live music here on Saturday and Sunday. ⊠ *Apple Bay,* ☎ *809/495–4214.*

Stanley's Welcome Bar. It gets rowdy when crews stop by to drink and indulge in time-honored fraternity-type high jinks, such as piling up on the tire swing outside. ⊠ *Cane Garden Bay,* ☎ *284/495–4520.*

Exploring Tortola

Although Tortola's 10 sq mi can be explored in a few hours—the island does not have many historical sites to visit—opting for such a whirlwind tour is surely a mistake. Life in the fast lane has no place among some of the Caribbean's most breathtaking panoramas and prettiest beaches. So hop in a car and take a leisurely drive around the island. If you don't stop, the following drive will take two hours; if you do—and you should—it will take half a day.

Numbers in the text correspond to numbers in the margin and on the Tortola map.

A Good Drive

Start your tour in **Road Town** ①. You can park your car next to the Ferry Dock on Waterfront Drive, and then walk across the street to the **Sir Olva Georges Square,** stroll down Main Street and Waterfront Drive, and head east to the **B.V.I. Tourist Board** office, where you can pick up a detailed map of the island and hotel and sightseeing brochures. You'll spot the office just where the road curves sharply to the left. You can walk from here to the **J. R. O'Neal Botanic Gardens** for a look at local flora.

Head back to your car and take Waterfront Drive west out of town. In about a mile (just as the road takes a major turn to the right) you'll see a steep driveway leading up to a fortresslike structure tucked into the side of a hill. This is **Fort Burt** ②, which is now a hotel. Drive up and walk out on the terrace for a great view.

Continue heading west along the coast-hugging road toward West End for about 6 mi. As you drive along, you'll see stunning views of islands off to your left—first Peter Island, then Norman Island, and then St. John in the U.S.V.I. About a mile after you have passed through the little settlement of Sea Cows Bay (where the road leaves the shore for a few minutes) start looking to the left for the sign that indicates the Villas of Fort Recovery Estate. Drive in for a look at the ruins of **Fort Recovery** ③, and while you are there take a good look at the views across Sir Francis Drake Channel.

It's just 2 mi farther to the lefthand turnoff for **Frenchman's Cay** ④. After you cross the little bridge, bear right and you'll come to a marina and a complex of pastel buildings with gingerbread trim that showcases art galleries, clothing stores, and a Pusser's store and restaurant.

Head back across the little bridge, turn right, and then take your first left and head over the hill on Zion Road. Honk as you take the blind curve that plunges down to the north side of the island. Once back to sea level, you'll be facing the foamy surf of Apple Bay. Take a left onto North Shore Drive, and head abruptly up over the hill for a great view of **Long Bay Beach** and **Belmont Point** ⑤, the green hill in the distance that looks just like a gumdrop.

Drive east back over the hill and just a few feet past Zion Hill Road you'll spot a pile of junk on your left. That's **Bomba's Surfside Shack** ⑥, arguably the most popular nightspot in the B.V.I. Stop in and see if Bomba is around.

About a mile farther down the road is the **North Shore Shell Museum** ⑦, where you'll find a rather casual display of seashells and driftwood.

The drive from Carrot Bay toward East End along Tortola's north side will take you over several very steep hills with exquisite views of the nearby islands of Jost Van Dyke and Sandy Cay. Eventually you'll come to **Cane Garden Bay** ⑧, exceptionally calm and crystalline.

After you leave Cane Garden Bay, follow the road as it goes up (which it will do for several miles). When it finally flattens out, watch for a sign off to the right for Ridge Road and **Sage Mountain National Park** ⑨, on Tortola's highest peak. Here you will see mahogany trees, white cedars, and elephant ear vines plus a huge number of birds.

Return to the intersection of Cane Garden Bay Road and Ridge Road and continue a mile farther on Ridge Road until you come to the sign for **Skyworld** ⑩. Head up to the observatory for a 360°-view of the B.V.I. You'll feel as if you are looking down from the window of a plane.

Keep driving east along Ridge Road for about a mile and look for the sign to Brewers Bay and **Mount Healthy National Park** ⑪. It's a bit of a bumpy drive, but you'll come to a well-preserved historic 18th-century windmill.

Retrace your steps to Ridge Road and head east 5 mi until the road finally drops down and ends at the town of East End. Pick up Waterfront Drive heading east until you come to the **Queen Elizabeth II Bridge** ⑫, where you'll get to meet the toll-taker. Once on Beef Island, you might want to spend some time at Long Beach (East) before taking the low road back to Road Town.

Finally, perhaps on another day, get on a boat and take a snorkel or dive to the **RMS *Rhone*** ⑬, a shipwreck that is one of the world's best snorkeling sights.

Sights to See

⑤ Belmont Point. This is a sugar-loaf promontory that is often described as a giant green gumdrop. It's at the west end of Long Bay, a mile-long stretch of white sand, home to the Long Bay Beach Resort, one of Tortola's more appealing resorts. The large island visible in the distance is Jost Van Dyke.

⑥ Bomba's Surfside Shack. One of the Caribbean's most famous bars is on the north shore of Tortola, and it's worth a look even if you generally skip bars. The shack is festooned with everything from license plates to crepe paper leis to colorful graffiti. It's hard to believe that this ramshackle place is one of the liveliest nightspots on Tortola and home of the famous Bomba Shack "Full Moon" party. Every full moon, bands play here all night long and people flock here from all over Tortola and from other islands. ⊠ *North Coast Rd.,* ☎ *284/495–4148.* ⊘ *Daily 11–11 or later.*

⑧ Cane Garden Bay. Exceptionally calm crystalline waters and a silky stretch of sand here make this enticing beach one of Tortola's most popular getaways. Its existence is no secret, however, and it can get crowded, especially when cruise ships are in Road Harbour.

② Fort Burt. The most intact historic ruin on Tortola was built by the Dutch in the early 17th century to safeguard Road Harbour. It sits on a hill on the western edge of town and is now the site of a small hotel and restaurant. The foundations and magazine remain, and the structure offers a commanding view of Road Town. ⊠ *Waterfront Dr., no phone.* ⊒ *Free.* ⊘ *Daily dawn–dusk.*

③ Fort Recovery. The unrestored ruins of the 17th-century Dutch historic fort, 30 ft in diameter, sit amidst a profusion of tropical greenery on the grounds of the Villas at Fort Recovery Estates. There are no guided tours, but the public is welcome to stop by. ⊠ *Waterfront Dr.,* ☎ *284/485–4467.* ⊒ *Free.*

④ Frenchman's Cay. On this little island connected by a causeway to Tortola's West End, there's a marina and a captivating complex of pastel West Indian–style buildings with shady second-floor balconies, colonnaded arcades, shuttered windows, and gingerbread trim that showcase art galleries, boutiques, and restaurants. **Pusser's Landing** is a lively place where you can stop for a cold drink (many are made with Pusser's famous rum) and a sandwich and watch the boats come and go from the harbor.

⑪ Mount Healthy National Park. The remains of an 18th-century sugar plantation are visible here. The windmill structure has been restored, and you can see the ruins of a mill round, a factory with boiling houses, storage, stables, hospital, and many dwellings. ⊠ *Ridge Rd., no phone.* ⊒ *Free.* ⊘ *Daily dawn–dusk.*

⑦ North Shore Shell Museum. On Tortola's north shore, this casual museum has a very informal exhibit of shells, unusually shaped driftwood, fish traps, and traditional wooden boats. ⊠ *North Shore Rd., no phone.* ⊒ *Free.* ⊘ *Daily dawn–dusk.*

⑫ Queen Elizabeth II Bridge. You'll have to pay a toll (50¢ for passenger cars, $1 for vans and trucks) to cross this narrow bridge connecting Tortola and Beef Island. It's worth it if only for the sight of the toll-taker extending a tin can attached to the end of a board through your car window to collect the fee.

⑬ RMS *Rhone.* Get yourself some snorkeling gear and hop a dive boat to the wreck, off Salt Island (just across the channel from Road Town).

This is your chance to float on crystal-clear water over or near one of the world's best wrecks: a royal mail steamer 310 ft long that sank here in a hurricane in 1867 and was later used in the movie *The Deep*. Its four parts are at various depths from 30 to 80 ft. Nearby Rhone Reef is only 20–50 ft down. Every dive outfit in the B.V.I. runs superlative scuba and snorkel tours here. For timid snorkelers, simple and safe flotation devices are available, and the scuba supervisors will keep an eye on you. Call **Baskin in the Sun** (☎ 284/494–2858), **Underwater Safaris** (☎ 284/494–3235), **DIVE B.V.I.** (☎ 284/495–5513), **Blue Water Divers** (☎ 284/494–8097), **Island Diver, Ltd.** (☎ 284/494–3878), or **Caribbean Images** (☎ 809/495–2563).

① **Road Town.** The laid-back capital of the B.V.I. is on the south side of the island of Tortola and looks out over Road Harbour. It takes only an hour or so to stroll down Main Street and along the waterfront checking out the shops and the traditional pastel-painted West Indian buildings with high-pitched, corrugated tin roofs, bright shutters, and delicate fretwork trim.

Choose a seat on one of the benches in **Sir Olva Georges Square,** and watch the people come and go from the ferry dock and customs office across the street. Also keep an eye out for the clock on the post office, which borders the other side of the square. Its hands permanently pointed to 10 minutes to 5 until last year, when they mysteriously started pointing to 5 minutes to 12, rather appropriate in this drowsy town, where time does seem to be standing still. ⊠ *Waterfront Dr.*

For hotel and sightseeing brochures and the latest information on everything from taxi rates to ferry boat schedules, stop in the **B.V.I. Tourist Board** office in downtown Road Town. ⊠ *Wickham's Cay I,* ☎ *284/494–3134.* ☉ *Weekdays 9–5.*

The 2.8-acre **J. R. O'Neal Botanic Gardens** showcases lush gardens of tropical plant life. There are sections devoted to prickly cacti and succulents, hothouses for ferns and orchids, gardens of medicinal herbs, plants that bloom around Christmas, and plants and trees indigenous to the seashore. From the tourist board office, cross Waterfront Drive and walk one block over to Main Street and turn right. Keep walking until you see the B.V.I. High School. The gardens are on your left. ⊠ *Station Ave.,* ☎ *284/494–4557.* ☜ *Free.* ☉ *Mon.–Sat. 8–4, Sun. noon–5.*

⑨ **Sage Mountain National Park.** At 1,716 ft, Sage Mountain is the highest peak in the B.V.I. From the parking area, a trail will lead you in a loop not only to the peak itself but also to the island's small rain forest, sometimes shrouded in mist. Most of the island's forest was cut down over the centuries to clear land for sugarcane, cotton, and other crops, as well as pastureland and timber. But in 1964 this park was established to preserve the remaining rain forest. Up here you can see mahogany trees, white cedars, mountain guavas, elephant-ear vines, mamey trees, and giant bulletwoods, to say nothing of such birds as mountain doves and thrushes. Take a taxi from Road Town or drive up Joe's Hill Road and make a left onto Ridge Road toward Chalwell and Doty villages. The road dead-ends at the park. ⊠ *Ridge Rd., no phone (contact tourist office for information).* ☜ *Free.*

⑩ **Skyworld.** Drive up here and climb the observation tower for the B.V.I.'s highest—and absolutely stunning—360°-view of numerous islands and cays. Even St. Croix (40 mi away) and Anegada (20 mi away) can be seen on a clear day. ⊠ *Ridge Rd., no phone.* ☜ *Free.*

Tortola A to Z

Emergencies
Emergencies (☎ 999).

Hospital: Peebles Hospital (☎ 284/494–3497) is in Road Town.

Pharmacies: In Road Town, try **J. R. O'Neal Drug Store** (☎ 284/494–2292) or **Lagoon Plaza Drug Store** (☎ 284/494–2498).

Getting Around
BY BUS
For information about rates and schedules, call **Scato's Bus Service** (☎ 284/494–2365). Taking the bus is a great way to meet locals, albeit at a bumpy snail's pace.

BY CAR
Avis (☎ 284/494–3322) rents four-wheel-drive vehicles and cars in Road Town. **Budget** (✉ Wickham's Cay I, ☎ 284/494–2639; ✉ Wickham's Cay II, ☎ 284/494–5150), which rents both cars and four-wheel drives, has two offices in Road Town. **Hertz** (☎ 284/495–4405) rents four-wheel drives and cars at their office at West End.

BY TAXI
Your hotel staff will be happy to summon a taxi for you when you want one. There is a B.V.I. Taxi Association stand in Road Town near the ferry dock (☎ 284/494–2875) and Wickham's Cay I (☎ 284/494–2322), as well as one at the airport on Beef Island (☎ 284/495–2378). You can also usually find a taxi at the ferry dock at Soper's Hole, West End, where ferries arrive from St. Thomas.

Guided Tours
If you'd like to do some chauffeured sightseeing on Tortola, get in touch with the **B.V.I. Taxi Association** (minimum three persons, ☎ 284/494–2875 or 284/495–2378). **Style's Taxi Service** (☎ 284/494–2260 during the day or 284/494–3341 at night) offers tours around the island and boat tours. **Travel Plan Tours** (☎ 284/494–2872) can arrange island tours, boat tours, and yacht charters. **Scato's Bus Service** (☎ 284/494–2365), in Road Town, provides public transportation, special tours with group rates, and beach outings.

Visitor Information
On Tortola there is a **B.V.I. Tourist Board Office** at the center of Road Town near the ferry dock, just south of Wickham's Cay I (✉ Box 134, Road Town, Tortola, ☎ 284/494–3134). For all kinds of useful information about these islands, including rates and phone numbers, get a free copy of *The Welcome Tourist Guide,* available at hotels, restaurants, and stores.

VIRGIN GORDA

Virgin Gorda, with its mountainous central portion connected by skinny necks to southern and northern appendages—on a map they look like the slightest breeze would cause them to splinter—is quite different from Tortola. The pace here is even slower than on its larger, sister island, for example. The island receives less rain, so some areas are more arid and home to scrub brush and cactus. Goats and cattle own the right of way, and the unpretentious friendliness of the local people is winning.

Lodging

Virgin Gorda's charming hostelries appeal to a select, appreciative clientele. Repeat business is extremely high here. Visitors who prefer Sheratons, Marriotts, and the like may feel they get more for their money on other islands. But the peace and pampering offered on Virgin Gorda are priceless to the discriminating traveler.

Hotels and Inns

$$$$ ⊞ **Biras Creek Hotel.** A longtime guest purchased Biras Creek in 1995
★ and turned it into one of the classiest resorts in the B.V.I. Virtually everything was redone and it still feels as if it is brand-new. Each unit has a bedroom and a living room area decorated in bright Caribbean colors and fabrics. The floors are Mexican tile. Units are discreetly hidden among the trees, and, if you leave the air-conditioning off, you can let the sound of the waves lull you to sleep. Bike paths and trails winding through woods lead to the various beaches and restaurants. The new general manager, Jamie Holmes, brings years of Caribbean hotel experience to this 150-acre secluded hideaway. The hilltop open-air bar and restaurant area is made of stonework and offers stunning views of North Sound. A "Sailaway" package includes two nights on a private yacht. ⊠ *Box 54, North Sound,* ☎ *284/494–3555,* FAX *284/494–3557. 34 rooms. 2 restaurants, bar, pool, 2 tennis courts, hiking, beach, snorkeling, windsurfing, boating, bicycles. AE, MC, V.*

$$$$ ⊞ **Bitter End Yacht Club and Marina.** Stretching along the coastline of
★ North Sound, and accessible only by boat, the BEYC enjoys panoramic views of the sound, Leverick Bay, and nearby islands. Accommodations range from exceptionally comfortable hillside or beachfront villas to liveaboard yachts. The BEYC extends a friendly, unpretentious welcome to all its guests, and your day can include as many or as few activities as you wish. There are daily snorkeling and diving trips to nearby reefs, cruises, windsurfing lessons, excursions to local attractions, and lessons at the Nick Trotter Sailing School. Regarded as the best sailing instruction in the Caribbean, the school helps both seasoned salts and beginners sharpen their nautical skills. When the sun goes down, the festivities continue at the Clubhouse, an open-air restaurant overlooking the Sound. This is the liveliest and most convivial hotel in the B.V.I. ⊠ *Box 46, North Sound,* ☎ *284/494–2746,* FAX *284/494–4756. 100 rooms. Restaurant, bar, pool, beach, snorkeling, windsurfing, waterskiing. AE, MC, V.*

$$$$ ⊞ **Little Dix Bay.** Relaxed elegance is the hallmark of this longtime fa-
★ vorite, which for 30 years has remained one of the outstanding resorts in the Caribbean. It's tucked among the mangroves, along the edge of a sandy beach. The hexagonally shaped rooms have stone and wood walls and are decorated in Caribbean prints. The spacious open-air library offers stateside daily newspapers if you want to stay in touch. Lawns are beautifully manicured; the reef-protected beach is long and silken; and the candlelight dining in an open peak-roof pavilion is a memorable experience. Tennis, sailing, snorkeling, waterskiing, and bicycling are included in the rate. Popular with honeymooners, and older couples who have been coming back for years, Little Dix is a quiet place favored by couples. The accommodations are superb, the service thoughtful and attentive, and the setting unforgettable. ⊠ *Box 70,* ☎ *284/495–5555,* FAX *284/495–5661. 102 rooms. 3 restaurants, 2 bars, 7 tennis courts, beach. AE, MC, V.*

$$–$$$$ ⊞ **Olde Yard Inn.** Owners Charlie Williams and Carol Kaufman have
★ cultivated a refreshingly unique atmosphere at this quiet retreat just outside Spanish Town. Classical music plays in the bar; books line the walls of the octagonal library cottage. The dinner restaurant's French-accented menu is lovingly prepared and served with style in the high-ceiling dining rooms. The lunch restaurant overlooks the pool and features fresh

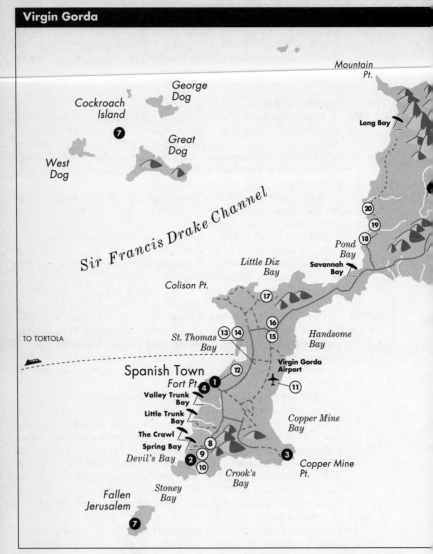

Mountain Pt.

George Dog

Cockroach Island

7

Great Dog

West Dog

Long Bay

Sir Francis Drake Channel

20
19
18

Pond Bay

Little Dix Bay

Savannah Bay

Colison Pt.

17

TO TORTOLA

St. Thomas Bay

Handsome Bay

13 **14**
16
15

Spanish Town
Fort Pt.

Virgin Gorda Airport

12

4 **1**

11

Valley Trunk Bay

Little Trunk Bay

Copper Mine Bay

The Crawl

Spring Bay

Devil's Bay

8

2 **9**

10

3

Copper Mine Pt.

Crook's Bay

Fallen Jerusalem

Stoney Bay

7

Exploring
The Baths, **2**
Coastal Islands, **7**
Copper Mine Point, **3**
Leverick Bay, **6**
Little Fort
National Park, **4**
Spanish Town, **1**
Virgin Gorda Peak
National Park, **5**

Dining
The Bath and Turtle, **12**
Biras Creek, **24**
The Clubhouse, **25**
Crab Hole, **13**
Drake's
Anchorage, **26**
The Flying Iguana, **11**
Giorgio's Italian
Restaurant, **18**

Little Dix Bay, **17**
Mad Dog's, **10**
Olde Yard Inn, **16**
Pusser's at Leverick
Bay, **21**
Sip and Dip Grill, **15**
Teacher's Pet
Ilma's, **14**
Top of the Baths, **9**

Lodging
Biras Creek Hotel, **24**
Bitter End Yacht Club
and Marina, **25**
Drake's
Anchorage, **26**
Guavaberry Spring Bay
Vacation Homes, **8**

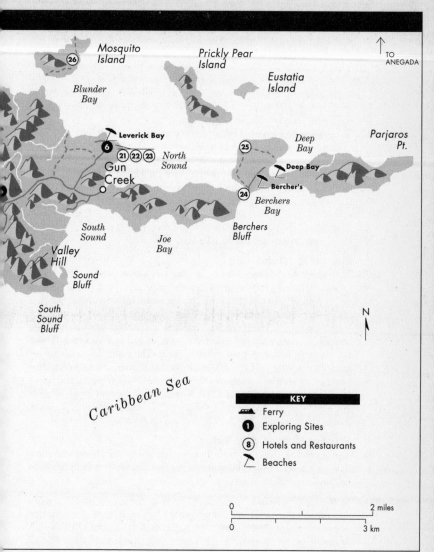

Mosquito Island
26

Blunder Bay

Prickly Pear Island

Eustatia Island

TO ANEGADA

Leverick Bay
6
21 22 23
North Sound

Gun Creek

25

Deep Bay

Parjaros Pt.

Deep Bay

Bercher's

24

Berchers Bay

South Sound

Joe Bay

Berchers Bluff

Valley Hill

Sound Bluff

South Sound Bluff

N

Caribbean Sea

KEY

🚌 Ferry

❶ Exploring Sites

❽ Hotels and Restaurants

⊱ Beaches

0   2 miles

0   3 km

salads, excellent chili, and hamburgers and sandwiches. Guest rooms are cozy and simply furnished. Arrangements can be made for day sails and scuba diving excursions. There's a large pool and a health club where you can work out, take exercise classes, and receive massages. The inn is not on the beach, but free transportation is provided. In the warmer months you may want to request an air-conditioned room; the hotel's location means trade winds are less noticeable here. ⊠ *Box 26, Spanish Town,* ☎ *284/495–5544,* FAX *284/495–5986. 14 rooms. Restaurant, bar, pool, croquet, library. AE, MC, V.*

$$–$$$ 🔟 **Leverick Bay Hotel.** The hillside rooms at this small hotel are decorated in pastels and with original artwork. All rooms have refrigerators, balconies, and views of North Sound; four two-bedroom condos are also available. A Spanish colonial–style main building houses a restaurant and store, both of which are operated by Pusser's of Tortola. The resort's office has books, games, and tennis rackets for guests to borrow. ⊠ *Box 63,* ☎ *284/495–7421,* FAX *284/495–7367. 20 rooms. Restaurant, bar, pool, beauty salon, tennis court, beach, dive shop, snorkeling, coin laundry. AE, D, MC, V.*

Mosquito Island

$$$$ 🔟 **Drake's Anchorage.** Set on the edge of its own private island, this
★ small, secluded getaway provides the true privacy and pampering you'd find in some of the more elegant resorts, but without the formality. Dinner attire here means changing from bathing suit to comfortable cottons. The three West Indian–style, waterfront bungalows contain 10 comfortably furnished rooms, including two suites. There are also two fully equipped villas for rent. The resort has a highly regarded restaurant, hiking trails, water-sports facilities, and four delightful beaches, as well as hammocks here and there—a truly peaceful, rejuvenating experience. ⊠ *Box 2510, North Sound, Virgin Gorda,* ☎ *284/ 494–2254 or 800/624–6651,* FAX *284/494–2254. 8 rooms, 2 suites, 2 villas. Restaurant, bar, beach, snorkeling, boating. AE, MC, V.*

Private Homes and Villas

Those craving seclusion would do well at one of the clusters of villas or even a private home, both of which offer comfortable lodgings with full kitchen and maid service.

$$$–$$$$ 🔟 **Mango Bay Resort.** Sparkling white villas framed by morning glory and frangipani, handsome contemporary Italian decor, and a gorgeous ribbon of golden sand that all but vanishes at high tide make this an idyllic family retreat. Even for Virgin Gorda it's a study in isolation. ⊠ *Box 1062, Virgin Gorda,* ☎ *284/495–5672. 5 villas. Beach. No credit cards.*

$$$–$$$$ 🔟 **Paradise Beach Resort.** These one-, two-, and three-bedroom beachfront suites and villas are handsomely decorated in pastel colors and Caribbean style and feature outdoor showers. Four-wheel-drive vehicles are included in the daily rate. ⊠ *Box 534, Virgin Gorda,* ☎ *284/ 495–5871. 9 units. Beach. No credit cards.*

$$$–$$$$ 🔟 **Virgin Gorda Villa Rentals.** This company manages the adjacent Leverick Bay Resort, so it's perfect for those who want to be close to some activity. Many villas have private swimming pools; all are well maintained and have spectacular views. ⊠ *Box 63, Virgin Gorda,* ☎ *284/ 495–7421. 21 villas, from studios to 3-bedrooms. AE, D, MC, V.*

$$–$$$$ 🔟 **Guavaberry Spring Bay Vacation Homes.** Spending time in these unusual hexagon-shape cottages perched on stilts makes you feel as if you are in a tree house as you listen to the chirping birds and the sound of trees swaying in the breeze. These one- and two-bedroom units are on a hill, a short walk down to a tamarind-shaded beach and not far from the mammoth boulders and cool basins of the famed Baths, which ad-

join this property. ⊠ *Box 20, Virgin Gorda,* ☎ *284/495–5227. 21 units. Beach. No credit cards.*

Dining

There are a number of excellent restaurants on Virgin Gorda. Hotels that are accessible only by boat will arrange transport in advance upon request for nonguests who wish to dine at their restaurants. It is wise to make dinner reservations almost everywhere, and don't be put off if the restaurant also wants your order before you arrive. They just want to be sure they have the necessary ingredients. If they don't, they'll head to the store!

\$\$\$ ✕ **Biras Creek.** This hilltop restaurant, built of island stonework and
★ with its signature turret roof, is one of the most stunning settings for a meal in all the B.V.I. Broad steps lead up to an open-air lounge and restaurant with beautiful views of North Sound. The gourmet menu changes daily but includes four or five choices each for appetizer, entrée, and dessert. Grilled local wahoo with ginger and carrot sauce, lobster with spicy Caribbean sauce, and roast duck with plum sauce are some of the enticing entrées offered. Delightful desserts include key lime pie, a warm treacle tart, and hot brownies with chocolate sauce. ⊠ *North Sound,* ☎ *284/494–3555. Reservations essential. AE, MC, V.*

\$\$\$ ✕ **Drake's Anchorage.** Actually on Mosquito Island (ferry service avail-
★ able free from Leverick Bay), this is a romantic candlelit setting right at the water's edge. Dine on local lobster, local dorado encrusted with bananas and bread crumbs, rack of lamb, or steak au poivre, and velvety chocolate mousse. ⊠ *Mosquito Island,* ☎ *284/494–2254. AE, MC, V.*

\$\$\$ ✕ **Little Dix Bay.** For an elegant evening out, you can't do better than
★ this—the candlelight in the main open-air pavilion is enchanting, the menu sophisticated, the service attentive. The dinner menu changes daily, but there is always a fine selection of superbly prepared seafood, meat, and vegetarian entrées from which to choose. The lunch buffet here is one of the best in the Caribbean. ⊠ *Spanish Town,* ☎ *284/495–5555, ext. 174. AE, MC, V.*

\$\$\$ ✕ **Olde Yard Inn.** Dinner here is a civilized and charming affair, as the intimate dining room is suffused with gentle classical melodies and the scent of herbs. A cedar roof covers the breezy, open-air room decorated with old-style Caribbean charm. The French-accented cuisine includes lamb chops with mango chutney, chicken breast in a rum cream sauce, garlic shrimp, grilled local fish, steaks, and lobster. For great chili, burgers, or tortellini salad stop by the poolside ☞ **Sip and Dip Grill** during lunch. ⊠ *The Valley, north of the marina,* ☎ *284/495–5544. AE, MC, V.*

\$\$\$ ✕ **Pusser's at Leverick Bay.** This two-level restaurant looks out over picturesque North Sound. The upstairs is more formal, although the menu is a combination of steak house and English pub. Below, the Beach Bar offers light fare all day and a nightly "theme." Thursday is \$1 Heineken night. Tuesday is pizza-and-beer night. ⊠ *Leverick Bay Resort,* ☎ *284/495–7369. AE, MC, V.*

\$\$–\$\$\$ ✕ **The Clubhouse.** The Bitter End's open-air, waterfront restaurant is a favorite rendezvous for the sailing set, with lavish buffets for breakfast, lunch, and dinner, and fresh fish and lobster à la carte. It's a popular, busy spot day and night. ⊠ *The Bitter End Yacht Club, North Sound,* ☎ *284/494–2746. AE, MC, V.*

\$\$–\$\$\$ ✕ **Giorgio's Italian Restaurant.** Gaze out at the stars and listen to the water lap against the shore while dining on penne arrabbiata, veal scaloppine, filet mignon with mushrooms, or fresh local fish. Pizzas and sandwiches are the fare at lunch at this pleasant, casual establishment. ⊠ *Mango Bay, 10 minutes north of Yacht Harbour,* ☎ *284/495–5684. MC, V.*

$$ ✕ **The Bath and Turtle.** This informal patio tavern with a friendly staff
★ is a popular spot where diners sit back and relax. Burgers, well-stuffed
sandwiches, pizzas, pasta dishes, and daily specials round out the ca-
sual menu. Live entertainers perform on Wednesday and Sunday nights.
⊠ *Virgin Gorda Yacht Harbour,* ☏ *284/495–5239. MC, V.*

$$ ✕ **The Flying Iguana.** Lifelike iguanas perch in the plants of the comfortable lounge at this charming restaurant. The dining room is open-
air and looks out over Virgin Gorda's tiny airport to the sea. Sandwiches
and thick, juicy hamburgers are served for lunch. The dinner menu includes a pasta special, grilled chicken, and steaks. ⊠ *At the airport,*
☏ *284/495–5277. AE, MC, V.*

$$ ✕ **Teacher's Pet Ilma's.** Delightful local atmosphere and delicious na-
tive-style family dinners, including local goat, fresh grouper or snap-
per, pork, and chicken, are givens at the restaurant in this small house.
⊠ *The Valley,* ☏ *284/495–5355. Reservations essential. No credit
cards. No lunch.*

$–$$ ✕ **The Crab Hole.** This homey hangout serves West Indian specialties such
as callaloo soup, salt fish, stewed goat, curried chicken roti, rice and peas,
and green bananas. ⊠ *The Valley,* ☏ *284/495–5307. No credit cards.*

$–$$ ✕ **Sip and Dip Grill.** The pool at the Olde Yard Inn is the setting for
★ this pleasant, informal lunch spot. Come here for grilled fish, pasta salads, chilled soups, and ice cream. Sunday evening it has a barbecue
and live entertainment. ⊠ *The Valley,* ☏ *284/495–5544. Reservations
not accepted. AE, MC, V. No dinner Mon.–Sat.*

$–$$ ✕ **Top of the Baths.** At the entrance to the Baths, this open-air restau-
rant serves food all day long, starting at 8 AM. Hamburgers, salads,
and sandwiches are served at lunch. Conch seviche and lentil soup are
among the dinner appetizers. Entrées include Cornish hen with wild
rice and grilled swordfish with fresh rosemary sauce. For dessert, you
can choose from such delectables as lemon cheesecake, pecan pie, and
black fruit cake. ⊠ *The Valley,* ☏ *284/495–5497. AE, MC, V.*

$ ✕ **Mad Dog's.** Piña coladas are the specialty at this breezy bar just
outside of The Baths. The all-day menu includes BLTs, hot dogs, and
burgers. ⊠ *The Valley,* ☏ *284/495–5830. Reservations not accepted.
MC, V.*

Beaches

The best beaches are most easily reached by water, although they are
also accessible on foot, usually after a moderately strenuous hike of
10 to 15 minutes. Either way, your persistence is amply rewarded.

Anybody going to Virgin Gorda must experience swimming or snorkeling among its **unique boulder formations** (⊠ Lee Rd.). But why go to
The Baths, which is usually crowded, when you can catch some rays
just north at **Spring Bay Beach,** which is a gem, and, a little farther
north, at the **Crawl?** Both are easily reached from The Baths on foot
via Lee Road, or by swimming.

From Biras Creek or Bitter End on the north shore, you can walk to
Bercher's Beach and along the windswept surf.

Footpaths from Bitter End and foot and bike paths from Biras Creek
lead to **Deep Bay,** a calm, well-protected swimming beach.

Mosquito Island's **Hay Point Beach** is a broad band of white sand accessible only by boat or by path from the dock at Drake's Anchorage
resort.

Leverick Bay (⊠ Leverick Bay Rd.) is a small, busy beach-cum-marina
that fronts a resort restaurant and pool. Don't come here to be alone,
but do come if you want a lively little place and a break from the is-

land's noble quiet. The view of Prickly Pear Island is an added plus, and there's a dive facility right here to motor you out to beautiful Eustatia Reef just across North Sound.

It's worth going out to **Long Bay** (near Virgin Gorda's northern tip, past the Diamond Beach Club), for the snorkeling (Little Dix Bay resort has outings here). The drive takes about a half hour after the turnoff from North Sound Road, and a dirt road makes up part of the route. ⊠ Plum Tree Bay Rd.

For a wonderfully private beach close to Spanish Town, try **Savannah Bay** (⊠ North Sound Rd.). It may not always be completely deserted, but it's a lovely long stretch of white sand.

Prickly Pear Island has a calm swimming beach at **Vixen Point Beach.**

Outdoor Activities and Sports

Cricket

Cricket matches can be seen at the **Recreation Grounds in Spanish Town** from February through April. Contact the tourist office (☎ 284/494–3134) for more information on specific game dates and times.

Sailboarding

The **Nick Trotter Sailing School** (⊠ Bitter End Yacht Club, North Sound, ☎ 800/872–2392). Both beginner and advanced courses are offered here.

Sailing

☞ Chapter 3, Sailing in the Virgin Islands.

Snorkeling and Diving

☞ Chapter 2, Diving and Snorkeling in the Virgin Islands.

Sportfishing

Captain Dale (⊠ Biras Creek, North Sound, ☎ 284/495–7248) takes people out on *Classic*, his 38-ft Bertram.

Tennis

The **Biras Creek Hotel** has two Astroturf courts. Courts and lessons are available to guests, and to nonguests for a fee. Lighted, pro. ⊠ *North Sound, ☎ 284/494–3555.*

Shopping

On Virgin Gorda most boutiques are within individual hotel complexes. One of the best is the one in Little Dix Bay. Other properties—Biras Creek, the Bitter End, Leverick Bay, and nearby Mosquito Island's Drake's Anchorage—have small but equally select boutiques, and there's a more than respectable and diverse scattering of shops in the minimal adjacent to the bustling yacht harbor in Spanish Town.

Art

Olde Yard Inn Boutique (⊠ The Valley, ☎ 284/495–5544) carries locally crafted sculpture, pottery, jewelry, and paintings; books on the islands; and some clothing and gift items.

Thee Artistic Gallery (⊠ Virgin Gorda Yacht Harbour, ☎ 284/495–5761) features Caribbean jewelry, 14kt-gold nautical jewelry, maps, collectible coins, and some crystal.

Clothing

DIVE B.V.I. (⊠ Virgin Gorda Yacht Harbour, ☎ 284/495–5513) sells books about the islands as well as men's and women's sportswear, sunglasses, and beach bags.

Island Silhouette in Flax Plaza (✉ Near Fischer's Cove Hotel, no phone) is the place to go for resortwear handpainted by Virgin Gorda artists, and locally made tie-dyed T-shirts.

Next Wave (✉ Virgin Gorda Yacht Harbour, ☎ 284/495–5623) sells bathing suits, T-shirts, and canvas tote bags.

Pavilion Gift Shop (✉ Little Dix Bay Hotel, ☎ 284/495–5555) has the latest in resortwear for men and women, as well as jewelry, books, and expensive T-shirts.

Pelican's Pouch Boutique (✉ Virgin Gorda Yacht Harbour, ☎ 284/495–5599) is where you'll find a large selection of swimsuits plus cover-ups, T-shirts, and accessories.

Pusser's Company Store (✉ Leverick Bay, ☎ 284/495–7369) offers its trademark line of rum products, gift items, and sportswear for men and women.

Tropical Gift Collections (✉ The Baths, ☎ 284/495–5380) specializes in locally made handicrafts, including hats, bags, and pottery. Island spices are also for sale.

Food and Drink

Bitter End's Emporium (✉ North Sound, ☎ 284/494–2745) is the place to look for such edible treats as local fruits, cheeses, and bakery goods.

Virgin Island Bakery (✉ Virgin Gorda Yacht Harbour, no phone) bakes bread, rolls, muffins, and cookies and has sandwiches and sodas to go.

Gifts

Palm Tree Gallery (✉ Leverick Bay, ☎ 284/495–7421) sells attractive handcrafted jewelry, paintings, and one-of-a-kind gift items, plus books about the Caribbean.

The Reeftique (✉ Bitter End, North Sound, ☎ 284/494–2745) carries a variety of gift items, including island crafts and jewelry, clothing, and nautical odds and ends with the Bitter End logo.

Local Crafts

Virgin Gorda Craft Shop (✉ Virgin Gorda Yacht Harbour, ☎ 284/495–5137) features the work of island artisans and carries West Indian jewelry and crafts styled in straw, shells, and other local materials. It also stocks clothing and paintings by Caribbean artists.

Nightlife

The Bath and Turtle (✉ Virgin Gorda Yacht Harbour, ☎ 284/495–5239) is a good spot to rub elbows with local music aficionados as well as boaters. One of the liveliest spots on Virgin Gorda, this informal pub hosts island bands on Wednesday and Sunday evenings. The entertainment begins at 8 and goes until midnight.

Chez Bamboo (✉ Across from Virgin Gorda Yacht Harbour, ☎ 284/495–5752) is the place to go for jazz Thursday and Saturday nights.

Little Dix Bay (☎ 284/495–5555) and **Bitter End Yacht Club** (☎ 284/494–2746) have live entertainment several nights a week in season. Call for schedules.

Pirate's Grill (☎ 284/495–9638) on Saba Rock has a nightly jam session. Bring your own instrument or use one of theirs.

Pirate's Pub at Andy's Chateau (✉ Fischer's Cove Beach Hotel, the Valley, ☎ 284/495–5252) offers live music and the closest thing to a disco here Friday, Saturday, and Sunday nights.

Pusser's at Leverick Bay (✉ Leverick Bay, ☎ 284/495–7370) has live bands on Saturday night and Sunday afternoon.

Sip and Dip Grill (✉ Olde Yard Inn, ☎ 284/495–5544) has live entertainment Sunday night.

Exploring Virgin Gorda

One of the most effective ways to see Virgin Gorda is by sailboat. Paved roads are few and far between, alternative routes are limited, and most byways do not follow the scalloped shoreline. The main road also sticks resolutely to the center of the island, linking The Baths at the tip of the southern extremity with Gun Creek and Leverick Bay in the north and providing exhilarating views from its higher points. The panorama of a craggy shoreline, scissored with grottoes and fringed by palms and the island's trademark boulders, possesses a primitive beauty. If you choose to drive, the island is small enough that a single day of touring will allow plenty of time to explore all of the sights.

Numbers in the text correspond to numbers in the margin and on the Virgin Gorda map.

A Good Drive

A good place to start is the south end of the island, in **Spanish Town** ①. This is the largest "town" on Virgin Gorda. Pick up maps and brochures at the **B.V.I. Tourist Board** on the west side of the little Yacht Harbour complex. To find out what is happening on the island, check the bulletin board in the parking lot.

Turn right out of the Yacht Harbour parking lot and head south as far as you can go. In about 2 mi you will reach the circular drive that marks the entrance to **The Baths** ②. You can take the little hike down to the water and swim or snorkel or wander through the small shopping complex.

Back in the car, head back toward town on Lee Road. Take a right as soon as you pass the school. When the road ends take another right onto Copper Mine Road and drive 3 mi to **Copper Mine Point** ③, where you will find the ruins of an old copper mine.

Return to Lee Road and turn right and immediately look for signs on the left for the **Little Fort National Park** ④, which is a wildlife sanctuary. Here you will see giant boulders similar to the ones at The Baths.

For great views of nearby islands and of Virgin Gorda's own eccentric shape, drive back through Spanish Town and north on North Sound Road, which runs across Virgin Gorda's hilly center. About 4 mi from Spanish Town (2 mi past Savannah Bay), watch for small signs on the left that indicate the entrance to **Virgin Gorda Peak National Park** ⑤. There's a trail to the top worth hiking, but it's a bit strenuous and you'll need sturdy shoes. Continue driving north for stunning views of **North Sound.**

The road eventually drops down from its lofty heights, and just before the final plunge, there's a turn off to the left to **Leverick Bay** ⑥, where you will find a little cluster of shops, a restaurant, a hotel, and a water sports center. If you continue north on North Sound Road, you'll reach the tiny settlement of Gun Creek, where you can catch ferries to Biras Creek Hotel and the Bitter End Yacht Club and Marina. Returning, as you drive south over the hill, you will see The Valley in the distance, looking flat and almost like a separate island.

You can't drive to the **Coastal Islands** ⑦, but they are so close that it is definitely worth contacting a local dive shop and taking a boat over.

Sights to See

② **The Baths.** It's well worth your time to visit Virgin Gorda's most celebrated site. Giant boulders, brought to the surface eons ago by a vast volcanic eruption, are scattered about the beach and in the water. Some are almost as large as small houses and form remarkable grottoes. Climb between these rocks to swim in the many pools. Early morning and late afternoon are the best times to visit, since the Baths and the beach here are usually crowded with cruise-ship passengers and day-trippers visiting from Tortola. (If it's privacy you crave, follow the shore north for a few hundred yards to reach several quieter bays—**Spring,** the **Crawl, Little Trunk,** and **Valley Trunk**—or head south along the trail to **Devil's Bay.** These beaches have the same giant boulders as those found at The Baths.) At The Baths, it's a 35-yard walk from the parking lot to the beach. ⊠ *Lee Rd., no phone.* ☎ *Free.*

⑦ **Coastal Islands.** You can easily reach the quaintly named islands of **Fallen Jerusalem** and the **Dog Islands** by boat. Their seductive beaches and unparalleled snorkeling display the B.V.I. at their beachcombing, hedonistic best. Contact **DIVE B.V.I.** (⊠ Virgin Gorda Yacht Harbour, ☎ 284/495–5513) for expert diving instruction, certification, and day trips. *No phone.* ☎ *Free.*

③ **Copper Mine Point.** Here you'll see a tall, stone shaft silhouetted against the sky and a small stone structure that overlooks the sea. These are the ruins of a copper mine established here 400 years ago and worked first by the Spanish, then by English miners until the early 20th century. This is one of the few places in the B.V.I. where you won't see islands along the horizon. ⊠ *Copper Mine Rd., no phone.* ☎ *Free.*

⑥ **Leverick Bay.** A resort, a tiny beach and marina, a restaurant, a cluster of shops, and some luxurious hillside villas are here. This is also where a launch picks up passengers for Drake's Anchorage, a resort on nearby Mosquito Island.

④ **Little Fort National Park.** A 36-acre wildlife sanctuary and the ruins of an old fort can be found here. Piles of giant boulders similar to those found at The Baths are scattered throughout the park. ⊠ *Spanish Town Rd., no phone.* ☎ *Free.*

① **Spanish Town.** Virgin Gorda's main settlement, on the island's southern wing, is a peaceful village so tiny that it barely qualifies as a town at all. Also known as the Valley, Spanish Town is home to a marina, a small cluster of shops, and a couple of car-rental agencies. Just north of town is the ferry slip. At the **Virgin Gorda Yacht Harbour** you can enjoy a stroll along the dockfront or do a little browsing in the shops.

⑤ **Virgin Gorda Peak National Park.** A small sign on North Sound Road marks the trail up to the 265-acre park and the island's summit at 1,359 ft. Sometimes the sign is missing, so keep your eyes open for a set of stairs that disappears into the trees. It's about a 15-minute hike up to a small clearing, where you can climb a ladder to the platform of a wood observation tower. If you're keen for some woodsy exercise or just want to stretch your legs, go for it. Unfortunately, the view at the top is somewhat tree-obstructed. ⊠ *North Sound Rd., no phone.* ☎ *Free.*

Virgin Gorda A to Z

Emergencies

Emergencies (☎ 999).

Clinics: On Virgin Gorda, there is a clinic in Spanish Town, or the Valley (☎ 284/495–5337). There is also a clinic on Virgin Gorda at North Sound (☎ 284/495–7310).

Pharmacy The Spanish Town pharmacy is **Medicure** (☎ 284/495–5479).

Getting Around

BY CAR

The taxi companies on Virgin Gorda also provide rentals. A four-wheel-drive vehicle is best for negotiating some of the rougher terrain. Virtually none of the roads are marked, so be prepared to stop and ask for directions. Puck, who owns **Mahogany,** goes out of his way to provide good service.

BY TAXI

Mahogany Rentals and Taxi Service (☎ 284/495–5469) provides taxi service all over the island. **Andy's Taxi and Jeep Rental** (☎ 284/495–5252 or 284/495–5353) offers taxi service from one end of the island to the other.

Guided Tours

Guided tours on Virgin Gorda can be arranged through **Andy's Taxi and Jeep Rental** (☎ 284/495–5252 or 284/495–5353) and **Mahogany Rentals and Taxi Service** (☎ 284/495–5469).

Visitor Information

The **B.V.I. Tourist Board** is in Virgin Gorda Yacht Harbour, Spanish Town (☎ 284/495–5182).

JOST VAN DYKE

Named after an early Dutch settler, Jost Van Dyke is a small island northwest of Tortola, and a worthwhile destination for those travelers who *truly* want to get away from it all. Mountainous and lush, the 4-mi-long island—home to only about 140 people—has one tiny hotel, two campgrounds, and fewer than a dozen informal eateries. With only a handful of cars and a single road the island makes visitors feel as if they've stepped back in time. This is one of the most popular anchorages in the Caribbean, and there is a disproportionately large collection of informal bars and restaurants, which together have helped earn Jost its reputation as "Party Island" of the B.V.I.

Lodging

$$–$$$ 🏨 **Sandcastle.** This tiny, four-cottage hideaway, with a staff of eight, is set on a half mile of white-sand beach on remote White Bay. There's "nothing" to do here, except maybe relax in a hammock, read, walk, swim, and enjoy sophisticated cuisine by candlelight. Arrangements can be made for diving, sailing, and sportfishing trips. ⌧ *White Bay,* ☎ *284/775–5262,* FAX *284/775–3590. 4 cottages. Restaurant, bar, beach. MC, V.*

$$–$$$ 🏨 **Sandy Ground Estates.** This collection of eight privately owned one- and two-bedroom houses is tucked into the foliage along the edge of a beach at the east end of Jost Van Dyke. Each one is architecturally different, and interiors range from spartan to stylish. The fully equipped kitchens can be prestocked if you supply a list of groceries (consider doing this—supplies are limited on the island), and there are four very

casual restaurants within walking distance on the other side of the hill. ⊠ *Sandy Ground,* ☎ *284/495–3391. 8 houses. Beach. No credit cards.*

Campgrounds

⚠ **White Bay Campground.** On remote White Bay beach, this simple campground has bare sites ($15 per couple, per night), equipped tent sites (tents with electricity and one lamp; $25 per couple), and screened cabins ($35 per couple). The owners will take you on nature walks and can arrange island tours and sailing and diving trips. ⊠ *White Bay,* ☎ *284/495–9312. 8 bare sites, 4 prepared sites. Restaurant, bar, beach. No credit cards.*

Dining

Restaurants on Jost Van Dyke are charming but very informal. Some serve meals family style, at long tables. The island is a favorite charter stop, and you're bound to hear people exchanging stories about the previous night's anchoring adventures. Most restaurants do not take reservations, and in all cases, dress is informal.

$$$ ✕ **Sandcastle.** Candlelit dinners here in the tiny beachfront dining room are four-course, prix-fixe affairs. The menu changes but can include a West Indian pumpkin or a curried apple soup, curried shrimp or three-mustard chicken, and, for dessert, rum bananas or key lime pie. Reservations are requested by 4 PM. Sandwiches are served at lunch at the **Soggy Dollar Bar,** famous for allegedly being the birthplace of the lethal Painkiller drink. ⊠ *White Bay,* ☎ *284/495–9888. MC, V.*

$$ ✕ **Rudy's Mariner Rendezvous.** This eatery at the western end of the beach specializes in lobster and other seafood dishes and has live entertainment several nights during the week. ⊠ *Great Harbour,* ☎ *284/495–9282. No credit cards.*

$–$$ ✕ **Abe's Little Harbour.** Specialties at this informal, popular spot include fresh lobster, conch, and spare ribs. During most of the winter season, there's a pig roast every Wednesday night. ⊠ *Little Harbour, no phone (use VHF Channel 16). No credit cards.*

$–$$ ✕ **Club Paradise.** The dinner menu at this casual beachfront establishment includes grilled local fish such as mahimahi, red snapper, and grouper; grilled steak; and barbecued chicken and ribs. Hamburgers, West Indian conch stew, and curried chicken are the luncheon fare. Be sure to try the excellent black bean soup. There's a pig roast with live entertainment every Wednesday night. ⊠ *Great Harbour,* ☎ *284/495–9267. No credit cards.*

$–$$ ✕ **Foxy's Tamarind.** One of the true "hot spots" in the B.V.I., and a
★ "must stop" for yachters all over the world, it hosts the madcap Wooden Boat Race every August or September and throws big parties on New Year's Eve, April Fools' Day, and Halloween. This lively place serves local dishes and the best barbecue, and it makes a rum punch that's all its own. Foxy himself plays the guitar and delights in creating calypso ditties about his guests. Next door is Foxy's Store, which sells clothing, sundries, souvenirs, and cassettes of Foxy performing. ⊠ *Great Harbour,* ☎ *284/495–9258. AE, MC, V. No lunch.*

$–$$ ✕ **Harris' Place.** Owner Harris Jones is famous for his Monday, Thursday, and Saturday pig roast buffets and Monday night's Lobstermania. Harris' Place is a great spot to rub elbows with some of the local citizenry and the charter-boat crowd. There's live reggae music Thursday and Saturday. ⊠ *Little Harbour,* ☎ *284/495–9302. AE, MC, V.*

$–$$ ✕ **Sydney's Peace and Love.** Here you'll find great lobster, barbecue, and (for the B.V.I.) a sensational jukebox. The cognoscenti sail here for dinner since there's no beach—meaning no sand fleas, which are especially irksome in the evenings. ⊠ *Little Harbour,* ☎ *284/495–9271. No credit cards.*

$ ✕ **Happy Laurry.** A great choice for a quick meal—snacks, fritters, fish, chicken, and chips. Try a Painkiller, the house-specialty tropical drink. There's live entertainment some nights. ⊠ *Great Harbour, no phone (use VHF Channel 16). No credit cards.*

Beaches

White Bay, on the south shore, west of Great Harbour, has a long stretch of white sand. Just offshore, the little islet known as **Sandy Cay** is a gleaming scimitar of white sand, with marvelous snorkeling.

PETER ISLAND

A dramatic, hilly island with wonderful anchorages and beautiful beaches, Peter Island is about 5 mi directly south across the Sir Francis Drake Channel from Road Town, Tortola. Set amid the string of small islands that stream from the southern tip of Virgin Gorda, the island is an idyllic hideaway replete with white sand beaches, stunning views, and the exclusive Peter Island Resort. It can be reached by sailing in on your own craft or by launch from the Peter Island dock just east of Road Town, Tortola ($15 each way or free if you're coming for dinner).

Lodging

$$$$ ⊞ **Peter Island Resort and Yacht Harbour.** There's lots to do at this luxury resort: Facilities include a stunning pool, a tennis program run by Peter Burwash, a water-sports center, mountain bicycles, a fitness trail, and a 5-star PADI dive facility. The 50 guest rooms, in four-unit cottages tucked among beds of radiant tropical flowers, are either on the beach or near the pool. Beachfront units are beautiful stone-and-wood structures that open out on one of the loveliest beaches anywhere. The less expensive ocean-view and garden-view rooms, which are smaller and could use a bit of refurbishing, look across the pool toward the hills and twinkling lights of Tortola. A spectacular hilltop villa, the Crow's Nest, rents for about $3,500 a day and includes four bedrooms, living room, state-of-the-art kitchen, dining room, terrace, inner courtyard, fully stocked entertainment systems, domestic help, vehicles, and a private swimming pool overlooking the marina on one side and Dead Man's Bay on the other. Those seeking seclusion should be aware that the resort's beaches are on bays that are popular anchorages and the island can be somewhat crowded with day-trippers and the charterboat crowd. For the last several years, there has been a constant turnover of resident managers, and service here is somewhat inconsistent. ⊠ *Box 211, Road Town, Tortola,* ☎ *284/495–2000 or 800/346–4451,* FAX *284/495–2500. 50 rooms, 2 villas. 2 restaurants, 2 bars, pool, 4 tennis courts, exercise room, a 20-station fitness trail, beach, windsurfing, mountain bikes, helipad. AE, MC, V.*

Dining

$$$$ ✕ **Tradewinds Restaurant.** Peter Island Resort's open-air dining room overlooking the Sir Francis Drake Channel provides an enchanting setting for dinner. The à la carte menu offers a variety of mostly Continental selections, with subtle Caribbean touches. Every Saturday night there's a seafood buffet. During or after dinner, dance under the stars to soft, rhythmic tunes performed by local musicians three or four nights

a week in season. ⊠ *Peter Island Resort,* ☎ *284/495–2000. Reservations essential. AE, MC, V. No lunch.*

$$$–$$$$ ✕ **Deadman's Bay Bar and Grill.** This more casual grill on the beach serves lunches of ribs, burgers, grilled fish, and a bountiful salad bar. Sunday lunch features a lavish West Indian buffet and a steel band. A dinner with a choice of grilled local fish, steak, chicken, or chicken roti, is served most evenings. Try one of the many delicious frozen tropical drinks. ⊠ *Peter Island Resort,* ☎ *284/495–2000. Reservations essential. AE, MC, V.*

Beaches

Palm-fringed **Dead Man's Bay,** called one of the world's 10 most romantic beaches, is just a short hike from the dock. Snorkeling is good at both ends of the beach, and you'll find a bar and restaurant for lunch.

If you feel like taking a hike instead of heading down to Dead Man's Bay, follow the road up, and when it levels off bear right and head down to the other side of the island and secluded **White Bay.**

ANEGADA

Anegada lies low on the sea about 14 mi north of Virgin Gorda. Unlike the other islands of the chain, it is not volcanic but rather a coral and limestone atoll with no hills. Nine miles long and 2 mi wide, the island rises no more than 28 ft above sea level. In fact, by the time you are able to see it, you may have run your boat onto a reef. More than 300 other captains, unfamiliar with the waters, have done exactly that since the exploration days. Because of the dangerous reefs, many bare-boat companies don't allow their vessels to head to Anegada without a trained skipper. The scores of shipwrecks that encircle the island make it popular with scuba divers. The northern and western shores of Anegada have long stretches of stunning white-sand beach. The island's population of about 150 is clustered in a small village called the Settlement, and many of the inhabitants are fishers who will take visitors out bonefishing. Snorkeling, especially in the translucent waters around Loblolly Bay on the north shore, is a transcendent experience. It is possible to float in totally reef-protected calm water only several feet deep and several feet from shore and see one coral formation after another, each shimmering with a rainbow of colorful fish. Combine that with miles of white sand as fine as pancake batter and one lone beach bar serving wondrous home cooking and frosty beers, and you have a formula that should satisfy anyone's fantasy of being marooned on a desert island.

Lodging

$$$–$$$$ ⌂ **Anegada Reef Hotel.** This is the only hotel on the island, and it has just 16 simply furnished rooms. It has its own narrow strip of beach, but beach lovers will want to spend their days on the beautiful deserted beaches on the other side of the island; you can be dropped off with a picnic lunch or be picked up and returned to the hotel for lunch. A bathing suit and something warmer for the evening are all the clothes you'll need. The outdoor bar is a great spot for a cool island drink or a cold beer, and the restaurant is one of the best spots for sampling Anegada's famous local lobster grilled or in cold salads. Snorkeling and diving are as good on Anegada as anywhere in the islands. Bonefishing in the flats is a favorite activity, and deep-sea fishing trips can be arranged. If you favor laid-back living with no schedules, this is the spot for you. ⊠ *Anegada,* ☎ *284/495–8002,* FAX *284/495–9362. 16 rooms. Restaurant, bar, beach. No credit cards.*

$$ 🏨 **Neptune's Treasure.** This little guest house offers double and single rooms with private baths and also tents with foam mattresses and linens. There's a restaurant and a little gift shop on the premises. ⊠ *Between Pomato and Saltheap points,* ☎ *284/495–9439. 4 rooms, 6 tents. Restaurant, beach. AE, MC, V.*

Campground

🏕 **Anegada Beach Campground.** The tents (8-by-10 ft or 10-by-12 ft) are put up in a marvelously serene setting. Sites cost $7 per person, per night. ⊠ *The Settlement, Anegada,* ☎ *284/495–8038. Restaurant, bar, beach. No credit cards.*

Dining

There are between three and six restaurants open at any one time, depending on the season and also on whim. Check when you're on the island.

$$ ✕ **Anegada Reef Hotel.** Seasoned yachters gather nightly at the bar here to join conversations and dine with the hotel guests. Dinner is by candlelight and always includes famous Anegada lobster, steaks, and chicken, all prepared on the large grill by the little open-air bar. ⊠ *Anegada Reef Hotel,* ☎ *284/495–8002. Reservations essential. No credit cards.*

$$ ✕ **Neptune's Treasure.** The owners catch, cook, and serve the seafood at this casual bar and restaurant. Lobster is the specialty. ⊠ *Between Pomato and Saltheap points,* ☎ *284/495–9439. AE.*

$$ ✕ **Pomato Point.** This relaxed restaurant and bar is on a narrow beach, a short walk from the Anegada Reef Hotel. Entrées include steak, chicken, lobster, and fresh-caught seafood. Owner Wilfred Creque displays various island artifacts, including shards of Arawak pottery and 17th-century coins, cannonballs, and bottles. ⊠ *Pomato Point,* ☎ *284/495–8038. Reservations essential. No credit cards.*

Shopping

Pat's Pottery (☎ 284/495–8031) sells bowls, plates, cups, candlestick holders, and original watercolors in soft pastels—made locally.

V n J's Souvenir & Gift Shop (☎ 284/495–8018) makes and sells handcrafted pottery, handpainted T-shirts, and gift items.

OTHER BRITISH VIRGIN ISLANDS

Cooper Island

Cooper Island, a small hilly island on the south side of the Sir Francis Drake Channel, about 8 mi from Road Town, Tortola, is a popular stop for the charter-boat crowd. There are no roads or cars but there's a beach restaurant, a casual, little hotel, a few privately owned houses (some of which are available for rent), and great snorkeling at the south end of Manchioneel Bay.

Dining

$$–$$$ ✕ **Cooper Island Restaurant.** Ferry service from Road Town is available only to guests of the hotel, but this restaurant is a popular stop for boaters. Come here for great ratatouille (it's a main course at lunch, an appetizer at dinner); grilled local fish, chicken, and steak; and conch Creole. For lunch, there are also hamburgers, conch fritters, and pasta salad. ⊠ *Cooper Island, no phone (VHF Channel 16). Reservations essential. AE, MC, V.*

Lodging

$$-$$$ 🏨 **Cooper Island Beach Club.** Two West Indian–style cottages house 12 no-frills units with a living area, a small but complete kitchen, and a balcony. This is a wonderful place to lead a somewhat back-to-basics existence: The only water available is rain collected in a cistern, and because of the limited amount of electricity, you won't be able to use a hair dryer, an iron, or any other electric appliance. There is ample opportunity to mingle, however, at the bar, which fills nightly with a new group of boaters. ⊠ *Box 859, Road Town, Tortola,* ☎ *413/659–2602 or 800/542–4624. 12 rooms. Restaurant, beach, dive shop. MC, V.*

Guana Island

Guana Island is very quiet and *very* private. Guana Island Club sends its private launch to pick up guests arriving at Beef Island. If you're not a guest, you'll have to rely on your own boat to get here, and once you're onshore you'll be restricted to the beaches that ring the island. Guests of the resort, however, can use the numerous hiking trails throughout the island.

Lodging

$$$$ 🏨 **Guana Island Club.** Guana Island is owned entirely by the hotel, and as a result, the hotel is very private. Lack of facilities available to the public keeps it even more so. Guests are met at Beef Island by the hotel's launch, the only organized access to the island. The hotel is situated on the top of a hill, from where it is a 10-minute walk to the beach. Fifteen rustic but comfortable guest rooms are spread among seven separate houses scattered along the hillside. The houses are decorated in Caribbean style, with rattan furniture and ceiling fans, and each has its own porch. More than 50 species of bird can be observed on the island, and the terrain is a verdant collection of exotic tropical plants ringed by six deserted beaches. Guests mingle during cocktail hour, and meals are served at several large tables, but there are several tables for two if you prefer to dine as a couple. ⊠ *Box 32, Road Town, Tortola,* ☎ *284/494–2354,* FAX *914/967–8048. 15 rooms. Restaurant, tennis court, croquet, hiking. No credit cards.*

Necker Island

Necker Island is a private island just north of Virgin Gorda. It has rooms for 20, but they can be rented only as a block—with the whole island.

Lodging

$$$$ 🏨 **Necker Island.** You and up to 19 friends can rent out the whole island, including its five beaches, many walks, tennis court, and luxurious villa with 20 spacious guest rooms. ⊠ *Necker Island,* ☎ *284/494–2757. Beach, boating. AE, MC, V.*

Pusser's Marina Cay

Pusser's Marina Cay is a beautiful little island in Trellis Bay, not far from Beef Island and its airport. It can sometimes be seen from the air during the approach to the airport: a very dramatic sight, with large J-shape coral reefs engulfing the cay. With only 6 acres, this islet is considered small even by B.V.I. standards. There's a Pusser's Restaurant, Pusser's Store, and a six-unit Pusser's Hotel here. Ferry service is free from the dock on Beef Island.

Lodging

$$-$$$ 🏨 **Pusser's Marina Cay Hotel.** The tiny island's only hotel has six double rooms and two suites, all with lovely views of the water and neighboring islands. Each has its own porch. Ferry service is free from the

dock on Beef Island. Call for ferry times, which vary with the season. ⊠ *Box 76, Road Town, Tortola,* ☎ *284/494–2174,* FAX *284/494–4775. 6 units. Restaurant, bar, beach. AE, D, DC, MC, V.*

Dining

$–$$ ✕ **Pusser's Marina Cay Restaurant.** Ferry service is available from Beef Island dock to this beachfront restaurant on a tiny islet. The dinner menu ranges from fish and lobster to steak, chicken, and barbecued ribs. Pusser's Painkiller Punch is the house specialty. ⊠ *Pusser's Marina Cay,* ☎ *284/494–2174. AE, MC, V.*

BRITISH VIRGIN ISLANDS A TO Z

Arriving and Departing

AIRPORTS AND AIRLINES

No nonstop service is available from the United States mainland to the B.V.I.; connections are usually made through San Juan, Puerto Rico, or St. Thomas, U.S.V.I. Airlines serving both San Juan and St. Thomas include **American** (☎ 800/433–7300), **Continental** (☎ 800/231–0856), and **Delta** (☎ 800/323–2323). **American Eagle** (☎ 800/433–7300) flies from San Juan to Tortola. **Air St. Thomas** (☎ 284/495–5935) flies between St. Thomas and Virgin Gorda. Regularly scheduled flights between the B.V.I. and most other Caribbean islands are provided by **Leeward Islands Air Transport (LIAT)** (☎ 284/495–1187). Many Caribbean islands can also be reached through **Gorda Aero Service** (⊠ Tortola, ☎ 284/495–2271), a charter service.

Both the Beef Island/Tortola and Virgin Gorda airports are classic Caribbean—always sleepy, and all but dead when there are no flights. Service desks can be slow at Beef Island when the airport gets crowded before departures: Give yourself at least an hour.

BETWEEN THE AIRPORTS AND HOTELS

Most hotels will provide transport if you call prior to arrival. At the Beef Island/Tortola airport, there is usually a group of taxi drivers hovering at the exit from customs to meet flights. Fares are officially set and are not negotiable and are lower per person for more than one passenger. Figure about $15 for up to three people and $5 for each additional passenger for the 20-minute ride to Road Town, and about $20–$30 for the 45-minute ride to West End. Expect to share your taxi, and be patient if your driver searches for people to fill his cab—only a few flights land each day and this could be your driver's only run. You can also call the **B.V.I. Taxi Association** (☎ 284/495–2378). On Virgin Gorda call **Mahogany Taxi Service** (☎ 284/495–5469). Rates will vary depending on your destination. If you're staying anywhere on the North Sound in Virgin Gorda, you can fly to Beef Island/Tortola and catch the nearby North Sound Express (☞ Getting Around, *below*), or you can fly to Virgin Gorda and take a taxi to North Sound. From there a hotel launch will meet you, but you must have made arrangements with your hotel before your arrival. Don't get nervous if your land taxi leaves you by yourself on a deserted dock and tells you to wait for your skipper. They are very reliable and someone will show up. If your destination is Leverick Bay, your land taxi will take you there directly.

From the U.S. by Ship

Mostly smaller ships, and a few larger ones, call at the B.V.I. The most popular ports are Tortola, Virgin Gorda, and Jost Van Dyke. Smaller ships often stop at more than one of the islands; larger ones usually make only one port call during the course of an eastern Caribbean sailing. Among the ocean liners that call in the B.V.I. are ships from

Cunard Line (✉ 555 5th Ave., New York, NY 10017, ☎ 800/528–6273),
Carnival Cruise Lines (✉ Carnival Pl., 3655 N.W. 87th Ave., Miami,
FL 33178, ☎ 800/327–9501), **Holland America** (✉ 300 Elliott Ave.
W, Seattle, WA 98119, ☎ 800/426–0327), **Norwegian Cruise Line** (✉
95 Merrick Way, Coral Gables, FL 33134, ☎ 800/327–7030), **Princess
Cruises** (✉ 10100 Santa Monica Blvd., Los Angeles, CA 90067, ☎
310/553–1770), and **Royal Caribbean Cruise Line** (✉ 1050 Caribbean
Way, Miami, FL 33132, ☎ 800/327–6700). Itineraries and ship de-
ployments change frequently, so contact your cruise line for the latest
scheduled sailings. Many luxury yachts visit the islands. Contact **Re-
naissance Cruises** (✉ 1800 Eller Dr., Suite 300, Box 350307, Fort
Lauderdale, FL 33335, ☎ 800/525–5350), **Royal Viking Line** (✉ 95
Merrick Way, Coral Gables, FL 33134, ☎ 800/422–8000), or **Seabourn
Cruise Line** (✉ 55 San Francisco St., San Francisco, CA 94133, ☎
800/351–9595). Sail-powered ships also frequent the B.V.I. Contact **Club
Med** (✉ 40 W. 57th St., New York, NY 10019, ☎ 800/258–2633), **Tall
Ship Adventures** (✉ 1010 S. Joliet St., Suite 200, Aurora, CO 80012,
☎ 800/662–0090), **Windjammer Barefoot Cruises** (✉ Box 190120,
Miami Beach, FL 33119, ☎ 800/327–2602), or **Windstar Cruises**
(✉ 300 Elliot Ave. W, Seattle, WA 98119, ☎ 800/258–7245).

From the U.S.V.I. by Ferry

Various ferries connect St. Thomas, U.S.V.I., with Tortola and Virgin
Gorda. **Native Son, Inc.** (☎ 284/495–4617) operates three ferries (*Na-
tive Son, Oriole,* and *Voyager Eagle*) and offers service between St.
Thomas and Tortola (West End and Road Town) daily. **Smiths Ferry
Services** (☎ 284/494–4430 or 284/494–2355) carries passengers be-
tween downtown St. Thomas and Road Town and West End daily.
Speedy's Ferries (☎ 284/495–5240) runs between Virgin Gorda, Tor-
tola, and St. Thomas on Tuesday, Thursday, and Saturday. **Inter-Island
Boat Services'** *Sundance II* (☎ 284/776–6597) connects St. John and
West End, Tortola, daily.

Dining

The most popular choices in B.V.I. restaurants are seafood dishes. Unfortunately, some restaurants have found that it's cheaper to serve fish
imported frozen from Miami than local fresh fish. You'll find a greater
range of eateries on Tortola than on more remote Virgin Gorda and
the other islands, where most hotels offer a meal plan.

CATEGORY	COST*
$$$$	over $35
$$$	$25–$35
$$	$15–$25
$	under $15

*per person for three courses, excluding drinks and service; there is no sales
tax in the B.V.I.*

Getting Around

By Boat

Speedy's Fantasy (☎ 284/495–5240) makes the run between Road
Town, Tortola, and Spanish Town, Virgin Gorda, daily. Running daily
between Virgin Gorda's North Sound and Beef Island/Tortola are
North Sound Express (☎ 284/494–2746) boats. The **Peter Island Ferry**
(☎ 284/495–2000) runs daily between Peter Island's private dock on
Tortola (just east of Road Town) and Peter Island. **Jost Van Dyke Ferry
Service** (☎ 284/494–2997) makes the Jost Van Dyke–Tortola run sev-
eral times daily.

By Car

Driving on Tortola and Virgin Gorda is not for the timid. Roller-coaster roads with breathtaking ascents and descents and tight turns that give new meaning to the term "hairpin curves" are the norm, but the ever-changing views of land, sea, and neighboring islands are among the most spectacular in the Caribbean. Most people will strongly recommend renting a four-wheel-drive vehicle. Roads tend to be named by where they lead to (e.g., Joe's Hill) but don't count on their being marked with signs. The numerous curves can trick even the greatest of pathfinders into taking a wrong turn (and heading down ever-narrowing dirt roads to a final dead end), so be sure to get a map at the rental agency and ask for suggested routes. Some roads are in better shape than others. It helps to keep track on the map of where you think you might be so you'll know when to look for a turn.

Driving is *à l'Anglais,* on the left side of the road, but the steering wheel is on the left. It's easy if you drive slowly, think before you make a turn, and pay attention when driving in and out of the occasional traffic circle, locally called round-a-bouts. Speed limits are 30–40 mph outside of town, 10–15 mph in residential areas. A valid B.V.I. driver's license is required and can be obtained for $10 at car-rental agencies. You must be at least 25 and have a valid driver's license from another country.

By Plane

Gorda Aero Service (☎ 284/495–2271) flies between Tortola and Anegada Monday, Wednesday, and Friday and offers charter flights between Tortola, Virgin Gorda, and Anegada, and to other Caribbean islands.

Lodging

There is a reassuring sense of intimacy about B.V.I. resorts. None are large—only four have more than 50 rooms. The soaring lobbies, anonymous guest rooms, and long check-in lines found in the high-rise behemoths on other Caribbean islands don't exist here. Guests are treated as more than just room numbers.

Don't be surprised—even at the more expensive resorts—if your room is missing some of the amenities you take for granted, such as a television or telephones. Some visitors find this a minor inconvenience, but for others it's a welcome surprise. Indeed, many, many visitors return to the B.V.I. year after year, making booking a room at many of the more popular resorts difficult even during the off-season. This is true despite the fact that nearly half the island visitors stay aboard their own boats during their vacations.

Some hotels also lack air-conditioning, relying instead on ceiling fans to capture the almost constant trade winds. Nights are cool and breezy, even in midsummer, and never reach the temperatures or humidity levels that are so common in much of the United States during the summer.

CATEGORY	COST*
$$$$	over $225
$$$	$150–$225
$$	$75–$150
$	under $75

All prices are for a standard double room in high season, excluding 7% hotel tax and 10% (sometimes 12% or higher on Virgin Gorda) service charge.

Mail

There are post offices in Road Town on Tortola and in Spanish Town on Virgin Gorda. (It might be noted that postal efficiency in the B.V.I. is not first-class.) Postage for a first-class letter to the United States is 35¢ and for a postcard 20¢. For a small fee, **Rush It** in Road Town (☎ 284/494–4421) and in Spanish Town (☎ 284/495–5821) offer most U.S. mail and UPS services (via St. Thomas the next day).

Opening and Closing Times

Stores are generally open Monday through Saturday 9–5. Bank hours are usually Monday through Thursday 9–2:30 and Friday 9–2:30 and 4:30–6.

Telephones

The area code for the B.V.I. is now 284. At press time, the official date of the switch from 809 was set at October 1, 1997; the 809 area code should work for six months past that date. To call anywhere in the B.V.I. once you've arrived, dial only the last five digits: Instead of dialing 494–1234, just dial 4–1234. A local call from a public pay phone costs 25¢. Pay phones are frequently on the blink; a handy alternative (if you will be in the islands long enough or plan to make a lot of calls) is a Caribbean Phone Card, available in $5, $10, and $20 denominations. It's sold at most major hotels and many stores and can be used to call all over the Caribbean and to access USADirect from special phone-card telephones.

For credit card or collect long-distance calls to the United States, use a phone-card telephone or look for special **USADirect** phones, which are linked directly to an AT&T operator. For access dial 800/872–2881, or dial 111 from a pay phone and charge the call to your MasterCard or Visa. USADirect and pay phones can be found at most hotels and in towns.

Tipping

Service charges are generally added to the hotel bill. Porters and bell-hops should be tipped $1 per bag. A tip is usually not necessary for cabbies, because most taxis are owned independently; add 10%–15% if they exceed their duties. Some service (10%) is often included at restaurants; if it is included, and you liked the service, it is customary to leave an additional 5%; if no charge is added, 15% is customary.

Visitor Information

Information about the B.V.I. is available through the **British Virgin Islands Tourist Board** (✉ 370 Lexington Ave., Suite 313, New York, NY 10017, ☎ 212/696–0400 or 800/835–8530) or at the **British Virgin Islands Information Offices** in San Francisco (✉ 1804 Union St., Suite 305, San Francisco, CA 94123, ☎ 415/775–0344; nationwide, ☎ 800/232–7770). British travelers can write or visit the **B.V.I. Information Office** (✉ 110 St. Martin's La., London WC2N 4DY, ☎ 071/240–4259).

6 Portraits of the Virgin Islands

Beach Picnic

Me? The Dad? On a Spring-Break Cruise?

Further Reading

BEACH PICNIC

AS THE BOAT from St. Thomas neared St. John, it occurred to me again that I might have made a serious mistake leaving behind my ham. You could say, after all, that our entire trip had been based on that ham. In our family, the possibility of renting a house for a week on St. John had been kicking around for years; Abigail and Sarah were so strongly for it that I sometimes referred to them as "the St. John lobby." We had been on St. John briefly during the week we'd spent on St. Thomas, only a short ferry ride away. St. Thomas is known mainly for recreational shopping—its principal town, Charlotte Amalie, had already been a tax-free port for a century and a half when the United States bought St. Thomas and St. John and St. Croix from Denmark toward the end of the five or six thousand years of human history now thought of as the pre-credit-card era—and what I remember most vividly about our week there was trying to explain to Abigail and Sarah that the mere existence of a customs exemption of $800 per person does not mean that each person is actually required to spend $800. ("I happen to know of a man who was permitted to leave even though he had purchased only $68.50 worth of goods. He is now living happily in Metuchen, New Jersey.") I was rather intent on getting the point across because according to what I could see from the shopping patterns on St. Thomas, our family would ordinarily have been expected to buy $3,200 worth of perfume—enough perfume, I figured, to neutralize the aroma of a fair-sized cattle feedlot.

What Abigail and Sarah remembered most vividly were rumless piña coladas—it was their first crack at rumless piña coladas—and the spectacular beaches on St. John. The beaches are accessible to everyone through inclusion in the Virgin Islands National Park, which covers nearly three quarters of the island, and, just as important, going to the beach is pretty much all there is to do—a state of affairs that Abigail and Sarah would think of as what ham purveyors call Hog Heaven. We had talked about it a lot, but the conversation usually ended with a simple question: What would we eat?

The question went beyond the dismal food we had come to expect in Virgin Islands restaurants. (On St. Thomas, the restaurants had seemed to specialize in that old Caribbean standby, Miami frozen fish covered with Number 22 sunblock, and my attempts to find some native cooking had resulted mainly in the discovery of bull-foot soup.) In a house on St. John, we would presumably have our own kitchen, but we'd be dependent on the ingredients available in the island stores. Our only previous experience in that line—in the British Virgin Islands, where we had once rented a house when Abigail was a baby—had produced the shopping incident that I have alluded to ever since when the subject of Caribbean eating comes up. On a shopping trip to Roadtown, the capital, Alice ordered a chicken and asked that it be cut up. When we returned from our other errands, we found that the butcher had taken a frozen chicken and run it through a band saw, producing what looked like some grotesque new form of lunch meat.

The memory of that chicken caused a lot of conversations about St. John rentals to fizzle and die. Then, during one of the conversations, my eye happened to fall on a country ham that was hanging in our living room. Maybe I'd better explain the presence of a ham in our living room; Abigail and Sarah seem to think it requires an explanation whenever they bring friends home for the first time. Now and then, we have arranged to buy a country ham from Kentucky. The ham often arrives with a wire attached to it, and since we have a couple of stalking cats, I put the ham out of their reach by attaching the wire to a living room beam in what seems to be a natural hanging place—a spot where we once briefly considered hanging a philodendron. The first time I hung a ham in the living room, Alice pointed out that some

The individual customs exemption has been increased from $800 to $1,200.

of the people expected at a sort of PTA gathering about to be held at our house didn't know us well enough to see the clear logic involved in the ham's presence, so I put a three-by-five card of the sort used in art galleries on a post next to the ham. The card said, "Country ham. 1983. J. T. Mitchum. Meat and wire composition." Since then, I've found that even without the card many guests tend to take the country ham as a work of art, which, at least in the view of people who have eaten one of Mr. Mitchum's, it is.

Contemplating that ham, I found my resistance to renting a house in St. John melting away. We could take the ham along to sustain us, in the way a band of Plains Indians, living in happier times, would have brought their newly killed buffalo to the next camp site. We would bring other provisions from the neighborhood. We would not be dependent on frozen chicken lunch meat. We made arrangements to rent a house for a week on St. John.

Then I left the ham at home. Not because it slipped my mind. A country ham is not the sort of thing you simply forget. Alice had argued that it was terribly heavy, that it was more than we needed, that she didn't feel like making biscuits on St. John (because the American Virgin Islands are U.S. territory, the federal law against eating country ham without biscuits applies). I finally agreed, although I couldn't resist pointing out that the remark about its being more than we needed was directly contradicted by the number of times I've heard people who have just finished off a plateful of country ham and biscuits say, "That's exactly what I needed."

I don't mean we arrived in St. John empty-handed. I had brought along an extra suitcase full of provisions. There were some breakfast necessities—tea and the seven-grain bread that Alice likes in the mornings and, of course, a dozen New York bagels. We also had smoked chicken breasts, a package of a Tuscan grain called farro, a couple of packages of spaghetti, sun-dried tomatoes, a package of pignoli nuts, an Italian salami, several slices of the flat Italian bread called focaccia that a man near our house makes every morning, a jar of olive paste, and what Alice usually refers to as her risotto kit—arborio rice, fresh Parmesan cheese, olive oil, wild mushrooms, a head of garlic, a large onion, and a can of chicken broth. Better safe than sorry.

FINDING A PLACE TO RENT had turned out to be relatively simple. St. John is organized on the premise that a lot of visitors will want to rent a house. The only hotels of any size on the island are Caneel Bay, one of the first of the resorts that the Rockefellers built for those who feel the need of being cosseted for a few days in reassuringly conventional luxury, and a new resort called the Virgin Grand, a touch of flash that is always mentioned in the first 30 seconds of any discussion about whether the island is in danger of being ruined by development.

The de facto concierges of St. John are a dozen or so property managers, each of whom presides over a small array of houses that seem to have been built with renting in mind—which is to say that you can usually count on your towels being of a uniform color and you don't have to toss somebody else's teddy bears off the bed to go to sleep. Most of the houses are tacked onto the side of a hill—the side of a hill is about the only place to build a house on St. John, which has so many ups and downs that its old Indian name was probably Place Where You're Always in First Gear—and have decks whose expansive views are measured by how many bays are visible. Our house was a simple but cheery two-bedroom place with what I would call a one-and-a-sliver-bay view. It had a kitchen more than adequate for the preparation of an arrival supper of grilled smoked-chicken sandwiches on focaccia. As I ate one, I tried to keep in mind that out there in the dark somewhere people were probably eating Miami frozen fish with sunblock. We weren't safe yet.

I think it was the phrase "fresh fish" that gave me the first hint that sustaining life on St. John might be easier than I had anticipated. For years, the American Virgin Islands have been known for being surrounded by fish that never seem to make it onto a plate. The first sunny news about fresh fish came accompanied by a small black cloud: local fishermen, I was told, showed up on Tuesday and Thursday mornings on a dock behind the customs shed in Cruz Bay, the one place on St.

John that more or less passes as a town, but some of the coral-feeding fish they catch had lately been carrying a disease called ciguatera, which attacks your central nervous system. There was conflicting information around on the subject of ciguatera. I met people in St. John who said that they don't hesitate to eat coral-feeders, and I met someone who said she had been horribly ill from eating one kingfish. I met someone who said that in Japan ciguatera, which isn't detectable by taste or smell, is avoided by putting the fish in a bucket of water with a quarter and discarding it if the quarter tarnishes. I decided to pass. The phrase "attacks your central nervous system" tends to dull my appetite; also, I kept wondering what all those American quarters were doing in Japan.

I T TURNED OUT, THOUGH, that a store in Cruz Bay called Caribbean Natural Foods sold fresh deep-water fish like tuna—not to speak of soy sauce and rice wine and sesame oil for the marinade. Caribbean Natural Foods was one of two or three small but ambitious food stores that had opened since our previous visit to St. John, and among them the island had available California wine and Tsingtao beer and Silver Palate chocolate sauce and Ben & Jerry's ice cream (including my daughters' favorite flavor, Dastardly Mash) and New York bagels and real pastrami and a salad identified as "tortellini with walnut pesto sauce and sour cream." I suppose there are old St. John hands who grumble that the world of exotic beers and gourmet ice cream was what they were trying to get away from, but there must be a lot of regular visitors who feel like celebrating the expansion of available foodstuffs with an appropriately catered parade.

Leading the parade would be people serious about picnics. On St. John, the pleasantness of beaches tends to vary roughly in direct proportion to how hard it is to get there. Anyone who chooses a beach on St. John because it has a convenient parking lot or a commissary or a marked underwater trail or plenty of changing rooms may find himself thinking at some point in the afternoon that he should have paid more attention to what his mother said about the rewards that come to those willing to make a little extra effort. (A difficult road, though, is not an absolute guarantee of peacefulness: someone who has been reading a novel on what seemed like an out-of-the-way beach may look up from his book and find that 20 boats of one sort or another have materialized in a line across the bay, prepared to disgorge a small but expensively outfitted invasion force.) Once you're settled in at the beach, the prospect of going back to Cruz Bay for lunch can provoke the great bicultural moan: *"Quel schlep!"* I don't know what people used to do about lunch at a beach like Francis Bay, where a beach-lounger can watch pelicans as they have a go at the flying fish and a snorkeler with a little patience can usually spot a giant sea turtle. By the time we got there, you could reach into the ice chest for a seafood-salad sandwich and a bottle of Dos Equis.

At Salt Pond, a spectacular beach on the more remote eastern end of the island, we did leave for lunch one day in order to go to Hazel's, where Hazel Eugene, whose wanderings after she left St. Lucia included New Orleans, was said to serve what she sometimes called Caribbean Creole cooking. Hazel's turned out to be on the ground floor of a sort of aqua house that had goats wandering around the back and a neighbor who seemed to be the island's leading collector of auto bodies. Its signs identified it as SEABREEZE: GROCERY, RESTAURANT, BAR, and while we were there Hazel would occasionally leave the kitchen to pour a couple of shots or to fill a shopping list that might consist of a box of Kraft Macaroni & Cheese dinner, a bottle of rum, and a beer for the ride home. She also waited on tables, and in that role she began a lot of sentences with "I could do you . . ." as in "I could do you some of my fried chicken with cottage fries" or "I could do you some codfish fritters and some of my special pumpkin soup to start." Hazel did us all of that, plus some blackened shark and some seafood creole and some puffed shrimp and some chicken curry and a plate of assorted root vegetables that tasted an awful lot better than they sounded or looked. When it was over, I was just about ready to admit that I might have sold St. John short.

I don't mean I regretted bringing along the extra suitcase. Hazel's was too far to drive at night. Places to eat dinner were limited, although at least one restaurant in Cruz Bay, the Lime Inn, had fish from the

Caribbean, of all places, and served it grilled, without even a dash of sunblock on the side. And, of course, we had one dress-up evening in the main dining room at Caneel Bay. What was being sold there, I realized, was simulation of membership in the most prominent country club in town—at a cost that might seem considerable but is, I assume, nothing compared to the kick of the real club's annual dues. The food is of the sort that is described by the most enthusiastic members as "not highly seasoned," and the waiters, playing the role of old club retainers, serve it in a manner so true to the rituals of the upper-middle-class past that you even get a little tray of olives and carrot sticks to nibble on while you're waiting for your shrimp cocktail. The night we were there, the menu offered a marinated conch appetizer as the single reminder that we were on an island rather than in one of the better suburbs, and it listed some California wines as the single reminder that we hadn't found ourselves, willy-nilly, in 1954.

All of which means that we often ate dinner at the place with a one-and-a-sliver-bay view—grilled tuna with some pasta on the side, a great meal of spaghetti with garlic and oil and sun-dried tomatoes, and, finally, the fruits of Alice's risotto kit. It occurred to me, as we ate the risotto and talked about risotto in Milan, that behind our shopping there may have been an unconscious desire to create the Italian West Indies. In fact, I informed those at the table, it hadn't been a bad try—although it might have been improved by bringing along a little more focaccia for the picnics.

Back home, we decided that surviving on St. John had been easy enough to merit a return engagement. A few months later we heard that Hazel had closed her restaurant and taken her talent for Caribbean Creole cooking elsewhere. It was a blow, but not a blow severe enough to change our minds about going back. After all, we still had the country ham.

— Calvin Trillin

ME? THE DAD? ON A SPRING-BREAK CRUISE?

ON A PERFECT MORNING in the British Virgin Islands, I am sitting alone in the cockpit when two young fellows, who are rowing by not quite as accidentally as they would like it to appear, rest on their oars long enough to ask me where my crew and I are headed.

"Norman Island," I answer pleasantly, albeit untruthfully.

Our actual destination is Trellis Bay, at the other end of the BVI from Norman Island. But over the past few days I've learned that evasive tactics are sometimes necessary when you are cruising with a college-age daughter and a few of her girlfriends. I've learned that if I were to be truthful to all the young men who have taken an interest in where we were going to anchor each night, there wouldn't be any room for us to anchor.

Besides, even though the girls had been polite to these particular two young fellows when we'd talked to them a shore on the preceding evening, I'd seen Kris roll her eyes in that meaningful way I'd come to understand means "total dweebs." And I'd heard one of the other girls label them with an even more damning epithet: "high school boys."

The idea for a spring-break cruise with my daughter had been mine. I wanted to share with her one of the things I enjoy most— visiting tropical waters aboard a sailboat when everyone at home is complaining about how cold the weather is. I wanted to do it in a way that would make her feel she was the focus of our adventure, not just tagging along. And I wanted some time to get caught up with how her life was going—not, of course, by asking her, which, as most parents know, is a singularly unenlightening method of intelligence gathering, but by taking advantage of the small confines of a boat to listening in on her conversations with her friends.

Even though the idea had been mine, Kris was keen on it from the start. That's one of the reasons I was so looking forward to it. She was finally beyond the age when kids consider the ideal distance between parent and offspring on vacation to be two or three states. Either that, or she was wise enough to see that spring break in the Virgin Islands is worth a certain amount of sacrifice.

But she did have one concern. After I explained that I'd pay all expenses except her friends' airfare, she said she feared that most of her friends, who were "poor college students," probably would not be able to afford the price of a ticket to the Caribbean. That fear lasted about 24 hours, after which she called me and asked, "How many people did you say was the maximum I could bring?"

We finally signed on two: Carol, whose enrollment in a sailing course at school left me in constant fear that she would ask me to demonstrate a knot I would not remember how to tie; and Missy, who, apparently somewhat dubious about details of the cruise ending up in print, throughout the week made such statements as "Don't quote me on this, but has anybody seen my eyeliner?"

The boat I chartered was a Bénéteau 41S, from Sunsail, which is based at Soper's Hole, at the west end of Tortola. With three double cabins plus the main saloon, the beamy French design could have accommodated more. In fact, based on charters by college-age groups I've seen over the years, the typical number aboard a 41-ft boat is about a dozen—with the crew sleeping all over the deck and, in at least one instance I remember, in the dinghy. But I was glad we were only four, because knowing that my crew had little sailing experience and not knowing how enthusiastic they would be about galley chores, I'd hired a paid captain for a few days, to be followed for a few days after that by a paid cook.

The captain, a young local named David, worked out well. He had what seems to me the most important quality of a paid hand—the ability to get along pleasantly with strangers on a small boat (although he himself admitted that with our crew he didn't find it a particularly tough assignment).

He ably handled the girls' sailing instruction for the first few days and was also handy to have aboard whenever I had a question about the boat's systems. His knowledge actually added a half-day to the time we could spend cruising, because we didn't have to be checked out before Sunsail let us go off on our own. David checked us out while we were under way. And his presence allowed us to solve a few small problems that might otherwise have required me to spend more of the cruise than I cared to reading service manuals.

He had local knowledge that we benefited from immediately. He showed us, almost within sight of the dock, a great day anchorage on Little Thatch Island, which he said most people overlooked because they were in a hurry to get either into or away from Soper's Hole. As the less fortunate waited for their pre-cruise briefings, we let the chain rattle out over a white sand bottom that proved an excellent spot for introducing the girls to snorkeling, windsurfing, and, eventually, lunch as prepared by "The Dad," as I was to overhear various young men call me throughout the week.

And, as we motored into The Bight at Norman Sound just before sunset on that first day, and David said, "Look at how those boats are turned every which way; I'm going to be poppin' my head out the hatch all night," his presence allowed me the pleasant realization that I just might be sleeping better than I usually do on a charter.

At Gorda Sound, on Virgin Gorda, the ferry service that runs between the Bitter End Resort and Tortola made it simple for us to get David back home and pick up the cook whom Sunsail had assigned to us. She was an Englishwoman named Val, whom, to my great relief, the girls got along with splendidly, and not just, as they hinted, because it meant that I would no longer be cooking.

Again, Val's ability to get along with strangers was her best quality. Not counting, of course, her willingness to do all the dish washing. None of our crew were gourmets, and none of us had spent a lifetime being the one expected to cook, so I can't really judge those aspects of having a professional aboard, which my wife and about half the human race have told me can make the difference between a true va-cation and simply moving the work load to a new venue. But I do know that at the end of the time we had planned to keep her, our crew decided we needed to convince Val to stay until the end of the cruise.

The crew, I am happy to report, were themselves a joy to have aboard. As I've said, they arrived with little experience, but they set about everything they did—learning how to steer a course, set a sail, handle the dinghy, wash their hair in a rainsquall—with nearly as much enthusiasm as they exhibited when getting ready to go ashore on the evenings when young men were likely to be present.

Of course, we did have our small differences. My inability to appreciate some of their music left me with the uncomfortable feeling that I might be—well, getting old. And they didn't care much for some of my music either. Not even what they called the classical stuff, such as Jimmy Buffett. But mostly what we had was one of the most pleasant cruises I can remember.

IT WAS PLEASANT introducing my daughter and her friends to places I'd visited and enjoyed a dozen times before: the sea caves on Norman Island, where rumors still persist of buried treasure; the Baths, on Virgin Gorda, where cathedral light and the ocean's swell bounce gently back and forth beneath church-size rocks; Cane Garden Bay, on Tortola, where the evening sun turned the palm trees golden: Sandy Cay, which has a beach as beautifully white as the image its name conjures up; the Bitter End Yacht Club in North Sound, on Virgin Gorda, where (I'd never really noticed before) the boys are; and Foxy's Tamarind Bar, on Jost Van Dyke, where in the afternoon, while we were picking out lobsters for our end-of-the-cruise evening meal ashore, Foxy himself played his guitar for us and told us how he had planned to travel to America and become a big star—and would have, too, he said, if he hadn't learned at the last moment that in order to board the airplane he would be required to wear shoes.

It was pleasant sailing with a crew whose neophyte's enthusiasm helped me remember what it was like to feel a boat come alive in my hands for the first time. Yet a crew so unafraid that they delighted in taking turns at the wheel when the wind attempted to put us on our ear during a beat up Sir Francis Drake Channel. And a crew that by the end of the week, as we reached across a gentle blue sea from Jost Van Dyke to Little Thatch for one more quick swim and a tidying up before heading back into Soper's Hole, had become so competent that I had nothing to do but what I fancy myself as doing best—serving in a supervisory capacity.

Most of all, it was pleasant to think that if Kris and her friends were still as enthusiastic about their spring-break cruise when they got back to school as they were when I saw them off at the airport, she might occasionally remember it was an adventure she had shared with her dad.

Oh, and if those guys from the sailing team who sat up in our cockpit half the night are still looking for the steering wheel that somebody removed from their boat, I don't know anything about it.

— Bob Payne

FURTHER READING

If you have the time before your trip, read James Michener's *Caribbean;* it will enhance your visit. *Don't Stop the Carnival* by Herman Wouk is a classic Caribbean book, though some of its 1950s perspectives seem rather dated.

Once you get to the Virgin Islands, take time to book-shop; there are some prolific U.S.V.I. writers and artists publishing on every subject from pirates to architecture. Look for books, art prints, and cards by Mapes de Monde, published by Virgin Islands native son Michael Paiewonsky, who splits his time between Rome and the U.S.V.I. Mapes de Monde also publishes *The Three Quarters of the Town of Charlotte Amalie* by local historian Edith Woods. It is richly printed and illustrated with Woods's fine pen-and-ink drawings. Photography buffs will want to look for the book of internationally known St. Croix photographer Fritz Henle. For B.V.I. history buffs, Vernon Pickering's *Concise History of the British Virgin Islands* is a wordy but worthy guide to the events and personalities that shaped the region. Pickering also produces the *Official Tourist Handbook* for the B.V.I. Pick up a copy of *A Place Like This: Hugh Benjamin's Peter Island,* the charming and eloquent personal account of the Kittitian's past two decades in the British Virgin Islands. The book was written in collaboration with Richard Myers, a New York writer.

For children there's *Up Mountain One Time* by Willie Wilson, and a *St. John Historical Coloring Book.*

For linguists, *What a Pistarckle!* by Lito Valls gives the origins of the many expressions you'll be hearing, and historians will enjoy *St. John Backtime* by Ruth Hull Low and Rafael Valls, and *Eyewitness Accounts of Slavery in the Danish West Indies* by Isidor Paiewonsky. For sailors, Simon Scott has written a *Cruising Guide to the Virgin Islands.*

INDEX

X = *restaurant*, ☒ = *hotel*

NOTES

NOTES

NOTES

NOTES

NOTES

NOTES

NOTES

NOTES

What's hot,
where it's hot!

Fodor's Travel Publications

Available at bookstores everywhere, or call 1–800–533–6478, 24 hours a day.

Gold Guides

U.S.

Alaska	Florida	New Orleans	Seattle & Vancouver
Arizona	Hawai'i	New York City	The South
Boston	Las Vegas, Reno, Tahoe	Pacific North Coast	U.S. & British Virgin Islands
California	Los Angeles	Philadelphia & the Pennsylvania Dutch Country	USA
Cape Cod, Martha's Vineyard, Nantucket	Maine, Vermont, New Hampshire	The Rockies	Virginia & Maryland
The Carolinas & Georgia	Maui & Lāna'i	San Diego	Walt Disney World, Universal Studios and Orlando
Chicago	Miami & the Keys	San Francisco	Washington, D.C.
Colorado	New England	Santa Fe, Taos, Albuquerque	

Foreign

Australia	Europe	Montréal & Québec City	Scotland
Austria	Florence, Tuscany & Umbria	Moscow, St. Petersburg, Kiev	Singapore
The Bahamas	France	The Netherlands, Belgium & Luxembourg	South Africa
Belize & Guatemala	Germany	New Zealand	South America
Bermuda	Great Britain	Norway	Southeast Asia
Canada	Greece	Nova Scotia, New Brunswick, Prince Edward Island	Spain
Cancún, Cozumel, Yucatán Peninsula	Hong Kong	Paris	Sweden
Caribbean	India	Portugal	Switzerland
China	Ireland	Provence & the Riviera	Thailand
Costa Rica	Israel	Scandinavia	Toronto
Cuba	Italy		Turkey
The Czech Republic & Slovakia	Japan		Vienna & the Danube
Eastern & Central Europe	London		
	Madrid & Barcelona		
	Mexico		

Special-Interest Guides

Adventures to Imagine	Fodor's Gay Guide to the USA	Halliday's New Orleans Food Explorer	Rock & Roll Traveler USA
Alaska Ports of Call	Fodor's How to Pack	Healthy Escapes	Sunday in San Francisco
Ballpark Vacations	Great American Learning Vacations	Kodak Guide to Shooting Great Travel Pictures	Walt Disney World for Adults
Caribbean Ports of Call	Great American Sports & Adventure Vacations	National Parks and Seashores of the East	Weekends in New York
The Official Guide to America's National Parks	Great American Vacations	National Parks of the West	Wendy Perrin's Secrets Every Smart Traveler Should Know
Disney Like a Pro	Great American Vacations for Travelers with Disabilities	Nights to Imagine	
Europe Ports of Call		Rock & Roll Traveler Great Britain and Ireland	
Family Adventures			

Fodor's Special Series

Fodor's Best Bed & Breakfasts

America

California

The Mid-Atlantic

New England

The Pacific Northwest

The South

The Southwest

The Upper Great Lakes

Compass American Guides

Alaska

Arizona

Boston

Chicago

Colorado

Hawaii

Idaho

Hollywood

Las Vegas

Maine

Manhattan

Minnesota

Montana

New Mexico

New Orleans

Oregon

Pacific Northwest

San Francisco

Santa Fe

South Carolina

South Dakota

Southwest

Texas

Utah

Virginia

Washington

Wine Country

Wisconsin

Wyoming

Citypacks

Amsterdam

Atlanta

Berlin

Chicago

Florence

Hong Kong

London

Los Angeles

Montréal

New York City

Paris

Prague

Rome

San Francisco

Tokyo

Venice

Washington, D.C.

Exploring Guides

Australia

Boston & New England

Britain

California

Canada

Caribbean

China

Costa Rica

Egypt

Florence & Tuscany

Florida

France

Germany

Greek Islands

Hawaii

Ireland

Israel

Italy

Japan

London

Mexico

Moscow & St. Petersburg

New York City

Paris

Prague

Provence

Rome

San Francisco

Scotland

Singapore & Malaysia

South Africa

Spain

Thailand

Turkey

Venice

Flashmaps

Boston

New York

San Francisco

Washington, D.C.

Fodor's Gay Guides

Los Angeles & Southern California

New York City

Pacific Northwest

San Francisco and the Bay Area

South Florida

USA

Pocket Guides

Acapulco

Aruba

Atlanta

Barbados

Budapest

Jamaica

London

New York City

Paris

Prague

Puerto Rico

Rome

San Francisco

Washington, D.C.

Languages for Travelers (Cassette & Phrasebook)

French

German

Italian

Spanish

Mobil Travel Guides

America's Best Hotels & Restaurants

California and the West

Major Cities

Great Lakes

Mid-Atlantic

Northeast

Northwest and Great Plains

Southeast

Southwest and South Central

Rivages Guides

Bed and Breakfasts of Character and Charm in France

Hotels and Country Inns of Character and Charm in France

Hotels and Country Inns of Character and Charm in Italy

Hotels and Country Inns of Character and Charm in Paris

Hotels and Country Inns of Character and Charm in Portugal

Hotels and Country Inns of Character and Charm in Spain

Short Escapes

Britain

France

New England

Near New York City

Fodor's Sports

Golf Digest's Places to Play

Skiing USA

USA Today The Complete Four Sport Stadium Guide